Research and Development in Intelligent Systems XXVIII

T0144987

Max Bramer · Miltos Petridis · Lars Nolle
Editors

Research and Development in Intelligent Systems XXVIII

Incorporating Applications and Innovations
in Intelligent Systems XIX

Proceedings of AI-2011, The Thirty-first
SGAI International Conference on Innovative
Techniques and Applications of Artificial
Intelligence

 Springer

Editors
Prof. Max Bramer
University of Portsmouth
UK

Miltos Petridis
University of Brighton
UK

Dr. Lars Nolle
Nottingham Trent University
UK

ISBN 978-1-4471-2317-0   e-ISBN 978-1-4471-2318-7
DOI 10.1007/978-1-4471-2318-7
Springer London Dordrecht Heidelberg New York

British Library Cataloguing in Publication Data
A catalogue record for this book is available from the British Library

Library of Congress Control Number: 2011940852

Printed on acid-free paper

Springer is part of Springer Science+Business Media (www.springer.com)

PROGRAMME CHAIRS' INTRODUCTION

M.A.BRAMER, University of Portsmouth, UK
M.PETRIDIS, University of Brighton, UK

This volume comprises the refereed papers presented at AI-2011, the Thirty-first SGAI International Conference on Innovative Techniques and Applications of Artificial Intelligence, held in Cambridge in December 2011 in both the technical and the application streams. The conference was organised by SGAI, the British Computer Society Specialist Group on Artificial Intelligence.

The technical papers included new and innovative developments in the field, divided into sections on Planning, Evolutionary Algorithms, Speech and Vision, and Machine Learning.

This year's Donald Michie Memorial Award for the best refereed technical paper was won by a paper entitled "Random Prism: An Alternative to Random Forests" by F. Stahl and M. Bramer (University of Portsmouth, UK).

The application papers included present innovative applications of AI techniques in a number of subject domains. This year, the papers are divided into sections on Knowledge Discovery and Data Mining, Machine Learning and AI in Action.

This year's Rob Milne Memorial Award for the best refereed application paper was won by a paper entitled "Web Community Knowledge Extraction for myCBR 3" by C.Sauer and T.Roth-Berghofer (University of Hildesheim, Germany).

The volume also includes the text of short papers presented as posters at the conference.

On behalf of the conference organising committee we would like to thank all those who contributed to the organisation of this year's programme, in particular the programme committee members, the executive programme committees and our administrators Mandy Bauer and Bryony Bramer.

Max Bramer, Technical Programme Chair, AI-2011
Miltos Petridis, Application Programme Chair, AI-2011

ACKNOWLEDGEMENTS

AI-2011 CONFERENCE COMMITTEE

Dr. Lars Nolle   (Conference Chair)
Nottingham Trent University

Prof. Max Bramer   (Technical Programme Chair)
University of Portsmouth

Dr. Daniel Neagu   (Deputy Technical Programme Chair)
University of Bradford

Prof. Miltos Petridis   (Application Programme Chair and UK CBR
University of Brighton   Organiser)

Dr. Jixin Ma   (Deputy Application Programme Chair)
University of Greenwich

Dr. Aladdin Ayesh   (Real AI Day Organiser)
De Montfort University,
Leicester

Prof. Adrian Hopgood   (Workshop Organiser)
Sheffield Hallam University

Rosemary Gilligan   (Treasurer)

Dr Nirmalie Wiratunga   (Poster Session Organiser)
The Robert Gordon University

Dr. Alice Kerly   (FAIRS 2011)
SELEX Systems
Integration Ltd

Prof. Max Bramer, Richard   (Machine Intelligence Competition)
Ellis, Dr. John Gordon

Dr. Ariadne Tampion   (Publicity Officer)

Mandy Bauer   (Conference Administrator)
BCS

Bryony Bramer   (Paper Administrator)

TECHNICAL EXECUTIVE PROGRAMME COMMITTEE

Prof. Max Bramer, University of Portsmouth (Chair)

Dr. Frans Coenen, University of Liverpool

Prof. Adrian Hopgood, Sheffield Hallam University

Dr. John Kingston (Health and Safety Laboratory)

Dr. Daniel Neagu, University of Bradford (Vice-Chair)

Dr. Lars Nolle, Nottingham Trent University

Dr. Nirmalie Wiratunga, Robert Gordon University

APPLICATIONS EXECUTIVE PROGRAMME COMMITTEE

Prof. Miltos Petridis, University of Brighton (Chair)

Mr. Richard Ellis (Helyx)

Ms. Rosemary Gilligan (University of Hertfordshire)

Dr Jixin Ma (University of Greenwich)

Dr. Richard Wheeler (University of Edinburgh)

TECHNICAL PROGRAMME COMMITTEE

Andreas A Albrecht (Queen's University Belfast)

Ali Orhan Aydin (Macquarie University)

Yaxin Bi (University of Ulster)

Mirko Boettcher (University of Magdeburg, Germany)

Max Bramer (University of Portsmouth)

Krysia Broda (Imperial College, University of London)

Ken Brown (University College Cork)

Frans Coenen (University of Liverpool)

Bruno Cremilleux (University of Caen)

Madalina Croitoru (University of Montpellier, France)

Ireneusz Czarnowski (Gdynia Maritime University, Poland)

John Debenham (University of Technology; Sydney)

Stefan Diaconescu (Softwin, Romania)

Nicolas Durand (University of Aix-Marseille 2)

Frank Eichinger (SAP Research Karlsruhe, Germany)

Sandra Garcia Esparza (University College Dublin, Ireland)

Adriana Giret (Universidad Politécnica de Valencia)

Nadim Haque (QinetiQ)

Arjen Hommersom (University of Nijmegen, The Netherlands)

Zina Ibrahim (Kings College, London, UK)

Konstantinos Kotis (University of the Aegean)

Ivan Koychev (Bulgarian Academy of Science)

Fernando Lopes (LNEG-National Research Institute, Portugal)

Peter Lucas (University of Nijmegen)

Michael Madden (National University of Ireland, Galway)

Daniel Manrique Gamo (Universidad Politecnica de Madrid)

Stephen G. Matthews (De Montfort University, UK)

Roberto Micalizio (Universita' di Torino)

APPLICATION PROGRAMME COMMITTEE

Hatem Ahriz (Robert Gordon University)

Tony Allen (Nottingham Trent University)

Ines Arana (Robert Gordon University)

Mercedes Argüello Casteleiro (University of Salford)

Ken Brown (University College Cork)

Richard Ellis (Helyx SIS Ltd)

Lindsay Evett (Nottingham Trent University)

Rosemary Gilligan (University of Hertfordshire)

Adrian Hopgood (Sheffield Hallam University)

Stelios Kapetanakis (University of Greenwich)

Alice Kerly (SELEX Systems Integration Ltd)

Shuliang Li (University of Westminster)

Jixin Ma (University of Greenwich)

Lars Nolle (Nottingham Trent University)

Miltos Petridis (University of Brighton)

Rong Qu (University of Nottingham)

Miguel Salido (Universidad Politécnica de Valencia)

Wamberto Vasconcelos (University of Aberdeen)

Richard Wheeler (Edinburgh Scientific)

CONTENTS

Research and Development in Intelligent Systems XXVIII

MACHINE LEARNING

SHORT PAPERS

Applications and Innovations in Intelligent Systems XIX

SHORT PAPERS

Research and Development in Intelligent Systems XXVIII

BEST TECHNICAL PAPER

Random Prism: An Alternative to Random Forests

Frederic Stahl and Max Bramer

Abstract Ensemble learning techniques generate multiple classifiers, so called base classifiers, whose combined classification results are used in order to increase the overall classification accuracy. In most ensemble classifiers the base classifiers are based on the Top Down Induction of Decision Trees (TDIDT) approach. However, an alternative approach for the induction of rule based classifiers is the Prism family of algorithms. Prism algorithms produce modular classification rules that do not necessarily fit into a decision tree structure. Prism classification rulesets achieve a comparable and sometimes higher classification accuracy compared with decision tree classifiers, if the data is noisy and large. Yet Prism still suffers from overfitting on noisy and large datasets. In practice ensemble techniques tend to reduce the overfitting, however there exists no ensemble learner for modular classification rule inducers such as the Prism family of algorithms. This article describes the first development of an ensemble learner based on the Prism family of algorithms in order to enhance Prism's classification accuracy by reducing overfitting.

1 Introduction

One of the most well-known ensemble learning methods is the Random Forests (RF) classifier from Breiman [7]. RF is inspired by the Random Decision Forests (RDF) approach from Ho [15]. Ho argues that traditional trees often cannot be grown over a certain level of complexity without risking a loss of generalisation caused by overfitting on the training data. Ho proposes inducing multiple trees in randomly selected

Frederic Stahl
School of Computing, Buckingham Building, Lion Terrace, PO1 3HE e-mail: Frederic.Stahl@port.ac.uk

Max Bramer
School of Computing, Buckingham Building, Lion Terrace, PO1 3HE e-mail: Max.Bramer@port.ac.uk

M. Bramer et al. (eds.), *Research and Development in Intelligent Systems XXVIII*,
DOI 10.1007/978-1-4471-2318-7_1, © Springer-Verlag London Limited 2011

subsets of the feature space. He claims that the combined classification will improve, as the individual trees will generalise better on the classification for their subset of the feature space. Ho evaluates his claims empirically. RF makes use of the basic RDF approach by combining it with Breiman's bagging (**B**ootstrap **agg**regat**ing**) method [6]. Bagging is intended to improve a classifier's stability and classification accuracy. A classifier is unstable if a small change in the training set causes major variations in the classification.

Research on ensemble learning technologies for classification in order to overcome overfitting is still ongoing. For example [13] generate ensembles of heterogeneous classifiers using stacking. [11] proposed a framework for generating hundreds of thousands of classifiers in parallel in a distributed environment using small subsamples of the dataset. Chan and Stolfo's [9, 10] Meta-Learning framework partitions the data into subsamples that fit into the memory of a single machine and developed a classifier in each subset separately. These classifiers are then combined using various algorithms in order to create a final classifier. This can easily be run in parallel using the independent multi-sample mining approach [19]. A recently developed prototype of ensemble learners, based on Hoeffding Trees [17] and incremental Naive Bayes, for the classification of datastreams in an ad hoc network of mobile phones is discussed here [27, 26]. The overall data mining framework is called 'Pocket Data Mining' [30]. Pocket Data Mining employs weighted majority voting in order to combine the different classifiers induced on different mobile phones. This work uses the terms 'ensemble learner' and 'ensemble classifier' interchangeably, referring to ensemble learners for classification unless stated otherwise.

There are two general approaches to the induction of classification rules, the 'divide and conquer' approach, also known as TDIDT [20, 21] and the 'separate and conquer' approach [31]. 'Divide and conquer' induces classification rules in the intermediate representation of a decision tree. 'Separate and conquer' induces a set of *IF..THEN* rules rather than a decision tree. 'Separate and conquer' can be traced back to Michalski's AQ system in the 1960s [16]. However the most notable development using the 'separate and conquer' approach is the Prism family of algorithms [8, 3, 4]. It produces modular rules that do not necessarily fit into a decision tree. It produces a comparable classification accuracy to and in some cases outperforms decision trees, especially in noisy domains. Recent developments on the Prism family of algorithms includes frameworks for parallelising Prism algorithms for rule induction on massive datasets [23, 25, 24] and rule pruning methods in order to reduce overfitting [28, 4]. In general Prism algorithms have been shown to be less vulnerable to overfitting compared with decision tree classifiers, especially if there is noise in the data and missing values [3]. Yet most ensemble learning approaches are either based on decision trees or a heterogeneous setup of base classifiers. Some ensemble approaches consider heterogeneous classifiers, such as Meta-Learning [9, 10], yet in practice their application mostly makes use of algorithms that follow the 'divide and conquer' approach.

The fact that Prism classifiers tend to overfit less compared with decision trees motivates the development of ensemble learners based on Prism algorithms. This paper presents the first attempt to build a Prism based ensemble learner inspired

from RF called *Random Prism* in order to improve Prism's classification accuracy further. A prototype implementation is evaluated empirically. This paper is structured as follows: Section 2 introduces the Prism family of algorithms in comparison with decision tree classifiers and describes the newly developed *Random Prism* ensemble learner; Section 3 evaluates Random Prism on several datasets and compares it with a standalone Prism classifier. Section 4 highlights some ongoing and future work, notably some variations of the Random Prism approach and a parallel version of Random Prism. Section 5 concludes the paper with a brief summary and some concluding remarks.

2 Random Prism

This section describes our Random Prism ensemble learner. It first introduces the Prism Family of algorithms in Section 2.1 and compares them with the 'divide and conquer' approach used by RF. Section 2.2 then highlights the Random Prism approach based on the RF ensemble learner.

2.1 The Prism Family of Algorithms

As mentioned in Section 1, the representation of classification rules differs between the 'divide and conquer' and 'separate and conquer' approaches. Rule sets generated by the 'divide and conquer' approach are in the form of decision trees whereas rules generated by the 'separate and conquer' approach are modular. Modular rules do not necessarily fit into a decision tree and normally do not. The rule representation of decision trees is the main drawback of the 'divide and conquer' approach, for example rules such as:

$$IF\ A = 1\ AND\ B = 1\ THEN\ class = x$$

$$IF\ C = 1\ AND\ D = 1\ THEN\ class = x$$

cannot be represented in a tree structure as they have no attribute in common. Forcing these rules into a tree will require the introduction of additional rule terms that are logically redundant, and thus result in unnecessarily large and confusing trees [8]. This is also known as the replicated subtree problem [31]. Cendrowska illustrates the replicated subtree using the two example rules above in [8]. Cendrowska assumes that the attributes in the two rules above comprise three possible values and both rules predict class x, all remaining classes being labelled y. The simplest tree that can express the two rules is shown in Figure 1. The total set of rules that predict class x encoded in the tree is:

$IF\ A = 1\ AND\ B = 1\ THEN\ Class = x$
$IF\ A = 1\ AND\ B = 2\ AND\ C = 1\ AND\ D = 1\ THEN\ Class = x$

IF A = 1 AND B = 3 AND C = 1 AND D = 1 THEN Class = x
IF A = 2 AND C = 1 AND D = 1 THEN Class = x
IF A = 3 AND C = 1 AND D = 1 THEN Class = x

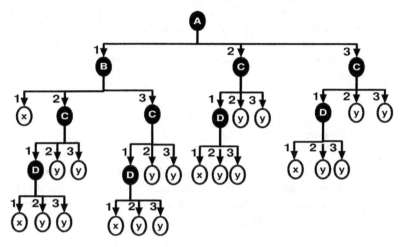

Fig. 1 Cendrowska's replicated subtree example.

Cendrowska argues that situations such as this which cause trees to be needlessly complex make the tree representation unsuitable for expert systems and may require unnecessary expensive tests by the user [8].

'Separate and conquer' algorithms avoid the replicated subtree problem by inducing directly sets of 'modular' rules, avoiding unnecessarily redundant rule terms that are induced just for the representation in a tree structure. The basic 'separate and conquer' approach can be described as follows, where the statement

```
Rule_set rules = new Rule_set();
```

creates a new rule set:

```
Rule_Set rules = new Rule_set();
While Stopping Criterion not satisfied{
    Rule = Learn_Rule;
    Remove all data instances covered from Rule;
    rules.add(rule);
}
```

The *Learn_Rule* procedure generates the best rule for the current subset of the training data where best is defined by a particular heuristic that may vary from algorithm to algorithm. The stopping criterion is also dependent on the algorithm used. After inducing a rule, the rule is added to the rule set, all instances that are covered by the rule are deleted and a new rule is induced on the remaining training instances.

In Prism each rule is generated for a particular Target Class (TC). The heuristic Prism uses in order to specialise a rule is the probability with which the rule covers

the TC in the current subset of the training data. The stopping criterion is fulfilled as soon as there are no training instances left that are associated with the TC.

Cendrowska's original Prism algorithm selects one class as the TC at the beginning and induces all rules for that class. It then selects the next class as TC and resets the whole training data to its original size and induces all rules for the next TC. This is repeated until all classes have been selected as TC. Variations exist such as PrismTC [5] and PrismTCS (Target Class Smallest first) [4]. Both select the TC anew after each rule induced. PrismTC always uses the majority class and PrismTCS uses the minority class. Both variations introduce an order in which the rules are induced, where there is none in the basic Prism approach. However unpublished experiments by the current authors show that the predictive accuracy of PrismTC cannot compete with that of Prism and PrismTCS. PrismTCS does not reset the dataset to its original size and thus is faster than Prism. It produces a high classification accuracy and also sets an order in which the rules should be applied to the test set.

The basic PrismTCS algorithm is outlined below where A_x is a possible attribute value pair and D is the training dataset. The statement

```
Rule_set rules = new Rule_set();
```

creates a new rule set which is a list of rules and the line

```
Rule rule = new Rule(i);
```

creates a new rule with class i as classification. The statement

```
rule.addTerm(Ax);
```

will append a rule term to the rule and

```
rules.add(rule);
```

adds the finished rule to the rule set.

```
        D' = D;
        Rule_set rules = new Rule_set();
Step 1: Find class i that has the fewest instances in the training
        set;
        Rule rule = new Rule(i);
Step 2: Calculate for each Ax p(class = i| Ax);
Step 3: Select the Ax with the maximum  p(class = i| Ax);
        rule.addTerm(Ax);
        Delete all instances in D' that do not cover rule;
Step 4: Repeat 2 to 3 for D' until D' only contains instances
        of classification i.
Step 5: rules.add(rule);
        Create a new D' that comprises all instances of D except
        those that are covered by all rules induced so far;
Step 6: IF (D' is not empty){
              repeat steps 1 to 6;
        }
```

We will concentrate here on the more popular PrismTCS approach but all techniques and methods outlined here can be applied to any member of the Prism family.

2.2 Random Prism Classifier

The Random Prism classifier is based on the principles of the RF ensemble learner, hence this section first introduces the Random Forests classifier briefly and then discusses the new Random Prism ensemble classifier.

As mentioned in Section 1 RF are inspired by the RDF approach from Ho [15]. RDF induces multiple trees in randomly selected subsets of the feature space in order to make the trees generalise better. RF uses RDF's approach plus bagging [6] in order to improve the classifiers' accuracy and stability. Bagging means that a sample with replacement is taken for the induction of each tree.

The basic principle of RF is that it grows a large number of decision trees (a forest) on samples produced by bagging, using a random subset of the feature space for the evaluation of splits at each node in each tree. If there is a new data instance to be classified, then each tree is used to produce a prediction for the new data instance. RF then labels the new data instance with the class that achieved the majority of the 'votes'.

The Random Prism ensemble learner's ingredients are the RDF's random feature subset selection, RF's bagging and PrismTCS as base classifier.

Using Prism as base classifier is motivated by the fact that Prism is less vulnerable to clashes, missing values and noise in the dataset and in general tends to overfit less compared with decision trees [3] which are used in RF and RDF. In particular PrismTCS is used, as PrismTCS is also computationally more efficient than the original Prism while in some cases producing a better accuracy [29]. A good computational efficiency is needed as ensemble classifiers induce multiple classifiers and thus place a high computational demand on CPU time. In the context of Random Prism, the terms PrismTCS and Prism may be used interchangeably in this paper, both referring to PrismTCS unless stated otherwise.

Given a training dataset D, using bagging a sample D_i if i is the ith classifier is created, using random sampling with replacement [6]. This means that the data samples may overlap, as in D_i a data instance may occur more than once or may not be included at all. From each D_i a classifier C_i is induced. In order to classify a new data instance, each C_i predicts the class, and the bagged classifier counts the votes and labels the data instance with the class that achieved the majority of the votes. An ensemble classifier created using bagging often achieves a higher accuracy compared with a single classifier induced on the whole training dataset D and if it achieves a worse accuracy it is often still close to the single classifier's accuracy [14]. The reason for the increased accuracy of bagged classifiers lies in the fact that the composite classifier model reduces the variance of the individual classifiers [14]. The most commonly used bootstrap model for bagging is to take a sample of size n if n is the number of instances. This will result in samples that contain on average 63.2% of the original data instances. The fact that bagged classifiers can achieve a higher accuracy than a single classifier induced on the whole dataset D, as mentioned above, motivates the use of bagging in the Random Prism ensemble classifier proposed here.

The RDF approach by Ho [15] induces multiple trees on randomly selected subsets of the feature space. Again a composite model is generated and it has been shown in [15] that they generalise better than a single tree induced on the complete feature space, as the are less prone to overfitting. Inspired from RDF, Breiman's RF randomly selects a subset of the feature space for each node of each tree. Feature subset selection similar to the one used in RF is incorporated in Random Prism as well, inspired from the fact that random feature subset selection generalises the ensemble classifier better and thus makes it likely to produce a higher classification accuracy.

The pseudo code below describes the adapted version of PrismTCS for the use in Random Prism based on PrismTCS's pseudo code in Section 2.1. M is the number of features in D:

```
          D' = random sample with replacement of size n from D;
          Rule_set rules = new Rule_set();
Step 1:   Find class i that has the fewest instances in the training
          set;
          Rule rule = new Rule(i);
Step 2:   generate a subset F of the feature space of size m where
          (M>m>0);
Step 3:   Calculate for each Ax in F  p(class = i| Ax);
Step 4:   Select the Ax with the maximum  p(class = i| Ax);
          rule.addTerm(Ax);
          Delete all instances in D' that do not cover rule;
Step 5:   Repeat 2 to 4 for D' until D' only contains instances
          of classification i.
Step 6:   rules.add(rule);
          Create a new D' that comprises all instances of D except
          those that are covered by all rules induced so far;
Step 7:   IF (D' is not empty){
                repeat steps 1 to 7;
          }
```

The pseudo code above is essentially PrismTCS incorporating RDF's and RF's random feature subset selection. For the induction of each rule term for each rule, a fresh random subset of the feature space is drawn. Also the number of features considered for each rule term is a random number between 1 and M. The PrismTCS version above is called *R-PrismTCS*, *R* for denoting **R**andom sample and feature selection.

The basic Random Prism approach is outlined in the pseudo code below, where k is the number of *R-PrismTCS* classifiers to be induced and i is the *ith* classifier:

```
double weights[] = new double[k];
Classifiers classifiers = new Classifier[k];
for(int t = 0; t < k; t++){
    Build R-RrismTCS classifier r;
    TestData T = instances of D that have not been to induce r;
    Apply r to T;
    int correct = number of by r correctly classified instances in T;
    weights[t] = correct/(number of instances in T);
}
```

Please note that in the Random Prism pseudo code above not only a set of classifiers is created but also a set of weights. Random Prism does not employ a simple voting system like RF or RDF, but a weighted majority voting system as in the

Pocket Data Mining System [27, 26], where each vote is weighted according to the corresponding classifier's accuracy on the test data. As mentioned earlier in this section, the sampling method used for each classifier selects approximately 63.2% percent of the total number of data instances, which leaves approximately 36.8% of the total number of data instances which are used to calculate the individual *R-PrismTCS* classifier's accuracy and thus weight. Also the user of the Random Prism classifier can define a threshold *N*, which is the precentage of classifiers to be used for prediction. Random Prism will always select those classifiers with the highest weights.

For example consider classifiers and weights listed in Table 1.

Table 1 Example data for weighted majority voting

Classifier	Weight
A	0.55
B	0.65
C	0.55
D	0.95
E	0.85

Assume that the classifiers in Table 1 are already the best classifiers selected according to the user's defined threshold. Further assume that for a new unseen data instance classifiers *A*, *B* and *C* predict class *Y* and classifiers *D* and *E* predict class *X*. Random Prism's weighted majority vote for class *Y* is 1.75 (i.e. $0.55 + 0.65 + 0.55$) and for class *X* is 1.80 (i.e. $0.95 + 0.85$). Thus Random Prism will label the data instance with class *X*.

The *R-PrismTCS* pseudo code above does not take pruning into consideration, however a pre-pruning method *J-pruning* presented in [4] is implemented in *R-PrismTCS* in order further generalise the base classifiers. J-pruning is based on the J-measure. According to Smyth and Goodman [22] the average information content of a rule of the form *IF Y = y THEN X = x* can be quantified by the following equation:

$$J(X;Y = y) = p(y) \cdot j(X;Y = y) \quad (1)$$

The J-measure is a product of two terms. The first term *p(y)* is the probability that the antecedent of the rule will occur. It is a measure of hypothesis simplicity. The second term *j(X;Y=y)* is the j-measure or cross entropy. It is a measure of the goodness-of-fit of a rule and is defined by:

$$j(X;Y = y) = p(x \mid y) \cdot log_2(\tfrac{p(x|y)}{p(x)}) + (1 - p(x \mid y)) \cdot log_2(\tfrac{(1-p(x|y))}{(1-p(x))}) \quad (2)$$

If a rule has a high J-value then it tends to have a high predictive accuracy as well. The J-value is used to identify when a further specialisation of the rule is likely to result in a lower predictive accuracy due to overfitting. The basic idea is to induce a rule term and if the rule term would increase the J-value of the current rule then the rule term is appended. If not then the rule term is discarded and the rule is finished.

3 Evaluation of Random Prism Classification

Random Prism has been evaluated on 15 different datasets retrieved from the UCI data repository [2]. For each dataset a test and a training set has been created using random sampling without replacement. The training set comprises 70% of the total data instances. Please note that the training set is sampled again by each R-PrismTCS base classifier, in order to incorporate bagging. Hence, as stated in Section 2.2 approximately 63.2% of the training data is used for the actual training and 36.8% is used to calculate the individual classifiers' weights. The percentage of the best classifiers to be used was 10% and the total number of R-PrismTCS classifiers induced was 100 for each dataset.

Table 2 shows the accuracy achieved using Random Prism classifier and the accuracy achieved using a single PrismTCS classifier.

Table 2 Accuracy of Random Prism compared with PrismTCS.

Dataset	Accuracy PrismTCS	Accuracy Random Prism
monk1	0.79	1.0
monk3	0.98	0.99
vote	0.94	0.95
genetics	0.70	0.88
contact lenses	0.95	0.91
breast cancer	0.95	0.95
soybean	0.88	0.65
australian credit	0.89	0.92
diabetes	0.75	0.89
crx	0.83	0.86
segmentation	0.79	0.71
ecoli	0.78	0.78
balance scale	0.72	0.86
car evaluation	0.76	0.71
contraceptive method choice	0.44	0.54

As can be seen in Table 2 Random Prism outperforms PrismTCS in 9 out of 15 cases; in two cases Random Prism achieved the same accuracy as PrismTCS; and in only 4 cases Random Prism's accuracy was below that of PrismTCS. However, looking into these four cases with a lower accuracy, which is for datasets 'car evaluation', 'segmentation', 'soybean' and 'contact lenses', it can be seen that the accuracies for 'car evaluation' and 'contact lenses' is still very close the PrismTCS's accuracy. In

general Random Prism outperforms its single classifier version PrismTCS in most cases and in the remaining cases its accuracy is often very close to PrismTCS's accuracy.

4 Ongoing and Future Work

Ongoing and future work comprises a distributed / parallel version of Random Prism and several variations of the Random Prism approach itself.

4.1 Parallel Random Prism Classifier

Random Prism like any other ensemble learner has a higher demand on CPU time than its single classifier version. Table 3 lists the runtimes of PrismTCS and Random Prism for the evaluation experiments outlined in Section 3. As ensemble learners are designed to reduce overfitting, they should be able to be executed on larger datasets as well, as the likelihood that noisy data instances are present is higher the larger the training data is.

Table 3 Runtime of Random Prism on 100 base classifiers compared with a single PrismTCS classifier in milli seconds.

Dataset	Runtime PrismTCS	Runtime Random Prism
monk1	16	703
monk3	15	640
vote	16	672
genetics	219	26563
contact lenses	16	235
breast cancer	32	1531
soybean	78	5078
australian credit	31	1515
diabetes	16	1953
crx	31	2734
segmentation	234	15735
ecoli	16	734
balance scale	15	1109
car evaluation	16	3750
contraceptive method choice	32	3563

It can be seen that as expected the runtimes are much larger for Random Prism than for PrismTCS. This is because Random Prism induces 100 base classifiers whereas PrismTCS is only a single classifier. One would expect the runtimes of Random Prism to be 100 times longer than for PrismTCS as Random Prism induces 100 base classifiers, however the runtimes are much shorter than expected. The rea-

son for this is that the base classifiers use a subset of the feature space and thus have fewer features to scan for the induction of each rule term.

Future work will address the problem of scalability of the Random Prism classifier. Google's Parallel Learner for Assembling Numerous Ensemble Trees system [18] addresses this problem in the context of decision tree based ensemble classifiers using the MapReduce [12] model of distributed computation. MapReduce builds a cluster of computers for a two-phase distributed computation on large volumes of data. First in the map-phase the dataset is split into disjoint subsets, which are assigned together with a user specified map function to workers (mappers) in the MapReduce cluster. Each mapper then applies the map function on its data. The output of the map function (a key-value pair) is then grouped and combined by a second kind of worker, the reducers, using a user defined reduce function.

For Random Prism the MapReduce model will be used to distribute the induction of the R-PrismTCS base classifiers using mappers. The individual R-PrismTCS classifiers are then combined using the reducers to the final Random Prism Classifier. Thus the CUP intense part, the induction of many base classifiers can easily be distributed to a computing cluster of workstations. A open source implementation of the MapReduce model called Hadoop is available [1].

4.2 Variations of the Random Prism Ensemble Classifier

There are many possible variations of the Random Prism approach that may achieve better classification accuracy, for example different versions of Prism could be used as base classifiers. Also it would be possible to use a diverse mix of all existing Prism classifiers, such as Prism, PrismTC or PrismTCS. Some Prism classifiers may perform well on certain samples, some may perform worse, thus a larger variety of Prism classifiers per sample may well increase Random Prism's classification accuracy.. Also it is possible to use several Prism and decision tree base classifiers for each sample.

4.3 Intelligent Voting System

Random Prism's classification accuracy may be further improved by employing a more intelligent voting system. For example a classifier may have in general a moderate predictive accuracy. However, concerning its predictions for class A, the classifier may have a very high predictive accuracy. Such cases could be addressed by calculating individual weights for each class for this particular classifier. Implementing more than one weight for a classifier must also be addressed in the selection of the best classifiers according to a user defined percentage. A similar approach called 'Combining' has been used by the Meta-Learning system [9, 10].

5 Conclusions

This work presents the Random Prism ensemble classifier based on the Prism family of algorithms as base classifier. Most ensemble learners are based on decision trees as base classifiers and aim to reduce the overfitting of the model in order to achieve a higher classification accuracy. However alternative base classifiers exist, such as the Prism family of algorithms. It has been discussed that Prism algorithms already perform better on noisy datasets compared with decision trees, as they tend to overfit less. The motivation behind Random Prism is that an ensemble classifier based on the Prism family of algorithms may further reduce the overfitting and thus achieve a higher classification accuracy compared with single Prism classifiers.

First the Prism family of algorithms has been introduced and compared with decision trees and next the well known Random Forests approach has been reviewed. Random Prism is inspired from the Prism family of algorithms, the Random Decision Forests and Random Forests approaches. Random Prism uses the PrismTCS classifier as base classifier with some modifications called R-PrismTCS. The modifications were in order to use the Random Decision Forests' feature subset selection approach. Random Prism also incorporates J-pruning for R-PrismTCS and Random Forests' bagging approach. Contrary to Random Forests and Random Decision Forests, Random Prism uses a weighted majority voting system instead of a plain majority voting system, in order to take the individual classifier's classification accuracy into account. Also Random Prism does not take all classifiers into account, the user can define the percentage of classifiers to be used for classification. Random Prism will select only the classifiers with the highest classification accuracy for the classification task.

Random Prism has been evaluated on 15 datasets from the UCI repository and has been shown to produce a better classification accuracy on 9 cases compared with PrismTCS. In two cases the classification accuracy was the same as for PrismTCS. In two further cases the classification accuracy was slightly below PrismTCS's accuracy and only in two cases was it much worse than PrismTCS's accuracy.

Ongoing work on Random Prism comprises the development of a distributed / parallel version in order to make Random Prism scale better on large datasets. For this the MapReduce framework is considered in order to distribute the induction of the individual classifiers to different machines in a cluster of workstations. This could be realised using a open source implementation of MapReduce called Hadoop. Furthermore a variety of Random Prism versions are planned, comprising different Prism classifiers as base classifiers or even hybrid ensemble learners comprising different versions of Prism in one ensemble learner or possibly a mix of decision tree and Prism classifiers.

Acknowledgements We would like to acknowledge Mohamed Medhat Gaber for his advice during the implementation of the Random Prism algorithm.

References

1. Hadoop, http://hadoop.apache.org/mapreduce/ 2011.
2. C L Blake and C J Merz. UCI repository of machine learning databases. Technical report, University of California, Irvine, Department of Information and Computer Sciences, 1998.
3. M A Bramer. Automatic induction of classification rules from examples using N-Prism. In *Research and Development in Intelligent Systems XVI*, pages 99–121, Cambridge, 2000. Springer-Verlag.
4. M A Bramer. An information-theoretic approach to the pre-pruning of classification rules. In B Neumann M Musen and R Studer, editors, *Intelligent Information Processing*, pages 201–212. Kluwer, 2002.
5. M A Bramer. Inducer: a public domain workbench for data mining. *International Journal of Systems Science*, 36(14):909–919, 2005.
6. Leo Breiman. Bagging predictors. *Machine Learning*, 24(2):123–140, 1996.
7. Leo Breiman. Random forests. *Machine Learning*, 45(1):5–32, 2001.
8. J. Cendrowska. PRISM: an algorithm for inducing modular rules. *International Journal of Man-Machine Studies*, 27(4):349–370, 1987.
9. Philip Chan and Salvatore J Stolfo. Experiments on multistrategy learning by meta learning. In *Proc. Second Intl. Conference on Information and Knowledge Management*, pages 314–323, 1993.
10. Philip Chan and Salvatore J Stolfo. Meta-Learning for multi strategy and parallel learning. In *Proceedings. Second International Workshop on Multistrategy Learning*, pages 150–165, 1993.
11. Nitesh V. Chawla, Lawrence O. Hall, Kevin W. Bowyer, and W. Philip Kegelmeyer. Learning ensembles from bites: A scalable and accurate approach. *J. Mach. Learn. Res.*, 5:421–451, December 2004.
12. Jeffrey Dean and Sanjay Ghemawat. Mapreduce: simplified data processing on large clusters. *Commun. ACM*, 51:107–113, January 2008.
13. Saso Dzeroski and Bernard Zenko. Is combining classifiers with stacking better than selecting the best one? *Machine Learning*, 54:255–273, 2004.
14. Jiawei Han and Micheline Kamber. *Data Mining: Concepts and Techniques*. Morgan Kaufmann, 2001.
15. Tin Kam Ho. Random decision forests. *Document Analysis and Recognition, International Conference on*, 1:278, 1995.
16. R S Michalski. On the Quasi-Minimal solution of the general covering problem. In *Proceedings of the Fifth International Symposium on Information Processing*, pages 125–128, Bled, Yugoslavia, 1969.
17. Domingos P. and Hulten G. Mining high-speed data streams. In *In International Conference on Knowledge Discovery and Data Mining*, pages 71–81, 2000.
18. Biswanath Panda, Joshua S. Herbach, Sugato Basu, and Roberto J. Bayardo. Planet: massively parallel learning of tree ensembles with mapreduce. *Proc. VLDB Endow.*, 2:1426–1437, August 2009.
19. Foster Provost. Distributed data mining: Scaling up and beyond. In *Advances in Distributed and Parallel Knowledge Discovery*, pages 3–27. MIT Press, 2000.
20. R J Quinlan. *C4.5: programs for machine learning*. Morgan Kaufmann, 1993.
21. Ross J Quinlan. Induction of decision trees. *Machine Learning*, 1(1):81–106, 1986.
22. P. Smyth and R M Goodman. An information theoretic approach to rule induction from databases. *Transactions on Knowledge and Data Engineering*, 4(4):301–316, 1992.
23. F T Stahl, M A Bramer, and M Adda. PMCRI: A parallel modular classification rule induction framework. In *MLDM*, pages 148–162. Springer, 2009.
24. Frederic Stahl, Max Bramer, and Mo Adda. J-PMCRI: a methodology for inducing pre-pruned modular classification rules. *IFIP Advances in Information and Communication Technology*, 331:47–56, 2010.

25. Frederic Stahl, Max Bramer, and Mo Adda. Parallel rule induction with information theoretic pre-pruning. In *Research and Development in Intelligent Systems XXVI*, volume 4, pages 151–164. Springerlink, 2010.
26. Frederic Stahl, Mohamed Medhat Gaber, Max Bramer, and Phillip S. Yu. Distributed hoeffding trees for pocket data mining. In *The 2011 International Conference on High Performance Computing and Simulation*, Istanbul, Turkey, in Press (2011).
27. Frederic Stahl, Mohamed Medhat Gaber, Han Liu, Max Bramer, and Phillip S. Yu. Distributed classification for pocket data mining. In *19th International Symposium on Methodologies for Intelligent Systems*, Warsaw, Poland, in Press (2011). Springer.
28. Frederic T. Stahl and Max Bramer. Induction of modular classification rules: Using jmax-pruning. In *SGAI Conf.'10*, pages 79–92, 2010.
29. Frederic T. Stahl, Max Bramer, and Mo Adda. Parallel induction of modular classification rules. In *SGAI Conf.*, pages lookup–lookup. Springer, 2008.
30. Frederic T. Stahl, Mohamed Medhat Gaber, Max Bramer, and Philip S. Yu. Pocket data mining: Towards collaborative data mining in mobile computing environments. In *ICTAI (2)'10*, pages 323–330, 2010.
31. I H Witten and F Eibe. *Data Mining: Practical Machine Learning Tools and Techniques with Java Implementations*. Morgan Kaufmann, 1999.

PLANNING

Exploiting Automatic Validation in Human Mission Planning

Pietro Torasso and Gianluca Torta

Abstract In this paper we describe an approach to support human operators in UAV mission planning, derived from our participation to the Industrial Research Project SMAT-F1, which focused on UAV missions for monitoring the territory for civil purposes. First of all, we propose a rich modeling language for expressing the complex structure of mission plans, as well as the quantitative and qualitative constraints needed to validate human-crafted plans. Then, we describe an automatic validation module which provides the operator with feedback on the flaws in the plan she is specifying and, when possible, also with explanations of such flaws and suggestions for fixing them. An initial evaluation of the approach is performed on several scenarios that could occur during the validation of mission plans.

1 Introduction

While automated planning can successfully address many real world problems, there are critical domains in which the planning is still mostly done by humans. One of such scenarios is mission planning (e.g. for space missions or Unmanned Aircraft Vehicle missions), where the human expert responsible for the task is still expected to have a wider and deeper domain knowledge and better reasoning skills w.r.t. an automatic planner.

However, manually building a mission plan is a very complex activity, where the operator must consider both quantitative constraints (time, space, resources) and qualitative constraints. Therefore, automatic tools to assist the human operator are needed, and some proposals have started to appear in the literature, most notably in the field of space missions [2, 1], while the role that automated tools could/should have in mission planning and monitoring of UAV missions is actively debated (see e.g. [5, 6]).

Pietro Torasso and Gianluca Torta
Dipartimento di Informatica, Università di Torino, Italy, e-mail: {torasso,torta}@di.unito.it

M. Bramer et al. (eds.), *Research and Development in Intelligent Systems XXVIII*,
DOI 10.1007/978-1-4471-2318-7_2, © Springer-Verlag London Limited 2011

In this paper we describe an approach to support human operators in UAV mission planning, derived from our participation to a Research Project (named SMAT-F1) which involve several aeronautics industries and was focused on UAV missions for monitoring the territory for civil purposes. In particular, we propose an *automatic validation* (AV) module that can be invoked by the operator to get feedback on the flaws in the plan she has built and, when possible, also explanations of such flaws and suggestions for fixing them.

In section 2 we introduce the rich modeling language that we have defined in order to express the complex structure of mission plans, as well as the quantitative and qualitative constraints needed to validate human-crafted plans.

In section 3 we describe the mission planning process, an iterative, interactive activity between the human operator and the automatic validation tool. At the most abstract level, the process is divided in two phases: the creation of an high-level sketch of the plan, and its refinement into a fully detailed plan.

In sections 4 and 5 we give details about the automatic check of plans, explanation of failures and suggestion of repairs during the two phases of the planning process. In section 6 we discuss the outcome of some tests performed with an implemented prototype of our approach. Finally, in section 7 we briefly compare our proposal to related work and point to further research directions.

2 Modeling

2.1 Problem Specification and Mission Plan

Let us start with the description of the requirements the mission has to fulfil.

Definition 1. The planning problem is specified by a *Problem Specification*

$$PS = \{MAP, UAV, TrgList, TrgOrder, TrgAnalysis, \\ Source, Dest, StartTime, EndTime\}$$

where:

- *MAP* describes the area interested by the mission. The map contains at least info about the main infrastructures present in the area (airports, roads, towns, rivers, etc.) and may also indicate "stay out" zones for the UAV
- *UAV* specifies the type of UAV to be used during this mission
- *TrgList* contains a list of targets to be covered during the mission and each target is specified with an *id* and the coordinates on the map defined by parameter *MAP*
- *TrgOrder* is a (partial) order specifying in which sequence the targets have to be reached by the UAV
- *TrgAnalysis* specifies for each target the kind of activity and analysis to be performed for the target
- *Source* and *Dest* (which can coincide) represent the facilities (typically airports) where the mission starts with the take-off and ends with a landing

- *StartTime* and *EndTime* represent the time envelop for the mission, and implicitly define the maximum duration as $(EndTime - StartTime)$

Given a problem specification *PS*, the final result of the planning activity is a mission plan *MP* which specifies what activities constitute the mission plan, which route has to be followed by the UAV in performing the mission and how to use the sensors on board of the UAV for analysing the targets.

A mission plan is an ordered list of tasks $MP = (Tsk_0, Tsk_1, \ldots, Tsk_n)$ describing the entire mission, while each Tsk_i describes a specific task. A task Tsk_i is characterized by the main activity $Tsk_i.act$ to be carried on (*take-off, landing, monitor, transfer*, etc.) and can cover at most one target T_j, denoted with $Tsk_i.trg = T_j$.

Each task is also characterized by a route to be flied by the UAV: more specifically $Tsk_i.route$ is an ordered list of way points $(WP_{i,1}, \ldots WP_{i,n})$; we also denote waypoint $WP_{i,1}$ as $Tsk_i.SWP$ (start waypoint) and, similarly, $WP_{i,n}$ as $Tsk_i.FWP$ (final waypoint), and we require that at least $Tsk_i.SWP$ and $Tsk_i.FWP$ are specified, while the other waypoints are optional. Moreover, if Tsk_i and Tsk_{i+1} are adjacent tasks in *MP*, then $Tsk_i.FWP = Tsk_{i+1}.SWP$.
Each way point *WP* is specified in terms of its coordinates $WP.long$, $WP.lat$ on the map, but also contains other types of information such as the altitude $WP.alt$ and speed $WP.speed$ of the UAV when it flies over *WP*.

In case a task Tsk_i involves the monitoring of the target T_j, it is necessary to specify which sensor has to be used via an assertion $Tsk_i.sns = S_k$; moreover, it is possible to specify some parameters about the sensor usage (for example *azimuth* and *elevation* angles).

The entire mission plan as well as each Tsk_i can be further characterized by additional information (such as the duration of the mission and the tasks, the length of the route, etc.) but these values are not explicitly represented inside the *MP* since they depend on other data contained in the plan description, and can be computed or estimated from such data. We will come back to this point when we discuss the predictive models in section 2.2.

A mission plan *MP* can be considered as a solution to a problem specification *PS* just in case *MP* satisfies the requirements put by *PS*. Let us denote with *DM* the *Domain Model*, i.e. the background constraints specifying knowledge about the UAVs, the sensors, and the missions. While the contents of *DM* will be discussed in detail in the next section, we define the validity of a mission plan *MP* w.r.t. *PS* as:

$$DM \cup PS \cup MP \not\vdash \bot$$

i.e. given the domain model *DM* and the problem specification *PS*, a mission plan *MP* is a valid plan for *PS* iff *MP* satisfies all the constraints put by *DM* given *PS*.

2.2 Domain Model

The constraints that relate the elements of a mission plan *MP*, the requirements of a problem specification *PS*, and other background information are contained in the domain model *DM*. We group such constraints into three main categories.

Physical and operative characteristics. An important source of knowledge concerns the basic characteristics of the UAVs and of the sensors. This knowledge can be further subdivided into:

- constraints concerning the UAVs, e.g. max speed, max fuel capacity, max altitude, max payload, etc.; these constraints also include typical (i.e. *nominal*) operative values of some parameters, such as cruise speed and flying altitude
- constraints concerning the sensors, e.g. max zoom, max resolution, max azimuth and elevation etc.
- constraints relating sensors and UAVs, e.g. what kind of sensors can be embarked on a specific UAV

Predictive models. With this term we denote numerical, discrete or qualitative models able to compute/estimate the value of certain relevant quantities from the values of other parameters. Let us consider the duration of a task $dur(Tsk_i)$. This quantity is not given explicitly by the human operator and is not included directly into the *MP*, but can be predicted (with some degree of approximation) from the route associated with Tsk_i, the speed at the different way points, the altitude, etc.

It is worth noting that the predictive models may require a mix of numerical and logical inference. One relevant example is estimate-coverage($T_j, Tsk_k, WP_{k,i} WP_{k,i+1}$):

this predictive model verifies whether a target T_j is covered when the UAV is flying the portion of the route between two consecutive waypoints (i.e. $WP_{k,i}, WP_{k,i+1}$)) of the task Tsk_k. For performing such a check, the predictive model performs some geometric reasoning for computing the footprint from a specific position of the UAV according to the method described in [3]. Such a computation requires that the route is approximated (for example, the route is a linear interpolation between the two specified waypoints); the other relevant parameters such as the altitude of the UAV, the FOV (field of view) of the sensor used for monitoring the target, and the azimuth/elevation of the sensor w.r.t. the UAV have to be retrieved from the plan *MP* (and in case they are not specified, default values are used by considering the pieces of information contained in the "physical and operative characteristics").

Similar considerations can be done for the estimation of other parameters, such as length of the route, fuel consumption, etc. The accuracy of such estimates depends on the specific kind of model adopted. At the planning time, simple predictive models are usually preferred since they allow to get a first estimate without requiring the knowledge of the exact value of many parameters which are difficult to be given at the planning time.

Mission plan constraints. The third component of the domain model *DM* refers to the mission plan constraints. This kind of knowledge plays an essential role in

specifying the relation between the assignment of values to the parameters of MP and the requirements contained in the problem specification PS. Because of the variety of constraints, it is useful to group them in two classes, namely local and global constraints.

Local constraints involve just parameters that refer to the same task. Some of them are related to the role of the task inside the mission; for example:

$$T sk_0.act = take - off$$
$$\forall T sk_i, T_j : \ T sk_i.trg = T_j \Rightarrow T sk_i.act = monitoring$$

Other constraints relate the values of some parameters of the entities specified for a task: let us suppose the route $T sk_i.route$ contains the waypoints $WP_{i,1}, \ldots WP_{i,n}$. The constraint stating that:

$$\forall T sk_i : \ |WP_{i,k+1}.alt - WP_{i,k}.alt| \leq \Delta_{alt}$$

puts a restriction on the difference of altitude for two consecutive way points of the same task.

Global constraints involve one or more variables for all the tasks of a mission. Some of these constraints relate properties of each task with a global property the mission plan has to exhibit. For example:

$$\{T_i : \ \exists T sk_j (T sk_j.trg = T_i)\} \equiv TrgList$$

states that all the targets T_i listed in $TrgList$ have to be covered by some task.

Similarly, the ordering constraints $TrgOrder$ on the targets specified in PS have to be matched by the sequence of tasks. formally we have that:

$$\forall T_i, T_j : (T_i < T_j) \Rightarrow \exists T sk_k \exists T sk_l \ (T sk_k.trg = T_i) \wedge (T sk_l.trg = T_j) \wedge (T sk_k < T sk_l)$$

Some other global constraints require that a global parameter is satisfied. As an example let us consider:

$$\sum dur(T sk_i) \leq Maxdur$$

which requires that the total duration of the mission (computed as the sum of the duration of all the tasks involved in the mission) is less than the maximum duration $Maxdur$. Similar constraints can be put on other global properties, such as length of the mission (in terms of flown kilometers), total fuel consumption, etc.

3 Mission Planning Process

As stated in the introduction, mission planning is a complex task, and so far most of the activities are carried out by human operators who take responsibilities also with Aviation authorities. For these reasons the role of automated tools is constrained, and currently consists in supporting human decision making.

Figure 1 shows a sketch of how the human operator OP and the automatic validator AV cooperate in the mission planning process.

Starting from a problem specification PS, OP creates a *high-level* plan HP containing the following basic information:

- the sequence of tasks

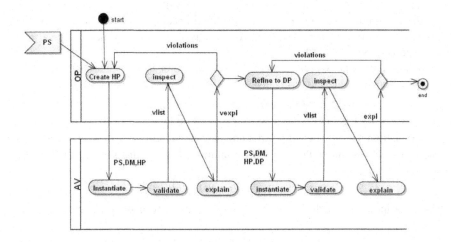

Fig. 1 Mission Planning Process.

- the main activity of each task and (when appropriate) the associated target and the type of sensor used for monitoring the target
- a first indication about the route to be flown, containing the geographical coordinates of the starting and final waypoints for each task

The high level plan should be consistent with both the problem specification *PS* and the background constraints described in the *DM*; therefore, *OP* calls the validator *AV* with *DM*, *PS* and *HP* as arguments.

First of all, *AV* instantiates the generic constraints in *DM* to specific constraints based on plan *HP*. This process is essential since constraints in *DM* are given in an intensional form (by using quantified variables), while the actual check of satisfiability is done on instantiated constraints (see next section for an example).

After the instantiation step, *AV* checks each constraint and returns to *OP* the list *vlist* of all the violated constraints.

If *vlist* is not empty, *OP* can inspect it and ask *AV* for a set of explanations *vexpl*; then she goes back to modify *HP* in order to fix the violations (or to change *PS*), thus repeating this part of the process until *HP* satisfies all the constraints.

When *HP* has been successfully validated, it is up to *OP* to refine *HP* in a number of directions:

- a more precise specification of the route in terms of additional waypoints
- altitude and desired speed of the UAV at each WP
- parameters for the sensors

The detailed plan *DP* is derived by *HP* via the application of *refinement* operations chosen by the human operator:

- *RefineRoute*$(Tsk_i, WP_{i,1}, \ldots, WP_{i,n})$: specifies that the route $Tsk_i.route$ (initially specified just with the starting and final waypoints $Tsk_i.SWP$ and $Tsk_i.FWP$) has to be flown via the intermediate waypoints $WP_{i,1}, \ldots, WP_{i,n}$
- *SetWpParam*(WP, P, V) sets the parameter P at waypoint WP to the value V, e.g. *SetWpParam*$(WP1.speed, 40m/s)$ sets the speed of the UAV at the way point $WP1$ to 40 meters per second
- *SetSensParam*(Tsk_i, S, P, V) sets the parameter P of the sensor S during the execution of task Tsk_i to the value V, e.g. *SetSensParam*$(Tsk_i, S1, azimuth, 90)$ sets the azimuth of sensor $S1$ to 90 degrees during task Tsk_i

Once *OP* has completed the refinement, the validator *AV* is called with *DM*, *PS*, *HP* and *DP* as arguments. After instantiating the generic constraints in *DM* to specific constraints based on plan *DP*, *AV* checks each constraint and returns to *OP* the list *vlist* of all the violated constraints.

Also in this phase, if *vlist* is not empty, *OP* can inspect it and ask *AV* for a set of explanations *vexpl* before going back to modify *DP* in order to fix the violations, until *DP* satisfies all the constraints and the mission planning process can terminate. In the following sections we will describe with more detail the two phases.

4 Validation of High-Level Plans

As sketched in the previous section, the validation of a high level plan is possible just after the *OP* has provided a *HP* for the *PS*. Let us assume that the mission planning problem *PS* is characterized in terms of the following requirements:

- three targets to be covered T_1, T_2 and T_3 in sequence, i.e. $T_1 < T_2 < T_3$
- the kind of analysis is given by $T_1.analysis = scanning$, $T_2.analysis = detect$, $T_3.analysis = scanning$
- the starting and final point of the mission is the airport A_0

The geographical positions of the targets and of the airport are reported in figure 2. The *PS* also states that the mission has to be performed by aircraft *UAV1* with a maximum duration MAX_{dur} of *30 min*.

Let us suppose that *OP* provides a high level plan *HP* which involves 7 tasks (namely $Tsk_0, \ldots, Tsk_6$) whose order is $Tsk_0 < Tsk_1 < Tsk_2 < Tsk_3 < Tsk_4 < Tsk_5 < Tsk_6$. The relation between tasks and targets is given by means of the following assertions:

$$(Tsk_1.trg = T_1), \ (Tsk_3.trg = T_2), \ (Tsk_4.trg = T_3)$$

(e.g., target T_3 is monitored during Tsk_4). The main activity carried on within each task is specified as:

$$(Tsk_0.act = takeoff), \ Tsk_1.act = monitor), \ (Tsk_2.act = transfer),$$
$$(Tsk_3.act = monitor), \ (Tsk_4.act = monitor), \ (Tsk_5.act = transfer),$$
$$(Tsk_6.act = landing)$$

The initial plan has also to provide some information about the route, in particular for each task the final waypoint (and initial waypoint of the next task) has to be defined. Let us suppose that this information is as follows:

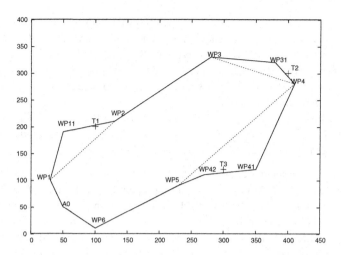

Fig. 2 Mission Plan Route.

$Tsk_0.FWP = WP_1$, $Tsk_1.FWP = WP_2$, $Tsk_2.FWP = WP_3$, $Tsk_3.FWP = WP_4$
$Tsk_4.FWP = WP_5$, $Tsk_5.FWP = WP_6$, $Tsk_6.FWP = A_0$

where the positions of the way-points on the map are reported in figure 2.

The high level plan is completed with information concerning the use of sensors in specific tasks; in particular:

$$(Tsk_1.sns = S_1), \ (Tsk_3.sns = S2), \ (Tsk_4.sns = S1)$$

Once the high level plan has been provided, the human operator can activate the automatic validation for checking the consistency between the high level plan HP and the mission requirements. This process will involve first the automatic instantiation of the generic constraints; for example:

$$\forall Tsk_i, T_j \ : \ Tsk_i.trg = T_j \Rightarrow act(Tsk_i) = monitoring$$

is instantiated to the specific constraints:

$$Tsk_1.act = monitoring; \ Tsk_3.act = monitoring; \ Tsk_4.act = monitoring$$

since HP associates targets with tasks Tsk_1, Tsk_3 and Tsk_4. This set of constraints is satisfied by HP.

Note that some of the constraints in DM may have no instances, due to lack of information in HP; for example, the generic constraint:

$$\forall Tsk_i : \ |WP_{i,k+1}.alt - WP_{i,k}.alt| \leq \Delta_{alt}$$

can't be checked at this stage, since the flight altitudes are not specified in HP.

The instantiation of the general constraint on HP:

$$\{T_i \ : \ \exists Tsk_j \ : \ Tsk_j.trg = T_i\} \equiv TrgList$$

produces the requirement:

$$\{T_1, T_2, T_3\} \equiv TrgList$$

which is immediate to check (all targets are considered).

In the same way it is easy to verify that the instantiation of the constraint about the ordering of the targets:

$$\forall T_i, T_j : (T_i < T_j) \Rightarrow \exists Tsk_k, Tsk_l (Tsk_k.trg = T_i) \wedge (Tsk_l.trg = T_j) \wedge (Tsk_k < Tsk_l)$$

is satisfied by the current plan HP.

Similar checks are done for the use of sensors and the correspondence between the activity performed by a task and the kind of service required for the targets.

Let us now consider the verification of the global constraint stating:

$$\sum dur(Tsk_i) < MAX_{dur}$$

In HP there is no information about the duration of the tasks, so in principle it is not possible to point out any constraint violation.

However, the automatic validator AV is able to reason also in presence of incomplete information by exploiting the predictive models and by making assumptions. In particular, a very rough route can be estimated by linearly interpolating the starting and final waypoints of each task. By computing the length of such a route and by assuming the cruise speed for $UAV1$, we can determine an estimate of $dur(Tsk_i)$ (the duration of take-off and landing in a specific airport are constant values taken from an appropriate database). Assuming that, under these assumptions, the constraint concerning max duration is violated, AV makes a last try by assuming that the speed at each WP is set to maxspeed: AV computes the lower bound $LB_{dur}(Tsk_i)$ for the duration of each task and, consequently, the lower bound $LB_{dur} = \sum LB_{dur}(Tsk_i)$ for the duration of the entire mission.

Following this method, we get that the length of the route exceeds 110 Km, and by considering that the max speed of $UAV1$ is 60 m/sec, it is easy to verify that the constraint on the maximum duration is violated, since LB_{dur} exceeds 38 min

This kind of inference is sufficient for AV to conclude that there is no way to satisfy the requirements with the current high level plan HP and this piece of information is provided to the human operator.

Let us suppose that the human operator reacts to this piece of information by setting MAX_{dur} to 60 min. This means that the problem specification PS has been revised into a new specification and therefore the high level plan HP has to be checked again. It is worth noting that the max duration constraint is now not only satisfied by considering LB_{dur}, but also by the much more realistic assumption that the UAV is flying at the cruise speed of 40 m/sec instead of the maximum speed. In particular, this estimate NOM_{dur} of 53 min satisfies the new max duration constraint of 60 min.

5 Validation of Refined Plans

The process for validating a detailed plan DP is similar to the process for validating a high level plan since also in this case AV has first to instantiate the general constraints and then to check them. It is worth noting that some classes of constraints that were not checked at the high level because of lack of information are now checked, since the plan has been refined and more information has been provided.

ExplainLocal($C(p_1, \ldots, p_n)$, Tsk, DP, DM)
1   plist = OrderParameters($p_1, \ldots, p_n$)
2   **while** (!empty(plist))
3   p = head(plist); plist = tail(plist)
4   set p to default value dv
5   **if** recheck $C(p_1, \ldots, p_n)$ with $p = dv$ **return** (p,dv)
6   set p to max/min value mv
7   **if** recheck $C(p_1, \ldots, p_n)$ with $p = mv$ **return** (p,mv)
8   **wend**
9   **return** FAIL

Fig. 3 Implementation of ExplainLocal.

In the following we will focus on the mechanism of explaining the violations, since this is the most interesting process where a significant role is played by the existence of an high level plan *HP* which satisfies both *PS* and *DM*. In fact, *HP* is an important source of information since it provides a baseline for comparing a *DP* (when it violates at least one constraint) with a consistent plan.

When *OP* requires *AV* to provide an explanation for a violation $v \in vlist$, *AV* has first to identify the kind of constraint the violation v refers to. In fact, the reasoning mechanism involved for explaining a violation of a local constraint is somewhat different from the one used for dealing with global constraints.

Figure 3 sketches the process for explaining the violation of the constraint C which involves the parameters $(p_1, \ldots, p_n)$. Since C is a local constraint, it is easy lo single out for which task Tsk such a violation occurs.

The basic idea of *ExplainLocal* consists in searching for a new assignment in one of the parameters $(p_1, \ldots, p_n)$ such that the new assignment satisfies C.

In order to reduce the search space, only one parameter per time is considered for change and the order is given by the function *OrderParameters* which, according to a heuristics h_L, considers parameters in the following order:

- sensor parameters (e.g. *zoom*, *azimuth*, *elevation*, ...)
- UAV parameters (e.g. *speed*, *climb rate*, *altitude*, ...)
- route definition (i.e. *waypoints* associated with the task)

This ordering prefers to check first changes of the parameters related to sensors, since they have the minimum impact on the whole plan, then the parameters of the UAV (whose impact is medium) before considering changes in the route since the revisions of the way points can have a serious impact also on some global aspects (such as length of the route).

For the first two classes of parameters (sensor and UAV), the *ExplainLocal* rechecks the satisfiability of C by setting p to the default (nominal) value dv (while all other parameters are left unchanged) and, in case of failure, it sets p to the min/max value as specified in *DM*.

In case an assignment satisfying the constraint C is found, this is reported to the user as an explanation of the violation. If no of such an assignment exists, then the checker informs the user that there is no simple repair for the violated constraint.

ExplainGlobal$(C(p_1,\ldots,p_n), DP, HP, DM)$
1   tsk = SelectCulpritTask$(C(p_1,\ldots,p_n), DP, HP)$
2    $pset$ = SelectCulpritParams$(C(p_1,\ldots,p_n), tsk, DP, HP)$
3   set each $p \in pset$ to corresponding value hv in HP
4   **if** recheck $C(p_1,\ldots,p_n)$ with $\forall p \in pset : p = hv$ **return** (pset,hv)
5   set each $p \in pset$ to default value dv
6   **if** recheck $C(p_1,\ldots,p_n)$ with $\forall p \in pset : p = dv$ **return** (pset,dv)
7   set each $p \in pset$ to max/min value mv
8   **if** recheck $C(p_1,\ldots,p_n)$ with $\forall p \in pset : p = mv$ **return** (pset,mv)
9   **return** FAIL

Fig. 4 Implementation of `ExplainGlobal`.

As an example, let us suppose that there is a violation of the constraint C requiring that the target T_2 is correctly covered when the UAV is flying the portion of the route defined by $WP3.1$ and $WP4$) of the task Tsk_3 (that is the estimate-coverage$(T_2,Tsk_3, WP3.1, WP4)$ returns fail) Since C is a local constraint, the *ExplainLocal* tries first to change a sensor parameter (such as azimuth and elevation) and then a UAV parameter (such as altitude). For the considered parameter, *AV* first looks for the default value (in case of altitude the default value for a specific UAV is 3000m , while the max altitude is 5000m). For each setting of the parameter the footprint is computed by estimate-coverage$(T_2,Tsk_3, WP3.1, WP4)$ and the *AV* checks whether the target T_2 is included in the footprint.

Figure 4 sketches the behavior of the *AV* when the violated constraint C is a global one. The first step in *ExplainGlobal* is to single out the most probable portion of the plan responsible for the violation. The *SelectCulpritTask*$(C(p_1,\ldots,p_n),$ $DP, HP)$ performs a sort of localization of the problem by adopting the following heuristics h_G. Let us suppose that the violated constraint C has the form $\sum P(Tsk_i) \leq MAX_P$, where P is some measure associated with each task (e.g. duration). In case the C is satisfied in the HP plan, then h_G assumes that the culprit is the task Tsk_j for which $Tsk_j.P_{DP} - Tsk_j.P_{HP}$ is maximum. In other words the heuristic considers as culprit the task Tsk_j which has contributed the most relevant deviation to the value of P in DP w.r.t. the value of P in HP.

In case the constraint has not been checked in the high level plan because the value of the parameter P in the HP is unknown (the relevant pieces of information are missing in HP and cannot be estimated via predictive models), the heuristic selects as culprit just the task Tsk_j for which $Tsk_j.P_{DP}$ is max.

In general the value of $Tsk_j.P$ depends on other parameters $P_1, \ldots, P_n$ defined for the task Tsk_j. Let us suppose that P_i was set to v_i in the HP and that in the refinement phase the parameters $P_{i,1}$ $P_{i,k}$ have been added for task Tsk_j and are of the same type as P_i. The function *SelectCulpritParams* performs such an analysis and returns *pset*.

Then AV assigns value v_i to all these related parameters *pset* to see whether this tentative assignment is such as to make the constraint C satisfied while the value of all other variables is left unchanged. In case the constraint is still violated, AV tries

with the default value dv and, as last attempt, with the max/min values for all the parameters in *pset*.

In case an assignment v satisfying the constraint is found, $(pset, v)$ is reported to the operator as an explanation of the violation. If no such assignment exists, then the checker inform the user that there is no simple repair for the violated constraint.

From the above description is quite clear the automated checker explores just very few possibilities, but these are relevant either because it exploits as much as possible the fact that a given assignment has made the constraint C satisfied in the HP or because it considers the extreme cases (the most optimistic). Since these attempts are limited, the resulting computational cost is almost negligible. Moreover, in some cases the heuristic is able to suggest how to fix the problem.

Let us suppose that the human operator has refined the HP described above by inserting WP1.1 before WP2 in Tsk_1, WP3.1 before WP4 in Tsk_3, WP4.1 and WP4.2 in Tsk_4 (see figure 2). Moreover, the human operator sets the desired speed at some WP at a lower value than cruise speed. For example the speeds for WP1.1 , WP3.1, WP 5 are set to 30m/sec while for WP4.1 and WP4.2 are set to 20m/sec.

Such a refined plan DP has to be checked for consistency with PS and DM. While other checks do not signal a violation, we have that the global constraint on MAX duration is violated since the predictive model returns an estimated total duration of almost 65min. The occurrence of such a violation has to be reported to the human operator, but with additional information for explaining (if possible) the reason of such a failure.

Since the considered violation involves a global constraint, AV (according to the ExplainGlobal) has to look for the most plausible culprit. While in the high level plan HP, the estimated global duration is consistent with maxduration constraint, the refined plan is not, because of the parameter setting and the introduction of additional way points.

While several tasks have a duration time different from the one estimated in HP, the SelectCulpritTask singles out Tsk_4 as the most suspect since its duration has been significantly increased (from 662sec in the HP to 1156sec in DP). The AV analyzes the route length and the speed (the two main parameters involved in the computation of duration) in DP and in HP and realizes that the addition of WP4.1 and WP4.2 had an impact in lengthening the $Tsk_4.route$ as defined in HP. However the increase in length is modest (from 26500m to 29800m), so that the AV considers the speed as the most plausible culprit.

The SelectCulpritParams returns the *pset* list containing parameters WP3.speed, WP4.1.speed, WP4.2.speed, WP4.speed. Since in the HP the speed was assumed to be the cruise speed, the speed for WP3, WP4.1, WP.4.2, WP4 is now set to 40m/sec when the AV rechecks the duration constraint. This recheck shows that reverting the speed to the cruise speed is a suitable repair which removes the violation since the new total duration of mission is around 57 min (below the max duration) and the one of Tsk_4 is reduced to 745 sec. These pieces of information are provided as explanation to the operator, which obviously can accept the suggestion or can refine HP in an alternative way.

6 Experiments

As said above, the *AV* module is part of a large project involving many industrial partners and had to be integrated into a complex software architecture which is aimed both at planning and at monitoring (in real time) missions involving one or more UAVs. Most of the information used by *AV* is stored in a relational data base which is shared among different modules. The reasoning part of *AV* has been encoded using the rule-based expert system tool CLIPS [4], because of performance reasons. In fact the validation of a mission plan never takes more than 2-3 seconds.

The *AV* module has been tested in two different ways. In the formal testing of the whole software architecture, several mission plans for three different types of UAVs have been used. The detailed mission plans are quite complex, involving up to 25 waypoints and the related parameters. All the violations detected by *AV* were considered *actual* violations worth to be taken into account by the human operator.

We have also carried out a second preliminary experiment to test the capability of the *AV* in providing explanations. In particular, we started from the most representative high level plan *HP* consistent with a problem specification *PS*, and we refined it by causing at least one violation: in 20 cases, we injected the violation of a local constraint, and in 10 cases the violation of a global constraint.
In all cases the *AV* was able to detect the violation, and as concerns the *ExplainLocal*, in 18 cases it was able to find a parameter setting which satisfied the violated constraints. In 2 cases *AV* was unable to suggest a parameter setting for fixing the problem; both cases involved the estimation of the covering of targets. In particular, *AV* provided an explanation stating that no change of a single parameter (either UAV altitude or sensor elevation) is sufficient for covering the target; the only way for satisfying the constraint is a complex change of the route which may require the introduction of additional waypoints and/or the removal of other ones.

As concerns the *ExplainGlobal*, after locating the possible culprit task Tsk_i, in 6 out of the 10 cases it was able to single out which parameter changes on Tsk_i the tas were sufficient to satisfy the violated constraint. In the remaining 4 cases, *AV* concluded that a change of the route of Tsk_i was necessary; this piece of information was useful in 3 out of 4 cases because a human operator could actually revise such a route and remove the violation (i.e. *AV* had successfully located the culprit), while in one case this was not possible and a more global change involving the routes of two tasks was necessary.

These preliminary results show that the explanation facility is quite effective and informative since it presents a suggestion when the change of a parameter (or of a set of parameters in case of *ExplainGlobal*) is sufficient for solving the violation, and in the other cases it focuses the attention of the human operator on the part of route which is more critical for solving the problem.

7 Conclusions

In this paper we have described an approach to automatic mission plan validation capable of detecting violations in human-crafted plans and, in most cases, also to

provide explanations and suggestions for fixing the violations. The domain models we have defined for supporting plan validation exhibit a significant level of complexity, due both to the fact that the plans to be validated are rich, structured objects, and that the constraints to be checked are both numeric and qualitative. Moreover, some quantities needed in order to check the constraints are not explicitly contained in the plan, and need to be estimated by means of predictive models.

Also the approach described in [2] aims to generate explanations of mission plan flaws to the human operator, focusing on temporal constraints. While temporal constraints are fundamental in mission planning, our approach has considered explanations also for the violation of other important types of constrains, including spatial, physical and logical constraints. In [7], the authors describe a decision support functionality of a system which assists the human experts during the complete life cycle of mission plans for human space exploration. While the focus is mainly on the interactive exploration of alternatives (i.e. *what-if*), the system is also able to provide explanations for the commitments it makes; the explanations in our approach are different, in that they aim to explaining/solving flaws in human crafted plans.

The work can be extended in several directions. One such direction involves taking into account interrelated violations; in such cases, instead of providing a separate explanation and repair suggestion for each violation, it may be possible to provide a more meaningful single explanation and repair suggestion for the whole set of related violations. We would also like to consider a more flexible structure of preferences, where the user can instruct the validation tool about which changes she is more willing to make to a flawed plan in order to restore its consistency.

Acknowledgements

This reasearch was partially conducted within the project *SMAT-F1* coordinated by Alenia Aeronautica and partially funded by Regione Piemonte via the *Fondo Europeo di Sviluppo Regionale*. The authors are grateful to Sebastiano Caff for his contribution to develop the prototype of the validation tool.

References

1. Bresina, J.L., Morris, P.H.: Mixed-Initiative Planning in Space Mission Operations. AI Magazine **28**(2) (2007)
2. Bresina, J.L., Morris, P.H.: Explanations and Recommendations for Temporal Inconsistencies. In: Proc. Int. Work. on Planning and Scheduling for Space (2006)
3. Göktoğan, A.H., Sukkarieh, S., Cole, D.T., Thompson, P.: Airborne vision sensor detection performance simulation. In: Proc I/ITSEC, pp. 1682-1687 (2005)
4. CLIPS, http://clipsrules.sourceforge.net/
5. Cummings, M.L., Brzezinski, A., Lee, J.: Operator Performance and Intelligent Aiding in Unmanned Aerial Vehicle Scheduling. IEEE Int. Syst. **22**, pp. 52-59 (2007)
6. Gancet, J., Hattenberger, G., Alami, R., Lacroix, S.: Task planning and control for a multi-UAV system: architecture and algorithms. In: Proc. IROS Conference, pp. 1017-1022 (2005)
7. Kichkaylo, T., van Buskirk, C., Singh, S., Neema, H., Orosz, M., Neches, R.: Mixed-Initiative Planning for Space Exploration Missions. In: Proc. ICAPS Work. on Moving Plan. and Sched. Syst. into the Real World (2007)

Real-Time Path Planning using a Simulation-Based Markov Decision Process

M. Naveed, A. Crampton, D. Kitchin and T.L. McCluskey

Abstract This paper introduces a novel path planning technique called MCRT which is aimed at non-deterministic, partially known, real-time domains populated with dynamically moving obstacles, such as might be found in a real-time strategy (RTS) game. The technique combines an efficient form of Monte-Carlo tree search with the randomized exploration capabilities of rapidly exploring random tree (RRT) planning. The main innovation of MCRT is in incrementally building an RRT structure with a collision-sensitive reward function, and then re-using it to efficiently solve multiple, sequential goals. We have implemented the technique in MCRT-planner, a program which solves non-deterministic path planning problems in imperfect information RTS games, and evaluated it in comparison to four other state of the art techniques. Planners embedding each technique were applied to a typical RTS game and evaluated using the game score and the planning cost. The empirical evidence demonstrates the success of MCRT-planner.

1 Introduction

Real-Time Strategy (RTS) games are complex real-time concurrent systems where players build societies and engage in simulated combat to capture territory and explore the game world to collect resources. Path planning is a challenging task that is required frequently in RTS games by human or AI players. The key challenging aspects of path planning problems in RTS games are tight time constraints, limited CPU and memory, partial visibility, and large and dynamic game worlds. These domains require an automated planner to solve planning problems with non-

Munir Naveed, University of Huddersfield, e-mail: m.naveed@hud.ac.uk,
Andrew Crampton, University of Huddersfield, e-mail: a.crampton@hud.ac.uk,
Diane Kitchin, University of Huddersfield, e-mail: d.kitchin@hud.ac.uk,
Lee McCluskey, University of Huddersfield, e-mail: t.l.mccluskey@hud.ac.uk

M. Bramer et al. (eds.), *Research and Development in Intelligent Systems XXVIII*,
DOI 10.1007/978-1-4471-2318-7_3, © Springer-Verlag London Limited 2011

deterministic effects. Markov Decision Process (MDP) is a common planning formalism used to represent planning problems in nondeterministic domains. MDPs can be solved using either Dynamic Programming (DP) [3] or Monte-Carlo Simulations [19]. The current dynamic programming based planners such as mGPT [6] are applicable in domains that are modeled in a specific planning language (e.g. Probabilistic planning domain language) and all transition probabilities in the domain must be available before planning is started. The transition probabilities are used in DP to calculate the state values. Monte-Carlo (MC) planning requires only a simulation model that can generate a sequence of samples (of states or actions) according to the desired sampling distribution and a reward function to evaluate them. MC Planning uses the average rewards (of the samples) to estimate action (or state) values rather than using the pre-computed transition probabilities in a stochastic domain. Therefore, MC Planning does not need the availability of transition probabilities before the start of planning. The modeling of a RTS game in a planning language is a challenging task. MC planning is suitable for RTS games as it is easy to build a simulator for the game.

The main challenging issue in MC planning is the adjustment of the balance between the exploration of new actions and exploitation of the previously discovered promising actions. A recent MC planning approach called Upper Confidence bounds applied to Trees (UCT) [13] uses the selective action sampling approach to control the trade-off between exploration and exploitation. UCT exploits the best actions to generate the look-ahead search tree in a Monte-Carlo simulation. An action is best if its estimated value is higher than other applicable actions at a state. UCT maintains exploration by using a domain-dependent constant and the number of times an action is sampled since the start of the simulations. UCT has been an effective planning approach in domains where the reward of the state-action pairs is in the range of [0,1] e.g. Go [9]. In RTS games, the action values can be greater than this range [1]. UCT in its original form is not suitable for RTS games. The variations of UCT have been explored in RTS games for tactical assault planning [1] and path planning [18]. In this paper, we extend the work of [18] with the following contributions:

1. We introduce a new domain-independent way of controlling the trade-off between exploration and exploitation in the Monte-Carlo simulations. The new approach combines the exploration feature of rapidly-exploring random trees (RRT [17]) with the exploitation scheme of UCT. The look-ahead tree in a simulation is built by performing exploitation and exploration in a sequence. The new approach is called MCRT search.
2. The paper presents a new path planner - called MCRT Planner - that uses MCRT search. MCRT planner is a real-time path planner that interleaves planning and plan execution. MCRT planner also incrementally builds a tree to reuse the searching efforts.
3. We provide an empirical study of MCRT planner in a typical RTS game and compare its performance with its close rivals: UCT, RRT, Real-time Dynamic Programming (RTDP) [2] and LSS-LRTA* [14]. The performance is evaluated using the game score and the number of states explored during the planning.

The experimental results demonstrate the success of MCRT planner over its rival techniques.

2 Problem Formulation

The class of problems we consider are typical of autonomous agent path planning in RTS games. It is assumed an agent knows the size of the world, its position and velocity (collectively called its state), the position of its target goal states, and the set of obstacles that are within the pre set limits of its sight (which takes into account occlusion by obstacles blocking places it would normally see). The set of obstacles include both static and dynamic obstacles. The dynamic obstacles make the agent's moves non-deterministic. We formulate the path planning problem as a simulation-based Markov Decision Process (MDP) [19]. It is represented as (S, A, T, Q, s_o, G) where S is a finite set of states, A is a finite set of actions, T is a stochastic state transition function, $Q(s, a, h)$ represents the estimated value of the action $a \in A(s)$ over a finite horizon h at state s, s_o is the initial state and G is the set of the goal states. For any state $s \in S$, we define $A(s)$ to be the set of applicable actions at s where $A(s) \subset A$. The stochastic transition function T is a function of a state-action pair that randomly selects a next state for the input state-action pair. For example, for the current state s and action a, T selects a state s_{next} randomly from all successor states of s that are possible to reach with a.

$$s_{next} = T(s, a) \tag{1}$$

An action a is encoded as (dx, dy, u) where $dx \in \{-1, 0, 1\}$, $dy \in \{-1, 0, 1\}$ and u is the speed of the movable agent. $V(s)$ represents the value of the state s. The value of a state s is measured using the estimated action values.

$$V(s) = max_a Q(s, a, h) \tag{2}$$

The stochastic transition function T is built using a probability distribution P. P is used to estimate the transition probabilities in the state space. A transition probability $p(s_i, a, s_j) \in P$ represents the probability of moving an agent to s_j when $a \in A(s_i)$ is applied at s_i. P is updated during online planning using a frequency based approach [2] and is given in (3).

$$p(s_i, a, s_j) = N(s_i, a, s_j)/N(s_i, a) \tag{3}$$

where $N(s_i, a, s_j)$ is the total number of times action a is selected at s_i to move to s_j and $N(s_i, a)$ is the total number of times a is selected at s_i since the start of the planning task. The exception to this is that a move to an *occupied* state has the probability 0. In stochastic transition function T, the states with high transition probabilities have more chances of selection than the states with low probabilities.

3 The MCRT Search

MCRT search has been designed to find a new domain-independent way of handling the exploration and exploitation trade-off in the Monte-Carlo simulations and to introduce a multi-objective reward function. MCRT search evaluates an action with respect to two objectives. The first objective is to reduce the distance to the goal state and other is to avoid the collision with the static objects. Tuning the domain specific parameters (e.g. UCT uses one parameter) to balance the exploration and exploitation in a domain requires an offline empirical work. Such empirical work is a cumbersome and time-consuming task in RTS games. An investigation to find a domain independent way of managing the exploration and exploitation is crucial for RTS-type domains. Path planning in RTS games is not only required to find the shortest path but also to handle other issues e.g. to avoid areas occupied by static objects or enemy units. Intuitively, a multi-objective reward function is suitable for RTS games.

MCRT is a local search algorithm that is designed for planners that interleave planning and plan execution. MCRT search starts by finding the local search space for the current state of the planning agent. The size of the local space for a state s is $|A(s)|$. The value of each neighbouring state in the local space is measured at least once using the Monte-Carlo simulations. The Monte-Carlo simulations are performed for a fixed time duration. The simulation time is independent of the size of the search space. In every simulation, the look-ahead depth is kept finite and fixed to keep MCRT a real-time search method. In the simulations, the non-deterministic transition function is used to estimate the value and effects of sampled action. The value of each state is calculated using (2). At the end of the simulations, MCRT selects the action to move the agent to the neighbouring state that gains the highest value since the start of the simulations. Ties are broken by random selection.

3.1 Algorithmic Details

The MCRT technique borrows the idea of the generic Monte Carlo algorithm given in [13] and integrates it with the RRT sampling technique [17] for applications in path planning. Based on the problem formulation, the current state (i.e. s_c), and the current target goal (g), the MCRT function (Figure 1) returns the action it evaluates to be the most promising. It has access to system parameters that are calculated to take into account the real-time characteristics of the application to which MCRT is applied: the look-ahead depth, the time elapsed and its allowed cycle time. MCRT starts (line 1, Figure 1) by initialising the set S of ($state, reward$) pairs, where $state$ is a neighbour of s_c, the current state. The repeat loop iterates as long as the real-time constraints allow. The *ChooseNeighbour* function (line 3) selects which s_n will be used for expansion: the choice is initially random from the set of unexpanded neighbouring states of state s_c, but once all neighbouring states have been seen it selects the neighbouring state with the highest reward value currently recorded in

S. After each call to the *RewardSim* function is made (line 4), S is updated with a new reward value for a particular neighbour s_n. After the simulations have finished, line 7 determines s_{best}, the neighbour with the maximum estimated reward. Line 8 returns the action a which is aimed in the direction of neighbour s_{best}. We assume a is unique as the actions are directional (i.e. only one action at s_c is for the motion in the direction of s_{best}). Key to MCRT is the simulation procedure *RewardSim*

Function *MCRT*(s_c, g)
Read access $depth, timelimit$;
1. $S := \{(s, 0) : s \text{ is a neighbour of } s_c\}$;
2.   REPEAT
3. $s_n := ChooseNeighbour(s_c)$;
4. $r_n := RewardSim(s_n, g, depth, 1)$;
5.   Update S with (s_n, r_n)
6.   UNTIL $(ElapsedTime() > timelimit)$;
7.   find $(s_{best}, r_{max}) \in S : (s, r) \in S \Rightarrow r_{max} \geq r$;
8.   RETURN the action a that aims towards s_{best}
End *MCRT*

Fig. 1: High Level Design of MCRT

(Figure 2) which estimates the reward of moving to s_n. This is adapted from the generic Monte Carlo algorithm given in [13]. The latter work introduced a bandit algorithm for this, whereas we adapt the technique to RTS games using a novel reward estimator which takes into account potential collisions, and a static estimate involving distance from the goal. *RewardSim* expands a look-ahead tree from the neighbouring state s_n of current state s_c, by generating random samples of states, and accumulating rewards as it searches, as explained below. The main recursive

Function *RewardSim*$(s_n, g, depth, d)$
Read access MDP;
1.   IF $d \neq depth$ THEN
2. $s_{rand} := RandomSample()$;
3. $a := SelectAction(s_n, s_{rand})$;
4. $[s_{next}, rw] := SimulateAction(s_n, a, g)$;
5.   RETURN $rw + RewardSim(s_{next}, g, depth, d+1)$
6.   ELSE RETURN $1/dist(s_n, g)$
End *RewardSim*

Fig. 2: RewardSim: MCRT Look-ahead Search

loop of *RewardSim* starts in line 2 where a state position s_{rand} is chosen at random from any position on the map excluding (i) the agent's position (ii) the position of any obstacle that the agent can see. An action is selected to progress towards s_{rand} using a function called *SelectAction*. This finds the neighbour of s_n which is

nearest to s_{rand} using the Euclidean metric, and selects an action which is aimed towards the neighbour of s_n. A state s_{next} is generated that might be produced by the execution of this action in the *SimulateAction* explained below, and the estimated reward of that state is returned. The recursive call sums a series of rewards for each of the advancing states, with a base case calculating the reward statically as the inverse Euclidean distance from s to the target. The function *SimulateAction* returns

Function *SimulateAction*(s_n, a, g)
Read access MDP, W_d;
1. $s_{next} := Transition(s_n, a)$;
2. $rw := \|\{t : p(s_n, a, t)) > 0\}\| / (W_d * dist(s_{next}, g))$;
3. $return[s_{next}, rw]$
End *SimulateAction*

Fig. 3: Simulate Action

a randomly selected state s_{next} that the agent may occupy after execution of action a, and the estimate of the reward in moving to the new state s_{next}. The simulator uses the probability distribution P to estimate the outcome of an action. A state s_{next} is a possible new state after the execution of action a at s if $p(s_n, a, s_{next}) > 0$. *Transition* (line 1 in Figure 3) assembles a list of the possible new states, and selects the next state s_{next} randomly from the list, where the random choice takes into account the probability that the state is reached by the execution of a. Thus the higher the chance a state would be reached, the more likely it is to be chosen. In line 2 the reward for that state is calculated; the idea is that the larger the list of possible new states is for an action, then the higher the reward. This is based on the intuition that a larger list indicates there are likely to be less obstacles present in that action's direction of travel (and thus less chance of future collisions). The size of the list is divided by $dist(s_{next}, g)$, the Euclidean distance to the goal g from the new state s_{next}, as the further away, the less the reward. Finally the reward is given a scaling factor W_d which normalises the relationship between the collision-free path and distance to goal: for a particular application of MCRT, this would be tuned to balance the importance of directing towards collision free paths with minimising the Euclidean distance to goal states.

Figure 4 shows a grid example of MCRT search with look-ahead of depth 5. The search starts at S and determines the immediate neighbours of S (line 1, Figure 1). These neighbours are labeled as 1.1 in Figure 4 (in Figure 4, label X.Y means that the state is produced by Figure X in line Y). If S is seen for the first time, then a neighbour is selected randomly (line 3, Figure 1). Suppose the randomly chosen neighbour is E2. Then MCRT runs MC simulations (*RewardSim*) to estimate the reward for the transition from S to E2. *RewardSim* expands the look-ahead search using the RRT sampling approach. A state, say C9, is selected randomly at look-ahead depth $d = 1$ from the state space (according to line 2 of Figure 2). An action a is selected to expand E2 towards C9. The action a is simulated (line 4, Figure 2) and an outcome of a is estimated using the probability distribution. In the example, D3 is

Fig. 4 An MCRT Example:
S is the current state, G is
the goal state and d is the
look-ahead depth. The cells in
Black are the static obstacle.

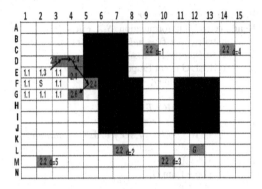

assumed as the estimated next state of E2 when action a is applied. The simulation
also estimates and stores a reward for the state-action pair i.e. (E2, a). The depth
of the look-ahead search is increased and *RewardSim* is run from the next state i.e.
D3. An action a at D3 is selected according to the second random sample, say L7,
and simulated to estimate the reward and the next state of D3 with action a, and this
reward is added to the previously stored reward. This process continues until look-
ahead search reaches a depth of five. The next state at depth five is a leaf node of the
look-ahead search. In Figure 4, G4 is the leaf node of the look-ahead search, and is
evaluated using line 6 of Figure 2. The evaluated value is added to the accumulated
reward and used as the final value of the reward for the transition from S to E2. The
simulations are continued for the maximum allowed time.

4 An MCRT-based Path Planner

In this section we describe how to embed the MCRT technique into a real-time path
planner with a list of goal states to visit. The planner is supplied with information
described in the "Problem Formulation" section above, and interleaves planning and
execution as follows. Lines 1 and 2 (Figure 5) initialise a RRT tree structure (T). At
the start of the planning loop in line 4, "pop g from G" has the effect of assigning
g to the head of list G, and reducing G. If G is found to be empty, then the "pop"
function will exit the loop and the program will end. The planner proceeds in two
stages: in the first stage (lines 5 - 10), the RRT tree structure is populated using
the MCRT technique, interleaved with action execution (line 9). The RRT structure
T builds up a *tree* of the collision free states of the search space within S, as it is
possible that s can be revisited if (a) states are retraced (b) $Execute(a, s)$ leaves s
unchanged - where there is an obstacle. T is expanded with an edge from s to s_{next} if
it passes the Valid test: this test returns true unless s_{next} already appears in T, or if s
already has a child edge in T that has a greater estimated reward than s_{next}. In either
case, the returned action is executed on s and the new state of the agent recorded.
After the first stage achieves the first goal, the planner enters the second stage. In

Procedure *MCRT Planner*
Read access MDP formulation (S, A, P, R, s_0, G);
1.   initialise tree $T := null$ and state $s := s_0$;
2. $T.AddRoot(s)$;
3.   WHILE G is not Empty
4.   pop g from G;
5.   REPEAT
6. $a := MCRT(s, g, d, n)$;
7. $s_{next} := Transition(s, a)$;
8.   IF $Valid(s_{next}, s, T)$ THEN $T.addnode(s, s_{next})$;
9. $s := Execute(a, s)$
10.   UNTIL $s.pos = g$;
11.   pop g from G;
12.   REPEAT
13. $a := LocalPlanningMethod(s, g, T)$;
14. $s_{next} := Transition(s, a)$;
15.   IF $ObstacleFree(s_{next})$
16.   THEN $s := Execute(a, s)$
17.   ELSE $T.remove(s_{next})$;
18.   IF $s.pos = g$ THEN pop g from G
19.   UNTIL $\neg ObstacleFree(s_{next})$
20.   END WHILE
End *MCRT Planner*

Fig. 5: MCRT-Planner

the second stage (lines 12 - 19), the planner exploits the fact that T has been built up in the first phase, searching T to find the path to the next goal state from the current location. The local planning method (line 13, Figure 5) is a breadth first search of fixed depth to find an action to the neighbouring state of the current state which reduces the distance to the next goal state. If the simulation of action a (utilizing the *Transition* described above) changes the agent's state to a state which is obstacle free, then that action is actually executed, otherwise the state is removed from the tree. The planner leaves the second stage and starts running the first stage again if s is occupied by an obstacle. This interchange between stage one and two continues until the end of the game when all goal states have been reached, or a fixed time bound is reached for the game.

5 An RTS game

As an application we use RC-RTS, a typical real-time strategy game that has been developed using the Open Real-Time Strategy (ORTS) game engine [8]. ORTS provides an appropriate environment for studying real-time AI problems such as path finding and imperfect information. RC-RTS is a resource (minerals) collection game characterised by multiple goals, partial observation, and non-deterministic actions.

Fig. 6 RC-RTS with Map 2.

It incorporates dynamically changing objects (tanks and bugs, which move randomly), and partially known static obstacles (ridges, water ponds, nurseries, geysers, communication towers and military barracks). An AI client controls workers who have to collect the minerals and return them to a control centre. With their vision restricted to only eleven tiles in any direction, they must find a path from their start location to the mineral cluster, pick up ten pieces of the minerals – gaining ten points for doing so – and then find a path from the mineral cluster back to the control centre. A worker who successfully returns minerals to the control centre gets a further twenty points. A sample of the game map is shown in figure 6.

6 Related Work

The path planning problem has been extensively studied in the area of computer games. Optimal path planning approaches like A* [10], way-points and navigational mesh are not applicable in the RTS games due to the time constraints and incomplete information of the game world. Learning real-time A* (LRTA) [15] is a real-time heuristic search planner that is designed for solving the planning problems in real-time. LRTA searches for an action using a look-ahead of depth one. LRTA also updates the heuristic value of the current state in a planning episode. The main drawback of LRTA is its easily getting trap into heuristic depression (HD) [12, 11]. HD makes real-time heuristic search get stuck in a small region due to the inappropriate heuristic values of the states in that region. It takes several searching efforts of the planner to escape a HD.

The recent variations of LRTA e.g. LRTS [7], LSS-LRTA* [14] and aLSS-LRTA [11] have been designed to escape HD. However, these variations require a lot of searching efforts to escape HD or to avoid it. LRTS increases the look-ahead depth to escape from HD. LSS-LRTA* [14] uses A* to identify the look-ahead search space of fixed depth in the current vicinity of the planning agent and then updates the heuristic values using Dijkstra's algorithm. LSS-LRTA is faster than LRTS because it updates the heuristic values of all the edges seen during the look-ahead search. An-

other notable characteristic of LSS-LRTA* is its better performance than D* Lite on static maps. aLSS-LRTA is a variation of LSS-LRTA that avoids HD by appropriately selecting the best state (in a look-ahead search). However, LSS-LRTA* and aLSS-LRTA do not decrease the action costs if required due to a dynamic change in the game world. Due to these drawbacks, LSS-LRTA* and its variation can be expensive for path planning in dynamic worlds. MCRT search does not get stuck in small regions due to its exploration capabilities. The action values of a state are decreased or increased by MCRT search according to the current settings of the environment. This makes MCRT search suitable for dynamic worlds. A variation of LRTA called Real-Time D* (RTD*) [4] handles the problem of the increase and decrease of an edge cost due to the dynamic change in the domain. Real-Time D* uses bidirectional search, combining real-time and dynamic search, which allows it to react to dynamic changes in the world and update the heuristic values accordingly. It seems a promising approach but the main reason for not using RTD* in our domain is its dependency on backward global search. MCRT is also applicable in the high dimensional search spaces [17] due to its RRT based sampling capabilities.

7 Experimental Setup

We have designed a set of experiments which test the MCRT technique against four of its main rivals: RRT, UCT, LSS-LRTA* and RTDP. Ten tests have been performed on three different game maps; each with a grid of size 60×60. The criteria that we have used to evaluate the performance of each planning method, within the RTS environment are: **Score** – which measures the total amount of mineral recovered by the workers and **Planning Cost** – which represents the total number of states visited by the planner during the planning process for the whole game. As success in many games is measured by who gets the highest score, we naturally consider the first of these to be the most important performance indicator. The level of difficulty is controlled by constructing maps with differing numbers of static and dynamic obstacles and by introducing a successively increasing number of narrow passages and ridges. The complexity of the environments created for each of the three test maps used in our experiments are shown in table 1. Each of the planners (except RRT) require

Table 1: Environment variables set for each test map.

Map	Static Obstacles	Dynamic Obstacles	Narrow Passages	Ridges	Water Tiles
Map 1	12	9	4	5	3
Map 2	16	10	5	5	3
Map 3	17	16	7	6	3

some parameters to be tuned off-line for an application domain, and in particular

we found that different planners perform better for different look-ahead depths. We decided to make the comparisons between planners with each one performing optimally. For UCT the trade-off parameter C_p was set to 0.1 (see [13]). A look-ahead depth of four was chosen for MCRT and UCT, a depth of seven for RTDP and a depth of nine for LSS-LRTA*. In our experiments, RRT has been implemented as detailed in [16]. The RRT structure is expanded heuristically, using random samples, towards a nearest neighbour. We use Euclidean distance as a heuristic to expand the tree. This means that given the current state, a neigbouring state that is nearest to the random state is selected and added into the tree if it is collision free (i.e., not occupied by a static obstacle). Once the first goal is achieved then RRT re-uses the constructed tree to plan the path to subsequent goals (this is a two stage planner similar to MCRT). The resulting tree can be thought of as having a similar structure to that of traditional way-points.

For UCT, we have implemented the algorithm given in [13] but with some variations. These variations are made due to the time-constraints and the presence of multiple goals in a planning problem. UCT uses the same reward function as given in MCRT. To reuse the outcomes of previous searches in UCT, the estimated action values for each goal are stored in a separate vector for future use. RTDP is implemented using the details given in [2] and [5]. RTDP formulates the path planning problem as a Markov Decision Process and tunes the policy (a mapping from states to actions) during the online search; we use hash tables to store the policy values. In our implementation, policy values are updated using a fixed number of iterations. Furthermore, we use a frequency based approach given in (3) to measure the probability distribution for RTDP, and Euclidean distance as the initial heuristic in all RTDP simulations. We use two hash tables to store the state values in RTDP - one for each goal in a planning problem - to reuse the efforts done in the previous search. To implement LSS-LRTA* in RC-RTS, we modify the A* implementation given with the ORTS download. The priority queue is implemented as a heap. The goal assigning task is simple. Each worker has its own goal. At the start of the game, all workers are assigned the same goal i.e. the minerals. Once a worker reaches the mineral cluster (and picks them up), the planner changes the goal of the worker to Control Centre and sets a boolean variable as true. This boolean variable is used to decide which data structure (hash tables or vectors) is to use for path planning in the case of UCT, LSS-LRTA* and RTDP. If a worker returns to the Control centre, the planner changes the goal of the worker and sets the boolean variable as false.

8 Results

A summary of the scores for each planner in the test games is given in table 2. We can see that in all of the test games, the MCRT technique, with the two-stage planner, achieves better observed scores than the other planners. The use of an incrementally built MCRT tree structure speeds up both the path planning and the motion of the workers. Although the RRT planner also incrementally builds up a similar tree dur-

ing planning in the first stage, it does not perform the same as MCRT. This is due to the huge size of the tree built by the RRT planner. The MCRT planner adds only the collision-free nodes into the incremental tree if they are found to be promising by the policy roll-out. This reduces the size of the tree structure by keeping the useful nodes only. The small size of the MCRT tree also minimises the time required to update it if the game world is changed during the game play. It is notable that the

Table 2: Scores for each planner on Maps 1-3.

Planner	Map	Minimum	Maximum	Mean	Planner	Map	Minimum	Maximum	Mean
MCRT	1	540	1130	752	RRT	1	30	210	117
	2	170	830	507		2	30	360	179
	3	280	850	486		3	10	130	72
UCT	1	30	150	80	LSS-LRTA*	1	190	290	230
	2	0	150	50		2	50	160	87
	3	0	160	52		3	20	80	57
RTDP	1	20	110	50					
	2	0	70	28					
	3	0	70	18					

minimum scores of the MCRT planner are higher than the maximum scores of its rivals; the closest rival is LSS-LRTA*. Furthermore, the deterministic planner LSS-LRTA* performs better than RRT, UCT and RTDP. This is due to the way in which A* is used to expand the look-ahead search. Though LSS-LRTA* has a deterministic approach to path planning, its behaviour looks non-deterministic in our game because of the interleaving of planning and execution and because of its ability to tune the heuristic function through learning. A worker's path that is controlled by the LSS-LRTA* planner changes its direction of movement when it collides with a tank or other dynamic obstacle. In general, it is observed that the scoring performance of the planners reduces as the difficulty level of the maps increase.

The planning cost of the planners for all test games are shown in table 3. We note that MCRT's minimum planning costs are significantly smaller than those of its rivals. This is a result of needing a small amount of search effort for the planner to determine a path plan. The MCRT planner is able to score higher than its rivals, whilst keeping the planning cost low, because of the way in which it uniquely re-uses the outcomes of the previous searching effort. This is achieved through the use of the incrementally built tree (of collision free nodes) which is later re-used by the MCRT planner to achieve subsequent goals. RTDP is also shown to have a reduced planning cost when compared to its rivals. However, we do not see a correspondingly high score as we do with MCRT. The minimum searching efforts by RTDP can be explained by the fact that the RTDP planner explores only a limited part of the state space during the simulations. The reasons for the minimum exploration in this case are i) a greedy action selection approach (i.e., best action) and ii) slow convergence (of the policy values). The average planning cost of MCRT is lower

Table 3: Planning Cost for each planner on Maps 1-3.

Planner	Map	Minimum	Maximum	Mean	Planner	Map	Minimum	Maximum	Mean
MCRT	1	320	1701	994	RRT	1	1257	2014	1885
	2	225	1766	1251		2	1390	2005	1812
	3	288	1789	1271		3	1261	2020	1884
UCT	1	1064	2017	1655	LSS-LRTA*	1	966	1893	1402
	2	490	1765	1287		2	1512	2191	1798
	3	496	1801	1348		3	1403	2208	1637
RTDP	1	485	629	542					
	2	439	619	520					
	3	505	656	568					

than both RRT and LSS-LRTA*. The RRT planner produces the highest planning cost due to its sampling approach, i.e., exploring the state space based on the random samples. The results also show that the planning cost of MCRT is related to the difficulty level of the map; the higher the difficulty levels the more planning cost it consumes. UCT keeps a balance between the exploration and the exploitation of the actions during the simulations, therefore, its planning cost is smaller than RRT and LSS-LRTA*. However, we observe from table 3 that the minimum planning cost of UCT has dropped for maps 2 and 3. This is due to the fact that when the complexity of the maps increase (i.e., an increase in static and dynamic obstacles) the planner is more likely to become stuck in local minima. This is further evidenced by the scores shown in table 2, where the zero scores indicate no goals achieved.

9 Conclusions

In this paper we have introduced a new real-time path planning algorithm which is aimed at finding paths for agents in applications as typified by real-time strategy games. Here the agents inhabit a world containing obstacles some of which continuously change positions; they have multiple sequential goal states to find, limited time to plan their next move, imperfect information about the effect of their move actions and partial information about the positions of obstacles. Our planner is founded on two key innovations:

- the MCRT search for finding the next action to execute. This technique is based on a fusion of two existing techniques (UCT and rapidly expanding random trees) together with a novel reward function which takes into account the likelihood of collisions along a path
- a two stage structure. During one stage, path finding to solve one goal using the MCRT planner builds up a RRT structure. This is then exploited in a second stage which uses a standard search technique until conditions change to invalidate the RRT, in which case the first stage is re-engaged and the tree restored.

These features of MCRT leverage the domain characteristics that multiple sequential goals have to be solved, and that reward estimates should be collision-sensitive, to make it superior to its rivals. In future work, we aim to explore the performance of MCRT planner on the pathfinding benchmark problems. MCRT is also extendable for path planning in the environments modeled as a Digital Elevation Model [20] by introducing a height parameter in the reward function.

References

1. Balla, R.K. and Fern, A.: UCT for Tactical Assault Planning in Real-Time Strategy Games. In: Poceedings of the 21st International Joint Conference on Artificial Intelligence, pp. 40-45 (2009)
2. Barto, A.G. and Bradtke, S.J. and Singh, S.P.: Learning to act using Real-time Dynamic Programming. Artificial Intelligence. **72**, 81–138 (1995)
3. Bellman, R.: The Theory of Dynamic Programming. Bulletin of The American Mathematical Society-BULL AMER MATH SOC. **60(6)**, 503 – 516 (1954)
4. Bond, D.M. and Widger, N.A. and Ruml, W. and Sun, X.: Real-Time Search in Dynamic Worlds. In: Proceedings of the Third Annual Symposium on Combinatorial Search, (2010)
5. Bonet, B. and Geffner, H.: Labelled RTDP: Improving the Convergence of Real-Time Dynamic Programming. In: Proceedings of ICAPS, pp. 12–21 (2003)
6. Bonet, B. and Geffner, H.: mGPT: A Probabilistic Planner Based on Heuristic Search. Journal of Artificial Intelligence Research. **24**, 933–944 (2005)
7. Bulitko, V. and Lee, G.: Learning in Real-Time Search: A unifying framework. Journal of Aritificial Intelligence Research. **25(1)**, 119–157 (2006)
8. Buro, M.: ORTS: A Hack-free RTS Game Environment. In: Proceedings of the International Computers and Games Conference. pp. 280–291 (2002)
9. Gelly, S. and Silver, D.: Combining Online and Offline Knowledge in UCT. In: ICML 2007. pp. 273-280 (2007)
10. Hart, P.E. and Nilsson, N.J. and Raphael, B.: A Formal Basis for the Heuristic Determination of Minimum Cost Paths. IEEE Transactions of Systems Science and Cybernetics. **4(2)**, 100–107 (1968)
11. Hernández, C. and Baier J.: Real-Time Heuristic Search with Depression Avoidance. In: Proceedings of the twenty-second international joint conference on Artificial Intelligence. (2011)
12. Ishida, T.: Moving target search with intelligence. In: Proceedings of the tenth national conference on Artificial intelligence (AAAI92). (1992)
13. Kocsis, L. and Szepesvári, Cs.: Bandit Based Monte-Carlo Planning. In: Proceedings of the 17th European Conference on Machine Learning. pp. 282-293 (2006)
14. Koenig, S. and Sun, X.: Comparing Real-Time and Incremental Heuristic Search for Real-Time Situated Agents. Journal of Autonomous Agents and Multi-Agent Systems. **18(3)**, 313–341 (2009)
15. Korf, R. E.: Real-Time Heuristic Search. Artificial Intelligence. **42**, 189–211 (1990)
16. Kuffner, J.J. and LaValle, S.M.: RRT-Connect: An Efficient Approach to Single-Query Path Planning. In: Proceedings of the IEEE International Conference on Robotics and Automation. pp. 995–1001 (2000)
17. LaValle, S.M.: Planning Algorithms. Cambridge University Press. (2006)
18. Naveed, M. and Kitchin, D. and Crampton, A.: Monte-Carlo Planning for Pathfinding in Real-Time Strategy Games. In: Proceedings of PlanSIG 2010. pp. 125-132 (2010)
19. Sutton, R.S. and Barto, A.G.: Reinforcement Learning An Introduction. MIT Press. (1998)
20. Wood, J.D.: The Geomorphological Characterisation of Digital Elevation Models. Phd Thesis. University of Leicester, UK. (1996)

Using a Plan Graph with Interaction Estimates for Probabilistic Planning

Yolanda E-Martín and María D. R-Moreno and David E. Smith

Abstract Many planning and scheduling applications require the ability to deal with uncertainty. Often this uncertainty can be characterized in terms of probability distributions on the initial conditions and on the outcomes of actions. These distributions can be used to guide a planner towards the most likely plan for achieving the goals. This work is focused on developing domain-independent heuristics for probabilistic planning based on this information. The approach is to first search for a low cost deterministic plan using a classical planner. A novel plan graph cost heuristic is used to guide the search towards high probability plans. The resulting plans can be used in a system that handles unexpected outcomes by runtime replanning. The plans can also be incrementally augmented with contingency branches for the most critical action outcomes.

1 Introduction

The success of plan graph heuristics in classical planners like FF [11] or HSP [3], has influenced research on heuristic estimators to deal with probabilistic planning problems. These kind of problems, represented in PPDDL [7], are characterized by full observability and non-deterministic effects of actions that are expressed by probability distribution.

A few probabilistic planners such as FF-Replan [15] or RFF [6] determinize the given probabilistic problem into a classical planning problem, and use heuris-

Yolanda E-Martín
Departamento de Automática, Universidad de Alcalá, e-mail: yolanda@aut.uah.es

María D. R-Moreno
Departamento de Automática, Universidad de Alcalá, e-mail: mdolores@aut.uah.es

David E. Smith
Intelligent Systems Division, NASA Ames Research Center, e-mail: david.smith@nasa.gov

M. Bramer et al. (eds.), *Research and Development in Intelligent Systems XXVIII*,
DOI 10.1007/978-1-4471-2318-7_4, © Springer-Verlag London Limited 2011

tic functions based on relaxed plans to guide a classical planner in the search for a deterministic plan. However, other probabilistic planners use plan graphs to compute estimates of probability that propositions can be achieved and actions can be performed [1, 8]. This information can be used to guide the probabilistic planner towards the most likely plan for achieving the goals.

The main motivation for this work is to find high probability deterministic seed plans. These plans can be used in a system that handles unexpected outcomes by runtime replanning. The plans can also be incrementally augmented with contingency branches for critical action outcomes. To find high probability seed plans, we use a relaxed-plan heuristic to guide a forward state space planner. Construction of relaxed plans is guided by probability estimates propagated through a plan graph. These probability estimates are more accurate than typical, as they make use of the notion of interaction introduced by Bryce & Smith in [5].

This approach has been implemented in the Parallel Integrated Planning and Scheduling System (PIPSS) [18]. PIPSS is the union of a heuristic search planner and a scheduling system. This paper starts by describing the translation technique from probabilistic planning domains into a deterministic domains. Then, we describe our plan graph cost estimator and the relaxed plan extraction procedure that guides the search. We follow with an empirical study of the techniques within PIPSS and compare with some other probabilistic planners. Finally, future work is discussed.

2 Conversion from PPDDL to PDDL

To convert from PPDDL to PDDL we follow the approach of Jimenez, Coles & Smith [14]. In general, the process consists of generating a deterministic action for each probabilistic effect of a probabilistic action. For each new action created, the probability of its outcomes is transformed in to a cost equal to the negative logarithm of the probability. This cost will be used to compute the probability of each proposition and action.

More precisely, if A is a probabilistic action with outcomes $O_1,...,O_i$ with probabilities $P_1,...,P_i$ respectively, we create a new deterministic action for each outcome. Each deterministic action A_i has all the preconditions of A. If the outcome O_i is conditional A_i will also have additional preconditions corresponding to the conditions of O_i. The effects of A_i are the effects in the outcome O_i, and A_i is given the cost $C_i = -Ln(P_i)$. Figure 1 shows an example of the conversion strategy . Figure 1(a) shows a probabilistic action that has two effects leading to the two deterministic actions shown in Figures 1(b) and 1(c).

```
(:action pick-up
 :parameters (?b1 ?b2 - block)
 :precondition (and (not(= ?b1 ?b2)) (emptyhand) (clear ?b1) (on ?b1 ?b2))
 :effect (probabilistic
    3/4 (and (holding ?b1) (clear ?b2) (not(emptyhand)) (not(clear ?b1))
             (not(on ?b1 ?b2)))
    1/4 (and (clear ?b2) (on-table ?b1) (not(on ?b1 ?b2)))))
```

(a) Probabilistic action in PPDDL

```
(:action pick-up-ALIAS-0
 :parameters (?b1 ?b2 - block)
 :precondition (and (not(= ?b1 ?b2)) (emptyhand) (clear ?b1) (on ?b1 ?b2))
 :effect (and (holding ?b1) (clear ?b2) (not(emptyhand))
              (not(clear ?b1)) (not(on ?b1 ?b2)) (increase (cost) 0.28)))
```

(b) Deterministic action I

```
(:action pick-up-ALIAS-1
 :parameters (?b1 ?b2 - block)
 :precondition (and (not(= ?b1 ?b2)) (emptyhand) (clear ?b1) (on ?b1 ?b2))
 :effect (and (clear ?b2) (on-table ?b1) (not(on ?b1 ?b2))
              (increase (cost) 1.38)))
```

(c) Deterministic action II

Fig. 1 Example of determinization of a probabilistic action.

3 Plan Graph Cost Heuristic

In this section we describe the plan graph heuristic, which guides the planner towards the lowest cost (highest probability) plan.

Given the deterministic actions created by the technique described in the previous section, we build a plan graph and propagate cost (probability) information through it. We start from the initial conditions and work progressively forward through each successive layer of the plan graph. The cost of performing an action will be the cost that its preconditions can be achieved. The cost of achieving a proposition in the next level of the plan graph will be the minimum cost among all the actions of the previous layer that generate the proposition. Typically, the cost of achieving a set of preconditions for an action is taken to be the sum of the costs of achieving the propositions. However, this can be an underestimate if some of the preconditions interfere with each other, and can be an overestimate if some of the preconditions are achieved by the same action. For this reason, we introduce the notion of *interaction* (L), which captures the degree of dependence (positive or negative) between pairs of propositions and actions in the plan graph [5].

3.1 Interaction

Interaction, is a value that determines how more or less costly (probable) it is that two propositions or actions are established together instead of independently. This concept is a generalization of the mutual exclusion concept used in classical plan graphs. Formally, the interaction, L, between two propositions or two actions (p and q) is defined as:

$$L(p,q) = Cost(p \wedge q) - (Cost(p) + Cost(q)) \qquad (1)$$

It has the following features:

$$L(p,q) \; is \; \begin{cases} < 0 & \text{if } p \text{ and } q \text{ are synergistic} \\ = 0 & \text{if } p \text{ and } q \text{ are independent} \\ > 0 & \text{if } p \text{ and } q \text{ interfere} \end{cases}$$

That is, L provides information about the degree of interference or synergy between pairs of propositions and pairs of actions in a plan graph. When $L(p,q) < 0$ (synergy) this means that the cost of establishing both p and q is less than the sum of the cost for establishing the two independently. However, this cost cannot be less than the cost of establishing the most difficult of p and q. As a result $L(p,q)$ is bounded below by $-min[cost(p), cost(q)]$. Similarly, $0 < L(p,q) < \infty$ means that there is some interference between the best plans for achieving p and q so it is harder (more costly) to achieve them both than to achieve them independently. In the extreme case, $L = \infty$, the propositions or actions are mutually exclusive.

Interaction is important because it provides information about the relation (independence, interference or synergy) between a pair of propositions or a pair of actions at each level of the plan graph. For this reason, instead of computing mutex information in the plan graph, we compute interaction information between all pair of propositions and all pair of actions at each level. Hence, this terms is taken into account in the cost propagation. In this way, we can establish a better estimation of the cost that two propositions or two action perform at the same time.

3.2 Plan Graph Estimator

This subsection describes the method to create the cost plan graph. The process consists of building a plan graph using a modified GraphPlan [2] algorithm in which the mutex calculation is replaced with interaction calculation.

The cost and interaction computation begins at level zero of the plan graph and sequentially proceeds to higher levels. For level zero we assume 1) the cost of each proposition at this level is $-Ln(Pr)$, where Pr is the probability of the proposition in the current state and 2) the interaction between pair of propositions is 0, that is, the propositions are independent. Neither of these assumptions are essential, but we

adopt them here for simplicity. With these assumptions, we start the propagation by computing the cost of the actions at level zero.

In the following subsections, we give the details of how to do this beginning at the initial proposition layer and working forward to actions, and finally to the next proposition layer.

Computing Action Cost and Interaction

Lets suppose that we have the cost and interaction information for propositions at a given level of the plan graph. We use this information to compute the cost and the interaction information for the subsequent action layer. Considering an action a at level l with a set of preconditions $prec_a$, the cost that an action is executed is the cost that all the preconditions are achieved plus the interaction between all pairs of preconditions:

$$Cost(a) = \sum_{\substack{(x_i,x_j) \in prec_a \\ j>i}} \left[Cost(x_i) + L(x_i,x_j) \right] \qquad (2)$$

As an example, consider one level of the plan graph shown in Figure 2, where we have three propositions q, r and s with costs .22, .43 and .69 respectively, and interaction values $L(q,r) = -.2$, $L(q,s) = .3$ and $L(r,s) = .6$ at level i. There are also two actions P and W which have outcomes with costs .26 and .3 respectively (these costs are the negative logarithm of the probabilities for those outcomes). The numbers above the propositions and actions are the costs associated with each one (those with * are the costs that will be computed in subsequent sections).

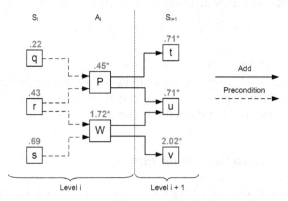

Fig. 2 A Plan Graph with Costs and Interaction Calculation and Propagation

For the example shown in Figure 2, the cost for actions P and W would be:

$$Cost(P) = Cost(q) + Cost(r) + L(q,r) = .22 + .43 - .2 = .45$$

$$Cost(W) = Cost(r) + Cost(s) + L(r,s) = .43 + .69 + .6 = 1.72$$

The next step is to compute the interaction between actions. If the actions are mutex by inconsistent effect, or effects clobbering preconditions, then the cost is ∞. Otherwise, the cost of performing two actions a and b will be the sum of their individual costs plus the cost of the interaction between their preconditions. We can define the interaction between two actions a and b at level l, with sets of preconditions $prec_a$ and $prec_b$ as:

$$L(a,b) = \begin{cases} \infty & \text{if } a \text{ and } b \text{ are mutex by inconsistent effects or effects clobbering preconditions} \\ Cost(a \wedge b) - Cost(a) - Cost(b) & \text{otherwise} \end{cases}$$

(3)

Where in the second case the interaction can be simplified as follows:

$$\begin{aligned} L(a,b) &= Cost(a \wedge b) - Cost(a) - Cost(b) \\ &= \left[Cost(a) + Cost(b) + \sum_{\substack{x_i \in prec_a - prec_b \\ x_j \in prec_b - prec_a}} L(x_i, x_j) \right] - Cost(a) - Cost(b) \\ &= \sum_{\substack{x_i \in prec_a - prec_b \\ x_j \in prec_b - prec_a}} L(x_i, y_j) - \sum_{\substack{(x_i, x_j) \in prec_a \cap prec_b \\ j > i}} \left[Cost(x_i) - L(x_i, x_j) \right] \end{aligned}$$

For the example in Figure 2, the interaction between actions P and W would be:

$$L(P,W) = L(q,s) - Cost(r) = .3 - .43 = -.13$$

The fact that $L(P,W) = -.13$ means that there is some degree of synergy between the actions P and W. This synergy comes from the fact that the two actions have a common precondition, r. However, this synergy is tempered due to the interference between the precondition q of P and the precondition s of W.

Computing Proposition Cost and Interaction

The next step consists of calculating the cost of the propositions at the next level. In this calculation we need to consider all the possible actions at the previous level that achieve each proposition. We make the usual optimistic assumption that we can use the least expensive action, so the cost is the minimum over the costs of all the actions that can achieve the proposition. More formally, for a proposition x at level l, achieved by the actions $Ach(x)$ at the preceding level, the cost is calculated as:

$$Cost(x) = \min_{a \in Ach(x)} [Cost(a) + Cost(x|a)] \qquad (4)$$

Where $Cost(x|a)$ is the cost of the outcome x for the action a.

In our example, the cost of the proposition u of the graph is:

$$\begin{aligned} Cost(u) &= \min[Cost(P) + Cost(u|P), Cost(W) + Cost(u|W)] \\ &= \min[.45 + .26, 1.72 + .3] \\ &= \min[.71, 2.02] = .71 \end{aligned}$$

Finally, we consider the interaction between a pair of propositions x and y. In order to compute the interaction between two propositions at a level l, we need to consider all possible ways of achieving those propositions at the previous level. That is, all the actions that achieve the pair of propositions and the interaction between them. Suppose that $Ach(x)$ and $Ach(y)$ are the sets of actions that achieve the propositions x and y at level l. The interaction between x and y is then:

$$L(x,y) = \min_{\substack{a \in Ach(x) \\ b \in Ach(y)}} [Cost(a) + Cost(b) + L(a,b) + Cost(x|a) + Cost(y|b)] - Cost(x) - Cost(y) \quad (5)$$

Returning to our example, consider the calculation of the interaction between t and u where the possible ways to achieve both are performing P or P and W. In this case, the interaction is calculated as follows:

$$\begin{aligned} I(t,u) &= \min[Cost(P) + Cost(u|P), Cost(P) + Cost(W) + L(P,W) + Cost(t|P) + Cost(u|W)] \\ &\quad - Cost(t) - Cost(u) \\ &= \min[.45 + .26, .45 + 1.72 - .13 + .26 + .3] - .71 - .71 \\ &= .71 - .71 - .71 = -.71 \end{aligned}$$

In this case, it is less costly to establish the propositions t and u through action P than P and W. This makes sense because executing a single action always has lower cost than performing two.

Taking the above calculations into consideration, we build a cost plan graph in the same way that an ordinary plan graph is created, replacing the mutex calculation with interaction calculation. The cost estimates for each action and proposition that appears in the graph, and the interaction value of every pair of propositions and every pair of operators are then used to compute the heuristic estimation that guides the planner towards low cost plans.

3.3 Heuristic Computation

As mentioned above, the plan graph and cost estimates are used to help guide a forward state-space planning search. Thus, initially the system builds a cost plan graph. For each state, the plan graph is updated and a relaxed plan is created to estimate the cost of achieving the goals from that state. The relaxed plan regression algorithm makes use of the cost and interaction information to make better choices for actions. In particular, the algorithm orders the goals at each level according to cost, and chooses the operator used to achieve each goal based on cost. More precisely:

- Arrange goals: the goals at each level are arranged from the highest cost to the lowest. That is, we begin analyzing the most expensive (least probable) proposition.
- Choose operators: if there is more than one operator that achieves a particular goal at a level, we choose the operator with the lowest cost (highest probability) given the other operators that have already been chosen at that level. Suppose that O is the set of operators selected in level l, and $Ach(g)$ is the set of actions that achieve the current goal g at level l. The operator we choose is:

$$\underset{a \in Ach(g)}{\text{argmin}} \left[Cost(a) + Cost(g|a) + \sum_{b \in O} L(a,b) \right] \qquad (6)$$

Figure 3 shows the algorithm used in the relaxed plan regression phase.

Function COSTESTIMATE (G,l)

G_l the set of goals at level l in the relaxed plan graph
g a goal proposition
l number of levels in the relaxed plan graph
A_l the set of actions at level l for an specific goal
a an action
O_l the set of operators selected at level l
π the set of actions selected
CCE the completion cost estimate of the current node

1. while $l \neq 0$
2.   while $G_l \neq \emptyset$
3. $g = \underset{g \in G_l}{\text{argmax}} (Cost(g))$
4. $A_l = \{a : g \in effect^+(a)\}$
5. $a = \underset{a \in A_l}{\text{argmin}} \left[Cost(a) + Cost(g|a) + \sum_{b \in O_l} L(a,b) \right]$
6. $O_l \leftarrow$ Add(a)
7. $\pi \leftarrow$ Add(a)
8. $G_{l-1} = G_{l-1} \cup preconditions(a)$
9. $G_l = G_l - \{g\}$
10. $l = l - 1$
11. $CCE(currentNode) = \sum_{i=1..n} Cost(\pi_i)$
12. return CCE

Fig. 3 The relaxed plan regression pseudo-algorithm.

To illustrate, consider the relaxed plan graph shown in Figure 4, where every operator and action has associated a cost value. Suppose that the set of goals is composed of the propositions r and p with cost .53 and .67 respectively, we start analyzing goal p and later r. In this way, we first deal with the highest cost goal. The proposition p is achieved by actions C and D and, we choose C because it has the lowest cost. Goal r is achieved by operator B and *noop-r*. In order to know which is the best choice, the cost of achieving r must be computed for both of these operators assuming operator C. Considering the action cost values shown in Figure 4, and the interactions and additive costs: $L(B,C) = 0$, $L(\text{noop-r},C) = 0$, $Cost(r|\text{noop-r}) = 0$ and $Cost(r|B) = 0.25$, the chosen operator would be:

$$\underset{a\in Ach(g)}{\text{argmin}} \quad [Cost(\text{noop-r}) + L(\text{noop-r},C) + Cost(r|\text{noop-r}), Cost(B) + L(B,C) + Cost(r|B)]$$

$$\underset{a\in Ach(g)}{\text{argmin}} \quad [0+0+0,0+0+0.25] = 0$$

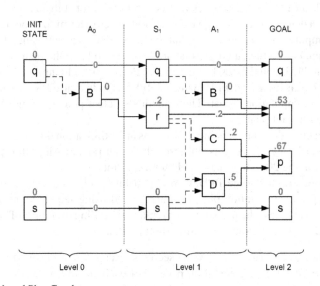

Fig. 4 A Relaxed Plan Graph

In this case the selected operator is *noop-r* because it would have the lowest cost.

The same technique is applied for the rest of the layers until the initial state is reached. Once the plan is extracted, we compute the heuristic estimation. That would be the sum of the cost of every action selected in the search plan process. In this way, we are considering the interaction information.

Supposing that the plan solution selected is composed of operators B and C, the heuristic would be $0 + .2 = .2$. In this way, the planner would guide the search process towards the low cost path thus achieving the low cost plan.

4 Experimental Results

In this section, we describe the experiments that demonstrate that the plan graph cost heuristic guides the search to high probability solutions for probabilistic planning problems. We have conducted an experimental evaluation on IPPC-06 [4] and IPPC-08 [12] fully-observable-probabilistic planning track (FOP) as well as the "probabilistically interesting" domains introduced by Little and Thiebaux [9]. For all the planners 30 trials per problem were performed with a total time limit of 30 minutes for the 30 trials. The test consists of running the planner and using the resulting plan in the MDP Simulator [7]. Unexpected outcomes are handled by runtime replanning. The planner and simulator communicate by exchanging messages: the simulator sends a message to the planner with the current state; the executive sends a message with the next action of the plan. When the planner receives an unexpected state it treats this by replanning.

Four planners have been used for the experimental evaluation:

- FFH [16]: an FF-Replan planner that converts the probabilistic domain definitions into a deterministic domain using all-outcomes determinization. It then uses FF to compute a solution plan. To handle unexpected states it generates contingency branches on the outcomes that are expected to be in the plan. The original FF-Replan [15] won the 2004 International Probabilistic Planning Competition.
- FFH+ [17]: an improved FFH with helpful methods that allow the planner to reduce its computational cost. These methods detect potentially useful actions and reuse relevant plans.
- FPG [13]: considers the planning problem as an optimization problem, and solves it using stochastic gradient ascent through the OLpomdp Algorithm [10]. This planner won the 2006 International Planning Competition.
- RFF [6]: determinizes the PPDDL problem into a classical planning problem and then produces solution plans that are treated using sequential Monte-Carlo simulations to assess the probability of replanning during execution. This planner won the 2008 International Planning Competition.

This section is divided into three subsections, each one corresponding to the set of domains used for experimental purposes. For each subsection, we show a table that represents the number of successful rounds. The results have been compared with those shown in [17]. We cannot compare computational time because some of the planners are not available.

4.1 The 2006 IPPC Domains

The Second International Probabilistic Planning Competition consisted of two tracks, one for conformant planning characterized by non-observability and non-deterministic effects (NOND track), and the other for probabilistic planning with

fully observable domains and probabilistic action outcomes (FOP track). We are concerned with the FOP track, which contains the following domains:

- Blocks World: this domain is similar to the classical BlocksWorld with additional actions. A gripper can hold a block or a tower of them or be empty. When trying to perform an action, there is a chance of dropping a block on the table.
- Exploding Blocks World: this is a dead-end version of the BlocksWorld domain described earlier where additionally the blocks can explode. The explosion may affect the table or other blocks.
- Elevators: this domain consists of a set of coins arranged in different levels. To collect them, the elevators can move among the levels. The movements can fail if the elevator falls down the shaft and finishes on a lower level.
- Tire World: in this domain a car has to move between two locations. When the car drives a part of the route, there is the possibility of a flat tire. When this occurs the tire must be replaced. However, spare tires are not available in all locations.
- Zenotravel: this domain has actions to embark and disembark passengers from an aircraft that can fly at two alternative speeds between locations. The actions have a probability of failing without causing any effects. So, actions must sometimes be repeated.

Results

There are 15 problems for each domain. So, the maximum number of successful rounds for each domain is $15 \cdot 30 = 450$. Table 1 shows the number of successful rounds for FFH, FFH+, FPG and PIPSS$_I$ planners in each domain. PIPSS$_I$ gets good results in three of the five domains. Concretely, the higher successful rates are obtained in those domains like Exploding BlocksWorld or TireWorld that have dead-end states despite PIPSS$_I$ does not deal with dead-end states yet. This is evidence that we are generating relatively low cost (high probability) plans. However, in classical domains like BlocksWorld or Zeno, PIPSS$_I$ perfoms poorly. Although we get good results in problems with dead end states, we are surprised that in classical problems we obtain worse results. Then, we need to analyze how the calculation of the interactions affects this type of problems.

Table 1 Successful Rounds on the IPPC-06

DOMAINS	PLANNERS			
	FFH	FFH+	FPG	PIPSS$_I$
Blocks World	256	335	283	113
Exploding Blocks World	205	265	193	180
Elevators	214	292	342	342
Tire World	343	364	337	351
Zeno Travel	0	310	121	50
TOTAL	1018	1566	1276	1003

4.2 The 2008 IPPC Domains

The Uncertainty Part of the 6th International Planning Competition had three different tracks: fully observable probabilistic (FOP), non-observable non-deterministic (NOND) and fully observable non-deterministic (FOND). Again we have used the FOP track, which contains the following domains:

- Blocks World: Similar to IPPC-06 Blocks World Domain.
- Exploding Blocks World: Similar to IPPC-06 Exploding-BlocksWorld Domain.
- 2-Tire World: Similar to IPPC-06 Tire World Domain but with slight differences in the definition to permit short but dangerous paths.
- Search and Rescue: in this domain there is a helicopter on a rescue mission. To achieve its mission, it has to explore several areas to find one that is landable and close to the human to rescue.
- SysAdmin-SLP: this domain consists of a system administrator that has to manage a network of servers that fail with a higher probability when a neighbouring server is down. The objective is to restart servers. However, there is the possibility that the network is completely down.

Results

There are 15 problems for each domain. So, the maximum number of successful rounds for each domain is $15 \cdot 30 = 450$. The results in Table 2 shown that again $PIPSS_I$ has a low successful rate in those domains with no dead end states like BlocksWorld. In the Exploding BlocksWorld domain, $PIPSS_I$ obtains better results than the winner planner of the IPPC, the RFF planner. However, it gets low number of successful rounds compare to the other two planners. In the 2-TireWorld domain, it gets a poorly rate. That is because, this domain leads on a high number of dead end states that are not supported by $PIPSS_I$. In the SysAdmin-SLP and Search and Rescue domains $PIPSS_I$ was unable to solve any problem because there are some PDDL expressions (i.e. exists, imply) that $PIPSS_I$ cannot yet handle.

Table 2 Successful Rounds on the IPPC-08

	PLANNERS			
DOMAINS	FFH	FFH+	RFF	PIPSS$_I$
Blocks World	185	270	364	120
Exploding Blocks World	131	214	58	85
2-Tire World	420	420	382	42
Search and Rescue	450	450	0	0
SysAdmin-SLP	0	0	117	0
TOTAL	1186	1354	921	247

4.3 Probabilistically Interesting Domains

Little and Thiebaux have created a number of very simple problems that explore the issue of probabilistic planning vs replanning. These problems lead to dead-ends. These may show the true behavior of the planner because several reasons as mentioned in [9]. First, the presence of dead-end states where the goal is unreachable. Second, the degree to which the probability of reaching a dead-end state can be reduced through the choice of actions. Third, the number of distinct trajectories from which the goal can be reached from the initial state. Finally, the presence of mutual exclusion of choices that exclude other courses of action later.

Results

There is one problem for each domain so, the maximum number of successful rounds for each domain is 30. Table 3 shows that in this test, $PIPSS_I$ completes all the rounds for the *Climb* domain and gets the highest successful rate for the *River* domain. For the *Tire* domain, when the number of tires is low, $PIPSS_I$ gets a good rate, but when this number increases it does not solve any round.

Table 3 Successful Rounds on Probabilistically Interesting Benchmarks

	PLANNERS				
DOMAINS	FF-Replan	FFH	FFH+	FPG	$PIPSS_I$
Climb	19	30	30	30	30
River	20	20	20	20	23
Tire1	15	30	30	30	21
Tire10	0	6	30	0	0
TOTAL	54	86	110	80	74

5 Conclusions and Future Work

In this paper we have presented a novel plan graph heuristic. This heuristic estimator is used to guide the search towards high probability plans. The resulting plans will be used in a system that handles unexpected outcomes by runtime replanning.

According to the results of the 2006 IPPC and 2008 IPPC, the combination of deterministic planning and replanning seems to be the best. Although our planner does not deal with dead-end outcomes, the results dealing with probabilistic planning problems have high success rates in several cases. This is evidence that we are generating relatively high probability seed plans. However, replanning is not enough to dealing with those cases in which the dead-end states cannot achieve a solution plan. For this reason, our future work involves analyzing the generated seed plans to find potential points of failure which will be identified as recoverable or unrecoverable. Recoverable failures will be left in the plan and will be repaired through replanning at execution time. For each unrecoverable failure, an attempt will be made to improve the chances of recovery, by adding precautionary steps such as taking along extra supplies or tools that would allow recovery if the failure occurs.

Acknowledgements This work is funded by the Junta de Comunidades de Castilla-La Mancha project PEII11-0079-8929. We want to thank Bonifacio Castaño for his help during the development of this work.

References

1. A. Blum and J. Langford. Probabilistic Planning in the Graphplan Framework. In Proceedings of The 5th European Conference on Planning. Durham, UK, 1999.
2. A. Blum and M. Furst. Fast Planning Through Planning Graph Analysis. Artificial Intelligence, vol. 90, pp: 281-300, 1997.
3. B. Bonet and H. Geffner. Planning as Heuristic Search. Artificial Intelligence, vol. 129, pp: 5-33, 2001.
4. B. Bonet and R. Givan. International Probabilistic Planning Competition.http://www.ldc.usb.ve/~bonet/ipc5, 2006.
5. D. Bryce and D. E. Smith. Using Interaction to Compute Better Probability Estimates in Plan Graphs. In Proceedings of The ICAPS-06 Workshop on Planning Under Uncertainty and Execution Control for Autonomous Systems. The English Lake District, Cumbria, UK, 2006.
6. F. Teichteil-Königsbuch and U. Kuter and G. Infantes. Incremental Plan Aggregation for Generating Policies in MDPs. In Proceedings of the 9th International Conference on Autonomous Agents and Multiagent Systems. Toronto, Canada, 2010.
7. H. L. S. Younes, M. L. Littman, D. Weissman and J. Asmuth. The First Probabilistic Track of the International Planning Competition. Journal of Artificial Intelligence Research, 24, pp: 841-887, 2005.
8. I. Little and S. Thiébaux. Concurrent Probabilistic Planning in the Graphplan Framework. In Proceedings of ICAPS-06 Workshop on Planning Under Uncertainty and Execution Control for Autonomous Systems. The English Lake District, Cumbria, UK, 2006.
9. I. Little and S. Thiébaux. Probabilistic Planning vs Replanning. In Proceedings of ICAPS-07 Workshop on Planning Competitions. Providence, Rhode Island, USA, 2007.
10. J. Baxter and P. L. Bartlett. Direct Gradient-Based Reinforcement Learning: I. Gradient Estimation Algorithms. Technical Report. Australian National University, 1999.
11. J. Hoffmann and B. Nebel. The FF Planning System: Fast Plan Generation Through Heuristic Search. Journal of Artificial Intelligence Research, 14, pp: 253-302, 2001.
12. O. Buffet and D. Bryce. International Probabilistic Planning Competition. http://ippc-2008.loria.fr/wiki/index.php/Main_Page, 2008.
13. O. Buffet and D. Aberdeen. The Factored Policy Gradient Planner. In Proceedings of the 5th International Planning Competition. The English Lake District, Cumbria, UK, 2006.
14. S. Jimenez, A. Coles and A. Smith. Planning in Probabilistic Domains using a Deterministic Numeric Planner. In Proceedings of the 25th Workshop of the UK Planning and Scheduling Special Interest Group. Nottingham, UK, 2006.
15. S. Yoon, A. Fern and R. Givan. FF-Replan: A Baseline for Probabilistic Planning. In Proceedings of the 17th International Conference on Automated Planning and Scheduling. Providence, Rhode Island, USA, 2007.
16. S. Yoon, A. Fern, R. Givan and S. Kambhampati. Probabilistic Planning via Determinization in Hindsight. In Proceedings of the 23rd AAAI Conference on Artificial Intelligence. Chicago, Illinois, USA, 2008.
17. S. Yoon, W. Ruml, J. Benton and M. B. Do. Improving Determinization in Hindsight for On-line Probabilistic Planning. In Proceedings of the 20th International Conference on Automated Planning and Scheduling. Toronto, Canada, 2010.
18. Y. E-Martín, M. D. R-Moreno and B. Castaño. PIPSS*: a System based on Temporal Estimates. In Proceedings of the 30th Annual International Conference of the British Computer Society's Specialist Group on Artificial Intelligence. Cambridge, UK, 2010.

EVOLUTIONARY ALGORITHMS

A Hybrid Parallel Genetic Algorithm for the Winner Determination Problem in Combinatorial Auctions

Dalila Boughaci[1], Louiza Slaouti and Kahina Achour

Abstract   In this work, we are interested in the optimal winner determination problem (WDP) in combinatorial auctions. Given a set of bundles bids, the winner determination problem is to decide which of the bids to accept. More precisely, the WDP is finding an allocation that maximizes the auctioneer's revenue, subject to the constraint that each item can be allocated at most once. This paper tries to propose a hybrid parallel genetic algorithm for the winner determination problem. Experiments on realistic data sets of various sizes are performed to show and compare the effectiveness of our approach.

1 Introduction

The winner determination problem (WDP) is a crucial problem in combinatorial auctions. The WDP is the problem of finding winning bids that maximize the auctioneer's revenue under the constraint that each item can be allocated to at most one bidder [17, 16]. The WDP can be stated as follows:

Let us consider a set of m items, $M =\{ 1, 2, ... m\}$ to be auctioned and a set of n bids, $B= \{B_1, B_2, ... B_n\}$. A bid B_j is a tuple (S_j, P_j) where S_j is a set of items, and P_j is the price of B_j $(P_j>0)$. Further, consider a matrix $a_{m \times n}$ having m rows and n columns where $a_{ij}=1$ iff the item i belongs to S_j, $a_{ij}=0$, otherwise. Finally the decision variables are defined as follows: $x_j=1$ iff the bid B_j is a winning bid and $x_j=0$ otherwise. The WDP can be modeled as the following integer program [1, 6].

[1]University of Sciences and Technology Houari Boumediène
Department of Computer Science-
LRIA Laboratory of Research in Artificial Intelligence

BP32, El-Alia, beb-Ezzouar, Algiers, 16111.
dalila_info@yahoo.fr, dboughaci@usthb.dz

M. Bramer et al. (eds.), *Research and Development in Intelligent Systems XXVIII*,
DOI 10.1007/978-1-4471-2318-7_5, © Springer-Verlag London Limited 2011

$$\text{Maximize} \quad \sum_{j=1}^{n} P_j \cdot x_j \quad \dots\dots\dots\dots(1)$$

$$\text{Under the constraints} \quad \sum_{j=1}^{n} a_{ij} \cdot x_j \leq 1$$

$$i \in \{1, \dots.m\}, \quad x_j \in \{0, 1\} \quad \dots\dots\dots\dots(2)$$

The objective function (1) maximizes the auctioneer's revenue which is equal to the sum of the prices of the winning bids. The constraints (2) express the fact that each item can be allocated to at most one bidder. Due to the free disposal assumption, some items could be left uncovered.

The winner determination problem is NP-Complete [12]. Several methods have been studied for the WDP. Among these methods, we can find the exact algorithms that permit to find an optimal solution and prove its optimality, given enough time. As examples, we cite: the Branch-on-Items (BoI), the Branch on Bids (BoB) [13, 14], and the Combinatorial Auctions BoB (CABoB) [15]. The CASS (Combinatorial Auction Structural Search) method is a Branch-and-Bound algorithm for WDP, proposed in [4]. Authors in [9] proposed CAMUS (Combinatorial Auctions Multi-Unit Search) which is a new version of the CASS for determining the optimal set of bids in general multi-unit combinatorial auctions.

The inexact methods, given enough time, may find optimal solutions, but they cannot be used to prove the optimality of any solution they find. In general, the inexact methods are based on heuristics or meta-heuristics and they are helpful for finding solutions of very large instances. The current well-known inexact algorithms for the WDP are: Hybrid Simulated Annealing SAGII [5, 6], Casanova [7], local search methods [2] and recently memetic algorithms [3].

The current work tries to propose a hybrid parallel genetic algorithm adapted to the winner determination problem. The objective is to obtain a good quality solution and optimize the time response.

The rest of this paper is organized as follows: The second section gives an overview of the parallel genetic algorithms. The third section proposes a parallel genetic algorithm hybridized with local search for the WDP. Some numerical results are given in the fourth section. Finally, the fifth section concludes the work.

2 Parallel Genetic Algorithms (PGA)

Genetic algorithms (GAs) have been applied successfully to solve various NP-hard problems. However, GA is a population- based method that suffers from

premature convergence. The parallelism is a good way that can be used for improving the efficiency of genetic algorithms and can be lead to achieve high quality solutions for complex problems [10, 11]. The three classical models of PGA are given in the following.

2.1 Parallel Genetic Algorithms (master-slaves)

This kind of algorithm makes use of a single population. The evaluation of the individuals of the population is distributed on processing nodes called slaves. Such a model is easy to implement on machine.

2.2 Parallel cellular genetic algorithms

This type of parallel genetic algorithm consists of a simple and structured population. It is designed to run on a parallel processing system, a computing system comprising a large number of calculus units and provides a very high speed. For example, the population of individuals in a cellular parallel genetic algorithm can be organized as a two-dimensional grid. Consequently, selection and crossover in these algorithms are limited to small groups. An individual can only communicate with its neighbors.

2.3 Parallel genetic algorithm multi-populations or PGA Island

The parallel genetic algorithm with multiple populations (or PGA Island) is composed of several subpopulations which exchange individuals occasionally. This exchange of individuals is called migration and it may be a function of several parameters.

2.4 The parallel hybrid genetic algorithms or hierarchical genetic algorithms

The various models of parallel genetic algorithms given above can be hybridized to produce hierarchical models (noted HPGA). For example, we can form a hierarchical parallel genetic algorithm by combining a multi-population parallel genetic algorithm (top level) and a parallel cellular genetic algorithm or master-

slave, or even another level of PGA Multi-populations (below level). In general, any combination of two or more of three classical forms of PGA is a HPGA.

3 The Proposed Approach

The genetic algorithms are used in solving various optimization problems. However such algorithms suffer particularly from the premature convergence. Numerous studies suggest the use of other techniques to improve the performance of the standard genetic algorithms such as: the expanding of the size of the population, the use of sub-populations (Parallel genetic algorithms PGA), and a hybridization of a PGA with SLS (stochastic local search) which can be implemented on a parallel architecture.

The PGASLS algorithm which we proposed in this work is a Parallel Genetic Algorithm combined with the Stochastic Local Search. We used three operators which are the selection, the crossover and the migration operators. The mutation is replaced by the local search algorithm SLS. The main components of the proposed method are given in the following.

3.1 The conflict graph

The conflict graph permits to move from a feasible solution to other ones in the search space. We implemented a conflict graph where the vertices are the bids, and the edges connect the pairs of conflicting bids those sharing items.

3.2 The individual representation

The individual representation is the same used in [3]. That is, an individual is represented by an integer vector A having a variable length bounded by the number of bids n, where the components of the vector A are the winning bids themselves.

3.3 The objective function

The objective function is one of the most important concepts in the proposed algorithm. It is also called fitness function or fitness. For each individual, a value

is associated that measures the quality of such individual in the population. The quality of an individual is given by the sum of the price of winning bids.

3.4 The selection Operator

The selection step permits to identify the best individuals of the population. Based on the fitness value, a set of high quality individuals is selected to build a new generation.

3.5 The Crossover Operator

The crossover operator is used to enrich the diversity of the population by manipulating the structure of existing individuals. The proposed crossover operator is planned with two parents and produces one child. The child is produced by concatenating the two parents randomly. We choose randomly an offer from the two parents and add it to the child if it does not cause any conflict with other offers already in the child. We repeated this process until all offers from both parents are examined.

Let us consider for example a set of five goods $M = \{1, 2, 3, 4, 5\}$ and five bids $B = \{B1, B2, B3, B4, B5\}$. The five bids are as follows:

- Bid 1: $B1 = (\{1, 2, 4\}, 500)$
- Bid 2: $B2 = (\{2, 5\}, 200)$
- Bid 3: $B3 = (\{3\}, 300)$
- Bid 4: $B4 = (\{5\}, 100)$
- Bid 5: $B5 = (\{1, 4\}, 100)$

We consider the two parents X and Y where:

- $X = \{B1, B3\}$ with a fitness value equals to 800
- $Y = \{B2, B3, B5\}$ with a fitness value equals to 600

To generate a child Z, we apply the crossover operator that works as follows:

We generate a random number $0 \leq r \leq 1$, suppose that r is greater than a given probability wc (determined empirically), then we take from the parent Y, the bid $B2$ and we add it to Z. Then, we generate a new random number r. We suppose that it is less than wc. In this case, the bid $B1$ of the parent X will be selected but it is discarded because $B1$ and $B2$ are in conflict (they share the same good 2). In the

same way, we generate a third random number r. we assume this time that r is less than wc. We add to child Z, the bid $B3$ from the parent X. We repeat this process until all the bids contained in the two parents X and Y are examined.

3.6 The Stochastic Local Search Method

To enhance the quality of the new trial individuals in the current generation, we use a stochastic local search method. The SLS performs a certain number of local steps that combines diversification and intensification strategies to locate a good solution. The intensification phase consists in selecting a best neighbor solution. The diversification phase consists in selecting a random neighbor solution. The diversification phase is applied with a fixed probability $wp>0$ and the intensification phase with a probability $1-wp$. The process is repeated until a certain number of iterations called *maxiter* is reached. The SLS method is sketched in Algorithm 1.

Algorithm 1: The SLS method.

Require: a WDP instance, an individual V, *maxiter*, wp
Ensure: an improved individual V
1: **for** $I = 1$ to *maxiter* **do**
2: r⇐ random number between 0 and 1;
3:    **if** $r < wp$ **then**
4:     bid = pick a random bid (*Step 1)
5:    **else**
6:     bid = pick a best bid; (*Step 2)
7:    **end if**
8: $V = V \square \{bid\}$;
9: Based on the conflict graph, remove from V any conflicting bids;
10: **end for**
11: **return** the best individual found.

3.7 The migration Operator

The migration process permits to move an individual of a subpopulation to another subpopulation. In this study, the choice of the individual to be moved is based on the fitness criterion where the best individual is selected for migration.

3.8 The proposed approach organigrams

The different steps of the sequential hybrid genetic algorithm are depicted in Figure 1. Figure 2 shows the parallel version of the hybrid genetic algorithm where the population is subdivided into a set of subpopulations. On each subpopulation, we apply the genetic algorithm process.

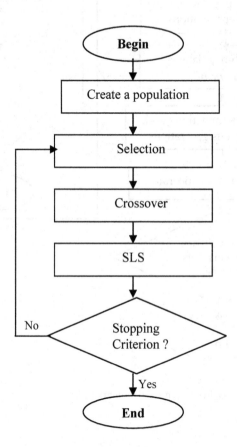

Figure 1 A sequential version of a hybrid genetic algorithm (SGASLS).

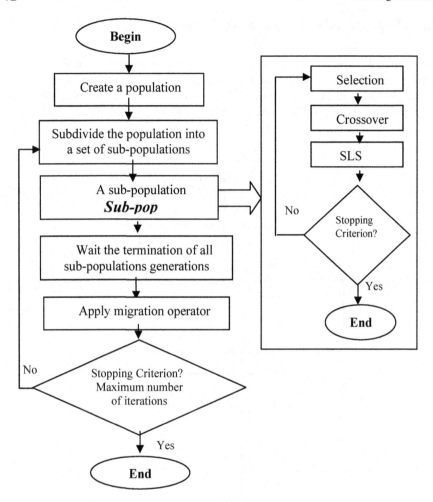

Figure 2 A parallel version of a hybrid genetic algorithm (PGASLS).

4 Experiments

This section gives some experimental results. The source code is written in Java and runs on a Core 2 Duo (1.60 GHz) with 2 GB of RAM.

4.1 Benchmarks

The different algorithms were tested on various benchmark problems commonly used in experimental tests [8]. The data set includes 500 instances and it is available at the Zhuyi's home page[2]. These instances can be divided into five different groups of problems where each group contains 100 instances given as following where m is the number of items and n is the number of bids.

- From in101 to in200: m = 500, n = 1000
- From in201 to in300: m = 1000, n = 1000
- From in401 to in 500: m = 1000, n = 500
- From in501 to in 600: m = 1000, n = 1500
- From in601 to in 700: m = 1500, n = 1500

4.2 Parameter Tuning

The adjustment of parameters of the proposed algorithms is fixed by an experimental study. The fixed values are those for which a good compromise between the quality of the solution obtained by the algorithm and the running time of the algorithm is found.

The PGASLS parameters are: the size of the population (*popsize*), the maximum number of generations of PGASLS (*maxPGA*), the maximum number of generations of the subpopulations (*maxgen*), the crossover probability *wc*. The SLS parameters are: the number of iterations (*maxiter)* and the walk probability *wp*.

To examine the impact of the population size on the effectiveness of the proposed method, several experiments were performed on the five groups of benchmarks. According to the experimental results (not detailed here), we have seen that the solution quality is improved when *popsize* is increased. However, the CPU time also increases when *popsize* is increased. The PGASLS is effective when applied on an average collection of individuals. We have also studied the impact of the *maxiter* parameter on the effectiveness of the PGASLS method. According to the experimental results (note detailed here), we can confirm that the solution quality is improved when we increase the *maxiter* value but the method needs more time.

Table 1 shows the impact of the parameters on the solution quality of PGASLS. The column μ_{PGASLS} corresponds to the arithmetic average solution of the 100 instances in each group, the column *time* corresponds to the average time in second. We can see that for each group of problems, the quality of solutions is

---

[2] (http://logistics.ust.hk/~zhuyi/instance.zip)

improved when *maxiter* and *maxgen* increase. Table1 shows that the CPU time of PGASLS grows when *maxiter* and *maxgen* increase.

Table 1. The impact of maxPGA, maxgen and maxiter on the efficiency of the PGASLS

Test set	*popsize*	*maxPGA*	*maxgen*	*maxiter*	*time*	μ_{PGASLS}
REL-1000-500	20	10	30	20	15,86	66537,54
REL-500-1000	20	10	30	20	9,46	85605,91
REL-1000-1000	20	10	30	20	12,12	88827,13
REL-1500-1000	20	10	30	20	12,18	88116,41
REL-1500-1500	20	10	30	20	12,35	105080,42
REL-1000-500	**20**	**10**	**50**	**60**	**39,56**	**67675,02**
REL-500-1000	**20**	**10**	**50**	**60**	**16,13**	**87543,42**
REL-1000-1000	**20**	**10**	**50**	**60**	**26,68**	**89020,1**
REL-1500-1000	**20**	**10**	**50**	**60**	**29.4**	**95744,42**
REL-1500-1500	**20**	**10**	**50**	**60**	**30,61**	**107072,63**
REL-1000-500	20	15	75	60	85,72	68938,77
REL-500-1000	20	15	75	60	28,75	91291,76
REL-1000-1000	20	15	75	60	56,26	92950,94
REL-1500-1000	20	15	75	60	61,33	104585,75
REL-1500-1500	20	15	75	60	66,71	113662,86
REL-1000-500	20	20	100	100	212,5	70552,26
REL-500-1000	20	20	100	100	6	95296,07
REL-1000-1000	20	20	100	100	66,85	98300,19
REL-1500-1000	20	20	100	100	144,0	108346,69
REL-1500-1500	20	20	100	100	2	110702,53
					159,3	
					4	
					171,6	
					5	

4.3 Comparison with the sequential (SAGSLS)

To show the effectiveness of the parallel approach PGASLS, we made a comparative study with the sequential variant (SAGSLS). The parameters of the SGASLS algorithm are defined by an empirical study as follows: *maxgen* = 300, *popsize* = 13, *maxiter* = 300, *wc* = 0.5, and *wp* = 0.3. The parameters of PGASLS are: the population size *popsize* includes 20 individuals, the maximum number of iterations *maxAGP* is set to 10, the maximum number of generations *maxgen* is 50 and the number of iterations of SLS is 60, *wc* = 0.5, and *wp* = 0.3.

Table 2 shows the results found by both SGASLS and PGASLS methods on some WDP instances. The column *time* gives the CPU time in second and *Sol* is the quality solution. We can see that PGASLS outperforms SGASLS on almost of the tested instances from solution quality and CPU time point of view.

Table 2. SAGSLS Vs. PGASLS on some WDP instances

Instances	SAGSLS		PAGSLS	
	time	sol	time	sol
In401	24.08	72948.08	14.61	88884.0
In402	24.37	74469.08	15.94	78761.47
In403	24.85	74843.97	16.43	87568.03
In404	25.56	78761.69	15.23	101327.33
In405	25.12	74138.29	15.11	91126.52
In406	24.82	72863.33	14.55	88766.46
In407	27.42	76365.72	16.43	90647.23
In408	25.92	77018.83	16.09	77018.84
In409	22.79	73188.62	29.35	84868.91
In410	26.66	71791.58	19.54	89870.25
In411	25.26	71200.55	15.19	105450.98
In474	25.46	75439.37	15.38	86410.07
In475	24.03	75093.1	15.35	80007.49
In501	64.22	81302.69	16.28	110238.42
In502	64.84	80340.77	31.37	82151.32
In503	68.50	79010.71	34.70	108941.96
In504	69.87	81903.03	29.79	105583.86
In505	65.67	80658.36	29.09	84518.58
In506	52.40	79722.13	26.81	87542.07
In507	71.17	83484.53	35.32	88153.71
In508	63.36	85695.34	29.48	122164.72
In509	72.03	82672.27	30.02	90767.74
In510	56.20	79361.91	27.08	85562.51
In571	62.12	79372.83	28.00	85637.45
In572	68.26	83575.23	30.72	89239.56
In573	78.58	79867.37	33.02	107410.59
In574	67.02	79931.32	29.74	97264.55
In575	48.51	83197.26	26.05	90227.05
In576	78.83	79544.87	32.24	84565.43
In577	66.38	81154.19	31.14	82927.92
In578	62.95	80829.85	29.11	116368.08
In579	64.00	82571.39	29.01	98057.07
In580	63.40	79323.34	29.03	97565.98

To further illustrate the results of Table2, we give the comparative curves in Figures 3 and 4 to show and confirm the effectiveness of PGASLS in reaching good quality solutions of many instances in shorter time compared to SGASLS.

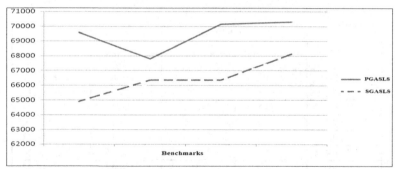

Figure 3. Comparison between PGASLS and SGASLS from quality solution point of view.

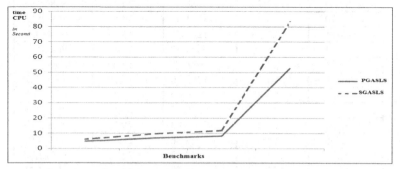

Figure 4. Comparison between PGASLS and SGASLS from CPU time point of view.

4.4 Further comparison

Tables 3 and 4 show the numerical result where the column μ corresponds to the arithmetic average solution of the 100 instances in each group, the column *time* corresponds to the average time in second. Table 3 shows that PGASLS gives a good improvement in results in comparison to SGASLS.

To show the effectiveness of the proposed approach in solving the WDP problem, we compared it with the memetic method (MA) proposed in [3], with Casanova [7] and with SAGII [5, 6].

The simulated annealing SAGII is a hybrid approach. It consists of Branch and-Bound, greedy and exchange moves. The Casanova is a stochastic local search proposed by Hoos and Boutilier [7]. The MA [3] method is an evolutionary metaheuristic. It applies a crossover operator to create new trial individuals which are enhanced by using a stochastic local search (SLS) component.

The parameters of MA were set as follows: a collection of ten individuals including five higher quality individuals and five diversified individuals, the population contains 100 individuals, the number of generations is fixed to 100 and the number of iterations of the local search is 500. More details on the MA method

are given in [3]. The PGASLS and SGASLS parameters are the same already given above in *section 4.3*.

According to the results depicted on Tables 3 and 4, we can see that PGASLS performs better than MA, Casanova and SAGII. It finds better solutions in shorter time. The results show good performances in favour of the PGASLS in solving the WDP compared to the others considered methods. PGASLS outperforms significantly MA, Casanova and SAGII on almost all of the checked instances of the WDP problem.

Table3. PGASLS Vs. SGASLS Vs. MA on WDP instances

Test set	PGASLS		SGASLS		MA	
	time	μ	time	μ	*time*	μ
REL-1000-500	**39,56**	**67675,02**	84.79	**67844.41**	56.64	65,740.25
REL-500-1000	**16,13**	**87543,42**	25.01	74836,99	5.91	73,604.62
REL-1000-1000	**26,68**	**89020,1**	56.85	85161,81	33.05	83,304.20
REL-1500-1000	**29.4**	**95744,42**	65.44	81218.45	24.51	79,644.64
REL-1500-1500	**30,61**	**107072,63**	68.84	101544.27	28.22	99,957.96

Table 4. PGASLS Vs. Casanova Vs. SAGII on WDP instances

Test set	PGASLS		Casanova		SAGII	
	time	μ	time	μ	*time*	μ
REL-1000-500	**39,56**	**67675,02**	119.46	37053.78	38.06	64922.02
REL-500-1000	**16,13**	**87543,42**	57.74	51248.79	24.46	73922.10
REL-1000-1000	**26,68**	**89020,1**	111.42	51990.91	45.37	83728.34
REL-1500-1000	**29.4**	**95744,42**	168.24	56406.74	68.82	82651.49
REL-1500-1500	**30,61**	**107072,63**	165.92	65661.03	91.78	101739.64

5 Conclusion

In this paper, we proposed a hybrid parallel genetic algorithm (PGASLS) for solving the winner determination problem (WDP) in combinatorial auctions. The method is implemented and evaluated on several benchmark problems with various sizes, and compared with a sequential genetic hybrid genetic algorithm (SGASLS), Casanova, SAGII and the memetic algorithm (MA). The experimental results are very encouraging. PGASLS provides competitive results and finds solutions of a higher quality than the sequential variant, Casanova, SAGII and MA. To improve the current results, we aim in future to implementing parallel variant of our methods on GPU platforms.

References

1. Andersson, A., Tenhunen, M., Ygge, F.: Integer programming for combinatorial auction winner determination. In: Proceedings of 4th International Conference on Multi-Agent Systems, pp. 39–46. IEEE Computer Society, July (2000).
2. Boughaci, D., Drias, H., Benhamou, B.: Stochastic local search for the optimal winner determination problem in combinatorial auctions. In: The International Conference on Constraint Programming, CP 2008. LNCS, pp. 593–597 (2008).
3. Boughaci, D., Drias, H., Benhamou, B.: A memetic algorithm for the optimal winner determination problem. In: Soft Computing—a Fusion of Foundations, Methodologies and Applications, vol. 13, no. 8–9, pp. 905–917. Springer, Berlin (2009).
4. Fujishima, Y., Leyton-Brown, K., Shoham, Y.: Taming the computational complexity of combinatorial auctions: optimal and approximate approaches. In: Sixteenth International Joint Conference on Artificial Intelligence, pp. 48–53 (1999)
5. Guo, Y., Lim, A., Rodrigues, B., Zhu, Y.: Heuristics for a brokering set packing problem. In: Proceedings of eighth international symposium on artificial intelligence and mathematics, pp. 10–14 (2004).
6. Guo, Y., Lim, A., Rodrigues, B., Zhu, Y.: Heuristics for a bidding problem. Comput. Oper. Res. 33(8), 2179–2188 (2006).
7. Hoos, H.H., Boutilier, C.: Solving combinatorial auctions using stochastic local search. In: Proceedings of the 17th National Conference on Artificial Intelligence, pp. 22–29 (2000).
8. Lau, H.C., Goh, Y.G.: An intelligent brokering system to support multi-agent web-based 4thparty logistics. In: Proceedings of the 14th International Conference on Tools with Artificial Intelligence, pp. 54–61 (2002).
9. Leyton-Brown, K., Tennenholtz, M., Shoham, Y.: An algorithm for multi-unit combinatorial auctions. In: Proceedings of the 17th National Conference on Artificial Intelligence, Austin, Games-2000, Bilbao, and ISMP-2000, Atlanta (2000).
10. Munawar, A.,Wahib,M.,Munetomo, M., Akama, K.: Optimization Problem Solving Framework Employing GAs with Linkage Identification over a Grid Environment. In: CEC 2007: Proceedings of IEEE congress on Evolutionary Computation, Singapore (2007).
11. Munawar, Wahib, M., A., Munetomo, M., Akama, K.: A General Service-Oriented Grid Computing Framework For Global Optimization Problem Solving. In: SCC 2008: Proceedings of the 2008 IEEE International Conference on Services Computing, Honolulu, Hawaii, USA. IEEE, Los Alamitos (2008).
12. Rothkopf, M.H., Pekee, A., Ronald, M.: Computationally manageable combinatorial auctions. Manage. Sci. 44(8), 1131–1147 (1998)
13. Sandholm, T.: Algorithms for optimal winner determination in combinatorial auctions. Artificial. Intelligence. 135(1–2), 1–54 (1999).
14. Sandholm, T., Suri, S.: Improved optimal algorithm for combinatorial auctions and generalizations. In: Proceedings of the 17th National Conference on Artificial Intelligence, pp. 90–97 (2000).
15. Sandholm, T., Suri, S., Gilpin, A., Levine, D.: CABoB: a fast optimal algorithm for combinatorial auctions. In: Proceedings of the International Joint Conferences on Artificial Intelligence, pp. 1102–1108 (2001).
16. Sandholm, T.: Optimal winner determination algorithms. In: Cramton, P., et al. (ed.), Combinatorial Auctions. MIT, Cambridge (2006).
17. Vries de S and R. Vohra, 'Combinatorial auctions a survey', In INFORMS Journal of Computing, Vol 15, pp. 284-309, (2003).

Validation Sets, Genetic Programming and Generalisation

Jeannie Fitzgerald and Conor Ryan

Abstract This paper investigates a new application of a validation set when using a three data set methodology with Genetic Programming (GP). Our system uses *Validation Pressure* combined with *Validation Elitism* to influence fitness evaluation and population structure with the aim of improving the system's ability to evolve individuals with an enhanced capacity for generalisation. This strategy facilitates the use of a validation set to reduce over-fitting while mitigating the loss of training data associated with traditional methods employing a validation set.

The method is tested on five benchmark binary classification data sets and results obtained suggest that the strategy can deliver improved generalisation on unseen test data.

1 Introduction

Since the early pioneering work of Koza [15], Genetic Programming has gone from being somewhat of an outsider in the machine learning world to its wide acceptance as an effective method for solving difficult problems, showing human competitive results across a wide variety of tasks. The GP paradigm is based around the Darwinian model of human evolution, where the fittest survive and have a greater opportunity to reproduce and so pass their genetic material to future generations. From time to time, mutations occur which while often fatal, occasionally introduce useful new genetic material which leads to some measurable improvement.

Typically a GP implementation involves randomly generating a population of individual computer programs comprised of functions and terminals which may be appropriate to the particular problem. Traditionally, GP programs are represented

Jeannie Fitzgerald
BDS Group, CSIS Department, University of Limerick, Ireland. e-mail: jeannie.fitzgerald@ul.ie

Conor Ryan
BDS Group, CSIS Department, University of Limerick, Ireland. e-mail: conor.ryan@ul.ie

M. Bramer et al. (eds.), *Research and Development in Intelligent Systems XXVIII*,
DOI 10.1007/978-1-4471-2318-7_6, © Springer-Verlag London Limited 2011

using tree based structures (but other representations have also been employed). In tree based GP, each internal node contains an operator and each terminal or leaf node is a place-holder for an operand. Tree structures are evaluated recursively substituting in operands specific to each problem instance.

The population of individuals is allowed to evolve over a number of iterations or generations. For each generation, every program is evaluated and is assigned a fitness value which depends on how successful it is at solving the given problem. Each new generation is populated with new individuals through the application of several GP processes: in GP terminology the processes of *reproduction, crossover* and *mutation* roughly correspond to the Darwinian notions of survival of the fittest, sexual reproduction and genetic mutation. Through these mechanisms, the population ideally evolves increasingly better solutions through the generations until an optimum solution is found, the individuals in the population are no longer showing significant improvement or a pre-set maximum number of generations has been reached.

In recent years several researchers [16, 12, 5] have expressed the opinion, that in the past, traditional GP research effort may not have put sufficient emphasis on the generalisation potential of a given proposed method. The authors point out that it was not uncommon for experiments to be carried out using a single data set: the training set. In the early days of GP, a great deal of effort was focused on finding new and better ways of tackling benchmark problems such as symbolic regression, parity, boolean multiplexer and artificial ant. As the focus of the effort was on proving that GP had the capability to solve the problems and in discovering the best GP strategies to do so, and as these are essentially "toy" problems, it is considered reasonable that a single data set was used in these cases [12].

The importance of generalisation comes to the fore when GP is used to tackle real world problems. Using a single data set approach tends to over fit, and may produce brittle solutions. So, it is desirable to test the evolved solutions against unseen data to provide an indication of their ability to solve the same problems on new instances. While this provides reassurance as to the robustness of the solution, it does not really help with the problem of over-fitting the training data. To address this issue, several researchers have used a third data set: the validation data set. The idea is that this data set can be employed to detect over-fitting and curtail the training phase once some pre-defined validation criteria has been met, such as a deterioration or lack of improvement in validation fitness. However, establishing consistent stopping criteria has been shown to be a non trivial task [30].

Using this approach program fitness is determined by the performance of the individual on training alone, and the validation set is used to determine when learning should cease. The main disadvantage of this method is that having now to divide the test data into three sets instead of two, the number of instances available for training are reduced. This may not be an issue if the available training data is statistically representative of the problem space, as, after a time, new instances will support existing patterns and will not add further information to the model. On the other hand, if the data set is too big and noisy learning will not succeed. But, in general the more data available for training the system the more accurate the generated solutions will be, with greater generalisation potential, whereas reducing the amount of

data available for training will negatively impact performance. Our method aims at overcoming this disadvantage.

The remainder of this paper is laid out as follows: Section 2 provides some background to this work with a particular focus on the application of a validation set; Section 3 explains the proposed technique, Section 4 details the experimental set-up, reports and discusses the results; and Section 5 outlines conclusions and future work.

2 Related Work

In recent years, several researchers have investigated the use of a validation set to detect over-fitting of the training data in order to terminate evolution at the appropriate time [29, 18]. Foreman and Evett [9], and later, Vanneschi et al [31] investigated over-fitting measures based on the relationship between training and validation fitness. In the latter, it was observed that the success of such measures may be highly dependant on how the data is partitioned unless some form of cross-validation is employed. In recent work which examined the effectiveness of "early stopping" in preventing over-fitting, Tuite et al. [30] concluded that while the strategy may be useful in improving generalisation, employing a "naive early stopping heuristic" can result in terminating too soon.

Also in the research, a validation set has been used in various ways to select a best of run individual or individuals. Thomas and Sycara [29] experimented with using a validation set to improve performance of financial trading rules. Firstly, they tested the best of run trading rule against the validation set and kept it if it produced positive returns. Next, they also tested all of the trading rules of the final training generation against the validation set and kept any that produced a positive return. The experiments did not yield any noticeable improvement and in several cases the results were actually worse. Gagne et al. [12] used a validation set to select the best of run individual from among the fittest trained individuals and reported that while their use of a validation set did not improve performance, it did deliver more stable solutions that had lower variance. Fitzgerald and Ryan [8] used validation performance as the main criterion for selecting the best of run individual, choosing the one with the best training score in the event of a tie. Robilliard and Fonlupt [27] proposed "backwarding" where whenever a new best individual with respect to the training set was discovered, this program was also compared to the last best one with respect to an independent validation set. A solution that improved on both sets was then stored and the last such solution was returned at the end of the GP process. The authors tested their approach on a regression task and on a real world remote sensing problem and reported that the system delivered robust solutions.

Miller and Thomson [22] were among the first to observe the beneficial effects of elitism on evolutionary learning. Since then it has become commonplace to use elitism in GP whenever a generational strategy is employed. The technique ensures that the best performing individuals remain in the population and are available to

pass on their desirable genetic material to the next generation. We propose to extend this idea so that individuals who perform best on the validation data are also maintained in the breeding pool. In the absence of such a strategy it is quite possible that their potentially useful genes will be lost if their performance on the training data falls below the threshold required for normal elite selection. Secondly, we investigate a technique of *validation pressure* whereby the individuals' validation score may be taken into account during selection for breeding or modification purposes.

Selection pressure is a vital component in the GP paradigm and could loosely be described as a means of directing the focus of the search operation. Usually when using tournament selection, this is achieved using tournament size: the larger the tournament, the more elitist or narrow the search strategy. Various adjustments have been employed to control aspects of the evolutionary process such as selecting the smallest of two individuals where they are tied on training fitness scores, or some other form of parsimony pressure [20] or diversity inducing tournaments [1]. As far as we are aware, this is the first time that validation elitism and validation pressure have been used to influence the evolutionary process.

3 Methodology

Our method employs a three data set methodology to reduce the risk of over-fitting while mitigating the potential loss of richness in the training data associated with a traditional three data set approach. We do this by leveraging the validation data set during the learning process. During evolution, we evaluate each individual against the validation set and use this information to provide additional training opportunities to the system.

The difference between our proposed method and standard approaches is that we envisage the role of the validation set as not only to determine when evolution should be curtailed, but also to influence the evolutionary process itself. This is achieved by comparing individuals' performance on the validation data when their performance on training data is identical(*validation pressure*) and by using *validation elitism*: maintaining a percentage of individuals with elite validation performance in the population.

Using a three data set methodology, in each generation, we evaluate each individual on both the training and validation sets. When it comes to tournament selection, if two competing individuals have the same training fitness, we chose the one with the best validation fitness. Also, during evolution, we use *validation elitism* to ensure that there is a good representation of the best so far validation scoring individuals in the breeding pool. Experiments were undertaken using various levels of validation elitism from 10%-50%. Our objective is to combine these techniques with the aim of breeding individuals that are less elitist with regard to either the training or validation data, rather they are good "all rounders". In this way, we may be able to make more efficient use of a validation set that allows the system to be flexible re-

garding appropriate termination without sacrificing richness in the available training opportunities.

For the purpose of the current experiments, in order to isolate potential effects of the new method, we have chosen to terminate evolution at the same generation number for each program run. We have elected to end each run at generation forty unless a perfect classification occurs earlier. It is likely that this approach prevents the system from delivering on its full potential as the choice of terminating generation may not be appropriate for a given classification problem while the competing baseline configuration could be said to be advantaged by implicitly reducing an inherent tendency to over fit.

We have elected to investigate the potential of our approach using binary classification tasks because GP is suitable for this type of task as it is flexible, expressive and domain independent. The flexibility of the system facilitates implementation of an experimental framework that can easily accommodate a wide range of different data sets. Also, there are a good number of well tested data sets available for research. The ones which we have selected have varying numbers of attributes of different ranges and exhibit varying degrees of perceived classification difficulty.

4 Experiments

4.1 Data Sets

Five benchmark data sets have been used for experiments, four from the medical domain and one from the financial domain. For each dataset, the ratio of negative to positive instances is preserved in the training, validation and test sets. In partitioning the data between training, validation and test sets, we discarded several records from any master set where the values did not divide evenly, in order to ensure equal sized sets with the correct proportions. All data sets used here were obtained from the UCI Machine Learning database [10].

Table 1: Data Sets

Data Set	Domain	Features	Instances
Blood Transfusion (BT)	Medical	5	768
Bupa Liver Disorders (BUPA)	Medical	7	345
German Credit (GC)	Financial	23	1000
Habermans Survival (HS)	Medical	4	306
Wisconsin Brest Cancer (WBC)	Medical	10	699

4.2 Function Sets

We have used a function set consisting of addition, subtraction, multiplication and protected division and have chosen not to use constants for our experiments, as the system should be capable of synthesising any values required using the function set together with the range of values in the existing terminal sets.

Table 2: GP Parameters

Parameter	Value
Strategy	Generational
Initialisation	Ramped half-and-half
Selection	Tournament
Tournament Size	5
Crossover (subtree)	90
Mutation (subtree)	10
Initial Minimum Depth	1
Initial Maximum Depth	6
Maximum Depth	17
Function Set	+ - * /
Population Size	300
Maximum Generations	40

In this investigation, we compare the results of a standard GP implementation with those achieved on the same data sets using the proposed methodology. The outlined parameter set applies to the baseline configuration. For the proposed method, an additional parameter: validation elitism is added, with values in the range 0-50%. In this case crossover and mutation rates are applied with probabilities detailed in the parameter table on the remainder of the population.

4.3 Experimental Set-up and GP Parameters

Genetic Programming(GP) parameters used for the experiments are detailed in Table 2. One hundred independent runs were undertaken for each configuration, giving a total of 4500 runs (five data sets with one hundred runs each for baseline, *validation pressure* combined with eight different *validation elitism* values, that is, 0, 10, 20, 25, 30, 35, 40 and 50 percent). The fitness measure used for evolution was the number of classification errors of each program. Final fitness values are converted to error rate and % classification accuracy for reporting and comparison purposes. The GP framework used was the Open Beagle Evolutionary Framework[11]. For the remainder of this document we will refer to the baseline configuration as "Base"

and the proposed method as "ValPE".

4.4 Results and Discussion

In this section, we outline results achieved using the Base and ValPE configurations. The best result in each category is in bold font.

4.4.1 Training, Validation and Test Fitness Scores

In Table 3 we compare results achieved using the ValPE configuration against the baseline configuration. For training and validation, we give average fitness and average best fitness, along with standard deviation, as well as best individual fitness at the final generation. Test scores represent average fitness, standard deviation and best individual resulting from testing the hundred best of run individuals on each task on the corresponding test data.

We have chosen to compare using the ValPE configuration with 30% validation elitism: for most of the examples improvement was at this fraction or higher, although, as can be seen in table 4, 30% was the optimal value for only one of the data sets.

Table 3: Training Validation & Test Fitness

Dataset	Method	Training				Validation				Test		
		Avg.	StdD	Best	High	Avg.	StdD	Best	High	Avg.	StdD	High
BT	*Base*	76.53	2.61	**82.29**	**84.74**	72.55	2.79	79.61	81.53	75.38	1.91	81.12
	ValPE	**76.59**	2.15	81.74	84.34	**75.58**	1.94	**81.46**	**83.13**	**75.79**	1.89	**81.52**
BUPA	Base	**74.91**	2.42	**81.38**	86.84	65.64	3.55	73.52	79.82	70.15	3.60	77.19
	ValPE	74.68	2.02	80.53	86.84	**69.78**	2.23	**76.42**	**82.46**	**73.51**	2.65	**80.70**
GC	Base	**74.92**	1.73	**78.60**	81.98	69.85	1.89	74.12	78.68	70.90	2.11	**76.57**
	ValPE	73.73	1.77	77.37	81.98	**72.39**	1.86	**76.41**	**83.18**	**71.64**	1.68	76.26
HS	Base	**78.64**	1.79	**83.09**	**88.24**	68.72	1.63	74.94	78.43	76.16	2.05	79.41
	ValPE	76.38	1.43	81.05	84.31	**71.46**	1.02	**77.25**	**80.39**	**76.67**	1.81	**81.37**
WBC	Base	93.53	1.69	97.02	**99.12**	93.15	1.99	97.52	**99.12**	95.46	1.56	98.67
	ValPE	**94.45**	1.71	**97.22**	98.24	**94.51**	1.51	**97.57**	98.68	**97.59**	0.82	**99.12**

[a] For Training and Validation, "Best" is the average of the best individuals, in all cases "High" is the best individual overall.

The baseline configuration produced the best results overall on training data: it had highest average fitness and highest average best fitness on four of the five tasks, and either outscores ValPE or shares the best score for best overall individual. However, for both validation and test results the ValPE configuration outscores Base on all

categories except best overall individual where the baseline configuration does better on validation for both WBC and GC on test data. In *all* cases, the average test performance is better with ValPE.

We expected that the proposed method would deliver improvements over the baseline configuration in cases where the data instances in the training and validation sets exhibited some dissimilarity. When we looked at the composition of the data for each problem, comparing the average and standard deviation of each attribute, we saw that the partitioning of the data into training and validation sets resulted in very similar sets for HS and GC, with more dissimilarity apparent for BUPA, WBC and BT. Generally, the results seem to be consistent with this, as the greatest improvement over the standard approach can be seen in the BUPA and WBC experiments. The BT experiment does not show a similar improvement, which may be because it is possible to obtain relatively good results with limited data for this task as the attribute values for positive and negative instances have good separation.

4.4.2 Validation Elitism

We experimented with various levels of validation elitism ranging from 0% to 50%. Results shown in Table 4 were recorded when the best of run individuals were applied on the test data sets of each problem. For clarity, we show only test results here.

Table 4: Test Fitness VP with Elitism

Data Set	0%	10%	20%	25%	30%	35%	40%	50%
BT	75.69	75.57	75.70	76.17	75.79	75.76	75.60	**76.29**
BUPA	70.86	73.34	73.53	73.26	73.51	73.61	**73.74**	73.40
GC	70.97	71.19	70.87	71.03	**71.64**	71.20	70.89	70.98
HS	**76.97**	76.20	76.84	76.46	76.67	76.64	76.77	76.87
WBC	95.67	97.56	97.48	97.14	97.59	97.56	**97.75**	97.46

[a] Average fitness on test data over 100 runs at each setting.

The application of validation elitism appears to have had a beneficial effect on most of the data sets with the exception of Haberman's Survival where the best score was achieved without any elitism. The effect was only mildly beneficial for BT and GC, but had a more significant impact on BUPA and WBC. In general, the pattern suggests that higher values are more effective than lower ones. Certainly, the method appears to do no harm and has the side benefit of smaller run times due to fewer evaluations.

In a similar experiment focused on the effects of varying degrees of standard elitism on program bloat, Poli et al.[26] observed that higher values of elitism tended to produce smaller programs and bloated more slowly during evolution, with elite fractions 30% and 50% behaving almost identically.

A cursory analysis of the HS underlying data instances in terms of average and standard deviation of the attribute values suggests that the partitioning of instances between the training and validation sets has resulted in the sets being very similar. One of the stated aims of our approach is to compensate for the loss of richness in test data that may result from having to partition the data into three data sets, thus reducing the number of training instances. However, as already discussed, if the partitioned data is representative (as seems to be the case here) then one would not expect the application of validation elitism to yield much in the way of improvement.

4.5 Comparison with other work

In this section, results obtained using the ValPE approach are compared with other work involving the same datasets, including non-EC approaches such as neural networks and SVMs. Results are expressed as either % classification accuracy or error rate as appropriate, to aid comparison with other work. The goal is to achieve high classification accuracy which corresponds to low error rate. Here again, for consistency, we are using the results of the 30% validation elitism configurations for comparison, although higher scores were achieved on four of the data sets with different elitism settings.

Lim et al.[17] compared the performance of over thirty classification algorithms including decision tree algorithms, statistical algorithms and neural networks. The best performing of these on the WBC and BUPA datasets reported error rates of 0.03 and 0.28. The corresponding error rates for ValPE of 0.02 and 0.26 are better.

Table 5: BUPA Comparative Data

Author (year)	Method	%Acc.
Cheung (2001)	BNND	61.83
Cheung (2001)	Naive Bayes	63.39
Yalçın and Yıldırım (2003)	GRNN	65.55
Cheung (2001)	C4.5	65.59
Van Gestel et al. (2002)	SVM with GP	69.70
Lee and Mangasarian (2001a)	SSVM	70.33
Yalçın and Yıldırım (2003)	MLP	73.05
Current work	**ValPE**	**73.51**
Lee and Mangasarian (2001b)	RSVM	74.86
Polat et al. (2005)	AIRS	81.00
Polat et al. (2005)	Fuzzy-AIRS	83.38

Table 6: HS Comparative Data

Algorithm	% Accuracy
KNN	68.27
NN	69.93
GMM	66.01
SVM	71.24
PSVM	72.54
ANFC	72.59
ANFC	73.35
ANFC-LH	74.51
BEC	74.90
ANFC-LH	75.31
ValPE	**76.67**

Looking at the Blood Transfusion problem, Badhran et al. reported average accuracies of 78.01% using a simple artificial neural network (SANN) and 76.14% with a functional link artificial neural network (FLANN). Darwiche et al. [6] reported classification accuracies between 74.7% and 77.3% using Support Vector Machines

and RPB Kernels, and 60.0% and 72.5% with multi layer perceptrons, depending on which attributes were chosen. The ValPE score of 75.79% delivers a competitive result.

Polat et al.[25] provides a comparison for the BUPA Liver Disorders task against a wide range of machine learning tools as shown in Table 5. The ValPE method ranks fourth highest in this table. In other work, Loveard and Ciesielski [19] experimented with GP using static and population based dynamic boundaries. They recorded a best test score of 69.2%. Muni et al. [23] reported a similar result. Recent research by Badhran and Rockett(2010) [2] applied GP with varying parameters and reported a test result of 74.86%. Overall, the ValPE result of 73.51% represents a very competitive performance.

For Habermans's survival data set we can compare our results with those recently (2010) published by Cetisli et al [4] as detailed in Table 6. In other work, Thommano and Moolwong [28] reported accuracy of 77.17% using a fascinating classification approach inspired by human social behaviour and Jabeen and Baig [13] achieved classification accuracies of 77.63% using GP and 82.12% using Particle Swarm Optimisation(PSO). With the exception of the PSO result, the performance of the ValPE configuration with a score of 76.67% has delivered results on a par with or superior to the available published results for this data set.

Turning our attention to the German Credit classification task where comparative scores are expressed as error rate the ValPE results are less convincing: Eggermont et al. [7] reported error rates of 0.278 using clustering GP, 0.271 using a standard GP implementation and 0.272 using C4.5. Meyer [21] compared the performance of SVMs against various other popular classification algorithms and reported average classification error of 0.236 for SVM, 0.232 using a generalised linear model(GLM), 0.273 for a multivariate regression model and 0.284 for learning vector quantization(LVQ). In other work, Baesens et al. [3] reported results of between 0.321 and 0.285 for several Bayesian Network Classifiers and 0.288 for C4.5. Overall, the ValPE score of 0.284 is not very competitive by comparison with the available research. Also, our baseline GP score of 0.291 compares poorly with that of [7]. It is possible that the small population, limited function set and termination condition we have chosen are insufficient for this particular problem. This will be addressed in future work.

Again, Polat et al.[25] compared the performance of various algorithms on the Wisconsin Breast Cancer classification problem as shown in Table 7. The ValPE score of 97.59% ranks third highest of those listed. In more recent work, Winkler et al. [32] reported test accuracy of 97.07% for an enhanced GP configuration, Johnson et al. [14] reported a test score of 95.71% using a linear regression approach to numerical simplification in Tree-Based Genetic Programming and Parrott et al. [24] achieved classification accuracy of 95.60% with a form of multi objective GP. Overall, the ValPE result compares favourably with those achieved using other methods.

Further details on the methods listed in the referenced results tables can be found in the cited works.

Table 7: WBC Comparative Data

Author (Year)	Method	%Acc.
Quinlan (1996)	C4.5	94.74
Hamilton et al. (1996)	RIAC	94.99
Nauck and Kruse (1999)	NEFCLASS	95.06
Abonyi and Szeifert (2003)	FuzzyClustering	95.57
Ster and Dobnikar (1996)	LDA	96.80
Goodman et al. (2002)	Big-LVQ	96.80
Bennet and Blue (1997)	SVM	97.20
Goodman et al. (2002)	AIRS	97.20
Pena-Reyes andSipper (1999)	Fuzzy-GA1	97.36
Current Work	**ValPE**	**97.59**
Setiono (2000)	Neuro-Rule 2a	98.10
Polat et al. (2005)	Fuzzy-AIRS	98.51

5 Conclusions and Future Work

In this paper, we have outlined the importance of generalisation in GP approaches to solving real world problems and highlighted both the usefulness and negative aspects of using a three data set approach. We have proposed a method in which we combine validation selection pressure and validation elitism in order to efficiently employ a three data set approach to improve generalisation ability while counteracting the potentially negative effect of partitioning the available data into three. The method has been tested on five binary classification problems and has been shown to deliver improvements in test performance over standard methods. We have compared our results with others achieved on the same data sets and the ValPE configuration has demonstrated a competitive and sometimes superior performance on four of the five problems.

In order to isolate any effects of employing the method, we chose to terminate the runs at generation forty. While this achieved the desired result, it is not an accurate reflection of how one would tackle these problems using GP in the field. Typically, in other work, using a standard approach, a greater proportion of the available data is used for training than for testing, and a larger number of generations are used. Also, by applying a "one size fits all" termination criterion to the ValPE method, it was not in a position to capitalise on its perceived natural advantage: the ability to determine the best point to stop the evolutionary process. This work is essentially a preliminary step in developing an approach that can facilitate early stopping to avoid over-fitting without sacrificing training opportunities.

A logical next step is to perform an 'in the field" comparison whereby the ValPE method is modified to allow the system to cease evolving once over-fitting occurs, compared with a baseline configuration where a larger proportion of the available data is used for training, and which terminates at a generation number that is consistent with other experiments in the research on the same data sets. We anticipate that detection and handling of over-fitting in a graceful and reliable way, using a three data set methodology, could be an interesting and challenging undertaking.

Acknowledgements

This work has been supported by the Science Foundation of Ireland.

References

1. R. M. A. Azad and C. Ryan. Abstract functions and lifetime learning in genetic programming for symbolic regression. In J. Branke, M. Pelikan, E. Alba, D. V. Arnold, J. Bongard, A. Brabazon, J. Branke, M. V. Butz, J. Clune, M. Cohen, K. Deb, A. P. Engelbrecht, N. Krasnogor, J. F. Miller, M. O'Neill, K. Sastry, D. Thierens, J. van Hemert, L. Vanneschi, and C. Witt, editors, *GECCO '10: Proceedings of the 12th annual conference on Genetic and evolutionary computation*, pages 893–900, Portland, Oregon, USA, 7-11 July 2010. ACM.
2. K. Badran and P. I. Rockett. The influence of mutation on population dynamics in multiobjective genetic programming. *Genetic Programming and Evolvable Machines*, 11(1):5–33, Mar. 2010.
3. B. Baesens, M. Egmont-Petersen, R. Castelo, and J. Vanthienen. Learning bayesian network classifiers for credit scoring using markov chain monte carlo search. In *Proceedings of the 16 th International Conference on Pattern Recognition (ICPR'02) Volume 3 - Volume 3*, ICPR '02, pages 30049–, Washington, DC, USA, 2002. IEEE Computer Society.
4. B. Cetisli. Development of an adaptive neuro-fuzzy classifier using linguistic hedges: Part 1. *Expert Syst. Appl.*, 37:6093–6101, August 2010.
5. D. Costelloe and C. Ryan. On improving generalisation in genetic programming. In L. Vanneschi, S. Gustafson, A. Moraglio, I. De Falco, and M. Ebner, editors, *Proceedings of the 12th European Conference on Genetic Programming, EuroGP 2009*, volume 5481 of *LNCS*, pages 61–72, Tuebingen, Apr. 15-17 2009. Springer.
6. M. Darwiche, M. Feuilloy, G. Bousaleh, and D. Schang. Prediction of blood transfusion donation. In *Research Challenges in Information Science (RCIS), 2010 Fourth International Conference on*, pages 51 –56, may 2010.
7. J. Eggermont, J. N. Kok, and W. A. Kosters. Genetic programming for data classification: Partitioning the search space. In *Proceedings of the 2004 Symposium on Applied Computing (ACM SAC'04)*, pages 1001–1005, Nicosia, Cyprus, 14-17 Mar. 2004.
8. J. Fitzgerald and C. Ryan. Drawing boundaries: using individual evolved class boundaries for binary classification problems. In N. Krasnogor and P. L. Lanzi, editors, *GECCO*, pages 1347–1354. ACM, 2011.
9. N. Foreman and M. Evett. Preventing overfitting in GP with canary functions. In H.-G. Beyer, U.-M. O'Reilly, D. V. Arnold, W. Banzhaf, C. Blum, E. W. Bonabeau, E. Cantu-Paz, D. Dasgupta, K. Deb, J. A. Foster, E. D. de Jong, H. Lipson, X. Llora, S. Mancoridis, M. Pelikan, G. R. Raidl, T. Soule, A. M. Tyrrell, J.-P. Watson, and E. Zitzler, editors, *GECCO 2005: Proceedings of the 2005 conference on Genetic and evolutionary computation*, volume 2, pages 1779–1780, Washington DC, USA, 25-29 June 2005. ACM Press.
10. A. Frank and A. Asuncion. UCI machine learning repository, 2010.
11. C. Gagné and M. Parizeau. Open beagle: A new c++ evolutionary computation framework. In *Proceedings of the Genetic and Evolutionary Computation Conference*, GECCO '02, pages 888–, San Francisco, CA, USA, 2002. Morgan Kaufmann Publishers Inc.
12. C. Gagné, M. Schoenauer, M. Parizeau, and M. Tomassini. Genetic programming, validation sets, and parsimony pressure. In P. Collet, M. Tomassini, M. Ebner, S. Gustafson, and A. Ekárt, editors, *Proceedings of the 9th European Conference on Genetic Programming*, volume 3905 of *Lecture Notes in Computer Science*, pages 109–120, Budapest, Hungary, 10 - 12 Apr. 2006. Springer.
13. H. Jabeen and A. Baig. A Framework for Optimization of Genetic Programming Evolved Classifier Expressions Using Particle Swarm Optimization. In a. n. u. e. l. GraÃa, Romay,

E. Corchado, and . Garcia, Sebastian, editors, *Hybrid Artificial Intelligence Systems*, volume 6076 of *Lecture Notes in Computer Science*, chapter 7, pages 56–63–63. Springer Berlin / Heidelberg, Berlin, Heidelberg, 2010.

14. M. Johnston, T. Liddle, and M. Zhang. A linear regression approach to numerical simplification in tree-based genetic programming. Research report 09-7, School of Mathematics Statistics and Operations Research, Victoria University of Wellington, New Zealand, 14 Dec. 2009.

15. J. R. Koza. Genetic programming: A paradigm for genetically breeding populations of computer programs to solve problems. Technical report, 1990.

16. I. Kushchu. Genetic programming and evolutionary generalization. *IEEE Transactions on Evolutionary Computation*, 6(5):431–442, Oct. 2002.

17. T.-S. Lim, W.-Y. LOH, and W. Cohen. A comparison of prediction accuracy, complexity, and training time of thirty-three old and new classification algorithms, 2000.

18. Y. Liu and T. M. Khoshgoftaar. Genetic programming model for software quality classification. In *Sixth IEEE International Symposium on High Assurance Systems Engineering, HASE'01*, pages 127–136, Boco Raton, FL, USA, Oct. 22-24 2001. IEEE.

19. T. Loveard and V. Ciesielski. Representing classification problems in genetic programming. In *Proceedings of the Congress on Evolutionary Computation*, volume 2, pages 1070–1077, COEX, World Trade Center, 159 Samseong-dong, Gangnam-gu, Seoul, Korea, 27-30 May 2001. IEEE Press.

20. S. Luke and L. Panait. Lexicographic parsimony pressure. In W. B. Langdon, E. Cantú-Paz, K. Mathias, R. Roy, D. Davis, R. Poli, K. Balakrishnan, V. Honavar, G. Rudolph, J. Wegener, L. Bull, M. A. Potter, A. C. Schultz, J. F. Miller, E. Burke, and N. Jonoska, editors, *GECCO 2002: Proceedings of the Genetic and Evolutionary Computation Conference*, pages 829–836, New York, 9-13 July 2002. Morgan Kaufmann Publishers.

21. D. Meyer. The support vector machine under test. *Neurocomputing*, 55(1-2):169–186, Sept. 2003.

22. J. F. Miller and P. Thomson. Aspects of digital evolution: Geometry and learning. In *Proceedings of the Second International Conference on Evolvable Systems*, pages 25–35. Springer-Verlag, 1998.

23. D. P. Muni, N. R. Pal, and J. Das. A novel approach to design classifier using genetic programming. *IEEE Transactions on Evolutionary Computation*, 8(2):183–196, Apr. 2004.

24. D. Parrott, X. Li, and V. Ciesielski. Multi-objective techniques in genetic programming for evolving classifiers. In D. Corne, Z. Michalewicz, M. Dorigo, G. Eiben, D. Fogel, C. Fonseca, G. Greenwood, T. K. Chen, G. Raidl, A. Zalzala, S. Lucas, B. Paechter, J. Willies, J. J. M. Guervos, E. Eberbach, B. McKay, A. Channon, A. Tiwari, L. G. Volkert, D. Ashlock, and M. Schoenauer, editors, *Proceedings of the 2005 IEEE Congress on Evolutionary Computation*, volume 2, pages 1141–1148, Edinburgh, UK, 2-5 Sept. 2005. IEEE Press.

25. K. Polat and S. Güneş. Artificial immune recognition system with fuzzy resource allocation mechanism classifier, principal component analysis and fft method based new hybrid automated identification system for classification of eeg signals. *Expert Syst. Appl.*, 34:2039–2048, April 2008.

26. R. Poli, N. F. McPhee, and L. Vanneschi. Elitism reduces bloat in genetic programming. In M. Keijzer, G. Antoniol, C. B. Congdon, K. Deb, B. Doerr, N. Hansen, J. H. Holmes, G. S. Hornby, D. Howard, J. Kennedy, S. Kumar, F. G. Lobo, J. F. Miller, J. Moore, F. Neumann, M. Pelikan, J. Pollack, K. Sastry, K. Stanley, A. Stoica, E.-G. Talbi, and I. Wegener, editors, *GECCO '08: Proceedings of the 10th annual conference on Genetic and evolutionary computation*, pages 1343–1344, Atlanta, GA, USA, 12-16 July 2008. ACM.

27. D. Robilliard and C. Fonlupt. Backwarding : An overfitting control for genetic programming in a remote sensing application. In P. Collet, C. Fonlupt, J.-K. Hao, E. Lutton, and M. Schoenauer, editors, *Artificial Evolution 5th International Conference, Evolution Artificielle, EA 2001*, volume 2310 of *LNCS*, pages 245–254, Creusot, France, Oct. 29-31 2001. Springer Verlag.

28. A. Thammano and J. Moolwong. Classification algorithm based on human social behavior. In *Proceedings of the 7th IEEE International Conference on Computer and Information Technology*, pages 105–109, Washington, DC, USA, 2007. IEEE Computer Society.

29. J. D. Thomas and K. Sycara. The importance of simplicity and validation in genetic programming for data mining in financial data. In A. A. Freitas, editor, *Data Mining with Evolutionary Algorithms: Research Directions*, pages 7–11, Orlando, Florida, 18 July 1999. AAAI Press. Technical Report WS-99-06.

30. C. Tuite, A. Agapitos, M. O'Neill, and A. Brabazon. A preliminary investigation of overfitting in evolutionary driven model induction: Implications for financial modelling. In C. Di Chio, A. Brabazon, G. Di Caro, R. Drechsler, M. Ebner, M. Farooq, J. Grahl, G. Greenfield, C. Prins, J. Romero, G. Squillero, E. Tarantino, A. G. B. Tettamanzi, N. Urquhart, and A. S. Uyar, editors, *Applications of Evolutionary Computing, EvoApplications 2011: EvoCOMNET, EvoFIN, EvoHOT, EvoMUSART, EvoSTIM, EvoTRANSLOG*, volume 6625 of *LNCS*, pages 121–130, Turin, Italy, 27-29 Apr. 2011. Springer Verlag.

31. L. Vanneschi, M. Castelli, and S. Silva. Measuring bloat, overfitting and functional complexity in genetic programming. In *Proceedings of the 12th annual conference on Genetic and evolutionary computation*, GECCO '10, pages 877–884, New York, NY, USA, 2010. ACM.

32. S. M. Winkler, M. Affenzeller, and S. Wagner. Using enhanced genetic programming techniques for evolving classifiers in the context of medical diagnosis - an empirical study. In S. L. Smith, S. Cagnoni, and J. van Hemert, editors, *MedGEC 2006 GECCO Workshop on Medical Applications of Genetic and Evolutionary Computation*, Seattle, WA, USA, 8 July 2006.

A Hyper-Heuristic Approach to Evolving Algorithms for Bandwidth Reduction Based on Genetic Programming

Behrooz Koohestani and Riccardo Poli

Abstract The bandwidth reduction problem is a well-known NP-complete graph-layout problem that consists of labeling the vertices of a graph with integer labels in such a way as to minimize the maximum absolute difference between the labels of adjacent vertices. The problem is isomorphic to the important problem of reordering the rows and columns of a symmetric matrix so that its non-zero entries are maximally close to the main diagonal — a problem which presents itself in a large number of domains in science and engineering. A considerable number of methods have been developed to reduce the bandwidth, among which graph-theoretic approaches are typically faster and more effective. In this paper, a hyper-heuristic approach based on genetic programming is presented for evolving graph-theoretic bandwidth reduction algorithms. The algorithms generated from our hyper-heuristic are extremely effective. We test the best of such evolved algorithms on a large set of standard benchmarks from the Harwell-Boeing sparse matrix collection against two state-of-the-art algorithms from the literature. Our algorithm outperforms both algorithms by a significant margin, clearly indicating the promise of the approach.

1 Introduction

Graph layout problems are a special class of combinatorial optimization problems aiming at discovering a linear layout of an input graph such that a certain objective function is optimized [11]. A linear layout is a labeling of the nodes of a graph with unique integers from the set $\{1, ..., n\}$ where n is the number of nodes in the graph.

Behrooz Koohestani
School of Computer Science and Electronic Engineering, University of Essex, Colchester, CO4 3SQ, UK. e-mail: bkoohe@essex.ac.uk

Riccardo Poli
School of Computer Science and Electronic Engineering, University of Essex, Colchester, CO4 3SQ, UK. e-mail: rpoli@essex.ac.uk

M. Bramer et al. (eds.), *Research and Development in Intelligent Systems XXVIII*,
DOI 10.1007/978-1-4471-2318-7_7, © Springer-Verlag London Limited 2011

The bandwidth minimisation problem (BMP) is a very well-known graph layout problem, which has connections with a wide range of other problems, such as finite element analysis of mechanical systems, large scale power transmission systems, circuit design, VLSI design, data storage, chemical kinetics, network survivability, numerical geophysics, industrial electromagnetics, saving large hypertext media and topology compression of road networks [6]. The BMP can be stated in the context of both graphs and matrices. The bandwidth problem for graphs consists of finding a special labeling of vertices of a graph which minimizes the maximum absolute difference between the (integer) labels of adjacent vertices. In terms of matrices, it consists of finding a permutation of rows and columns of a given matrix which ensures that the non-zero elements are located in a band as close as possible along the main diagonal. In fact, if the non-zero entries of a symmetric matrix and the permutations of rows and columns are identified with the edges of a graph and the flips of the vertex labels, respectively, then the bandwidth of the graph is equal to the bandwidth of the matrix [34].

One of the most common applications of bandwidth minimisation algorithms arises from the need to efficiently solve large systems of equations [35]. In such a scenario, more efficient solutions are obtained if the rows and columns of the matrix representing the set of equations can be permuted in such a way that the bandwidth of the matrix is minimized [35].

Unfortunately, the BMP has been proved to be NP-complete [33]. Hence, it is highly unlikely that there exists an algorithm which finds the minimum bandwidth of a matrix in polynomial time. It has also been proved that the BMP is NP-complete even for trees with a maximum degree of three, and only in very special cases it is possible to find the optimal ordering in polynomial time [15].

Due to the existence of strong links between the BMP and a wide range of other problems in scientific and engineering fields, a variety of methods have been proposed for reducing the bandwidth.

The first direct method for the BMP was proposed by Harary [21]. Cuthill and McKee [10] introduced the first heuristic approach to the problem. Their method is still one of the most important and widely used methods to (approximately) solve the problem. In this method, the nodes in the graph representation of a matrix are partitioned into equivalence classes based on their distance from a given root node. This partition is known as *level structure* for the given node. In Cuthill-McKee algorithm, the root node for the level structure is normally chosen from the nodes of minimum degree in the graph. The permutation selected to reduce the bandwidth of the matrix is then simply obtained by visiting the nodes in the level structure in increasing-distance order.

George [17] in the study of envelope reduction algorithms observed that renumbering the Cuthill-McKee ordering in a reverse way often yielded a result superior to the original ordering.[1] This algorithm is known as the Reverse Cuthill-McKee (RCM) algorithm. Experimental evidence confirming the superior performance of

---

[1] The envelope minimisation problem is a problem strongly related to the BMP which requires the reorganisation of the nodes in a graph or the rows and columns in a matrix, but with a slightly different objective (we will formally define the bandwidth and envelope in Sect. 3).

the RCM over Cuthill-McKee for matrices arising from the finite element method has been reported in [9, 29].

A few years later, Gibbs *et al.* [19] proposed an algorithm, known as GPS (which stands for "Gibbs, Poole and Stockmeyer"), that makes more extensive use of level structures. They also provided a novel heuristic algorithm for finding the endpoints of a pseudo-diameter (i.e., a pair of vertices that are at nearly maximal distance apart) to be used as an appropriate starting node. The algorithm is substantially faster than the Cuthill-McKee algorithm, and it can occasionally outperform it. However, GPS algorithm is more complex to implement.

Barnard *et al.* [3] proposed the use of spectral analysis of the Laplacian matrix associated with the graph representing the non-zero elements in a sparse matrix as an effective method for the reduction of the envelope of a graph. In particular, the method permutes the rows and columns of a matrix based on the eigenvector associated with the first non-zero eigenvalue of the Laplacian matrix. While the envelope is only indirectly related to the bandwidth of a matrix, this algorithm is very effective at reducing it. Further information on these and other classic methods for the BMP can be found in [7, 20].

Recently, meta-heuristic approaches have been tested to see if they can be viable alternatives to solve the BMP. For example, Tabu search was employed by Marti *et al.* [30], while Lim *et al.* [27] used a hybrid between genetic algorithm and hill-climbing to solve this problem. Lim *et al.* also introduced two other hybrid algorithms to solve the BMP: one combining ant colony optimization with hill-climbing [25] and one combining particle swarm optimization with hill-climbing [26]. More recently, simulated annealing has also been used to attack the problem [41].

In this paper, a genetic programming hyper-heuristic is presented for evolving bandwidth reduction algorithms. A hyper-heuristic is a higher-level search algorithm specialised in the production of search algorithms, heuristics, optimisers or problem solvers [5]. The algorithms generated from our hyper-heuristic are heuristic in nature and based on the level structures. In order to evaluate the performance of the generated heuristics, we test them against a high-performance version of the RCM algorithm contained in the MATLAB library and the spectral algorithm (also implemented in MATLAB) described earlier. To the best of our knowledge, no prior attempt to employ a hyper-heuristic in order to evolve BMP heuristics has been reported in the literature.

The paper is organised as follows. Sect. 2 provides some background information in relation to hyper-heuristics and genetic programming. Sect. 3 briefly describes graph and matrix definitions of the BMP. In Sect. 4, the proposed hyper-heuristic for the solution of the BMP is presented in detail. In Sect. 5, experimental results and related statistical analyses are reported. Finally, our conclusions are presented in Sect. 6.

2 Genetic Programming and Hyper-heuristics

Genetic Programming (GP) [24, 36] is an evolutionary algorithm inspired by biological evolution. GP has the potential to solve problems automatically without the need for the user to know or specify the form or structure of the solution in advance. It is actually a specialization of Genetic Algorithms (GAs) in which the evolving individuals are computer programs rather than a set of fixed length strings from a limited alphabet of symbols. GP has a random nature similar to GA and is able to stochastically transform populations of programs into new and, hopefully better populations of programs. In this study, GP is utilised as a hyper-heuristic.

The term *hyper-heuristic* was first introduced by Cowling *et al.* [8]. According to their definition, a hyper-heuristic manages the choice of which lower-level heuristic method should be applied at any given time, depending upon the characteristics of the heuristics and the region of the solution space currently under exploration. However, a *hyper-heuristic* could more simply and generally be defined as "heuristics to choose other heuristics" [5]. Here, a *heuristic* is considered as a rule-of-thumb or "educated guess" that reduces the search required to find a solution.

The difference between meta-heuristics and hyper-heuristics is that the former operate directly on the problem search space with the goal of finding optimal or near-optimal solutions. The latter, instead, operate on the heuristics search space (which consists of the heuristics used to solve the target problem). The goal then is finding or generating high-quality heuristics for a problem, for a certain class of instances of a problem, or even for a particular instance.

GP has been very successfully used as a hyperheuristic. For example, GP has evolved competitive SAT solvers [1, 2, 14, 23], state-of-the-art or better than state-of-the-art bin packing algorithms [4, 40], particle swarm optimisers [39], evolutionary algorithms [31], and TSP solvers [22, 32].

3 Bandwidth, Envelope and Level Structures

Let $G = (V, E)$ be a finite undirected graph, such that V is the set of vertices, E is the set of edges and $f : V \rightarrow \{1, \ldots, n\}$ is a labeling of its nodes where $n = |V|$, then the *bandwidth* of G under f can be defined as:

$$B_f(G) = \max_{(u,v) \in E} |f(u) - f(v)| \ , \qquad (1)$$

i.e., as the maximum absolute difference between the labels of the adjacent nodes (i.e., nodes connected by an edge). The BMP consists of finding a labeling f which minimises $B_f(G)$ while the easier *bandwidth reduction problem* requires finding any labeling which reduces $B_f(G)$. Since there are $n!$ possible labellings for a graph with n vertices, it stands to reason that the BMP is, in general, a very difficult combinatorial optimisation problem.

The BMP can also be stated in the context of matrices. If $A = [a_{ij}]_{n \times n}$ is a sparse matrix, its *bandwidth* is defined as

$$B(A) = \max_{(i,j):a_{ij} \neq 0} |i - j| \ . \tag{2}$$

The *matrix bandwidth minimisation problem* consists of finding a permutation of rows and columns which brings all non-zero elements of A into the smallest possible band around the diagonal. More formally, if σ is a permutation of $(1, 2, ..., n)$, and A_σ is the matrix obtained by permuting the rows and columns of A according to σ (i.e., $A_\sigma = [a_{\sigma_i \sigma_j}]$), then the problem can be formulated as

$$\min_\sigma B(A_\sigma) \ . \tag{3}$$

An important concept related to the *bandwidth* is the notion of *envelope*. Given a matrix A, its *envelope* is:

$$P(A) = \sum_{i=1}^{n} \max_{j:j<i, a_{ij} \neq 0} (i - j) \ . \tag{4}$$

Naturally, the *envelope* is also influenced by the permutations of A.

One of the most important concepts in many graph-theoretic bandwidth and envelope reduction algorithms is that of *level structure* [19]. A level structure, $L(G)$, of a graph G is a partition of the set $V(G)$ into levels $L_1, L_2, \ldots, L_k$ such that:

1. all vertices adjacent to vertices in level L_1 are in either level L_1 or L_2,
2. all vertices adjacent to vertices in level L_k are in either level L_k or L_{k-1},
3. for $1 < i < K$, all vertices adjacent to vertices in level L_i are in either level L_{i-1}, L_i, or L_{i+1}.

To each vertex $v \in V(G)$, there corresponds a particular level structure $L_v(G)$ called the *level structure rooted at v*. Its levels are determined by:

1. $L_1 = \{v\}$,
2. for $i > 1$, L_i is the set of all those vertices adjacent to vertices of level L_{i-1} not yet assigned to a level.

For any level structure, L, a numbering f_L of G assigns consecutive integers level by level, first to the vertices of level L_1, then to those of L_2, and so on [19].

In a nodal numbering scheme based on the level structures such as [10, 17, 19], there are then two important elements that influence performance. The first is the method used to specify a suitable starting vertex. This tends to be chosen from either the vertices of minimum degree or the *pseudo-peripheral vertices* [18] in a graph. The second element is the method of numbering the vertices located in each level. One of the most effective approaches is to number the vertices of each level based on their increasing degree. This is the method adopted by the RCM algorithm.

In this process, it is very likely that a level contains vertices with the same degree. The most common strategy for dealing with this issue is to break ties arbitrarily.

Algorithm 1 GHH for BMP

1: Randomly generate an initial population of programs from the available primitives.
2: **repeat**
3:   **for** each program $p \in$ population **do**
4:     $fitness[p] = 0$
5:   **end for**
6:   **for** each instance $i \in$ training set **do**
7:     Select a starting vertex s.
8:     Construct level structure L rooted at s.
9:     **for** each program $p \in$ population **do**
10:       Insert s into array $perm[1...n]$.
11:       **for** each level $l \in L$ **do**
12:         **for** each vertex $v \in l$ **do**
13:           Execute p.
14:         **end for**
15:         Create permutation σ represented by p.
16:         Sort vertices in l in order given by σ.
17:         Store the ordered vertices in $perm[]$ sequentially.
18:       **end for**
19:       Apply $perm[]$ to the adjacency list of the graph (or matrix) i, and generate a new adjacency list.
20:       Compute the *bandwidth* for the adjacency list thus obtained.
21:       $fitness[p] = fitness[p] + bandwidth(i, p)$.
22:     **end for**
23:   **end for**
24:   Perform selection to choose individual program(s) from the population based on fitness to participate in genetic operations.
25:   Create a new generation of individual programs by applying genetic operations with specified probabilities.
26: **until** the maximum number of generations is reached.
27: **return** the best program tree appearing in the last generation.

---

4 Proposed Hyper-heuristic for BMP

We propose to use GP as a hyper-heuristic for the BMP. In other words, in our system, which we will call GHH (for "Genetic Hyper-Heuristic"), GP is given a training set of matrices as input and produces a novel solver for BMPs as its output.

Naturally, the task is of a colossal difficulty. So, following the strategy adopted in [40] and to some extent also in [1], to make this feasible we provide GHH with the "skeleton" of a good solver (an enhanced version of the RCM graph-based BMP solver, mentioned in Sect. 1) and we ask GP to evolve the "brain" of that solver, that is the strategy by which it prioritises nodes in a level structure.

A description of the operations of the system is given in Algorithm 1. Below, the elements of the system are described in detail.

4.1 GP Setup

We used a tree-based GP system with some additional decoding steps required for the BMP. The system is implemented in C#. Individuals in our GP system are tree-like expressions which, for efficiency reasons, are internally stored as linear arrays using a flattened representation for trees. The primitive set used is shown in Table 1.

The initial population was generated randomly using a modified version of the ramped half-and-half method (which produces a mixture of full trees of different depths and randomly-grown trees) [24, 36]. In our system, during the process of tree initialisation, we artificially ensure that each program tree contains at least one instance of the primitive SDV. We will explain the motivation for this in Sect. 4.3.

In nodal numbering algorithms based on the level structures, the vertices in each level are numbered in order of increasing degree. We should note, however, that our primitive set does not include a function which returns the degree of the nodes in a graph. We did this for the following reason. In preliminary runs with such a primitive, we obtained relatively weak results. This is somehow surprising since the degree of a node is what the RCM algorithm uses for prioritising nodes within a level. We believe evolution found particularly difficult to use such a primitive due to the problem of ties.

In a level, there are often nodes with the same degree. As mentioned in Sect. 3, the normal strategy for dealing with this issue is to break ties arbitrarily. Although this can resolve the problem somehow, it leads to a strong non-determinism in the fitness evaluation. This may hamper the evolutionary search in that a lucky fitness evaluation may lead to an inferior individual to be selected over and over again. The problem is particularly severe if the number of ties is large.

By using the sum of the degrees of the vertices connected to a vertex, SDV, in place of a vertex degree, the likelihood of ties in a level is considerably reduced. Also, some additional information related to the vertices located in the following level is captured by the SDV, which is effectively equivalent to the product of a vertex degree and the mean degree of the vertex's children.

While the BMP can be stated both in terms of graphs (see Eq. (1)) and in terms of matrices (see Eq. (2)), in order to develop fast algorithms for sparse matrices, one really needs to calculate such quantities from graphs associated with the matrices. Therefore, we utilised the bandwidth as defined in Eq. (1) in our GP system as the fitness contribution of a problem. Naturally, the fitness of a program tree is then the total of the bandwidths of the solutions that it creates when run on each problem instance in the training set. Fitness, rather obviously, needs to be minimised by the GP system.

The parameters of the runs are presented in Table 2. We employed tournament selection to choose individual program(s) from the population based on fitness to participate in genetic operations. New individual programs were created by applying the genetic operations of reproduction, sub-tree crossover and point mutation with specified probabilities. We also used elitism to ensure that the best individual in one generation was transferred unaltered to the next. In addition, in order to control excessive code growth or bloat, the *Tarpeian method* (which artificially weeds out a

Table 1. Primitive set used in our GP system

Primitive set	Arity	Description
+	2	Adds two inputs
-	2	Subtracts second input from first input
*	2	Multiplies two inputs
N	0	Returns the number of vertices of a given graph (or the dimension of a given matrix)
SDV	0	Returns the sum of degrees of vertices connected to a vertex
Constants	0	Uniformly-distributed random constants with floating-point values in the interval $[-1.0, +1.0]$

Table 2. Parameters used in our experiments

Parameter	Value
Maximum Number of Generations	100
Maximum Depth of Initial Programs	3
Population Size	1000
Tournament Size	3
Elitism Rate	0.1%
Reproduction Rate	0.9%
Crossover Rate	80%
Mutation Rate	19%
Mutation Per Node	0.05%

proportion of above-average-size trees) [37, 38] was utilised in the GP system. The termination criterion used was based on the predetermined maximum number of generations to be run. Finally, the best program tree appearing in the last generation was designated as the final result of a run.

4.2 Training Set

We used a training set of 25 benchmark instances from the Harwell-Boeing sparse matrix collection (available at http://math.nist.gov/MatrixMarket/ data/Harwell-Boeing/dwt/dwt.html). This is a collection of standard test matrices arising from problems in finite element grids, linear systems, least squares, and eigenvalue calculations from a wide variety of scientific and engineering disciplines. The benchmark matrices were selected from 5 different sets in this collection, namely BCSSTRUC1 (dynamic analyses in structural engineering), BC-SSTRUC3 (dynamic analyses in structural engineering), CANNES (finite-element structures problems in aircraft design), LANPRO (linear equations in structural engineering), and LSHAPE (finite-element model problems) with sizes ranging from 24×24 to 960×960.

This training set was used only to evolve the heuristics. Performance of the evolved heuristics was then evaluated using a completely separate test set of 30 matrices taken from Everstine's sparse matrix collection (DWT) and BCSPWR, both included in the Harwell-Boeing database.

4.3 Numbering Vertices Located in Each Level

As shown in Algorithm 1, first, a level structure rooted at a suitable starting vertex is constructed (Step 8). The root vertex is assigned the number 1, and inserted
(Step 10) into the first position of array $perm[1...n]$, which is, in fact, the result
array.

For each vertex v located in level l, the GP interpreter is called k times, where k is
the number of vertices in l. Each call of the interpreter executes the selected program
with respect to the different values returned by SDV (Step 13). The outputs obtained
from each execution of the given program are stored in a one dimensional array. This
array is then sorted in ascending order while also recording the position that each
element originally had in the unsorted array. Reading such positions sequentially
from the sorted array produces the permutation associated with the original program (Step 15). The vertices located in l are then ordered based on the permutation
generated (Step 16).

The ordered vertices are sequentially assigned the number 2 for the first element,
number 3 for the second element, etc., and are stored in $perm[]$ (Step 17). This
process is repeated for each successive level in the rooted level structure until the
vertices of all levels have been numbered. Note that after the termination of this
process, the indices of $perm[]$ correspond to the numbers assigned to the vertices.
In order to compute the bandwidth, $perm[]$ should be applied to the adjacency list
of the initial graph (or the initial matrix) (Step 20).

In Sect. 4.1, we mentioned that each program tree in our GP system contains at
least one SDV primitive. Now, by considering our ordering method explained above,
the motivation behind this type of tree initialisation can be easily understood. Trees
without an SDV generate a constant output (the problem size, N, is constant for
each problem) and, thus, they represent a fixed permutation $\sigma = (1, 2, \cdots, n)$. Such
a permutation is useless, since numbering the vertices located in each level in the
order given by σ produces no change in the labels of vertices, and as a result, the
bandwidth remains unchanged.

5 Experimental Results

We performed ten independent runs of our GP system with the training set specified
above, recording the corresponding best-of-run individual in each. We then selected
as our overall best evolved heuristic the best program tree from these ten best-of-run
results. The simplified version of this evolved heuristic for ordering nodes in a level
is as follows:

$$0.179492928171 \times \text{SDV}^3 + 0.292849834929 \times \text{SDV}^2 - 0.208926175433 \times \text{N}$$
$$- 0.736485142138 \times \text{N} \times \text{SDV} - 1.77524579882 \times \text{SDV} - 1.75681383404$$

which is also shown graphically in Figure 1. What is interesting about this re-

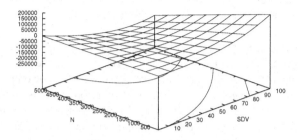

Fig. 1. Plot of the best heuristic evolved for BMP by GHH.

sult is that the function evolved is *not* monotonically increasing in SDV (for any given N). Indeed, the minimum of the function as N varies is given by SDV = $\sqrt{1.5863264966 \times \text{N} + 4.16677290311}/1.07695756903 - 0.543846560629$.

In other words, for small values of N, the system tries to select first nodes with minimum SDV, which is consistent with the standard strategy of sorting nodes by degree, as is done in RCM. However, as N increases, the heuristic function evolved by GHH becomes concave and the system starts favouring nodes with intermediate values of SDV over either very big or very small SDVs. Presumably, while preferring nodes with small degrees is generally a good strategy, it can sometimes force the algorithm along very narrow paths (where one low degree node is followed by another low degree node) which do not give enough choice to the algorithm.

We then incorporated this heuristic into a level structure system as explained in Sect. 3, and carried out a substantial number of experiments. In the experiments conducted in this study, we employed Everstine's sparse matrix collection (DWT) [13] as test problems. This collection consists of sparse matrices from NASTRAN (a finite element analysis program) users working in U.S. Navy, Army, Air Force and NASA laboratories. The collection has been widely used in benchmarks, and it is actually a subset of the well-known Harwell-Boeing sparse matrix collection. Since the DWT benchmark matrices have been collected from a diverse range of finite element grids in a variety of engineering disciplines, they seem large and diversified enough to be used reliably for assessing the performance of bandwidth reduction algorithms. DWT set is closely related to CANNES and LSHAPE sets used in our training set in terms of its discipline and the class of problems.

We also picked the six largest instances from BCSPWR set (power network patterns), which is totally in a different class compared to the training set used. We did this to observe how well the generated heuristic generalises in unseen situations.

In order to assess the performance of the heuristic generated, we compared it against two well-known and high-performance algorithms, i.e., the RCM contained

in the MATLAB library (RCMM), and spectral. RCMM is a highly enhanced version of the RCM algorithm, which is based closely on the SPARSPAK implementation described by George and Liu [16]. This algorithm is still one of the best and most widely used methods for bandwidth reduction. Indeed, the results reported in [12] and [28] indicate that RCMM is also superior to the well-known GPS [19] algorithm in terms of the quality of the solutions obtained.

All the experiments were performed on an AMD Athlon(tm) Dual-core Processor 2.20 GHz. In addition to reporting the bandwidth obtained by each method under test in each of the benchmark problems, we also measured the time required to solve the problem on this computer.

Table 3 shows a performance comparison of the algorithms under test. The results of the tests reveal that the heuristic generated by our GHH is far superior to both the RCMM algorithm and the spectral algorithm with respect to the mean of the bandwidth values, the run times and the number of the best results obtained under both criteria (shown in the "Wins/Draw" rows). A Wilcoxon signed-rank test, which is a reliable and widely used nonparametric test for paired data, revealed that the performance differences between the heuristic generated by GHH and these algorithms are highly statistically significant ($p = 0.000$).

6 Conclusions

In this paper, GHH — a hyper-heuristic approach based on genetic programming — has been proposed for evolving bandwidth reduction algorithms. To help GP in this difficult task, we constrained its search by providing it with the scaffolding of a good graph-based solver and asking it to only evolve the key element of the algorithm: its brain, i.e., the sorting strategy for nodes in a level structure.

The best solver produced by GHH is a very interesting and unconventional brain, which essentially goes against the accepted practice of ordering nodes by degree, particularly for large BMP instances. We compared this solver against two high-performance algorithms, the RCM contained in the MATLAB library and spectral, on a large set of standard benchmarks from the Harwell-Boeing sparse matrix collection. The best heuristic evolved performed extremely well both on benchmark instances from the same class as the training set and also (and perhaps even better) on large problem instances from a totally different class, confirming the efficacy of our approach.

In future work, we will investigate the possibility of further extending the primitive set used by GHH, we will test evolved solvers over even more diverse and large benchmark sets and we will also attack the envelope minimisation problem.

Table 3. Comparison of our GHH against the RCMM and Spectral algorithms. Numbers in bold face are best results.

Instance	Dimension	Bandwidth			Run time		
		RCMM	Spectral	GHH	RCMM	Spectral	GHH
DWT 59	59 × 59	**8**	10	**8**	0.00923	0.01445	**0.00169**
DWT 66	66 × 66	**3**	**3**	**3**	0.00608	0.03477	**0.00189**
DWT 72	72 × 72	**7**	12	**7**	0.00762	0.02110	**0.00210**
DWT 87	87 × 87	**18**	19	**18**	0.00951	0.03599	**0.00135**
DWT 162	162 × 162	**16**	26	**16**	0.00738	0.04329	**0.00273**
DWT 193	193 × 193	54	**45**	49	0.00965	0.06501	**0.00381**
DWT 209	209 × 209	**33**	52	34	0.01079	0.07493	**0.00318**
DWT 221	221 × 221	**15**	23	19	0.01220	0.07522	**0.00953**
DWT 245	245 × 245	55	90	**43**	0.00845	0.09125	**0.00844**
DWT 307	307 × 307	44	64	**39**	0.01178	0.21649	**0.00990**
DWT 310	310 × 310	15	18	**13**	0.01040	0.18425	**0.00932**
DWT 361	361 × 361	**15**	24	**15**	0.01054	0.32843	**0.00761**
DWT 419	419 × 419	34	65	**33**	0.01516	0.41680	**0.00754**
DWT 503	503 × 503	64	91	**51**	0.01707	0.86690	**0.00991**
DWT 592	592 × 592	42	101	**41**	0.01976	1.21548	**0.01009**
DWT 758	758 × 758	29	40	**26**	0.03121	2.49725	**0.01988**
DWT 869	869 × 869	43	149	**41**	0.03846	3.53698	**0.01102**
DWT 878	878 × 878	46	214	**44**	0.03831	3.73173	**0.01127**
DWT 918	918 × 918	57	82	**44**	0.04098	4.13962	**0.02502**
DWT 992	992 × 992	65	**60**	63	0.05488	4.44688	**0.01661**
DWT 1005	1005 × 1005	104	148	**101**	0.05092	5.86841	**0.01711**
DWT 1007	1007 × 1007	**38**	81	**38**	0.04824	5.56310	**0.02455**
DWT 1242	1242 × 1242	**92**	142	94	0.07462	9.96307	**0.02809**
DWT 2680	2680 × 2680	**69**	161	**69**	0.36711	91.7894	**0.03876**
Mean		40.25	71.67	37.87	0.03793	5.63420	0.01172
BCSPWR05	443 × 443	68	132	**56**	0.02329	0.460892	**0.01886**
BCSPWR06	1454 × 1454	126	204	**103**	0.10788	15.5191	**0.02912**
BCSPWR07	1612 × 1612	140	192	**119**	0.12310	19.1069	**0.03150**
BCSPWR08	1624 × 1624	135	341	**111**	0.12659	18.4791	**0.03898**
BCSPWR09	1723 × 1723	133	241	**126**	0.14560	22.4614	**0.04590**
BCSPWR10	5300 × 5300	285	554	**278**	3.19833	674.3833	**0.05982**
Mean		147.83	277.33	132.17	0.62079	125.06844	0.03736
Wins/Draws		3/8	2/1	17/8	0/0	0/0	30/0

References

1. Bader-El-Den, M., Poli, R.: Generating SAT local-search heuristics using a GP hyper-heuristic framework. In: Monmarché, N., Talbi, E.G., Collet, P., Schoenauer, M., Lutton, E. (eds.) Evolution Artificielle, 8th International Conference. Lecture Notes in Computer Science, vol. 4926, pp. 37–49. Springer, Tours, France (29-31 Oct 2007)
2. Bader-El-Den, M.B., Poli, R.: A GP-based hyper-heuristic framework for evolving 3-SAT heuristics. In: Thierens, D., Beyer, H.G., Bongard, J., Branke, J., Clark, J.A., Cliff, D., Congdon, C.B., Deb, K., Doerr, B., Kovacs, T., Kumar, S., Miller, J.F., Moore, J., Neumann, F., Pelikan, M., Poli, R., Sastry, K., Stanley, K.O., Stutzle, T., Watson, R.A., Wegener, I. (eds.) GECCO '07: Proceedings of the 9th annual conference on Genetic and evolutionary computation. vol. 2, pp. 1749–1749. ACM Press, London (7-11 Jul 2007)

3. Barnard, S.T., Pothen, A., Simon, H.D.: A spectral algorithm for envelope reduction of sparse matrices. In: Supercomputing '93: Proceedings of the 1993 ACM/IEEE conference on Super-computing. pp. 493–502. ACM, New York, NY, USA (1993)

4. Burke, E.K., Hyde, M.R., Kendall, G.: Evolving bin packing heuristics with genetic program-ming. In: Runarsson, T.P., Beyer, H.G., Burke, E., Merelo-Guervos, J.J., Whitley, L.D., Yao, X. (eds.) Parallel Problem Solving from Nature - PPSN IX. LNCS, vol. 4193, pp. 860–869. Springer-Verlag, Reykjavik, Iceland (9-13 Sep 2006)

5. Burke, E., Kendall, G., Newall, J., Hart, E., Ross, P., Schulenburg, S.: Hyper-Heuristics: An Emerging Direction in Modern Search Technology. In: Handbook of Metaheuristics, chap. 16, pp. 457–474. International Series in Operations Research & Management Science (2003)

6. Chinn, P.Z., Chvátalová, J., Dewdney, A.K., Gibbs, N.E.: The bandwidth problem for graphs and matrices — a survey. Journal of Graph Theory 6(3), 223–254 (1982)

7. Corso, G.D., Manzini, G.: Finding exact solutions to the bandwidth minimization problem. Computing 62(3), 189–203 (1999)

8. Cowling, P., Kendall, G., Soubeiga, E.: A hyperheuristic approach to scheduling a sales sum-mit. In: Burke, E., Erben, W. (eds.) Practice and Theory of Automated Timetabling III, Lecture Notes in Computer Science, vol. 2079, pp. 176–190. Springer Berlin / Heidelberg (2001)

9. Cuthill, E.: Several Strategies for Reducing the Bandwidth of Matrices, pp. 157–166. Plenum Press, New York (1972)

10. Cuthill, E., McKee, J.: Reducing the bandwidth of sparse symmetric matrices. In: ACM Na-tional Conference. pp. 157–172. Association for Computing Machinery, New York (1969)

11. Díaz, J., Petit, J., Serna, M.: A survey of graph layout problems. Computing Surveys 34, 313–356 (2002)

12. Esposito, A., Malucelli, F., Tarricone, L.: Bandwidth and profile reduction of sparse matrices: An experimental comparison of new heuristics. In: ALEX'98. pp. 19–26. Trento, Italy (1998)

13. Everstine, G. C.: A comparison of three resequencing algorithms for the reduction of matrix profile and wavefront. International Journal for Numerical Methods in Engineering. 14, 837–853 (1979)

14. Fukunaga, A.: Automated discovery of composite SAT variable selection heuristics. In: Pro-ceedings of the National Conference on Artificial Intelligence (AAAI). pp. 641–648 (2002)

15. Garey, M., Graham, R., Johnson, D., Knuth, D.: Complexity results for bandwidth minimiza-tion. SIAM Journal on Applied Mathematics 34(3), 477–495 (1978)

16. George, J.A., Liu, J.W.H.: Computer Solution of Large Sparse Positive Definite Systems. Prentice-Hall (1981)

17. George, J.A.: Computer implementation of the finite element method. Ph.D. thesis, Stanford, CA, USA (1971)

18. George, A., Liu, J. W. H.: An implementation of a pseudoperipheral node finder. ACM Trans-actions on Mathematical Software 5(3), 284–295 (1979)

19. Gibbs, N.E., Poole, W.G., Stockmeyer, P.K.: An algorithm for reducing the bandwidth and profile of a sparse matrix. SIAM Journal on Numerical Analysis 13(2), 236–250 (1976)

20. Gurari, E., Sudborough, I.: Improved dynamic programming algorithms for bandwidth min-imization and the min-cut linear arrangement problem. Journal of Algorithms 5, 531–546 (1984)

21. Harary, F.: Graph Theory. Addison-Wesley, Reading, Mass (1969)

22. Keller, R.E., Poli, R.: Linear genetic programming of parsimonious metaheuristics. In: Srini-vasan, D., Wang, L. (eds.) 2007 IEEE Congress on Evolutionary Computation. pp. 4508–4515. IEEE Computational Intelligence Society, IEEE Press, Singapore (25-28 Sep 2007)

23. Kibria, R.H., Li, Y.: Optimizing the initialization of dynamic decision heuristics in DPLL SAT solvers using genetic programming. In: Collet, P., Tomassini, M., Ebner, M., Gustafson, S., Ekárt, A. (eds.) Proceedings of the 9th European Conference on Genetic Programming. Lecture Notes in Computer Science, vol. 3905, pp. 331–340. Springer, Budapest, Hungary (10 - 12 Apr 2006)

24. Koza, J.R.G.P.: On the Programming of Computers by Means of Natural Selection. MIT Press, Cambridge, MA, USA (1992)

25. Lim, A., Lin, J., Rodrigues, B., Xiao, F.: Ant colony optimization with hill climbing for the bandwidth minimization problem. Applied Soft Computing 6(2), 180–188 (2006)
26. Lim, A., Lin, J., Xiao, F.: Particle swarm optimization and hill climbing for the bandwidth minimization problem. Applied Intelligence 26(3), 175–182 (2007)
27. Lim, A., Rodrigues, B., Xiao, F.: Integrated genetic algorithm with hill climbing for bandwidth minimization problem. In: Cantú-Paz, E., et al. (eds.) Proceedings of the Genetic and Evolutionary Computation Conference (GECCO). pp. 1594–1595. LNCS, vol. 2724, Springer, Heidelberg (2003)
28. Lim, A., Rodrigues, B., Xiao, F.: A centroid-based approach to solve the bandwidth minimization problem. In: 37th Hawaii international conference on system sciences (HICSS). p. 30075a. Big Island, Hawaii (2004)
29. Liu, W.H., Sherman, A.H.: Comparative analysis of the cuthill-mckee and the reverse cuthill-mckee ordering algorithms for sparse matrices. SIAM Journal on Numerical Analysis. 13(2), 198–213 (1976)
30. Marti, R., Laguna, M., Glover, F., Campos, V.: Reducing the bandwidth of a sparse matrix with tabu search. European Journal of Operational Research 135(2), 450–459 (2001)
31. Oltean, M.: Evolving evolutionary algorithms using linear genetic programming. Evolutionary Computation 13(3), 387–410 (Fall 2005)
32. Oltean, M., Dumitrescu, D.: Evolving TSP heuristics using multi expression programming. In: Bubak, M., van Albada, G.D., Sloot, P.M.A., Dongarra, J. (eds.) Computational Science - ICCS 2004: 4th International Conference, Part II. Lecture Notes in Computer Science, vol. 3037, pp. 670–673. Springer-Verlag, Krakow, Poland (6-9 Jun 2004)
33. Papadimitriou, C.H.: The NP-completeness of the bandwidth minimization problem. Computing 16(3), 263–270 (1976)
34. Papadimitriou, C. H., Steiglitz, K.: Combinatorial Optimization : Algorithms and Complexity. Prentice-Hall (1982)
35. Pissanetskey, S.: Sparse Matrix Technology. Academic Press, London (1984)
36. Poli, R., Langdon, W.B., McPhee, N.F.: A Field Guide to Genetic Programming (2008), published via http://lulu.com, with contributions by J. R. Koza
37. Poli, R.: A simple but theoretically-motivated method to control bloat in genetic programming. In: Ryan, C., Soule, T., Keijzer, M., Tsang, E., Poli, R., Costa, E. (eds.) Genetic Programming, Proceedings of EuroGP'2003. LNCS, vol. 2610, pp. 204–217. Springer-Verlag (14-16 Apr 2003)
38. Poli, R.: Covariant tarpeian method for bloat control in genetic programming. In: Riolo, R., McConaghy, T., Vladislavleva, E. (eds.) Genetic Programming Theory and Practice VIII, Genetic and Evolutionary Computation, vol. 8, chap. 5, pp. 71–90. Springer, Ann Arbor, USA (20-22 May 2010)
39. Poli, R., Langdon, W.B., Holland, O.: Extending particle swarm optimisation via genetic programming. In: Keijzer, M., Tettamanzi, A., Collet, P., van Hemert, J.I., Tomassini, M. (eds.) Proceedings of the 8th European Conference on Genetic Programming. Lecture Notes in Computer Science, vol. 3447, pp. 291–300. Springer, Lausanne, Switzerland (30 Mar - 1 Apr 2005)
40. Poli, R., Woodward, J., Burke, E.K.: A histogram-matching approach to the evolution of bin-packing strategies. In: Srinivasan, D., Wang, L. (eds.) 2007 IEEE Congress on Evolutionary Computation. pp. 3500–3507. IEEE Computational Intelligence Society, IEEE Press, Singapore (25-28 Sep 2007)
41. Rodriguez-Tello, E., Jin-Kao, H., Torres-Jimenez, J.: An improved simulated annealing algorithm for bandwidth minimization. European Journal of Operational Research 185(3), 1319–1335 (2008)

SPEECH AND VISION

Two stage speaker verification using Self Organising Map and Multilayer Perceptron Neural Network

Tariq Tashan and Tony Allen[1]

Abstract In this paper a two stage speaker verification system is presented. The first stage contains a modified Self Organising Map (SOM) that filters speech data using cluster information extracted from three selected vowels for a claimed speaker. Filtered frames from the first stage are then fed into the second stage which consists of three Multi Layer Perceptron (MLP) networks; these networks acting as individual claimed speaker vowel verifiers. Sixty four Discrete Fourier Transform (DFT) spectrum components are used as the input feature vectors. The system provides a verification performance of 94.54% when evaluated using 50 speakers from the Centre for Spoken Language Understanding (CSLU2002) speaker verification database.

1 Introduction

Speaker verification is an open set speaker recognition problem, where the primary function is to verify if a given test speech sample belongs to a claimed speaker or not. Speaker identification, on the other hand, is a closed set speaker recognition problem, where the main task is to identify a test speech sample to one speaker from a known speaker set. When developing a voice biometric authentication system there are several design parameters that need consideration- the first being what type of classifier to use. For the last two decades speaker recognition has been tackled using a wide range of methods; some of the popular approaches being: probabilistic models such as Hidden Markov Model (HMM) and Gaussian Mixture Model (GMM) classifiers [1], non-probabilistic binary linear models like Support Vector Machine (SVM) classifier [2] and non-linear statistical models i.e. Artificial Neural Networks (ANN) [3-10]. Different types of neural networks have been used in speaker recognition task such as MLP [3], Radial Basis Function [4],

---

1 Nottingham Trent University, NG11 8NS, UK
tariq.tashan@ntu.ac.uk; tony.allen@ntu.ac.uk

M. Bramer et al. (eds.), *Research and Development in Intelligent Systems XXVIII*,
DOI 10.1007/978-1-4471-2318-7_8, © Springer-Verlag London Limited 2011

Neural Tree Network [5], Auto Associative Neural Network [6], Recurrent neural networks [7], Probabilistic neural networks [8], Dynamic synapse based neural networks [9] and SOM [10].

Most modern voice biometric authentication systems employ GMM based methods in the verification engine; an offshoot of earlier research into the use of HMM algorithms for speech recognition systems. SOM based speaker recognition systems, on the other hand, are an attractive alternative to the conventional methods because they offer the prospect of being able to do away with the need for the speech recognition front-end commonly included in speaker recognition systems [11].

Having decided on the classifier methodology to use, the next major decision is which morphological level is to be used to extract the features. Since speech signals contain both language information as well as speaker identity information, speaker recognition can be achieved by processing the speech signal at a variety of levels (sentence, word, syllable or phoneme). It has been shown that more information about the identity of the speaker can be obtained by processing the speech at the phoneme level [12]. However, the disadvantage of processing at this level is that an efficient speech recognition algorithm is required in order to locate the positions of the phonemes within the speech signal prior to the feature extraction stage. The penalty for using such speech recognition tools in speaker recognition systems is the need for substantial speech data in order to train the speech recognition engine. As a consequence, the speaker recognition performance of such systems has been shown to fall dramatically when limited data training conditions are considered [13].

In addition to the level at which the speech recognition is processed, there are three major formats in which the features can be extracted from the speech sample. A straight forward and simple representation of the speech signal in the frequency domain is the DFT spectrum, this type of format is commonly used in speech and speaker recognition applications. The DFT spectrum is also used to derive some other feature formats. The DFT spectrum can be obtained by calculating the magnitude of the DFT vector [14]. Another feature format that preserve the speech signal characteristics are the Linear Prediction Coefficients (LPC's) which basically used for speech compression task. The LPC spectrum is calculated by taking the magnitude value at the output of the filter whose coefficients are represented by the LPC coefficients [14]. Mathematically, the LPC spectrum represents a smoothed version of the DFT spectrum. In speech and speaker recognition applications the most widely used feature format are MFCC. These features are calculated by firstly passing the DFT spectrum through a bank of triangular filters with Mel-frequency scale. The MFCC are then calculated by applying the Discrete Cosine Transform (DCT) to the logarithmic output of these filters [15].

Although the MFCC are the most preferred input feature formats in the literature, there is evidence to suggest that these may not be optimal for neural network based systems [11] [16]. A recent experiment was conducted to explore the use of the three feature formats mentioned above as input feature vector for a SOM based

speaker verification system [11], the experiment shows that the DFT spectrum is better than the MFCC and the LPC spectrum features with the system adopted.

The final design decision is then the sampling frequency that is to be used to produce the frames of data from which the features are to be extracted. Most modern systems are required to use 8kHz in order to be used over standard telecommunication channels.

In this paper, a two stage narrowband neural network speaker verification system is presented. The first stage consists of a modified SOM [11] that is used to filter the speech signal in order to select only those speech frames that are similar to enrolled vowel phonemes frames for the claimed speaker. This effectively replaces the speech recognition tool used in traditional speaker recognition systems and, in addition, performs coarse speaker verification. The second stage is then a triplet of conventional MLP networks that provide fine-grained speaker verification. 64 DFT spectrum components are adopted as the speech frame feature vectors.

Sections 1.1 to 1.3 of this paper present a brief summary of related publications on the use of MLP, SOM and SOM+MLP for speaker recognition. Section two then presents the proposed algorithm. The speech database used for evaluation purposes is described in section three, whilst section four presents the results of the conducted experiments. A final conclusion is provided in section five.

1.1 MLP

Multi-layer perceptrons are the most popular form of neural network; being used in a wide variety of recognition applications. D. P. Delacretaz and J. Hennebert investigated the use of specific phoneme MLP networks for a speaker verification task [17]. HMMs were used to extract the phoneme information from the speech data, and then each phoneme data was classified using an individual MLP network. Each MLP network consisted of 12 inputs, 20 hidden nodes and two outputs. Twelve Linear Prediction Coding (LPC) cepstrum coefficients were used as the feature vectors. The system was tested using 25 speakers from a Swiss German telephone database called HER. Their results suggest that for speaker verification, nasals, fricatives and vowels provide better speaker verification performance than plosives and liquids.

H. Seddik, et al. presented a phoneme based MLP network for closed-set speaker identification task [3]. Their paper investigated the use of different numbers of phonemes (up to 48 phonemes). The network contained 12 inputs, 45 hidden nodes and one output. Twelve Mel Frequency Cepstrum Coefficients (MFCC) were used as the input feature vector for each phoneme; each coefficient value representing the average value for that coefficient over the set of frames belonging to the phoneme. Speech was sampled at 16 kHz and segmented using a Hamming window. Phonemes positions were pre-extracted in the database. The system was

tested using a dataset of 20 speakers from the TIMIT database. Three experiments were performed using 5, 10 and 48 phonemes respectively and the claimed recognition rates are 98.57%, 97.05 and 87.23%. A fourth experiment, using only vowel phonemes, achieved only 77% recognition accuracy. Their results imply that using a small number of well separated phonemes produces better speaker verification results than using a large number of similar sounding phonemes.

K. Sri Rama Murty used an auto associative neural network in [18] to capture residual phase information in a closed-set speaker identification task. The network contains 40 linear input nodes, three nonlinear hidden layers of 48, 12 and 48 nodes respectively and 40 linear output nodes. Forty LPC samples were used as the input feature vector. Speech was sampled at 8 kHz. The system was tested using two datasets of 38 speakers and 76 speakers from the TIMIT database. Best claimed performance is 87% for the first dataset and 76% for the second dataset.

1.2 SOM

An SOM was proposed by E. Monte, et al. for closed-set speaker identification problem [10]. The paper uses a Kohonen SOM [19] version with size of 25 x 25. The decision making is made by comparing the histogram occupancy of each speaker's SOM with other speakers in the database. LPC and MFCC coefficient were investigated as feature vectors and the speech was segmented into 30 msec frames. The system was tested using 100 speakers from the TI database under different signal to noise ratio levels. The proposed system was compared with Arithmetic-Harmonic Sphere Measure and the best claimed results for clean speech was 100% when MFCC vectors were used with the SOM.

I. Lapidot, *et al.* presented an unsupervised speaker clustering system using an SOM [20]. The paper investigates the use of different SOM network sizes to recognise the number of speakers in given conversations. Speech was sampled at 16 kHz and segmented into 15 msec frames using a Hamming window. Twelve LPCC coefficients plus 12 ΔLPCC coefficients were used as the feature vector. The system was tested using two types of conversation. Conversations of nine speakers were recorded over a high quality channel and conversations of two speakers were recorded over a telephone quality channel. The sampling frequency was 8 kHz for the telephone quality channel. The optimised size of the SOM is 6 x 10. A comparison with time-series clustering approach is made and the claimed accuracy is over 80% using the proposed SOM.

A. T. Mafra and M. G. Simoes used an SOM for closed-set speaker identification [21]. The paper investigates different SOM sizes. Speech was sampled at 22.05 kHz and segmented into 32.22 msec frames using a Hamming window. Fourteen MFCC coefficients plus 14 ΔMFCC coefficients were used to provide a 28 components feature vector. The system was tested using a dataset of 14 speakers. Best claimed identification rate is more than 99% when the 16 x 16 SOM is

used; requiring 17.5 sec training speech data and more than 2.8 sec testing speech data.

In our previous work, the authors compared the performance of the three main feature formats used in speaker recognition systems (DFT, LPC & MFCC) when used as input feature vectors to an SOM + rule based scoring speaker verification system [11]. The results show that the DFT spectrum is better than the MFCC and the LPC spectrum features with the system adopted. In that paper, 64 DFT spectrum components were adopted as feature vector for the proposed system. In addition, a weighted Euclidian Distance (ED) measure was also suggested to compensate for the claimed speaker variability problem. The weighted ED included the weighting factor a, the effect of this factor was to increase the impact of the components with low variability on the total score, while decreasing the impact of high variability components.

1.3 SOM+MLP

As the MLP and SOM training methods are designed to achieve different aims – an MLP is trained to differentiate disjoint data patterns whilst SOMs are trained to cluster similar patterns – by combining the two methods a complementary system can be created that could potentially have a better speaker recognition performance than the two networks can achieve individually.

A two level classifier for closed-set speaker identification was presented by S. Hadjitodorov, *et al.* [22]. The paper investigates different versions of an SOM as a first stage classifier to obtain a prototype distribution map, and then use these maps to feed a second stage classifier of MLP network. The SOM is 15 x 15 in size, while the MLP contains two hidden layers. The first layer has 64 neurons and four neurons in the second layer, with one output neuron. Speech was sampled at 10.24 kHz, although framing information was not mentioned. Fifteen LPCC coefficients were used as feature vector. The system was tested using two datasets; the first being clean speech data of 68 speakers, while the second dataset consists of 92 speakers speech data recorded over telephone lines. The best claimed error rate with first dataset is 1.47% and 2.17% with the second dataset.

M. Inal and Y. S. Fatihoglu proposed a hybrid model that uses SOM and associative memory for closed–set speaker recognition application [23]. In their paper an SOM followed by associative memory neural network forms speaker classifier model. The paper investigates a 10 x 10 SOM for text dependent speaker identification and 20 x 20 SOM for text independent speaker identification. Twelve MFCC coefficients were used as feature vector. For the text dependent experiment the system was tested using a dataset of 10 speakers while for text independent experiment the system was tested using 38 speakers from the TIMIT database (results show performance for up to 20 speakers only). Speech was framed using 660

points Hamming window. Claimed performance for the first experiment is 97.45% and 96.3% for the second experiment using 20 speakers of the TIMIT subset.

It should be noted that the two examples referred to above are both closed-set speaker identification systems. This means that all test users have been seen during the training process. In real-world speaker verification systems it is necessary to demonstrate that the system is capable of dealing with unseen impostor data. However, the move to such an open-set application will have an impact on the classification performance of the system. Section 4 shows how the SOM + MLP system presented in this paper is evaluated in an open-set scenario.

2 Proposed SOM+MLP speaker verification system

The speaker verification algorithm presented in this section consists of two stages. The first stage is a frame filtering stage that uses the modified SOM, presented in [11] (and described in section 2.1), as a claimed user voice model for the three vowels considered in the experiment. The second stage then consists of three MLP networks (described in section 2.2); each of which has been trained to function as a claimed user vowel verifier. The main structure of the SOM+MLP system is shown in Fig. 1.

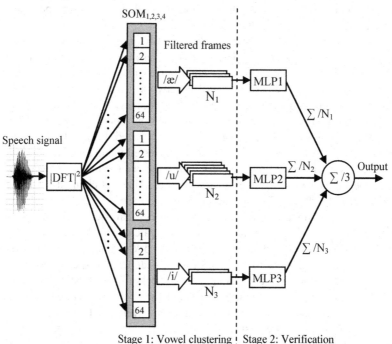

Fig. 1. SOM+MLP speaker verification.

Training phase: each individual speaker in the training set has four speech samples. From each sample a single three output vector SOM is trained to act as a vowel information filter for the enrolled user - producing four SOMs per speaker. After the SOM training has been completed, the four speech samples are then filtered using the same four SOMs to select only those speech frames that lie within the empirically optimised distance threshold (3.435) presented in [11]. The resultant speech frame sets N_1, N_2 and N_3 thus represent the filtered vowel information for the enrolled speaker, these sets are then used to train the three MLP networks.

Testing phase: to test a new speech sample, the sample is first passed to the four registration SOMs (for the claimed speaker). Any speech frame that is within the distance threshold of any of the four SOMs is passed through for testing in the MLP verification stage. The distance threshold used here is suggested to be (5.0). This is larger than the threshold value used in the training phase in order to overcome the real-user speaker variability seen between registration and verification sessions. The respective MLP networks are tested individually using the filtered frames of the test sample. As the number of the filtered frames given to each MLP network may differ, a normalisation process is required. To achieve this, the output of each MLP network is averaged over the number of filtered frames for that vowel in order to obtain a single output for each vowel. Finally the three averaged outputs of the three MLP networks are also averaged to achieve one output score for one test sample. Sections 2.1 and 2.2 explain the two verification stages of the proposed algorithm in greater detail.

2.1 A modified SOM for speaker verification system

As stated earlier, the authors have previously presented a novel one dimensional SOM as part of a hybrid SOM + rule based scoring speaker verification system [11]; the architectural details of which are repeated here for completeness. The SOM uses a single 64 DFT spectrum component feature vector as an input and three 64 weight vector nodes as output; each respectively representing one of the three selected vowels. Fig. 2 shows the modified SOM structure.

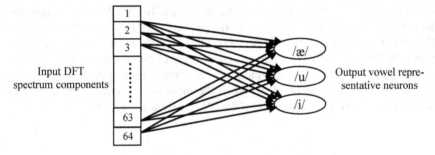

Fig. 2. modified SOM structure.

During its training phase the SOM is designed to update the winner neuron only if the input pattern lies within a specific distance region of the winner's current weight vector. Fig. 3 illustrates the training process of the three output neurons in two-dimensional weight space.

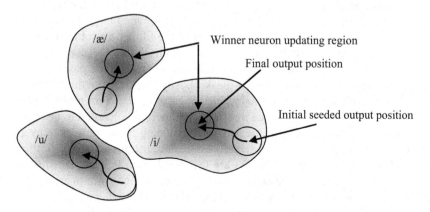

Fig. 3. SOM training process.

As shown in Fig. 3, at the onset of training, the weight vectors of the three output nodes of the SOM are first seeded with initial vowel information from predefined positions within the speech signal. As training progresses, the weight vectors of the output nodes respectively move through the weight space to a position representing the greatest density of input vectors for each vowel - exemplified by the darkest point in each vowel area in Fig. 3. At the end of training, the SOM thus represents a statistical three vowel voice model of the training speaker.

2.2 Fine MLP verifier

The second stage is consist of three MLP networks. Each MLP is trained individually by using the filtered frames from the first stage. The MLP network suggested for each vowel consists of two layers, an input layer of 64 nodes, representing the DFT spectrum vector of each frame successfully filtered by any of the four registration SOMs for that vowel, and an output layer of one neuron with supervised binary output of (1) when the input vowel frame information belongs to the claimed speaker and output of (0) when the input vowel frame information belongs to an impostor. The structure of the MLP is shown in Fig. 4.

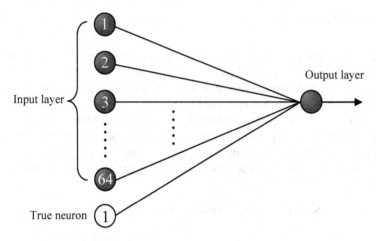

Fig. 4. MLP network structure.

A simple MLP network architecture is possible here because the SOM filtering stage removes noise, non-vowel data and undesired other vowels data. Each MLP network was trained using the standard back-propagation learning algorithm with a learning rate of (0.1) and a sigmoid activation function with a temperature of (1.0). To train and test the two stage speaker verification algorithm the same two sessions data from the CSLU2002 database, as used in the previous work, were used and divided as shown in the next sections.

3 Speech data

CSLU2002 is a commercially available speaker verification database from the Oregon Graduate Institute of Science and Technology Research Center in Spoken Language Technologies. The database consists of 91 speakers, from which 50 speakers were arbitrarily selected (27 females and 23 males) for use in this paper. The data were recorded over digital telephone lines with a sampling frequency of 8 kHz to produce 8-bit u-law files, which are then encoded into 8 kHz 16-bit wave format file. Two recording sessions samples are used for evaluation (the words two, five & eight), each session containing four samples for each speaker. More information on the CSLU2002 database can be obtained on the website "http://www.cslu.ogi.edu".

4 System evaluation

To train and test each MLP, two types of speech data are needed, claimed speaker speech data and impostor speech data. Each type is then divided into three parts, training, validation, and testing. Session 1 data was used only for training and validation while session 2 data was only used for testing.

The first 30 speakers were used to evaluate the performance of the algorithm. The remaining speakers were kept aside to provide validation and testing data for impostors. Fig. 5 explains how the data was divided to implement the algorithm for the first speaker. Note this data represent the filtered speech data (N_1, N_2 and N_3).

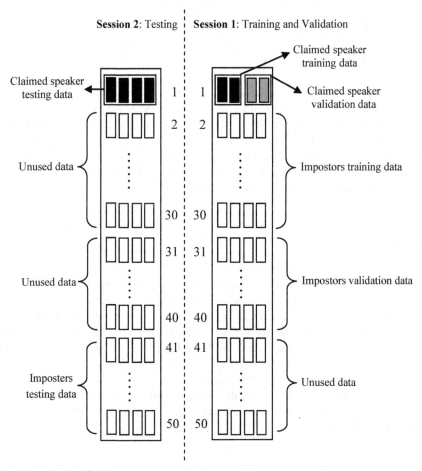

Fig. 5. Speech data division.

As shown in Fig. 5 the speaker data was split to provide training data for both claimed speaker and impostors, as well as to reserve unseen data for validation in session 1 and unseen testing data in session 2.

For each individual vowel MLP verifier, the network was trained to give an output of (1) for filtered frames corresponding to the claimed speaker training data, and an output of (0) for filtered frames corresponding to the impostors training data. At the end of each training epoch a validation error was calculated using the filtered validation data of the claimed speaker and impostors as shown in equation (1). The network stops the training, if the validation error increases.

$$E_{validation} = \frac{1}{2}\left[\frac{1}{M_1} \sum_i^{M_1} |T_i - A_i| + \frac{1}{M_2} \sum_i^{M_2} |T_i - A_i| \right] \qquad (1)$$

where M_1 and M_2 are the numbers of filtered validation data frames for claimed speaker and impostors respectively, T_i is the target output which is equal to (1) in the first term and equal to (0) in the second term and A_i is the actual output. In equation (1) the validation error is calculated individually for the claimed speaker and impostors to eliminate the effect of the unbalance between M_1 and M_2.

After training, the two stage speaker recognition system was tested using the unseen session 2 data samples of the claimed speaker and impostors. Each frame of a test sample was presented sequentially to the trained system to produce a final output, representing the average of the three MLP averaged outputs over the whole sample, as a number between 0 and 1. Note. Only filtered frames that are passed forward from the SOM stage are processed by the MLP stage, thus frames that were not passed forward by the first SOM stage do not contribute to the final output value. By applying speaker dependent variable thresholds to these values, the FRR and FAR can be calculated. Using the Minimum Average Error Rate (MAER) = min|(FRR+FAR)/2| the performance of the verification algorithm can be obtained as follows:

$$Performance\ (\%) = 100 - MAER \qquad (2)$$

For direct comparison purposes, the same 30 speakers set were enrolled using the SOM+ weighted ED scoring system presented in [11]. In addition, in order to gain an understanding of the results possible using an SOM only solution, the same data set was used to evaluate the performance of the SOM system in [11] with a conventional ED scoring. Fig. 6 shows the performance of the first 30 speakers using:

1. The SOM with ED scoring based system (SOM).
2. The SOM with weighted ED scoring based system (SOM+ weighted ED).
3. The proposed SOM+MLP algorithm (SOM+MLP).

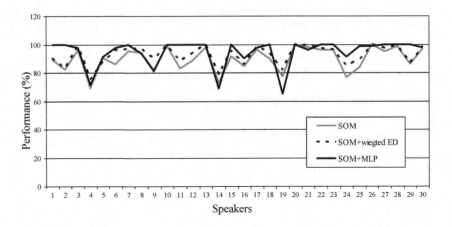

Fig. 6. Performance using: SOM, SOM+ weighted ED, SOM+MLP.

From Fig. 6, it is clear that the three investigated methods have the same behaviour towards many speakers in the dataset. Upon further investigation it was
found that the speakers (4, 14 and 19) with the lowest performance in the
SOM+MLP curve showed high variability across the registration and verification
sessions. The lowest performance occurs with speaker 19 when the SOM+MLP
system was trained with two low variability samples from session 1, i.e. the MLP
networks have lost some of their robustness against speaker variability. The average performance of the three algorithms is shown in Table 1.

Table 1. Speaker verification performance.

Method	Performance (%)
SOM	89.79
SOM+ weighted ED	92.73
SOM+MLP	94.54

From Table 1 it is clear that the SOM+MLP system has the best average performance rate. This is particularly impressive given that the SOM+ weighted ED
system saw four real-user samples during the training whereas the SOM+MLP
system saw only two real-user samples during the training. In addition, as the
SOM + MLP system is a more biologically plausible solution than the hybrid
SOM+ rule based weighted ED scoring method it can form the basis of further
work investigating the use of spiking neural networks for speaker recognition.

5 Conclusion

In this paper a two stage speaker verification system is proposed. The first stage employs a modified SOM to filter the input speech data into frames of three vowels information. The filtered frames are related to the claimed speaker since the SOM is designed to extract only claimed speaker vowel data frames. The second stage consists of three MLP networks, these networks act as fine-grained speaker verifiers, since they are trained with pure vowels information to accept the claimed speaker data frames and reject impostor data frames. The DFT spectrum was adopted as the input feature vector. Fifty speakers from the CSLU2002 speaker recognition database were used to evaluate the algorithm. Three experiments were conducted. The first experiment used an SOM and ED to compare its outputs. The second experiment used the SOM and weighted ED as described in [11]. The third experiment was applied using the proposed SOM and MLP system. The first experiment shows a performance of 89.7% while the second and the third experiments show performances of 92.7% and 94.54% respectively. In spite of being trained with 50% less speech data compared to the SOM+ weighted ED scoring based system, the proposed algorithm gives the best average performance over the 30 enrolled speakers.

In addition, since short speech data duration is used during training and testing in this paper, the experiment presented in this work can be considered as a limited data condition case. In a recent comparative study [13], different speaker recognition systems were investigated under limited data conditions. The study included popular speaker recognition systems such as GMM with universal background model, Learning vector quantisation, Fuzzy vector quantisation and SOM. It was shown there that the performance of these systems decreases dramatically when limited speech data (3 sec) is used for training and testing. It can be implied from that study that any other popular speaker recognition technique, which is normally trained using substantial speech data, may suffer from similar performance degradation when trained and tested using limited speech data. Thus the proposed system presented in this paper shows better limited data condition performance than all the traditional methods described in [13].

References

1. Reynolds, D.A. and R.C. Rose: Robust text-independent speaker identification using Gaussian mixture speaker models. Speech and Audio Processing, IEEE Transactions on, 1995. 3(1): p. 72-83.
2. Campbell, W.M., et al.: Support vector machines for speaker and language recognition. Computer Speech & Language, 2006. 20(2-3): p. 210-229.
3. Seddik, H., A. Rahmouni, and M. Sayadi: Text independent speaker recognition using the Mel frequency cepstral coefficients and a neural network classifier. in Control, Communications and Signal Processing, First International Symposium on. 2004.

4. Oglesby, J. and J.S. Mason: Radial basis function networks for speaker recognition. in Acoustics, Speech, and Signal Processing, ICASSP-91., International Conference on. 1991.
5. Farrell, K.R., R.J. Mammone, and K.T. Assaleh: Speaker recognition using neural networks and conventional classifiers. Speech and Audio Processing, IEEE Transactions on, 1994. 2(1): p. 194-205.
6. Kishore, S.P. and B. Yegnanarayana: Speaker verification: minimizing the channel effects using autoassociative neural network models. in Acoustics, Speech, and Signal Processing, ICASSP '00. Proceedings. IEEE International Conference on. 2000.
7. Mueen, F., et al: Speaker recognition using artificial neural networks. in Students Conference, ISCON '02. Proceedings. IEEE. 2002.
8. Kusumoputro, B., et al: Speaker identification in noisy environment using bispectrum analysis and probabilistic neural network. in Computational Intelligence and Multimedia Applications, ICCIMA 2001. Proceedings. Fourth International Conference on. 2001.
9. George, S., et al: Speaker recognition using dynamic synapse based neural networks with wavelet preprocessing. in Neural Networks, 2001. Proceedings. IJCNN '01. International Joint Conference on. 2001.
10. Monte, E., et al: Text independent speaker identification on noisy environments by means of self organizing maps. in Spoken Language, ICSLP 96. Proceedings., Fourth International Conference on. 1996.
11. Tashan, T., T. Allen, and L. Nolle: Vowel based speaker verification using self organising map. in The Eleventh IASTED International Conference on Artificial Intelligence and Applications (AIA 2011). 2011. Innsbruck, Austria: ACTA Press.
12. Han-Sheng, L. and R.J. Mammone: Speaker verification using phoneme-based neural tree networks and phonetic weighting scoring method. in Neural Networks for Signal Processing V. Proceedings of the IEEE Workshop. 1995.
13. Jayanna, H.S. and S.R.M. Prasanna: An experimental comparison of modelling techniques for speaker recognition under limited data condition. Sadhana-Academy Proceedings in Engineering Sciences, 2009. 34(5): p. 717-728.
14. Rabiner, L.R. and R.W. Schafer: Digital processing of speech signals. Prentice-Hall signal processing series. 1978, Englewood Cliffs, N.J.: Prentice-Hall.
15. Davis, S. and P. Mermelstein: Comparison of parametric representations for monosyllabic word recognition in continuously spoken sentences. Acoustics, Speech and Signal Processing, IEEE Transactions on, 1980. 28(4): p. 357-366.
16. Sun, F., B. Li, and H. Chi: Some key factors in speaker recognition using neural networks approach. in Neural Networks, IEEE International Joint Conference on. 1991.
17. Delacretaz, D.P. and J. Hennebert: Text-prompted speaker verification experiments with phoneme specific MLPs. in Acoustics, Speech and Signal Processing, Proceedings of the IEEE International Conference on. 1998.
18. Sri Rama Murty, K., S.R. Mahadeva Prasanna, and B. Yegnanarayana: Speaker-specific information from residual phase. in Signal Processing and Communications, SPCOM '04. International Conference on. 2004.
19. Kohonen, T.: The self-organizing map. Proceedings of the IEEE, 1990. 78(9): p. 1464-1480.
20. Lapidot, I., H. Guterman, and A. Cohen: Unsupervised speaker recognition based on competition between self-organizing maps. Neural Networks, IEEE Transactions on, 2002. 13(4): p. 877-887.
21. Mafra, A.T. and M.G. Simoes: Text independent automatic speaker recognition using selforganizing maps. in Industry Applications Conference, 39th IAS Annual Meeting. Conference Record of the IEEE. 2004.
22. Hadjitodorov, S., B. Boyanov, and N. Dalakchieva: A two-level classifier for text-independent speaker identification. Speech Communication, 1997. 21(3): p. 209-217.
23. Inal, M. and Y.S. Fatihoglu: Self organizing map and associative memory model hybrid classifier for speaker recognition. in Neural Network Applications in Electrical Engineering, NEUREL '02. 6th Seminar on. 2002.

Investigation into Computer vision methods to extract information for Context based image retrieval methods

Karen Le Roux[1]

Abstract This document investigates key issues in extracting information from images. Perimeters of objects are key features in human recognition, and are found through edge detection. Several edge detection methods are investigated in this paper, including fuzzy edge detection. Hough lines were drawn on the edges making use of 'Harris corner detection' to estimate the number of lines to draw. The lines were connected up into triangles and this was found to segment key parts of the images. The overall texture contained within a set images was analyzed, with it features being reduced by canonical variants. Classical classifiers and self organizing maps were used to analyze the textures, and showed very similar confusion.

1 Introduction

Context based image retrieval (CBIR), is a growing area of interest with many papers being published in the area. CBIR is a part of sub-field of multimedia mining, introduced by T. Kato in 19992. CBIR is an automatic method for extracting images from a database, using information such as colour, texture and edges [1]. Currently there is an increasing interest in CBIR, due to the limitations of textual methods for extracting images from image libraries. Textual search methods require all the images to be marked up by hand. This is a very labour intensive process that also requires good analysts to ensure the quality of the images. Ideally the images should be checked through by several analysts and then combined, before being entered into the data base.

Edges are important features contained in the image, as this is how human vision perceives the perimeters of objects. There are many ways of extracting edges from images. e.g. thresholds could be used if we were looking at the edges of a

1 De Montford University
p09171717@myemail.dmu.ac.uk

M. Bramer et al. (eds.), *Research and Development in Intelligent Systems XXVIII*,
DOI 10.1007/978-1-4471-2318-7_9, © Springer-Verlag London Limited 2011

white ball on a green field. This is a very simple example, as typically images have more detail than this. The Hough transform is another method of extracting lines from a binary image, however most images have a gray scale. Edges can be found in grey scale images, by processing differences in adjacent points in the image. Some examples of these algorithms are the Canny and Sobel edge detectors. As well as these traditional methods of edge detection, more recently there has been development of fuzzy edge detection. Fuzzy edge detection methods enhance edges for more difficult images where the edges are not clear. Example when the edges are broken or blurred. There many different approaches to implementing a fuzzy edge detector[2].

Another alternative approach to fuzzy edge detection was illustrated in [3], making use of Matlab's fuzzy logics toolbox. A fuzzy inference system was designed to take an input of a 2 by 2 block of pixels. The inputs from the pixels find their degree of membership to black and white using the triangle membership functions ranging from 0-255 as shown in Figure 1.

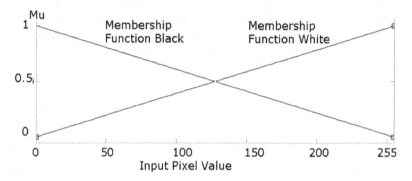

Figure 1 Fuzzy Sets of Input Pixels identical for all four inputs.

The degrees of membership from the 4 adjacent pixels are combined using the rules in Table 1, these rules are slightly different to [3].

Table 1. Fuzzy inputs, with rules and fuzzy outputs.

Fuzzy inputs	Fuzzy output
If all pixels are black	Black
If all pixels are white	White
If pixels are black and white	Edge

The rules are all combined using Madani inference to calculate the output, according to the output membership functions shown in Figure 2.

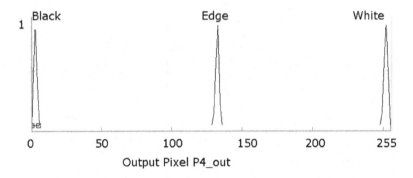

Figure 2 Fuzzy sets of Output Pixel.

2 Further extension of the Fuzzy edge detection

The fuzzy edge detection method show in [3], used fuzzy logic to create a fuzzy image that in turn strengthens the weaker edges, their analysis performed in only one direction. The resultant image from this process requires further processing to extract the actual edges. This paper investigated combining fuzzy enhanced images in the original orientation, next though 4 90 degree steps, giving four fuzzy images that were combined using the max function as follows:

$$best\ fuzzy\ image = \max\big(fi(0), fi(90), fi(180), fi(270)\big)$$

The best fuzzy image now requires processing to find the edges, the first stage of the process combines the x and y gradients of the image. The resultant gradient image still required the edges to be extracted; first Otsu method was used to calculate the threshold, on the gradient image. If the Otsu method was not successful, then fuzzy clustering was investigated as a method of finding the threshold of the gradient image [4]. Two clusters were extracted from the image, foreground and background. It was assumed that the fuzzy cluster with the largest membership of 1 was background. The threshold of the image was found by measuring the histogram of the background membership, in this case the histogram just had 10 bins this variable could be analyzed further. The bin next down to the maximum level was used to set the threshold. Figure 3 shows and example of setting a threshold based on membership, in this case the threshold is approximately 0.825, e.g. anything with a membership less than this in the image is considered an edge.

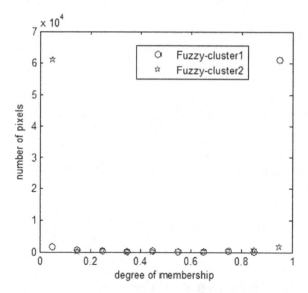

Figure 3 Example of setting threshold based on degree of membership.

Shown next in Figure 4 is an example of selecting the edges from the gradient image using Otsu and using fuzzy membership from fuzzy clustering. The fuzzy clustering method gives the best result.

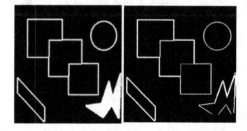

Figure 4 Threshold edges with Otsu and Fuzzy membership method (using test image).

Next the test image was used to validate the different edge detection methods, as shown in Figure 5. Shown first is the test image, next the gradient of the fuzzy image found using the fuzzy logic membership functions, note the different gray levels. Shown next is the fuzzy edge detection method, this appears to give the best edges out of all the four methods shown in this paper. The fuzzy edge detection algorithm implemented in this paper is computationally expensive, and could be speed up through parallel processing and other methods. So an alternative fuzzy edge method was investigated. This took the gradient of the image, and used fuzzy clustering to determine the edges, and this is shown next.

This alternative method was not as good as the initial method investigated in this paper. The alternative method was developed to help with some of the other experiments to be performed in this paper, due to the lack of computation time and power available. Also shown are the Sobel and Canny methods.

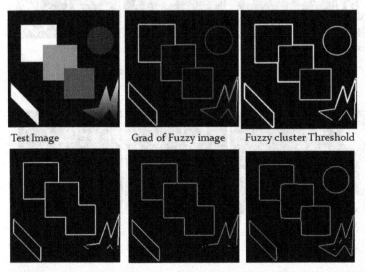

Test Image   Grad of Fuzzy image   Fuzzy cluster Threshold

Leaving out the fuzzy logic step   Sobel edge detection   Canny edge detection

Figure 5 Test Image and performance of the different edge detection methods.

The performance of the edge detection algorithms was evaluated using Pratt's figure of Merit [2][6]. Pratt's figure of measurement can only be measured with an image with known edges, e.g. one that has been ground truth by hand. The method uses equation 1. Where α is set to 1/9 this a default scaling value, N_A is the number of actual edges, N_l the number of edges the method finds in the image, d is the distance the edge found is from the ground truth edge.

$$F = \frac{1}{\max\{N_A, N_l\}} \sum_{k=1}^{N_A} \frac{1}{1 + \alpha d^2(k)} \tag{1}$$

Pratt's figure of merit was also investigated for the same images with Gaussian noise superimposed on the images. The edge detection response to the noisy images are shown next in Figures 6 and 7, table 2 shows the different in Pratt's figure of merit.

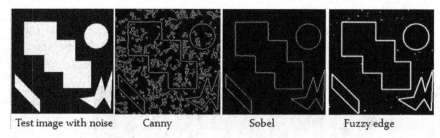

| Test image with noise | Canny | Sobel | Fuzzy edge |

Figure 6 Adding Gaussian noise to original test image mean =0 standard deviation 0.01

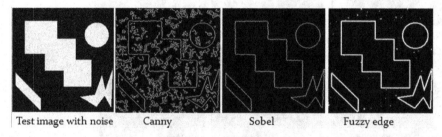

| Test image with noise | Canny | Sobel | Fuzzy edge |

Figure 7 Adding Gaussian noise to the original test image mean =0 and standard deviation 0.1.

Table 2. Analysis of Pratt's figure of merit comparing original image to noisy versions of the same images

Edge detection method	Original	Noise stdev 0.01	Noise stdev 0.1
Canny	0.6861	0.6444	0.6421
Sobel	0.7812	0.6672	0.6706
Fuzzy edge detection	0.9991	0.9458	0.8112

Shown next in Figure 8 and 9 are other examples of the fuzzy edge detection method compared to the Canny and Sobel methods. The Sobel method provides the lowest fidelity of edges, the Canny is sensitive to changes in the texture as shown in Figure 9, and these are not the most important edge features in the image to the human eye.

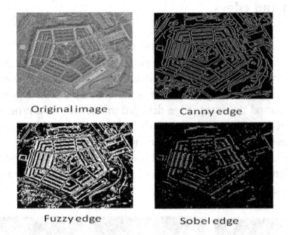

Figure 8 Example of different edge detection methods on the Pentagon image.

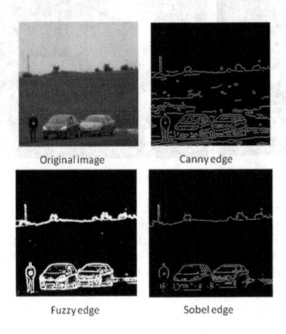

Figure 9 Original image next the Canny, fuzzy edge detection, and Canny.

Visual inspection of the edges shows the fuzzy edges gives the best detail with the lines being better connected around the important images in the scene.

3 Hough transform and edges

Edges to a machine are just a set of lines; the question is how to generate information from these edges that make up the perimeters of the objects in the image that are distinguishable by a human. The Hough transform allows a number of selected lines to be found in an image. But how many lines should the algorithm look for? As an initial method the fuzzy edge detected image was next processed by the Harris corner detections [7]. Harris corner detections could fall short as this method assumes that there are two lines to a corner, but depending on the angle there could be three lines to a corner. Figure 10, shows the Hough lines detected on the Fuzzy edge detection, also shown are the triangles created from drawing through lines that share a common end point.

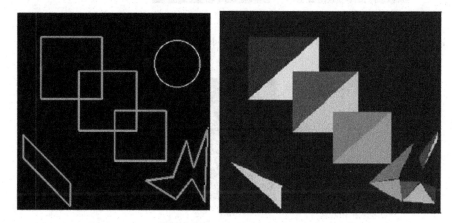

Figure 10 Hough lines found on Fuzzy edges, connecting the lines with triangles.

Note the circle only had one line marked on it, Hough circle detection could have be used to detect it. However, Hough circle detection is quite computationally expensive as each radius of each circle requires searching for. A simpler method could be derived for detection circles in the image by first filling in the objects and measuring the eccentricity of the objects, circles will have an eccentricity of typically about 1.

Fuzzy edge image with Hough lines , connect the Hough lines, use connect components

Figure 11 Hough lines found on the fuzzy edges, connecting them, and segment the regions in the image.

Figure 11 shows connecting Hough lines up as triangles segments the objects boundaries fairly well, however it has to be noted that some of the shadowing underneath the car as been attached to the two cars. Secondly both the cars have been attached together, this difficult problem, to a computer algorithms this might look like a bus if the two cars cannot be separated. An easy way of separating the cars would be to make use of their colour; this step has not been implemented yet. Show next is a simpler example with just one car in the image, again the shadow is being joined to the bottom of the car.

Fuzzy edge image with Hough lines , connect the Hough lines, use connect components

Figure 12 Hough lines found on the fuzzy edges, connecting them, and segment the regions in the image.

4 Texture measurement

For this analysis a set of images were downloaded from [9], and the following vehicle type images were selected for analysis: Air-ship, cannon, fire engine, motor bike, mountain bike, school bus, snowmobile, speedboat, aeroplanes and the side of a car.

The texture in the image was assessed by first measuring the gray-level co-occurrence metric of the input image. This matrix texture measurement was investigated for its interaction between different distances between the pixel of

interest and its neighbour, this is illustrated in Figure 13.

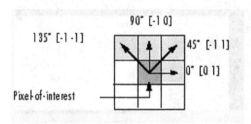

Figure 13 Investigating the pixels around the pixel of interest [8].

Next the following measurements, Contrast, Correlation, Energy, and Homogeneity, were extracted from the co-occurrence matrix and these became the texture features. Contrast is the measurement of intensity between a pixel and its neighbour over the whole image. Correlation measures how correlated the pixel of interest is with its neighbor all over the image. Energy returns the sum of the squares of the gray-level co-occurrence matrix. Homogeneity measure the closeness of the distribution of the elements of the diagonal of gray-level co-occurrence matrix.

Investigations of the grey-level co-occurrence showed that the best features were produced measuring up to an offset from 1- 3 from the pixel of interest; this is shown in Table 3. The results in Table 3 are form combining the performance of all ten images.

Table 3. Evaluating the optimum texture measurement.

Offset	Training Images (percentage correct)	Test Images (percentage correct)
1-2	64.60	57.17
1-3	69.80	58.90
1-4	74.30	58.60

4.1 Reducing the dimensionality of the features

The texture measurement found to give the optimum performance had 48 features, this is high dimensional feature for a classifier, and will suffer from the curse of dimensionality. The canonical projections were investigated to reduce the dimensionality of the features and 9 canonical features were found to give the best performance. Figure 14 compares the performance of a linear discriminator [10], by gradually increasing the number of canonical features used. These two figures also

show that some objects have a far more distinct texture and are clearly more recognizable.

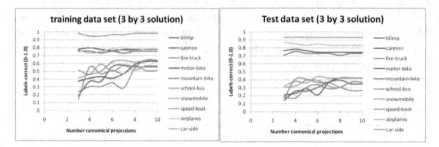

Figure 14 Performance of the linear discriminator per an object class.

Table 4. Confusion matrix using 9 canonical projections for texture measurements 1-3, training data set.

	Blimp	Cannon	Fire truck	Motor bike	Mountain bike	School bus	Snow mobile	Speed boat	Aeroplane	Side of car
Blimp	24	4	3	1	0	2	4	2.	3	0
Cannon	2	32	2	1	3	0	8	3	0	0
Fire truck	2	7	38	0	0	5	4	0	1	2
Motor bike	0	0	1	42	3	0	2	0	6	0
Mountain bike	0	8	0	0	31	1	1	0	0	0
School bus	0	5	15	0	0	25	1	1	0	2
Snow mobile	5	7	4	1	1	1	32	4	1	0
Speed boat	2	3	2	0	0	1	5	32	3	2
Aeroplane	4	0	0	2	0	0	1	6	47	0
Side of car	0	0	0	0	0	1	0	0	0	57

The aeroplane has a high level of texture performance as the planes are surrounded by sky. The school bus and fire engines are confused this is due to them being similar in shape and size, colour would be required in this case to tell the objects apart.

4.2 Analysis of features using Self Organizing Maps

Self Organizing Maps are a method of analyzing high dimensionality data for its spatial clustering. The SOM is an unsupervised neural network classifier. The SOMs were used to analyzed the 9 canonical projections. The response of the different size SOMs is shown in Table 5, there clearly is a limit to increasing the size of the map, the best size map was found to be a 5 by 5. Table 6 shows the confusion seen using the 4 by 4 SOM.

Table 5. Evaluating the optimum texture measurement with SOM.

Size of SOM	Training Images (percentage correct)	Test Images (percentage correct)
4 by 4	62.19	52.20
5 by 5	62.96	53.15
6 by 6	64.88	52.77
7 by 7	67.95	52.20
8 by 8	69.48	52.01
10 by 10	71.49	50.67

Table 6. Node discovered on a 4 by 4 SOM.

Node	1	2	3	4
1	Motor bike	Aeroplane	Motor bike	Side of car
2	Snow mobile	Speed boat	Speed boat	Blimp
3	Mountain bike	Snow mobile	Snow mobile	Fire truck
4	Cannon	Cannon	Fire truck	School bus

The performance of the SOM was found to be slightly lower than the linear discriminate classifier, this is due to the SOM being an unsupervised method.

5 Conclusion

Fuzzy edges clearly provide a better edge detection, and they were more robust to the addition of Gaussian noise. The fuzzy edges provided better lines to connect up to form triangles, this in turn has started the development of a segmentation algorithm. Presently this algorithm is computationally inefficient and could easily be implement into a parallel processing architecture. Some objects in images are difficult to separate when the edges overlap, for instance two cars parked adjacent to each other. If the cars are different colours this is a straight forward task to separate them but what if they are the same colours. It's possible that a method such as Kmeans could be used in conjunction with the fuzzy edges, Hough lines and triangles. Texture measurements from the whole images gave fairly good

results, but similar shaped objects were confused, for instance school-buses were confused fire-trucks. If colour was used as a feature this would improve the overall classification.

References

1. Yap-Peng Tan, Kim Hui Yap, Lipo Wang, "Intelligent Multimedia Processing with Soft Computing," Studies in Fuzziness and Soft Computing, vol. 168 ,Springer July 2004.
2. Tamalika Chaira, Ajoy Kumar Ray, Fuzzy Image Processing and Applications with Matlab, CRC Press, 2010, pp.109–123.
3. Er Kiranpreet Kaur,Er Vikram Mutenja,Er Inderjeet Singh Gill, "Fuzzy Logic Based Image Edge Detection Algorithm in Matlab", International Journal of Computer Applications . 2010, Volume 1 No.22, pp. 55-58
4. Dr G. Padmavathi, Mr Muthukumar, "Image segmentation using fuzzy c means clustering method with thresholding for underwater images", International Journal of Advanced Networking and Applications, 2010, volume 02, Issue 02, pp.514-518
5. Mark Nixon, Alberto, "Feature Extraction and Image Processing", 2008, second edition, Elsevier, pp.196-236
6. Karen A. Panetta, Eric J Wharton, "Logarithmic Edge Detection with Applications', Journal of Computers, September 2008, pp.11-19
7. Peter Kovesi, http://www.csse.uwa.edu.au/~pk/research/matlabfns/Spatial/harris.m
8. Matlab: Graycorprops::Functions(Image Processing Toolbox)
9. http://www.vision.caltech.edu/Image_Datasets/Caltech256/
10. "Linear Discriminant analysis," http://www.stat.psu.edu/~jiali/course/stat597e/notes2/lda.pdf

MACHINE LEARNING

A Multimodal Biometric Fusion Approach based on Binary Particle Optimization

Waheeda Almayyan[1] Hala Own[2] Rabab Abel-Kader[3] Hussian Zedan[1]

Abstract In this paper, we propose a novel fusion scheme of iris and online signature biometrics at feature level space. The features are extracted from the pre-processed images of iris and the dynamics of signatures. We propose different fusion schemes at feature level, which we compare on a database of 108 virtual people. Moreover, in order to reduce the complexity of the fusion scheme, we implement a binary particle swarm optimization (BPSO) procedure which allows the number of features to be significantly reduced while keeping the same level of performance. This paper studies the advantage of multimodal biometric system over unimodal biometric system. We also examine how the accuracy will be improved as several biometric data are integrated in an identification system. Results show a significant improvement in performance when classification performed at feature fusion level.

1 Introduction

Unimodal biometric systems based on single biometric trait often face limitations that negatively influence their overall performance. This is expected to a variety of reasons such as noisy data, intra-class variability, low distinctiveness, non-universality and unacceptable error rates due to the nature of relevant biometric traits [1]. Multimodality, that is the use of several biometric traits for individual authentication, is often seen as a way to solve some of the aforementioned difficulties [2]. The efforts in this area have been directed toward the development

1 Software Technology Research Laboratory, De Montfort University, UK
{walmayyan,hzedan}@dmu.ac.uk

2 Department of Solar and Space Research, National Research Institute of Astronomy and Geophysics, Cairo, Egypt
halaown@gmail.com

3 Electrical Engineering Department, Faculty of Engineering - Port-Said University, Port Fouad 42523, Port-Said, Egypt
rabab.ramadan58@gmail.com

M. Bramer et al. (eds.), *Research and Development in Intelligent Systems XXVIII*,
DOI 10.1007/978-1-4471-2318-7_10, © Springer-Verlag London Limited 2011

of fusing the information obtained from a range of independent modalities. In such approach, separate information from different modalities is combined to provide complementary information about the identity of the users. For example, a common approach is to combine face and speech modalities to achieve a more trustworthy recognition decision. In such cases, fusion normally takes place at the feature level or the score level. This is because the individual modalities provide different raw data types, and involve different classification methods for discrimination.

Any biometric system is usually divided into four basic modules: the sensor module acquires the biometric data, the feature extraction module process the biometric data in order to extract a discriminative representation of the data. The matching module compares input features to stored templates and after that the decision module issues an accept or reject decision based on the matching score. Consequently, the fusion in multimodal systems can take place at four possible levels: sensor, feature, matching and decision. The sensor and the feature levels are referred to as a pre-mapping fusion while the matching score and the decision levels are referred to as a post-mapping fusion [3]. In pre-mapping fusion, the data is integrated before any use of classifiers. While in post-mapping fusion; the data is integrated after mapping into matching score/decision space. Pre-mapping schemes include fusion at the sensor and the feature levels. Whereas post-mapping schemes include fusion at the match score, rank and decision levels. The later approach has attracted a lot of attention although that the amount of information available for fusion declined progressively after each layer of processing in a biometric system [4].

Fusion at the feature level is an understudied problem. Fusion at this level can be applied to the extracted features from the same modality or different multimodalities. Since the feature set contains richer information about the raw biometric data, integration at this level is expected to act better in comparison with fusion at the score level and decision level [2]. Nevertheless, fusion at this level is a challenging task due to a variety of reasons. Most feature sets gathered from multiple modalities may be incompatible such as in the case of combining Fourier Descriptor of gait's motion and eigen-coefficients of face's image. Moreover, concatenating several feature vectors may lead to construct a relatively large feature vector. This definitely increases the computational and storage resources demands and eventually requires more complex classifier design to operate on the concatenated data set at the feature level space [4]. Furthermore, poor feature representation, which mostly contains noisy or redundant data, may cause in degrading the overall performance. This difficulty can be overcome either by performing feature transformation or feature selection. Feature selection, also known as feature reduction, attribute selection or variable subset selection, is the technique of selecting a subset of relevant features for building robust learning models. By removing most irrelevant and redundant features from the data, feature selection helps improve the performance of learning model [5]. Assuming an original feature set of n features, the objective of feature selection is to identify the

most informative subset of m features ($m < n$). Common feature selection approaches, such as sequential forward selection (SFS), sequential backward selection (SBS), sequential floating forward selection (SFFS), genetic algorithms (GA) have been applied successfully to several optimization tasks [6]. Feature transformation, on the other hand, represents the feature vector in another vector space to improve the representativeness of the data. Moreover, only the significant "eigenvectors" are kept, inducing a subsequent reduction of dimension in the representation of the data. Finding such projection space requires a training phase on an adequate database. Principal Component Analysis (PCA), Linear Discriminant Analysis (LDA) and Independent Component Analysis (ICA) [7] are three main linear techniques used for data reduction and feature transformation. Whereas, kernel PCA (KPCA) has been successfully applied in extracting nonlinear structures in data [8].

In this paper, we are going to explore different fusion schemes at the feature level and we limit ourselves to two modalities, namely, iris and online signature. To the best of our knowledge, there is no reported research work combined iris and online signature. The main motive behind the selection of iris and online signature as biometric features for building a multimodal biometric system is that signature is being used in most of the daily applications for identity authentication since long time and iris offers an excellent recognition performance when used as a biometric. Therefore, in this paper, we aim to answer the following questions: which fusion strategy can bring the best results in terms of performance and how much improvement can we expect from a feature fusion scheme? Toward this objective, we will design different feature fusion schemes at different possible feature levels. Moreover, we will also address the complexity problem, in the sense that we will also raise the question whether it could be possible to reduce the dimension of the fusion feature space, through an appropriate selection procedure, while keeping the same level of performance. In order to achieve this goal, we deployed the binary particle swarm optimization (PSO) algorithm proposed in [9] to perform feature selection. Certainly PSO based feature selection has been shown to be very efficient in optimizing the feature selection process in large scale application problems [10, 11]. Therefore, implementing it for this biometric feature fusion problem of high dimension is another novelty of this paper.

This paper is organized as follows: Section 2 describes the iris and online signature unimodal biometric systems. Section 3 describes the different architectures that we have designed to perform iris and online signature fusion at feature level along with a presentation of the PSO algorithm and to its implementation in the context of this paper. Section 4 is concerned with the experimental setup, including the description of the databases and related experiments findings. Finally, Section 5 draws the conclusion.

2 Unimodal biometric systems

This section presents the general structure of the unimodal biometric systems deployed in this work. Individual identification systems with standard performance have intentionally been used to make the comparison of subsequent fusion strategies easier. In particular, the experiments have been carried out on our unimodal biometric system including the dual-tree complex wavelet transform-based iris verification subsystem described by Almayyan et al. (2010) and the online signature verification subsystem based on global features and Rough sets approach reported by Almayyan et al. (2011). A brief description of both systems is given in the following subsections.

2.1 Iris recognition system

Among biometric technologies, iris-based authentication systems bear more advantages than other biometric technologies do. Iris offers an excellent recognition performance when used as a biometric. Iris patterns are believed to be unique due to the complexity of the underlying the environmental and genetic processes that influence the generation of iris pattern. Iris recognition identifies a person by analysing the "unique" random patterns that are visible within the iris of an eye to form an iris code that is compared to iris templates stored in an existing database [14].

2.1.1 Iris preprocessing

Initially, the iris region is segmented by locating the boundaries between the pupil and iris region and between sclera and iris region using a method that based on canny edge detection and circular Hough Transform [15]. The eyelid and iris region were separated by a horizontal line which is constructed using combination of Radon transform and Hough transform techniques.

Processing iris images is a challenging task since the iris region can be occluded by eyelids or eyelashes and that generally leads to a significant dissimilarity between the intra- and inter-class comparisons [16]. Yet, locating the eyelashes and eyelids is a complex process and it requires a high level of computation load. Therefore, we decided to isolate the effect of the eyelids and eyelashes by simply extracting the left and right parts of the iris zone. Thus, with the intention of eliminating the translation variance, we first shifted the centroid of the image to the centre of the iris image and then we define the iris area. Next, we cropped the iris area above the upper boundary of the pupil and the area below the lower boundary of the pupil. Then, we applied histogram equalization to enhance

the contrast of the resulting images by transforming its intensity values. An illustration of this process is shown in Figure 1.

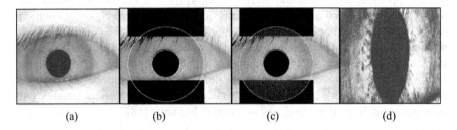

| (a) | (b) | (c) | (d) |

Figure 1 Localizing iris process, (a) original image, (b)(c) localized iris and the normalization region used for recognition, (d) enhanced and normalized iris image.

2.1.2 Iris feature extraction

The dual-tree complex wavelet transform (DTCWT) is an enhancement to the ordinary discrete wavelet transform (DWT), with important additional improved properties such as directionality and reduced shift sensitivity and it is approximately orientation invariant. The DT-CWT employs two real wavelet transforms in parallel where the wavelets of one branch are the Hilbert transforms of the wavelets in the other. In this manner any input image can be decomposed into its 6 directional subbands. At each scale, the DT-CWT generates 6 directional subbands with complex coefficients, oriented at $\pm 15°$, $\pm 45°$, and $\pm 75°$. The real (R_i) and imaginary (C_i) parts of complex wavelets in the 6 directional subbands [17]. We have applied the 2D-DTCWT on the normalized iris images and combined the features at different resolution scales to form a feature vector that represents the iris image.

2.2 Signature recognition system

Approaches related to signature recognition fall into two categories according to the acquisition technique: offline and online. In offline (static) technique, an image of the signature is digitized with a an optical scanner or CCD camera. Whereas, the online (dynamic) signature identification technique tracks down trajectory and other time-sequence variables using specially designed tablets or other devices during the process of signing. Compared to the static handwriting image of offline approach, online approach keeps track of dynamic information during signing and thus has relatively higher classification rate.

2.2.1 Signature feature extraction

In this approach, coordinate trajectories (x[n], y[n]), n = 1,...,N_s and number of pen-ups are considered in the feature extraction process, where N_s is the duration of the signature in time samples. Signature trajectories are then normalized by shifting the minimum and maximum scores to scale between 0 and 1, respectively. Primarily, our interest was to find the most reliable and suitable set of dynamic features to be used in our approach, so we decided to consider global features. To achieve this aim, we have selected a collection of 32 global statistical features that have been widely used, studied, and reported in literature [18].

2.2.2 Rough sets based feature reduction

We adapted a dynamic reduct technique to synthesize a decision rule from decision table. The process of computing dynamic reduct can be seen as a combining normal reduct computation with resampling techniques. Simply its idea consists of three steps. The first step randomly sampled a family of subsystems from the universe. In the second step, it computes the reduction of each sample. The final step is to keep the reduct that occur most frequently because it is the most stable one. For more information, reader can refer to reference [13].

3 Feature level fusion of iris and signature

The next step is to concatenate the two feature vectors obtained which will naturally lead to a significant increase in dimension. The advantage behind the fusion of different modalities is to get a better representation of the subject through varying and complementary details. So, to address this obstacle, we need to find a scheme that keeps the complementary information in the fused features and reduce redundancies by decrease the dimensionality of the fused features. Thus, it is necessary to use feature selection techniques to remove redundant parameters. In this work, BPSO algorithm was proposed since it has been proven very robust and efficient for the task of feature reduction [10]. This section describes several schemes that we propose for feature level fusion of iris and online signature.

3.1 Suggested feature level scenarios

In this paper, we propose a simple iris-signature multi biometrics system based on feature level fusion. In real-world application, the feature set is generally large in

terms of dimensionality. Usually, the fused feature vector may be noisy and contain irrelevant or redundant information about the target classes. This may possibly degrade the performance of the classifiers. Furthermore, large feature vector also increases the storage cost and requires more computation time to process it. Feature selection in this case, is crucial to select an "optimized" subset of features from the original feature set based on certain objective function. Overall, feature selection removes redundant or irrelevant data while retaining classification accuracy.

Figures 2 and 3 show the block diagram of the proposed feature selection and fusion, which starts with extracting the features of iris and online signatures separately. In feature fusion scheme I, the proposed scheme starts with concatenating of the two features vectors before applying the PSO to select the most dominant features from these concatenated features. But as the fused feature values of vectors of signature and iris may exhibit significant variations both in their range and distribution, feature vector normalization is carried out. The objective behind feature normalization (also called range-normalization) is to modify the location (mean) and scale (variance) of the features values and to independently normalize each feature component to the range between 0 and 1 [19]. Finally, we measure the similarity between the reference and test patterns using a number of classifiers. In order to compare our approach with one of the most common approaches to feature selection, we used the principal component analysis (PCA) algorithm prior to the final classification stage in Scheme II. PCA is used for feature extraction to generate the most distinguishing features. It aims to find the projection directions maximizing the variance of a subspace, equivalent to finding the eigenvalues from the covariance matrix. PCA has proven to be a powerful tool for analyzing data, identifying patterns and expressing the data to highlight their differences.

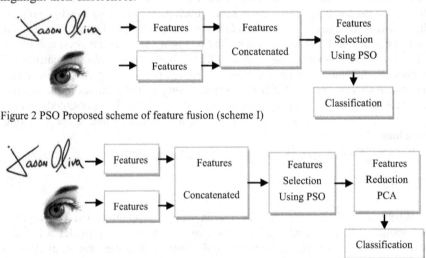

Figure 2 PSO Proposed scheme of feature fusion (scheme I)

Figure 3 PSO Proposed scheme of feature fusion including PCA (scheme II)

3.2 Feature selection using PSO

PSO is an evolutionary, stochastic, population-based optimization algorithm whose goal is to find a solution to an optimization problem in a search space. The PSO algorithm was developed by Kennedy and Eberhart in 1995 [20]. The main idea of PSO is inspired from the social behaviour of organisms, such as birds in a flock and fish in a school. The original intent was to simulate graphically the graceful but unpredictable movement of bird flocking. The PSO algorithm imitates the behaviour of flying birds and their means of information exchange to solve optimization problems. In PSO, each particle makes use of its own memory and knowledge gained by the swarm as a whole to find the best solution. Each potential solution is considered as a particle with a certain velocity, and "flies" through the problem space. Each particle adjusts its flight according to its own flying experience and its companions' flying experience [21]. Hence, the particle swarms find optimal path towards destination through the interaction of individuals in a population of particles.

PSO has been successfully applied to a wide range of difficult combinatorial optimization applications [22]. PSO proved to be both effective and efficient in feature selection applications in that particle swarms will discover the best feature combinations as they fly within the problem space.

3.2.1 Principles of PSO

The main objective of PSO is to optimize a given function called fitness function. Like evolutionary algorithms, PSO is initialized with a population of particles distributed randomly over the search space. Each particle corresponds to a point in the N-Dimension space. The ith particle is represented as $X_i = \{x_1, x_2, \ldots, x_N\}$. At every iteration, each particle is updated by two best values called pbest and gbest. pbest is the best position associated with the best fitness value of particle 'i' obtained so far and is represented as $p_{besti} = \{p_{besti1}, p_{besti2}, \ldots, p_{bestiN}\}$ with fitness function $f(pbesti)$. gbest is the best position among all the particles in the swarm. The rate of the position change (velocity) for particle 'i' is represented as $V_i = \{v_{i1}, v_{i2}, \ldots, v_{iN}\}$. The particle velocities are updated according to the following equations [20]:

$$v_{id}^{new} = w * v_{id}^{old} + C_1 * rand_1() * (p_{bestid} - x_{id}) + C_2 * rand_2() * (g_{bestg_{id}} - x_{id}) \qquad (1)$$

$$x_{id} = x_{id} + v_{id}^{new} \qquad (2)$$

Where id = 1, 2, . . . ,N. The inertia weight w controls the convergence behaviour of PSO. Optimizing the choice of inertia weights provides a balance between global and local explorations, and results in less iteration on average to find near optimal results. C1 and C2 are the acceleration constants used to pull each particle towards pbest and gbest. Adapting low values of C1 and C2 allows

the particle to roam far from best solutions, while adapting high values result in abrupt movements towards or past the target regions [23]. rand1() and rand2() are random numbers selected from a uniform distribution in the range [0.0, 1.0].

3.2.2 Binary PSO

PSO was originally developed for a space of continuous values and it therefore poses several problems for spaces of discrete values where the variable domain is finite. Kennedy and Eberhart [9] presented a discrete binary version of PSO for these discrete optimization problems. In the binary PSO, the particles are represented by binary values (0 or 1). Each particle velocity is updated according to the following equations:

$$S(V_{id}^{new}) = \frac{1}{1 + e^{-V_{id}^{new}}} \tag{3}$$

$$x_{id} = \begin{cases} 1 & if\ (rand < S(V_{id}^{new})) \\ 0 & otherwise \end{cases} \tag{4}$$

Where V_{id}^{new} denotes the particle velocity obtained from equation 1, function $S(V_{id}^{new})$ is a sigmoid transformation and *rand* is a random number selected from a uniform distribution U(0,1).

3.2.3 PSO-based feature selection algorithm

In this paper, the binary PSO searches for the most representative feature subset through the extracted feature space. The initial coding for each particle is randomly produced where each particle is coded to imitate a chromosome in a genetic algorithm; each particle was coded in a binary alphabetic string $P = F_1F_2 ...F_n$, $n = 1, 2, ..., m$; where m is the length of the fused feature vector. Each gene in the m-length chromosome represents the feature selection, "1" denotes that the corresponding feature is selected, otherwise denotes rejection. The m-genes in the particle represent the parameters to be iteratively evolved by PSO. In each generation, each particle (or individual) is evaluated, and a value of *fitness* is returned by a fitness function.

This evolution is driven by the fitness function F that evaluates the quality of evolved particles in terms of their ability to maximize the class separation term indicated by the scatter index among the different classes.

Let $w_1, w_2, ...w_L$ and $N_1, N_2, ...N_L$ denote the classes and number of samples within each class, respectively. Let and $M_1, M_2, ...M_L$ be the means of corresponding classes and the grand mean in the feature space, M_i can be calculated as:

$$M_i = \frac{1}{N_i} \sum_{j=1}^{N_i} W_j^{(i)}, \quad i = 1,2,...,L \tag{5}$$

where $W_j^{(i)}$, $i = 1,2,...,L$, represents the sample features from class w_i, and the grand mean M_o is:

$$M_o = \frac{1}{n} \sum_{i=1}^{L} N_i M_i \tag{6}$$

where n is the total number of images for all the classes. Thus the between class scatter fitness function F is computed as follows:

$$F = \sqrt{\sum_{i=1}^{L} (M_i - M_o)^t (M_i - M_o)} \tag{7}$$

As a result of this algorithm, the gene in the m-length chromosome which represents the feature selection is obtained. This gene is used to select features, where "1" denotes that the corresponding feature is selected, otherwise denotes rejection.

4 Experimental results

This section describes the experimental setup, including database and the assessment protocol that we have built in order to evaluate the proposed feature level fusion schemes.

4.1 Database

The first difficulty we are facing when working on multi-biometrics is the lack of real-user databases. As far our knowledge is concerned, there is no multimodal real-user database combining online signature and iris modalities available in the public domain. However, there exist few well established datasets for iris images, thus implying the combination of biometric modalities from different databases. Since both databases do not necessarily contain the same users, such combination results in the creation of virtual multimodal dataset, or so-called chimeric users.

Creating such chimeric users has lately been widely accepted and reasonable practice in the field of multimodal biometrics research as a way to overcome the problem of shortage of actual multimodal biometric databases. An investigation into the using of chimeric users to construct fusion classifiers in biometric authentication tasks was reported in [8] with the conclusion that a fusion operator derived from a chimeric-user database does not improve nor degrade the generalization performance (on real users) with respect to training it on real users.

We have created a 'virtual multimodal database' by aggregating two different database using online signature and iris modalities coming from two different

databases. A user from the online signature dataset is randomly associated with a user from the iris dataset, creating a virtual user with online signature and iris samples.

For online signature modality, we chose the database we have gathered in previous research [13]. From this database, we selected 108 different users from two different sessions. Each session consists of 10 samples for each user. For the iris modality, we chose the Chinese Academy of Sciences—Institute of Automation (CASIA) eye image database version 1.0 [26]. The CASIA database contains 756 frontal iris images of 108 classes with 7 images per each class taken from two sessions, and each session were taken with an interval of one month. In building our multimodal biometric database of online signature and iris, each virtual subject was associated with 7 samples of iris and online signature produced randomly from the iris and online signature samples of two subjects in the aforementioned databases. Thus, the resulting virtual multimodal biometric database consists of 108 subjects, so that each subject has 7 samples.

4.2 Results and discussion

As mentioned earlier, the first set of experiments (scheme I) is based on applying BPSO after fusing the features of the iris and signature. Whereas, the second feature fusion experiments (scheme II), study the effect of further reducing the same set of reduced set of features using PCA prior to classification. Note that for the feature fusion schemes I_a and II_a we have applied all the extracted signature features, while for the feature fusion schemes I_b and II_b we have applied the minimal reduced set of signature features. The classification phase was carried out to compare the performance of the: k-NN, Naïve Bayes and Support Vector Machine (SVM) classifiers.

Table 1 shows the best classification rate and the number of features, together with the classifier used for the of iris and signature features in unimodal system compared to the suggested fusion schemes. It is clear that the performance of the online signature unimodal system outperforms the iris unimodal model with FAR of 97.1% with 32 features and a FAR of 96.3% with 9 features using the Naïve Bayes classifier. Whilst, the iris achieved a FAR of 92.86% with a feature vector of 1040 2D-DTCWT coefficients using the SVM Gaussian RBF kernel.

Table 1. Comparative recognition rates of the different feature selection schemes

Method	Classifier	Number of features	Recognition Rate(%)
Iris alone	SVM-RBF	1040	92.86
Online signature alone	Naïve Bayes	32	97.1
Online signature alone	Naïve Bayes	9	96.3
Feature Fusion-Scheme I_a	SVM-RBF	50	98.14
Feature Fusion-Scheme I_b	SVM-RBF	45	93.78
Feature Fusion-Scheme II_a	k-NN	30	98.01
Feature Fusion-Scheme II_b	k-NN	72	96.29

Figure 4 shows the performance of feature fusion scheme I_a and scheme I_b. It is observed that, the best performance is noted for fusion scheme I_a was a FAR of 98.14% with the SVM-RBF kernel with a feature vector of 50, while the fusion scheme I_b registered a classification rate of 93.78% using 45 features using the SVM-RBF kernel.

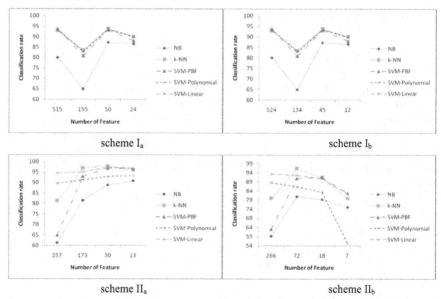

scheme I_a scheme I_b

scheme II_a scheme II_b

Figure 4 Graphical comparison of classification accuracies obtained from suggested schemes.

We also noticed that the BPSO-PCA-based fusion scheme shows similar performance as compared with the previous scheme. Nevertheless, the best performance is noted for fusion scheme II_a by k-NN classifier with a FAR of 98.01% and 30 features. It can be observed that the performance of any of the feature level fusion methods is superior to that of iris modality alone. More

importantly, the feature fusion schemes I_a and II_a showed a better performance as compared with the feature fusion schemes I_b and II_b. This indicates that the number of online signature features plays a significant role in classification.We also noticed that both schemes in most cases scored its best classification rates while using the 5th level of 2D DT-CWT decomposition with a feature vector of 80. It is worth noting that the BPSO-PCA-based fusion scheme (I_b and II_b) has slightly improved the classification performance. The best classification performance allows reducing the original feature space by 97% and hence it also reduces the computation time as compared with conventional methods. This demonstrates that the PSO based methods allow the same level of performance to be kept while reducing considerably the computation load.

5 Conclusion

In this paper, we have tackled the problem of feature level fusion in the context of multimodal biometrics. Our concern was to compare different fusion schemes and to provide an analysis of their comparative advantages in terms of performance and complexity. With this objective, we considered two independent modalities (iris and online signature) that are represented with different feature extraction techniques. We have shown that we can obtain a considerable improvement in terms of identification performance when appling the PSO feature selection scheme to the fused unimodal systems features before performing classification. The implementation of a BPSO algorithm reduced the number of features while keeping the same level of performance. Therefore, this paper offers new perspectives for multibiometric implementation for biometric traits which are efficiently represented in a high dimension feature space.

References

1. Ross, A. , Jain, A. K. :Multimodal Biometrics: An Overview. In Proc. of the 12th European Signal Processing Conf., pages 1221–1224, Sept. 2004.
2. Ross, A. , Nandakumar, K. , Jain, A. K. : Handbook of Multibiometrics. Springer- Verlag edition (2006).
3. Sanderson , C., Paliwal, K. K.: Information Fusion and Person Verification Using Speech and Face Information. Research Paper IDIAP-RR 02-33, IDIAP (2002).
4. Faundez-Zanuy, M. : Data fusion in biometrics. In: IEEE Aerospace and Electronic Systems Magazine, vol. 20, pp. 34-38 (2005).
5. Chen, Y., Li, Y., Cheng, X., Guo, L.: Survey and Taxonomy of Feature Selection Algorithms in Intrusion Detection System. In: Lipmaa, H., Yung, M., Lin, D. (eds.) Inscrypt 2006. LNCS, vol. 4318, pp. 153-167. Springer, Heidelberg (2006).
6. Krzysztof J. Cios, Witold Pedrycz, Roman W. Swiniarski and Lukasz A. Kurgan: Data Mining: A Knowledge Discovery Approach, pp. 133-233 (2007). Springer (2007).

7. Benediktsson, J. A. , Pesaresi, M. , Arnason, K. :Classification and feature extraction for remote sensing images from urban areas based on morphological transformations. IEEE Transactions on Geoscience and Remote Sensing, vol. 41, no. 9, pp. 1940-1949, Sept. 2003.
8. Li, W. Gang, W. , Liang and Y. , Chen W.: Feature selection based on KPCA, SVM and GSFS for face recognition. Proceedings of the International Conference on Advances in Pattern Recognition , pp. 344–350. (2005).
9. Kennedy, J. , Eberhart, R. C. :A discrete binary version of the particle swarm algorithm. In Proceedings of the IEEE International Conference on Computational Cybernetics and Simulation, pp. 4104 – 4108. (1997).
10. Wang, X., Yang, J. ,Teng, X., Xia, W., Jensen, B. :Feature selection based on rough sets and particle swarm optimization. Pattern Recognition Letters, vol. 28. pp. 459–471. (2007).
11. Garcia-Nieto, J. , Talbi, E.G. , Alba, E. , Jourdan, L. : A comparison between Genetic Algorithm and PSO approaches for Gene selection and classification of Microarray data. In: ACM (GECCO-07). pp. 427–429. (2007).
12. Almayyan, W. , Own, H.S.; Zedan, H. :Iris features extraction using dual-tree complex wavelet transform. International Conference of Soft Computing and Pattern Recognition (SoCPaR). pp.18-22, 7-10. (2010).
13. Al-Mayyan, W., Own, H.S., H. Zedan: Rough set approach to online signature identification. Digital Signal Processing 21(3): 477-485 (2011).
14. Daugman , J. : How iris recognition works, IEEE Trans. On Circuits and Systems for Video Technology. vol. 14, No. 1, pp. 21-30. (2004).
15. Wildes, R.P. : Iris recognition: an emerging biometric technology. Proceedings of the IEEE 85(9). pp. 1348–63. (1997).
16. Bowyer, K.W. , Hollingsworth, K. , Flynn, P. J. : Image Understanding for Iris Biometrics: A Survey. Computer vision and Image Understanding. vol. 110. Issue 2. pp. 281-307. (2008).
17. Kingsbury, N.: Image processing with complex wavelets. Philos. Trans. Roy. Soc. Lon. 357. pp. 2543–2560. (1999).
18. Kiran, G. V. , Kunte, R. S. R. , Samuel, S. : On Line Signature Verification System Using Probabilistic Feature Modelling. International Symposium on Signal Processing and its Application (ISSPA). pp.355-358, Kuala Lumpur, Malaysia, August 2001.
19. Nandakumar, k. : Integration of Multiple Cues in Biometric Systems. M.S. Thesis: Michigan State University (2005).
20. Kennedy, J. , Eberhart, R.C. : Particle swarm optimization. In: IEEE Int'l Joint Conf. on Neural Networks, Perth, Australia. (1995).
21. Venter, G. and Sobieszczanski-Sobieski, J.: Particle swarm optimization. Proceedings of the 43rd AIAA/ASME/ASCE/AHS/ASC Structures, Structural Dynamics, and Materials Conference, Denver, CO. (2002).
22. Shao-Rong , H. : Survey of particle swarm optimization algorithm. Computer Engineering and Design. Vol. 30, no. 8. pp. 1977-1980. (2009).
23. Raghavendra, R. , Drizzi, B. , Rao , A. , Kumar, H.: PSO versus AdaBoost for Feature Selection in Multimodal Biometrics. In Proceedings of the 3rd IEEE international conference on Biometrics: Theory, applications and systems. pp. 960-969. (2009).
24. Ramadan , R.M. , Abdel-Kader, R.F.: Face recognition using particle swarm optimization-based selected feature. International Journal of Signal Processing, Image Processing and Pattern Recognition. vol. 2, no. 2. pp. 51-65, June 2009.
25. Poh, N., Bengio, S.: Using chimeric users to construct fusion classifiers in biometric authentication tasks: An investigation. Technical report (2005).
26. Center for Biometrics and Security Research, CASIA Iris Image Database: http://www.sinobiometrics.com. (downloaded at 3.12.09).

Using Negation and Phrases in Inducing Rules for Text Classification

Stephanie Chua, Frans Coenen, Grant Malcolm, and Matías Fernando García-Constantino

Abstract An investigation into the use of negation in Inductive Rule Learning (IRL) for text classification is described. The use of negated features in the IRL process has been shown to improve effectiveness of classification. However, although in the case of small datasets it is perfectly feasible to include the potential negation of all possible features as part of the feature space, this is not possible for datasets that include large numbers of features such as those used in text mining applications. Instead a process whereby features to be negated can be identified dynamically is required. Such a process is described in the paper and compared with established techniques (JRip, NaiveBayes, Sequential Minimal Optimization (SMO), OlexGreedy). The work is also directed at an approach to text classification based on a "bag of phrases" representation; the motivation here being that a phrase contains semantic information that is not present in single keyword. In addition, a given text corpus typically contains many more key-phrase features than keyword features, therefore, providing more potential features to be negated.

Stephanie Chua
Department of Computer Science, University of Liverpool, Ashton Building, Ashton Street, L69 3BX Liverpool, UK, e-mail: s.chua@liverpool.ac.uk

Frans Coenen
Department of Computer Science, University of Liverpool, Ashton Building, Ashton Street, L69 3BX Liverpool, UK, e-mail: coenen@liverpool.ac.uk

Grant Malcolm
Department of Computer Science, University of Liverpool, Ashton Building, Ashton Street, L69 3BX Liverpool, UK, e-mail: grant@liverpool.ac.uk

Matías Fernando García Constantino
Department of Computer Science, University of Liverpool, Ashton Building, Ashton Street, L69 3BX Liverpool, UK, e-mail: mattgc@liverpool.ac.uk

M. Bramer et al. (eds.), *Research and Development in Intelligent Systems XXVIII*,
DOI 10.1007/978-1-4471-2318-7_11, © Springer-Verlag London Limited 2011

1 Introduction

Text mining is a well established component within the domain of Knowledge Discovery in Data (KDD) and especially data mining. One element of text mining is text classification where we wish to categorize documents according to a classifier generated using a training set. Many techniques have been proposed whereby the desired text classifier can be generated. Among the more popular techniques are the k-nearest neighbour (k-NN) [19], support vector machines (SVMs) [9], probabilistic Bayesian models [14, 19] and decision trees [8, 10] . The technique which is the focus of this paper is inductive rule learning (IRL) [1, 5]. The particular focus of the work described is IRL processes for text classification that incorporate an ability to dynamically include negated features in the rule learning process. The motivation here is twofold. Firstly, the inclusion of negated features in the IRL process can typically improve the quality of the resulting classifier. Indeed we can contrive text classification scenarios which can only be resolved by including negated features in the rule generation process (this was demonstrated in [4]). Secondly, the dynamic identification of candidate features that can be negated is seen as desirable as we do not wish to generate the complete set of potential negations a priori. In the case of datasets that have a small number of features, it is of course entirely feasible, and therefore justified, to include all potential feature negations as part of the "input"; however this is not justified in the case of datasets with very large numbers of features. The latter type of dataset is exemplified by the document collections to which text classification is typically applied. Such collections are typically represented, for text mining purposes, using the "bag of words" or "bag of phrases" representations. Document collections typically feature large numbers of keywords and even larger numbers of key-phrases. Consequently, the work described here is directed at the bag of phrases representation because this representation is likely to exhibit a greater number of potential features to be negated than in the case of the keyword representation. Thus, the objective of this paper is to evaluate the effectiveness of our proposed IRL mechanism against other machine learning techniques for text classification. In addition, the significance of using negation in IRL will be investigated, as well as, experimenting with the bag of phrases representation. An interesting point to evaluate include whether negated phrases can be more effective in text classification.

The potential inclusion of negated features in the IRL text classification process raises two issues. The first is the nature of the mechanism whereby we can identify the most appropriate negated features (without including all negated versions of the entire feature set). The second is the nature of the rule refinement strategies required to generate rules with and without negation (without using a fixed template as adopted in the case of some alternative approaches [15, 16]). A rule learning mechanism to include negation and a number of rule refinement strategies for addressing these issues are proposed and evaluated.

The rest of this paper is organized as follows. Section 2 describes some related work on IRL. Section 3 discusses our proposed mechanism for inductive rule learning with negation. Section 3.1 discusses the identification of negated features, and

Section 3.2 details the different rule refinement strategies used in our IRL approach. Section 4 discusses phrase extraction methods to extract phrases. The experimental setup is described in Section 5 and the results in Section 6. Section 7 concludes the paper.

2 Related Work

As noted in the previous section, many text classification techniques have been proposed. The technique at which the work described in this paper is directed is IRL. As in the case of some of the other techniques identified above, IRL offers the advantage that it is easily interpretable by human analysts. Many different IRL systems have been applied to the text classification problem. However, the focus in this paper is on systems that are capable of generating rules with negation. Examples of such systems include the Olex suite of systems [15, 16], and RIPPER (Repeated Incremental Pruning to Produce Error Reduction) [5].

The Olex suite was developed by Rullo et al. and is founded on the idea of using a fixed template that allows only one positive feature and zero or more negative features to generate rules. The suite includes Olex Greedy and OlexGA. OlexGreedy, as the name suggests, uses a "greedy", single stage, rule learning process [15]. One of the disadvantages of OlexGreedy, highlighted by the authors, is that the template approach is not able to express co-occurrences based on feature dependencies. Rullo et al. attempted to overcome this disadvantage by using conjunction of terms (coterms). However, the authors again reported that rules that were generated using the improved version could not share common features in the antecedent. Hence, the authors proposed OlexGA [16], which uses a genetic algorithm to induce a rule-based classifier. This version overcame the problems associated with OlexGreedy. However, the generated rules still adhere to the fixed template of "one positive feature , zero or more negative feature(s)". A criticism of Olex is that the use of such templates is somewhat restrictive. Our IRL system proposes a number of rule refinement strategies that impose no restrictions on the number of positive or negated features.

RIPPER is an IRL system which uses the covering algorithm to learn rules whereby, when a rule is generated, the examples "covered" by the rule are removed from the training set (the process then repeats until all examples are covered). RIPPER generates rules by greedily adding features to a rule until the rule achieves a 100% accuracy. This process tries every possible value of each feature and chooses the one with the highest information gain. Following this rule building phase is a rule pruning phase, whereby the generated rule is pruned using a pruning metric. On the surface, it does not look like RIPPER includes any mechanism for explicitly generating rules with negation. However, in the case of binary-valued features, a feature-value of zero (0) is interpreted as a negated feature (the absence of a feature). The approach proposed in this paper also uses the covering algorithm; however, for

reasons presented in Section 1, the search space does not include all possible negations of features from the feature set; instead these are identified as required.

3 Inductive Rule Learning with Negation

The proposed rule learning mechanism aims to improve the effectiveness of classifiers, comprising a small numbers of rules, by using both positive and negated features, while maintaining the simplicity and effectiveness of the covering algorithm. In the covering algorithm, rules are learned sequentially one at a time based on the training dataset. The documents "covered" by a rule learnt are then removed and the process is repeated until there are no more uncovered documents in the training set or there are no more unused features in the feature set. Rule refinement is a significant element of this approach. Suppose we have a rule $F \Rightarrow x$; in general, such a rule may cover both *positive* and *negative* documents: positive documents are documents in the training set that are correctly classified, while negative documents are those that are incorrectly classified. Rule refinement is used to obtain a more specialized rule $F \wedge l \Rightarrow x$. To prevent overfitting, or learning rules that are too precise, some stopping conditions to rule refinement were adopted. These conditions stop the rule refinement; (i) when a rule no longer covers negative documents, (ii) when the feature search space is empty or (iii) when the previous rule learnt has a higher or equal accuracy to that of the current rule learnt. Generating rules without negation is straightforward: we take l to be a conjunction of features that occur together in positive documents. However, generating rules with negation requires the identification of the feature to be negated. This will be discussed in Section 3.1. Our rule learning mechanism encompasses a number of strategies for rule refinement and these are discussed in Section 3.2.

3.1 Identifying Features

The discriminating power of a feature with respect to a class is usually evaluated using some statistical measure. In text classification, measures like chi-square (χ^2) and information gain (IG) are commonly used to select the most discriminating features with respect to a specific class.

We distinguish two strategies for feature selection: local and global. In local feature selection, ordered features that are local to a specific class are selected for learning. Global feature selection involves the selection of features from across all classes in a dataset. The maximum or weighted-average value of each feature's class-specific value is used to order and select features. In our experiments, despite a rigorous reduction factor of 0.9 (using only 10% of the features), global feature selection methods are still computationally expensive. We therefore focus on the local feature selection method.

In our proposed mechanism, during rule refinement, an appropriate feature is selected from the *local search space* of the rule. The search space contains features from both the positive and negative documents that are covered by the rule. Accordingly, we divide the search space into the following three sub-spaces.

1. **Unique Positive** (UP). Features that appear only in positive documents: we call these *unique positive* features.
2. **Unique Negative** (UN). Features that appear only in negative documents: we call these *unique negative* features.
3. **Overlap** (Ov). Features that are found in both positive and negative documents: we call these *overlap* features.

This division allows for the effective and efficient identification of positive or negated features to be used when refining rules. Note that for a given rule, the UP, UN and Ov sub-spaces may be empty, as the existence of these features depends upon the content of the documents covered by the rule.

When refining a rule, a feature from either the UP, UN or Ov sub-spaces can be selected to be added to the rule. If a UP or Ov feature is selected, it is simply added to the rule, and is not negated. If a UN feature is selected, then its negated form is added to the rule. When refining a rule with a UP or UN feature, we select the feature with the highest document frequency, i.e. the feature that occurs in the most covered documents. This ensures that the refined rule will cover the maximum possible number of positive documents at every round of refinement. When refining a rule with an Ov feature, we select the feature with the highest document frequency difference (i.e. positive document frequency minus negative document frequency). This is because an Ov feature occurs in both positive and negative documents and the feature that appears in the most positive documents and least negative documents will result in a refined rule that serves to maximise the number of positive documents.

3.2 Rule Refinement Strategies

There are a number of possible strategies for rule-refinement using the three sub-spaces, UP, UN and Ov. Here, we focus on eight of these. The first three strategies use only a single sub-space, from which they take their names: UP, UN and Ov. Table 1 shows a simple example of how the UP, UN and Ov strategies work.

Given that a sub-space may be empty, the UP, UN and Ov strategies may lead to refinement being prematurely halted in the absence of any features to be added to a rule. Two further strategies have been devised to address the empty sub-space problem: UP-UN-Ov and UN-UP-Ov. These strategies use a sequence of sub-space combinations and are labelled in the order that the sub-spaces are considered. Thus, UP-UN-Ov entails the use of UP features first; if the UP sub-space is empty, then UN features will be considered instead, and then the Ov features if the UN sub-space is also empty. The UN-UP-Ov strategy works in a similar manner, only inter-

Table 1 Example of rule refinement with UP, UN and Ov strategies

Feature set for class x = {bike, ride, harley, seat, motorcycles, honda}
Initial rule learnt = $bike \Rightarrow x$
The rule covers three documents (two positive documents and one negative document)

Doc 1 labelled class x = {bike, ride, motorcycles}
Doc 2 labelled class x = {seat, harley, bike, ride}
Doc 3 labelled class y = {bike, ride, honda}

Identify UP, UN and Ov features
UP feature(s) = {motorcycles, seat, harley}
UN feature(s) = {honda}
Ov feature(s) = {ride}

Strategies for rule refinement
Refine with UP = $bike \wedge motorcycle \Rightarrow x$
Refine with UN = $bike \wedge \neg honda \Rightarrow x$
Refine with Ov = $bike \wedge ride \Rightarrow x$

changing the order of UP and UN. In both cases, Ov is used last because using Ov features will always result in the coverage of at least one negative document. In both cases, if the first sub-space is not empty, then only features from that sub-space will be used for rule refinement. This means that the UP-UN-Ov strategy may produce the same results as the UP strategy, and similarly UN-UP-Ov may produce the same results as the UN strategy. For each rule to be refined, each of these five strategies may result in different rules. Our sixth strategy, BestStrategy, chooses the best rule (using accuracy with Laplace estimation) from the results of the first five strategies.

Each of the first five strategies refines a rule by selecting a feature from a particular sub-space; this refined rule is then further refined (using the same strategy) until some termination condition is met (e.g., the rule covers only positive documents, or further refinement produces a rule that is less accurate). Each of these strategies therefore corresponds to a depth-first search. A more exhaustive search through the possible rules is provided by our final two strategies. The first, BestPosRule, refines a rule by creating two versions of the original rule; one version by selecting a feature from the UP sub-space and another by selecting a feature from the Ov sub-space. Each of these rules is further refined in the same manner until the refined version is less accurate than the previous version. The rule with the best Laplace accuracy is then selected as the rule to be added to the ruleset. This strategy makes use of two sub-spaces during each refinement step and will only generate rules without negation. The second strategy, BestRule, is an extension of BestPosRule, where a third version of the rule to be refined is generated by selecting a feature from the UN sub-space. Thus, this strategy uses all three sub-spaces at each refinement step and may generate rules with negation. Rule refinement works in the same manner as in BestPosRule, but with an additional version where a feature from the UN sub-space is added. Again, the rule with the best Laplace accuracy will be the one added to the ruleset. Table 2 summarizes all the strategies described in this section.

Table 2 Summary of proposed rule refinement strategies

Strategy	Description	Sample rules
UP	Add a UP feature to refine a rule	$a \wedge b \Rightarrow x$
UN	Add a UN feature to refine a rule	$a \wedge \neg c \Rightarrow x$
Ov	Add an Ov feature to refine a rule	$a \wedge b \wedge d \Rightarrow x$
UP-UN-Ov	If UP is not empty, add a UP feature to refine a rule; Else If UN is not empty, add a UN feature to refine a rule; Else If Ov is not empty, add an Ov feature to refine a rule	$a \wedge b \Rightarrow x$
UN-UP-Ov	If UN is not empty, add a UN feature to refine a rule; Else If UP is not empty, add a UP feature to refine a rule; Else If Ov is not empty, add an Ov feature to refine a rule	$a \wedge b \wedge \neg c \Rightarrow x$
BestStrategy	Choose the best rule from the five rules generated by each UP, UN, Ov, UP-UN-Ov and UN-UP-Ov	$a \wedge b \wedge d \Rightarrow x$
BestPosRule	Generate two versions of rule; one refined with a UP feature and the other refined with an Ov feature. Choose the best between the two versions	$a \wedge b \wedge d \wedge e \Rightarrow x$
BestRule	Generate three versions of rule; one refined with a UP feature, one refined with a UN feature and the other refined with an Ov feature. Choose the best between the three versions	$a \wedge b \wedge \neg c \wedge \neg f \Rightarrow x$

4 The Bag of Phrases Representation

The use of the "bag of phrases" representation is motivated by the potential benefit of preserving semantic information that is not present in the "bag of words" representation. There are various methods that may be adopted to identify phrases for the bag of phrases representation. These methods tend to fall into two categories: linguistic phrase extraction and statistical phrase extraction. The former is based on linguistic patterns while the latter is based on statistical patterns.

Much previous work has reported on the use of phrases in text classification, albeit with mixed results. [6] investigated the use of linguistic phrases with both a naive bayes classifier (RAINBOW) and a rule-based classifier (RIPPER) and found that phrase features can improve classification at the expense of coverage. In [17], noun phrases and key phrases were extracted and used in RIPPER for text classification. The use of noun phrases was found to be only slightly better than the use of key words, while the use of key phrases was found to be slightly worse. In general, the authors reported no significant benefit from using phrases and concluded that more complex natural language processing methods were needed to identify them. In [2] phrases were extracted using a statistical word association based grammar, and an improvement over the use of the bag of words representation was reported using a naive bayes classifier. An n-gram word extractor was used in [13] to extract frequent phrases for classifying research paper abstracts using various classifiers; experiments showed that the bag of phrases representation was better than the bag of words representation for their dataset. [3] investigated the use of phrases for email classification and found that using phrases of size two gave the best classification

results. However, none of the above investigated the use of negated phrases with respect to IRL in text classification. For the work described here, two phrase extraction mechanisms were adopted.

The first approach was founded on n-gram extraction and operated as follows:

1. Preprocess the dataset by removing stop words, numbers, emails and symbols.
2. Extract n-grams from the preprocessed dataset.
3. Sort the extracted n-grams from each class in descending order according to their chi-square values.
4. Select the top 10% of the extracted n-grams from each class to be used as features for representation.

The experiments reported later in this paper extracted three different kinds of n-grams: 1-gram (which is essentially single keywords), 2-grams and 3-grams.

The second approach was a variation on the n-gram extraction approach:

1. Preprocess the dataset by removing numbers, emails and symbols. Stop words are not removed.
2. Extract all single keywords in the dataset (not including stop words).
3. Sort the extracted single keywords from each class in descending order according to their chi-square values.
4. Select the top 10% of the single keywords from each class and store in features list.
5. Based on the selected single keywords, extract phrases from the dataset that contain at least one keyword from the features list.
6. Sort the extracted phrases from each class in descending order according to their chi-square values.
7. Select the top 10% of the extracted phrases from each class to be used as features for representation.

This approach extracts sequences of words from the dataset that still had stop words in them. Each phrase that was extracted consisted of at least one single keyword. The experiments reported in the next section reported the use of a two-word (Phrase-2) and a three-word (Phrase-3) based phrase extraction.

5 Experimental Setup

The experiments that were conducted compared the use of our proposed rule learning mechanism and rule refinement strategies with that of JRip, NaiveBayes (NB) and Sequential Minimal Optimization (SMO) from the Waikato Environment for Knowledge Analysis (WEKA) machine learning workbench [7]. In addition, an OlexGreedy plug-in to WEKA [16] was also compared. χ^2 with a reduction factor of 0.9 was used as a dimensionality reduction method. Both the n-gram and phrase extraction methods described in the previous section were considered.

Two well known text classification datasets, the 20 Newsgroups [11] and Reuters-21578 Distribution 1.0 [12] were used for the evaluation. The 20 Newsgroups dataset is a collection of 19,997 documents, comprising news articles from 20 classes. There are 1,000 documents in each class with the exception of one class that contains 997 documents. In our experiments, this dataset was split into two non-overlapping datasets (hereafter, referred to as 20NG-A and 20NG-B), each comprising 10 classes (20NG-A has 10,000 documents and 20NG-B 9,997 documents). This dataset was split only for computational efficiency reasons as reported in Wang [18], by taking 10 classes for 20NG-A and the remaining 10 classes for 10NG-B. Therefore, 20NG-A and 20NG-B should be viewed as two separate datasets and the results should be considered in this context.

The Reuters-21578 Distribution 1.0 dataset is widely used in text classification. It consists of 21,578 documents and 135 classes. In our experiments for single-labelled text classification, the preparation of this dataset followed the method suggested by Wang [18], where the top ten most populated classes were identified and multi-labelled/non-text documents were removed from each class. This resulted in a dataset with only eight classes and 6,643 documents. Hereafter, this dataset is referred to as Reuters8.

Table 3 shows the number of features used with respect to each class in each dataset. The number of features used is the top 10% of the potential set of features ordered using χ^2 that can be used to describe a class. The number of features increases from 1-gram to 3-grams and similarly, less phrases are extracted for Phrase-2 as compared to Phrase-3.

6 Evaluation

This section details the evaluation of the results obtained from the experiments conducted. Our rule learning mechanism is denoted as RL with the identifier for the different rule refinement strategies used appended. The micro-averaged F1-measure from experiments using ten-fold cross validation are reported.

Table 4 gives the classification results for the 20NG-A dataset. The RL average was computed for ease of comparison with the other machine learning methods. In the RL mechanism, the strategies that generated rules with negation produced the best results using the 1-gram and Phrase-2 representations, while strategies that generated rules without negation came in top for all but 1-gram representation. Comparison of the n-gram approach when using the RL mechanism shows that when using the 2-grams representation the best results are produced, while the worst results were generated using the 3-grams representation. RL+BestStrategy produced slightly better results than all the other RL strategies when a 1-gram representation was used. It was also better than JRip, NaiveBayes and OlexGreedy but was slightly worse than SMO. For the 2-grams, 3-grams, Phrase-2 and Phrase-3 representations, the RL mechanism produced the top two best results as compared to JRip, NaiveBayes, SMO and OlexGreedy. When using JRip, NaiveBayes, SMO and OlexGreedy, the

Table 3 10% of all the total features extracted for each class in each dataset

Dataset/Classes	1-gram	2-grams	3-grams	Phrase-2	Phrase-3
20NG-A					
rec.motorcycles	1205	4666	5197	1631	3247
talk.religion.misc	1597	7743	8836	3269	7334
sci.electronics	1208	5231	5824	1914	3740
alt.atheism	1442	7522	8628	3252	7530
misc.forsale	1150	4256	4908	2003	3749
sci.med	1837	8408	9524	3250	6553
talk.politics.mideast	1922	11433	13270	5613	12494
comp.sys.ibm.pc.hardware	1069	4929	5892	2404	5281
rec.sport.baseball	1086	5439	6369	2650	5507
comp.windows.x	1713	8377	9934	4260	8769
20NG-B					
comp.graphics	1395	6638	7723	2938	5919
comp.sys.mac.hardware	1062	4685	5421	2036	4371
rec.sport-hockey	1250	6738	8295	3560	7208
sci.crypt	1539	8000	9333	3399	7487
sci.space	1629	8287	9487	3198	6453
talk.politics.guns	1676	8282	9536	3354	7417
comp.os.ms-windows.misc	2709	10945	13001	6427	13864
rec.autos	1231	5318	5986	1905	3909
talk.politics.misc	1769	10312	11937	4090	9350
soc.religion.christian	1640	9868	11344	4756	11386
Reuters8					
acq	1283	9236	12724	5153	12579
crude	630	3451	4397	1694	3825
earn	1040	5607	8132	3298	8074
grain	263	820	925	257	485
interest	340	1473	1830	688	1542
money-fx	526	2885	3632	1494	3440
ship	365	1164	1310	448	851
trade	597	3488	4451	1780	4210

best results were produced using the 1-gram (keyword only) representation and the worst using the 3-grams representation.

The performance for the RL mechanism in the case of the 20NG-B dataset in Table 5 showed that the strategies that generated rules with negation came in the top two for all the representations, while strategies that generated rules without negation came top for all the representations with exception of the 1-gram representation. The 2-gram representation was better than 1-gram and 3-grams for the RL mechanism. Similar to the 20NG-A dataset, when using JRip, NaiveBayes, SMO and OlexGreedy, the best results were produced when using the 1-gram representation and the worst using the 3-grams representation. The RL+BestRule strategy was slightly better than the other RL strategies, as well as the JRip, NaiveBayes and OlexGreedy for the 1-gram representation; but was worse than the SMO. The RL mechanism again came into the top two when the 2-grams, 3-grams, Phrase-2 and

Table 4 Micro-averaged F1-measure for the 20NG-A dataset using both n-grams and phrases representation (top two best results shown in **bold**)

Method/Rep	1-gram	2-grams	3-grams	Phrase-2	Phrase-3
RL + UP	0.800	0.828	0.786	**0.920**	**0.873**
RL + UN	0.810	0.832	0.793	0.898	0.859
RL + Ov	0.803	**0.836**	**0.796**	0.894	0.859
RL + UP-UN-Ov	0.800	0.826	0.783	**0.920**	**0.873**
RL + UN-UP-Ov	0.810	0.832	0.788	0.901	0.862
RL + BestStrategy	**0.830**	0.833	0.791	**0.911**	0.864
RL + BestPosRule	0.824	**0.837**	**0.794**	0.907	**0.866**
RL + BestRule	0.821	0.831	0.789	0.910	0.864
RL Average	0.812	0.832	0.790	0.908	0.865
JRip	0.760	0.665	0.612	0.785	0.665
NaiveBayes	0.636	0.603	0.480	0.704	0.587
SMO	**0.849**	0.814	0.759	0.905	0.853
OlexGreedy	0.824	0.729	0.580	0.862	0.714

Phrase-3 representations were used, as compared to JRip, NaiveBayes, SMO and OlexGreedy.

Table 5 Micro-averaged F1-measure for the 20NG-B dataset using both n-grams and phrases representation (top two best results shown in **bold**)

Method/Rep	1-gram	2-grams	3-grams	Phrase-2	Phrase-3
RL + UP	0.844	**0.873**	0.827	**0.933**	**0.891**
RL + UN	0.825	0.862	**0.830**	0.911	0.881
RL + Ov	0.824	0.866	**0.831**	0.908	0.880
RL + UP-UN-Ov	0.844	**0.873**	0.826	**0.933**	**0.891**
RL + UN-UP-Ov	0.823	0.862	0.828	0.914	0.882
RL + BestStrategy	0.861	**0.869**	0.829	**0.920**	**0.884**
RL + BestPosRule	0.858	**0.869**	0.829	0.917	0.882
RL + BestRule	**0.862**	**0.869**	**0.830**	0.919	0.883
RL Average	0.843	0.868	0.829	0.919	0.884
JRip	0.808	0.754	0.694	0.844	0.746
NaiveBayes	0.656	0.654	0.540	0.734	0.604
SMO	**0.892**	0.858	0.800	0.895	0.873
OlexGreedy	0.845	0.780	0.619	0.890	0.758

The results for the Reuters8 dataset in Table 6 showed a slightly different trend than that for 20NG-A and 20NG-B. In the RL mechanism, the strategies that generated rules with negation produced the best top two results for 2-grams and 3-grams while strategies that generated rules without negation came in the top two for Phrase-2 and Phrase-3 and top in 3-grams. Again, 2-grams was still the best repre-

sentation for the RL mechanism. However, 3-grams seemed to be slightly better for some of the strategies as compared to 1-gram. While JRip, SMO and OlexGreedy showed decreasing classification results in the order of 1-gram to 3-grams, Naive-Bayes had the best results when 2-grams was used, as opposed to 1-gram and 3-grams. The RL mechanism produced the best top two results for all representations except for 1-gram. In the 1-gram representation, the top two results were obtained using SMO and JRip. In fact, SMO had the best results for all the representations except for 3-grams.

Table 6 Micro-averaged F1-measure for the Reuters8 dataset using both n-grams and phrases representation (top two best results shown in **bold**)

Method/Rep	1-gram	2-grams	3-grams	Phrase-2	Phrase-3
RL + UP	0.822	0.879	0.851	**0.929**	**0.908**
RL + UN	0.842	0.873	0.862	0.908	0.887
RL + Ov	0.860	0.871	**0.867**	0.898	0.890
RL + UP-UN-Ov	0.822	0.879	0.851	**0.929**	**0.908**
RL + UN-UP-Ov	0.848	0.871	0.857	0.908	0.887
RL + BestStrategy	0.877	0.884	0.861	0.922	0.906
RL + BestPosRule	0.882	0.885	0.859	0.923	0.904
RL + BestRule	0.822	**0.887**	**0.863**	0.923	0.907
RL Average	0.847	0.879	0.859	0.918	0.900
JRip	**0.896**	0.844	0.735	0.907	0.854
NaiveBayes	0.775	0.802	0.698	0.843	0.799
SMO	**0.932**	**0.911**	0.840	**0.953**	**0.916**
OlexGreedy	0.883	0.875	0.787	0.915	0.875

The results obtained from the experiments suggested that when the RL mechanism was used to learn rules, the use of the phrase representations was beneficial with respect to text classification, particularly phrases of size two. This stemmed from the fact that, while the 1-gram representation was good enough as a representation for text classification, the rich nature of natural language text provided the use of phrases with the advantage of preserving semantic information that was not present in single keywords. However, three words appearing in sequence were likely to be occurring less frequently and too specific, and thus not appropriate for text classification. 2-grams in general could occur more frequently and serve to segregate two distinct classes when this could not be achieved using 1-gram. This however did not hold true for JRip, NaiveBayes, SMO and OlexGreedy where decreasing effectiveness was recorded when using 1-gram to 3-grams. All the techniques compared also showed that Phrase-2 was better than Phrase-3, strengthening the argument that any phrase longer than two was not effective for classification.

In the 20NG-A and 20NG-B dataset, the best RL strategy using the 1-gram representation was that which generated rules with negation and was competitive with SMO. In representations longer than one, strategies that generated rules without negation were slightly better in the 20NG-A and 20NG-B datasets. This suggests

that the use of negated features is more effective when single keyword representation is used and less effective when the phrase representation is used. Single keywords can be quite common across different classes and thus, the use of negated features which are unique to other classes to learn rules that exclude documents from other classes seems to be effective. However, when phrases are used in the representation, the use of negation becomes "redundant", due to the fact that a phrase itself can be unique enough to differentiate documents from other classes. A different scenario is depicted in the Reuters8 dataset though. For the Reuters8 dataset, the RL strategy which generated rules with negation was slightly better than the others when the 2-gram representations was adopted, but came in second for all the other representations. This could suggest that more common 2-grams occur across the different classes in the dataset.

As expected, SMO produced good classification results, as support vector machines have been shown to be one of the best techniques for text classification. It was the best technique for the 1-gram representation, but was outperformed by the RL mechanism for all the other representations for the 20NG-A and 20NG-B datasets. It was again the best technique for the Reuters8 dataset with respect to all representations except 3-grams. NaiveBayes consistently delivered the worst performance with respect to all datasets and all representations. The RL mechanism outperformed both JRip and OlexGreedy in all cases except for the 1-gram representation in the Reuters8 dataset where they were closely competitive.

7 Conclusion

An investigation into IRL with negation and phrases has been described. We have proposed an IRL mechanism, based on the covering algorithm, that includes a number of strategies for rule refinement. These strategies were devised based on the division of the search space into three different sub-spaces: UP, UN and Ov. A number of these strategies were designed to learn rules with negation. Experiments were carried out to evaluate the effectiveness of our IRL mechanism against that of other machine learning techniques. Interestingly, the evaluation showed that our IRL mechanism outperformed all the other machine learning techniques that were compared and was competitive with SMO. The experiments also aimed at investigating the effectiveness of rules with negation, as well as the bag of phrases representations for text classification. It was found that rules with negation were more effective when the single keyword representation was used and less prominent when the phrase representation was used. The use of phrases of size two was found to be beneficial for text classification while phrases longer than two seemed to be too unique to be useful.

References

1. Apté, C., Damerau, F. J., Weiss, S. M.: Automated learning of decision rules for text categorization. In: ACM Transactions on Information Systems **12**, 233-251 (1994)
2. Bakus, J., Kamel, M.: Document classification using phrases. In: Caelli, T. and Amin, A. and Duin, R. and de Ridder, D. and Kamel, M. (eds.): Structural, Syntactic, and Statistical Pattern Recognition, Lecture Notes in Computer Science, vol. 2396. Springer Berlin/Heidelberg, pp. 341-354 (2002)
3. Chang, M., Poon, C. K.: Using phrases as features in email classification. In: Journal of Systems and Software, Elsevier Science Inc., **82**, pp. 1036-1045 (2009)
4. Chua, S., Coenen, F, Malcolm, G.: Classification Inductive Rule Learning with Negated Features. In: Proceedings of the 6th International Conference on Advanced Data Mining and Applications (ADMA'10), Part 1, Springer LNAI, pp. 125-136 (2010)
5. Cohen, W.: Fast effective rule induction. In: Proceedings of the 12th Int. Conf. on Machine Learning (ICML), pp. 115-123, Morgan Kaufmann (1995)
6. Fürnkranz, J., Mitchell, T., Riloff, E.: A case study in using linguistic phrases for text categorization on the WWW. In: Working Notes of the AAAI/ICML Workshop on Learning for Text Categorization, AAAI Press, pp. 5-12 (1998)
7. Hall, M., Frank, E., Holmes, G., Pfahringer, B., Reutemann, P., Witten, I. H.: The WEKA data mining software: An update. In: SIGKDD Explorations **11** 10-18 (2009)
8. Holmes, G., Trigg, L.: A diagnostic tool for tree based supervised classification learning algorithms. In: Proceedings of the 6th Int. Conf. on Neural Information Processing (ICONIP), pp. 514-519 (1999)
9. Joachims, T.: Text categorization with support vector machines: Learning with many relevant features. In: Proceedings of the 10th European Conf. on Machine Learning (ECML), pp. 137-142 (1998)
10. Johnson, D. E., Oles, F. J., Zhang, T., Goetz, T.: A decision-tree-based symbolic rule induction system for text categorization. In: The IBM Systems Journal, Special Issue on AI **41** 428-437 (2002)
11. Lang, K.: Newsweeder: Learning to filter netnews. In: Proceedings of the 12th Int. Conf. on Machine Learning, pp. 331-339 (1995)
12. Lewis, D. D.: Reuters-21578 text categorization test collection, Distribution 1.0, README file (v 1.3). Available at http://www.daviddlewis.com/resources/testcollections/reuters21578/readme.txt (2004)
13. Li, Z., Li, P., Wei, W., Liu, H., He, J., Liu, T., Du, X.: AutoPCS: A phrase-based text categorization system for similar texts. In: Li, Q., Feng, L., Pei, J., Wang, S., Zhou, X., Zhu, Q.-M. (eds.): Advances in Data and Web Management, Lecture Notes in Computer Science, vol. 5446. Springer Berlin/Heidelberg, pp. 369-380 (2009)
14. McCallum, A., Nigam, K.: A comparison of event model for naive Bayes text classification. In: Proceedings of the AAAI-98 Workshop on Learning for Text Categorization, pp. 41-48 (1998)
15. Rullo, P., Cumbo, C., Policicchio, V. L.: Learning rules with negation for text categorization. In: Proceedings of the 22nd ACM Symposium on Applied Computing, pp. 409-416. ACM (2007)
16. Rullo, P., Policicchio, V., Cumbo, C., Iiritano, S.: Olex: Effective rule learning for text categorization. In: Transaction on Knowledge and Data Engineering, **21:8** 1118-1132 (2009)
17. Scott, S., Matwin, S.: Feature engineering for text classification. In: Proceedings of the 16th Int. Conf. on Machine Learning (ICML), pp. 379-388 (1999)
18. Wang, Y. J.: Language-independent pre-processing of large documentbases for text classifcation. PhD thesis (2007)
19. Yang, Y., Liu, X.: A re-examination of text categorization methods. In: Proceedings of the 22nd ACM Int. Conf. on Research and Development in Information Retrieval, pp. 42-49 (1999)

Choosing a Case Base Maintenance Algorithm using a Meta-Case Base

Lisa Cummins and Derek Bridge

Abstract In Case-Based Reasoning (CBR), case base maintenance algorithms remove noisy or redundant cases from case bases. The best maintenance algorithm to use on a particular case base at a particular stage in a CBR system's lifetime will vary. In this paper, we propose a meta-case-based classifier for selecting the best maintenance algorithm. The classifier takes in a description of a case base that is to undergo maintenance, and uses meta-cases—descriptions of case bases that have undergone maintenance—to predict the best maintenance algorithm. For describing case bases, we use measures of dataset complexity. We present the results of experiments that show the classifier can come close to selecting the best possible maintenance algorithms.

1 Introduction

In Case-Based Reasoning (CBR), *case base editing* is a form of *case base maintenance* in which algorithms use heuristics to select cases to delete from case bases. In the context of using CBR for classification, *noise reduction algorithms* seek to delete noisy cases, with the goal of increasing classification accuracy; *redundancy reduction algorithms* seek to delete redundant cases, with the goal of increasing retrieval efficiency while, as much as possible, not harming classification accuracy.

As is apparent from the previous paragraph, case base maintenance is a multi-objective optimization problem. An algorithm cannot, in general, maximize both the number of cases it deletes and the accuracy of the resulting case base. To see this in extreme form, imagine an algorithm that proposes deletion of all but one

Lisa Cummins
Department of Computer Science, University College Cork, Ireland, e-mail: lec1@cs.ucc.ie

Derek Bridge
Department of Computer Science, University College Cork, Ireland, e-mail: d.bridge@cs.ucc.ie

M. Bramer et al. (eds.), *Research and Development in Intelligent Systems XXVIII*,
DOI 10.1007/978-1-4471-2318-7_12, © Springer-Verlag London Limited 2011

case: deletion has been maximized but a case-based classifier will now incorrectly predict the class of all target problems whose true class is different from the class of the case that remains in the case base.

In our previous work, we proposed two strategies for investigating the trade-off between these two objectives [5]. One was to compute the *Pareto front*, i.e. those algorithms not dominated by any other algorithms. The other was to combine the percentage of cases deleted and the percentage accuracy of the case base after maintenance into a single number. We proposed to use their *harmonic mean*. The harmonic mean penalizes large differences between the two values so that a high mean is only produced if both individual values are high. In this way, we identify algorithms which have a high value for both accuracy and deletion. The disadvantage of the more conventional *arithmetic mean* is that it can produce similar values for, e.g., an algorithm with very high accuracy but very low deletion and an algorithm with medium deletion and accuracy. We found empirically that algorithms with high harmonic mean tended to correspond to the subset of those on the Pareto front which struck a good balance between deletion and accuracy.

Most case base maintenance algorithms are composites which combine a noise reduction phase and a subsequent redundancy reduction phase. The three most common are:

Brighton & Mellish's Iterative Case Filtering algorithm (ICF) [3]: ICF uses the Repeated Edited Nearest Neighbour algorithm (RENN) [26] to remove noisy cases. RENN regards a case as noisy if it has a different class from the majority of its k nearest neighbours. After running RENN, ICF then removes redundant cases. It regards 'interior' cases, i.e. ones within clusters of same-class cases, as redundant ones, and aims to retain cases on the boundaries between classes because these cases are important for classification accuracy. Specifically, the ICF redundancy reduction phase removes cases that are solved by more cases than they themselves solve.

McKenna & Smyth's algorithm (RC) [18]: RC, like ICF, uses RENN to remove noisy cases. But its redundancy reduction phase is quite different. It aims to retain a case if it is surrounded by many cases of the same class, while treating as redundant, and deleting, those that surround it.

Delany & Cunningham's Case Base Editing algorithm (CBE) [6]: CBE's first phase uses Blame-Based Noise Reduction (BBNR), which regards a case as noisy if it causes other cases to be mis-classified. CBE's second phase uses Conservative Redundancy Reduction (CRR), which, like ICF, regards 'interior' cases as redundant. But CRR has a different heuristic from ICF: CRR removes cases that solve other cases.

There are many other possible algorithms—indeed, in our own earlier work we defined a constructive framework called MACE (Maintenance by a Committee of Experts), using a grammar of maintenance algorithms, which defines an infinite set of case base maintenance algorithms [5].

Their different heuristics give case base maintenance algorithms different biases. It is well-known that the algorithms perform differently on different case bases (see,

e.g., [3, 5]): one size does not fit all in case base maintenance. Additionally, it may be that even the same case base may need to undergo maintenance by different algorithms at different points in its lifetime. For example, a case base developed from a legacy database may require noise removal in its early stages to make it cleaner, but redundancy removal as it matures and collects more experience. The research problem that we tackle in this paper is: how to choose a good maintenance algorithm for a given case base at a given time.

Imagine that we collect experience across the CBR community to say which algorithm or algorithms worked well for a case base at a particular stage in its lifetime. With this experience, we could train a decision-support system and then use this system to assist the human user in selecting maintenance algorithms in the future. In this paper we set out to build such a system and use it to help us to solve the problem of choosing which maintenance algorithm to use for a given case base.

In developing such a decision-support system we have a number of decisions to make. One decision is whether to formulate the problem as one of regression or of classification. We could run different maintenance algorithms on a sample of case bases and measure values such as the percentage of deletion and the difference between the original case base classification accuracy and the accuracy of the case base after maintenance. From this training data, we could then build a system that uses *regression* to predict deletion and accuracy values for a given maintenance algorithm and case base. Alternatively, if we could make a judgement about which algorithm works best for a given case base, we could run different algorithms on sample case bases and pick the best algorithm for each. From this training data, we could then build a system that uses *classification* to predict which algorithm is best to use for a given case base.

Another decision is what type of regression or classification system to use to make the predictions. We could use, for example, a neural net, a rule-based system, a decision tree or a CBR system.

We must decide also how we will describe case bases—both those in the training set from which the decision-support system is built, and those that are to undergo maintenance by an algorithm recommended by the decision-support system.

There is an obvious alternative to training a decision-support system using previous case base maintenance experience. Whenever it is deemed that a case base requires maintenance, we could simply run all maintenance algorithms on copies of the case base and choose whichever performs best, e.g. whichever has the highest harmonic mean of the percentage of cases deleted and post-maintenance accuracy. But this is only feasible if the case base is small, if the case base maintenance algorithms do not take long to run and, most especially, if there is only a small, finite number of case base maintenance algorithms. In general, however, there is a very large number of algorithms. As we said earlier, our MACE framework defined an infinite number. But even if we ignore the most complex algorithms that MACE defines, it is important to realise that we are still left with a large number—more than just the three that we use in the experiments that illustrate the feasibility of our approach in this paper.

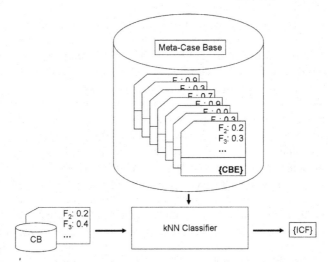

Fig. 1 Maintenance algorithm selection as meta-case-based classification

Our goals in this work are to find a way to describe case bases and then to establish the feasibility of training a decision-support system for choosing a maintenance algorithm for a given case base. Comparing different decision-support systems (regression versus classification, neural nets versus rules and so on), and using more than just three candidate maintenance algorithms, is left to future work. We focus on the feasibility of a decision-support system that is a classifier and we use case-based classification. We call this *meta-case-based classification*, since we are performing case-based classification but doing so for case base maintenance.

In Section 2, we describe our meta-case-based classifier for case base maintenance. Sections 3 and 4 describe two sets of experiments. Then Sections 5 and 6 describe related work and ideas for future work.

2 Maintenance Algorithm Selection as Meta-Case-Based Classification

To perform meta-case-based classification, we need to assemble a case base to use for predicting maintenance algorithms. This is a case base whose cases describe other case bases (Figure 1). We call such a case base a *meta-case base*, and we refer to the cases it contains as *meta-cases*. Each meta-case has a *meta-problem description* and a *meta-solution*. The meta-problem description is made up of the values for *meta-attributes*. A meta-case's meta-solution contains the name or names of the best maintenance algorithms (of those tested) for the case base that this meta-case describes.

2.1 Meta-Problem Description

Each meta-case describe a case base. Its meta-problem description comprises values for a set of meta-attributes. The meta-attributes must characterize the case base that the meta-case describes in a way that is likely to be predictive of the best case base maintenance algorithm. There is a body of work that describes dataset complexity measures, each of which characterizes a dataset in a different way. In this paper, we explore the feasibility of using these complexity measures as the meta-attributes in our meta-case based classifier.

Ho & Basu survey many of the geometrical dataset complexity measures [12, 13]. They divide the measures which they survey into three categories depending on what they focus on:

Measures of overlap of attribute values: These measures look at how effective the attributes are at discriminating between the classes.

Measures of separability of classes: These measures look at how separable the classes are by estimating the length and linearity of the class boundaries.

Measures of geometry, topology and density of manifolds: These measures characterize the position, shape, overlap and density of the manifolds that contain the instances of each class.

Subsequently, Orriols-Puig et al. have made available DCoL, the Data Complexity Library, which is an open-source C++ implementation of thirteen measures based on those in the Ho & Basu survey [19].[1] We have augmented these with four more, drawing from the CBR literature: we define two from Massie et al.'s complexity profile measure [17]; then there is Fornells et al.'s separability emphasis measure [8]; and we define another from Smyth & McKenna's notion of case base competence [24]. Table 1 summarizes these seventeen measures. Our four new measures are C_1, C_2, N'_5 and T_3. Their definitions can be found in [4]. Additionally, we found it necessary to make changes to the definitions of five of the measures to make them more fit for purpose. These are the ones with primes in their names (e.g. F'_2) in Table 1. The revised definitions can be found in [4].

Table 1 also indicates which measures can be computed for multi-class classification datasets (where there are more than two classes) and which can be computed on datasets whose attributes are symbolic-valued and not just numeric- or Boolean-valued. In this paper, we use just the twelve measures that can handle multi-class classification datasets and symbolic-valued attributes, since these are common in CBR. However, it is possible that not all of the complexity measures may be predictive of the best maintenance algorithm. Equally, two or more measures may compute very similar properties of the case base, rendering one or more measures redundant; to use several similar measures would give extra weight to that property of the case base. We use *feature selection* as a way to choose a good subset of the measures.

There has been much research done in the area of feature selection [1, 11, 16]. There are three types of feature selection algorithms: wrapper, filter and embedded

---

[1] http://dcol.sourceforge.net/

Table 1 The dataset complexity measures that we use as candidate meta-attributes

Measure	Description	Multi-class	Symbolic
F_1	Maximum Fisher's Discriminant Ratio	*Not DCoL*	No
F_2'	Volume of Overlap Region	Yes	Yes
F_3'	Maximum Attribute Efficiency	Yes	Yes
F_4'	Collective Attribute Efficiency	Yes	Yes
N_1'	Fraction of Instances on a Boundary	Yes	Yes
N_2	Ratio of Average Intra/Inter Class Distance	Yes	Yes
N_3	Error Rate of a 1NN Classifier	Yes	Yes
L_1	Minimized Sum of Error Distance of a Linear Classifier	*Not DCoL*	*Not DCoL*
L_2	Training Error of a Linear Classifier	*Not DCoL*	*Not DCoL*
C_1	Complexity Profile	Yes	Yes
C_2	Similarity-Weighted Complexity Profile	Yes	Yes
N_5'	Separability Emphasis Measure	Yes	Yes
L_3	Nonlinearity of a Linear Classifier	*Not DCoL*	No
N_4	Nonlinearity of a 1NN Classifier	Yes	No
T_1'	Fraction of Maximum Covering Spheres	Yes	Yes
T_2	Number of Instances per Attribute	Yes	Yes
T_3	Dataset Competence	Yes	Yes

[11]. Wrappers use a model to evaluate the predictive power of subsets of the attributes and choose the best attribute subset according to this model. Filters instead rely on general characteristics of the data to choose and evaluate a subset. Examples of these characteristics include correlation between attributes and mutual information. Embedded attribute selection methods are similar to wrappers in that they use a model to evaluate a set of attributes. However, with embedded methods, the feature selection is built into the learning process itself, while wrappers perform feature selection as a preprocessing step before learning takes place.

There are also three types of search strategies used by feature selection algorithms: complete, sequential and random. Complete search guarantees to find the optimal attribute subset. Sequential search gives up completeness and therefore may miss optimal subsets, but is faster than a complete search. Random search starts with a random subset and either continues with sequential search by adding or removing attributes, or generates another random subset and retains the better subset.

Since the predictive accuracy of a k-NN classifier is a suitable criterion to use to evaluate attribute subsets, we use a wrapper algorithm. We use a best-first search algorithm (hence, sequential search), which picks the most promising complexity measure at each point. It begins with an empty set and tests the accuracy of the classifier using each measure as a single meta-attribute separately. The accuracy of the classifier for each meta-attribute is measured by leave-one-out cross-validation. On the basis of the accuracies obtained by using each as a meta-attribute, the feature selection algorithm picks the best measure, and adds it to the empty set of selected meta-attributes. It repeats in order to choose further measures that become meta-attributes, stopping when there is no measure that can be added to the set of meta-attributes to improve accuracy.

2.2 Meta-Solution

The best maintenance algorithm or algorithms for a case base are taken to be the meta-solution in the corresponding meta-case. In this section we look at how to choose which maintenance algorithms are considered to be the best for a case base.

We have already acknowledged that there is an infinite number of maintenance algorithms which can be used to maintain a case base. However, since it is not possible to run an infinite number of maintenance algorithms on a case base to see which one works best, we need to choose a subset of candidate algorithms on which we base our predictions.

The set of candidate algorithms depends on what the person maintaining the case base hopes to achieve. If the focus is on deleting noise, the candidates might only contain noise reduction algorithms such as RENN and BBNR; if the focus is on aggressive deletion, the candidates may be composites like RC; for more careful and conservative deletion, candidates may be composites like CBE.

Once a set of candidate algorithms is chosen, each of the candidate algorithms is run on a sample of existing case bases. For each case base, we then need to decide which of the algorithms are 'winners' so that they can become the meta-solution. We have already discussed the problem of deciding on the best algorithm: an algorithm that does well in maintaining or improving accuracy may not perform much deletion, and an algorithm that deletes a large percentage of the case base may not maintain good accuracy. We have argued that the harmonic mean of the two provides a good balance [5]. Therefore a good choice for the meta-solution would be a set that contains the names of the maintenance algorithms whose resulting case bases give the highest harmonic mean value. Alternatively, a weighted harmonic mean can be used to bias the choice towards accuracy or deletion if either one was more of a priority for the person maintaining the case base.

2.3 Meta-Case-Based Classification

Assume that we have taken a sample of existing case bases. We have turned each one into a meta-case. Specifically, for each case base in the sample, we have computed the values of the dataset complexity measures, which become the values of candidate meta-attributes; we have run a set of candidate algorithms and the meta-solution is the set that contains the case base maintenance algorithm or algorithms with the highest harmonic mean. Then, on the meta-case base, we have run a feature selection algorithm to decide which of the candidate meta-attributes should be used by this classifier. Now we are ready to use this meta-case base for decision-support.

When we are presented with a case base that requires maintenance, we turn this case base into a query for our meta-case-based classifier. First, we compute the values of the dataset complexity measures on the case base. Obviously, we only need to compute the values of those measures that were selected by feature selection. This gives us the values of the meta-attributes of the query. We then use our meta-case

base to classify the query using k-NN: k similar cases are retrieved from the meta-case base and the predicted algorithm is the outcome of a similarity-weighted vote among the algorithms in the meta-solutions of these k cases. The result of the vote will be the maintenance algorithm or algorithms which the system considers to be the best one to use for that case base.

Since all the meta-attributes are numeric-valued, we measure similarity as the complement with respect to 1.0 of the Manhattan distance computed over the meta-attributes, range-normalising their values to make them comparable.

3 Holdout Experiments

We took 25 classification datasets: 19 from the UCI repository [10]; plus the Breathalyser dataset [7]; and five email datasets [6]. We divided each dataset randomly into three splits: a 60% training set, a 20% cross-validation set, and a 20% test set. We created 10 different splits of the data and we report all results as averages over the 10 splits.

Each of the 25 training sets becomes a meta-case in a meta-case base. On each training set, we compute the 12 complexity measures, and these are the values of the candidate meta-attributes. We run each of the candidate maintenance algorithms—which, in these experiments, are ICF, RC and CBE—on the training set. We record the percentage of cases deleted. We use the cross-validation set to compute the accuracy of the training set after maintenance by each of the algorithms. In other words, we take each case from the cross-validation set and treat it as a query. We present it to a k-NN classifier that uses the training set as its case base. We compute the percentage of the cross-validation set that the k-NN classifier correctly predicts. For each of the maintenance algorithms, we can now compute the harmonic mean of the percentage of cases deleted and the post-maintenance classifier accuracy on the cross-validation set. The algorithm or algorithms with highest harmonic mean are the best algorithms to use on this training set, and therefore a set containing these algorithms is the meta-solution for this meta-case. We do this for each of the 25 training sets to give us 25 meta-cases in our meta-case base.

At this stage, each meta-case has 12 candidate meta-attributes, one for each complexity measure. We run the feature selection algorithm on the meta-case base to decide which of the candidate meta-attributes to use in the rest of the experiment.

We apply a similar process to each of the 25 test sets. The goal here is to create queries that we can present to the meta-case-based classifier. It is important to keep in mind that the queries to this classifier are not individual cases; they are case bases that are to undergo maintenance (see Figure 1). For each test set, we compute the values of the complexity measures. The only measures we need are those that were selected by the feature selection algorithm previously. These become the values of the meta-attributes of the query.

We need to know the best maintenance algorithm to use on each test set—to act as the true class. So we run each of the candidate maintenance algorithms on the

Table 2 Repeated holdout experiment

Algorithm	Error (%)	Harmonic Mean	Accuracy (%)	Deletion (%)
Best Possible	0	76.02	71.68	85.09
Meta-CBR	43.2	69.79	69.53	78.21
RC	24.4	74.49	68.87	87.50
ICF	79.2	62.29	69.63	64.54
CBE	88.4	60.41	72.64	57.11

test set. We note the best algorithm or algorithms, i.e. those that have the highest harmonic mean of the percentage of cases deleted and post-maintenance accuracy on the cross-validation set.

At this point, we have a meta-case base of 25 meta-cases, and a meta-test set of 25 case bases that are to undergo maintenance. We take each case base in the meta-test set in turn. We present it to the meta-case-based classifier (henceforth referred to as the meta-CBR system), which uses 3-NN to predict an algorithm in the way described in Section 2.3.

In the experiment, we measure two things. We record the percentage of the meta-test set that the meta-CBR system incorrectly predicts—the error rate. A correct prediction is one in which the algorithm that the meta-CBR system predicts is the best algorithm—or, in general, it is one in which one of the algorithms that the meta-CBR system predicts is one of the best algorithms.

However, prediction error is not the whole story. Even if the meta-CBR system fails to choose the best algorithm (or one of the joint best algorithms), it may choose one that, when run, has a performance not too far below that of the best algorithm. So for each of the 25 case bases in the meta-test set, we run the meta-CBR system's predicted algorithm and record the percentage of cases deleted, the post-maintenance accuracy on the cross-validation set and their harmonic mean.

The results are shown in Table 2. The Table compares the meta-CBR system to four other options. One option is to always run the ICF algorithm, irrespective of the characteristics of the query case base. Similarly, we can instead always run RC or CBE. The other option (Best Possible) is a benchmark figure, which supposes we have an oracle available enabling us to always choose the best algorithm.

We see that RC is the best algorithm—or one of the best algorithms—in 75.6% of meta-cases and so always choosing RC gives an error rate of 24.4%. ICF and CBE are only rarely among the best algorithms and so always choosing them gives quite high error. Unfortunately, in terms of prediction error, in this experiment meta-CBR is performing poorly: it gets 43.2% of predictions wrong. But, as we said, this is not the whole story.

The results in Table 2 show that the highest possible harmonic mean value if we chose the best algorithm every time is 76.02. The algorithm that comes closest to this is RC, with a harmonic mean value of 74.49. Our meta-CBR classification system results in a harmonic mean value of 69.79, which is the next highest value after RC. What the mean hides is that our meta-CBR system results in case bases which, on average, exhibit post-maintenance classification accuracy that is slightly higher than

RC's, 69.53% compared to 68.87%. But, RC deletes over 9% more cases from the case bases on average, and this is why it ends up with the higher harmonic mean.

Always choosing CBE results in the highest classification accuracy (72.64%), higher even than choosing the algorithm with the best possible harmonic mean, but this is unsurprising given how conservative CBE is: it deletes by far the lowest proposition of cases. Always choosing ICF also results in a conservative mainte- nance strategy (although less conservative than CBE), hence its accuracy is higher than meta-CBR's too. But, because they delete a lower proportion of the case base, ICF and CBE have lower harmonic means than meta-CBR.

Although our meta-CBR system does not have a higher harmonic mean than RC, it has a higher harmonic mean than ICF and CBE. Additionally, it maintains a good level of accuracy at just 2% lower than the best possible on average. This is a promising result for our meta-CBR system.

There are reasons to believe that these results may not be wholly representative. Some of the case bases that we present as queries are very small. They comprise just 20% of their full datasets, which may themselves be small. Some of them may even end up containing cases all of the same class. A first problem is that they may not contain enough cases, or enough different-class cases, for the dataset complexity measures to be informative. For example, if all cases are of the same class, then all complexity measures should produce their lowest values. A second problem is that, if most or all of the cases are of the same class, then this will favour RC's aggressive redundancy reduction, and we are seeing this in the results Table 2. Accordingly, we decided to complement the holdout experiments with leave-one-out experiments, in which the case bases that we present as queries are larger and much less likely to contain cases all of the same class.

4 Leave-One-Out Experiments

In our leave-one-out experiments, we use the same splits of the 25 datasets. We use exactly the same meta-case bases as before—constructed from the 60% train- ing splits and having meta-solutions chosen with the assistance of the 20% cross- validation splits. We do not need a separate meta-test set, so we can discard the 20% test splits. (We could instead have re-split the datasets into just two parts, e.g. 70% training and 30% cross-validation, or 60% and 40%, but then we would have incurred the substantial cost of building new meta-case bases.)

In a fashion akin to classic leave-one-out cross-validation, we remove one meta- case from the meta-case base. We present this meta-case as a query to the meta-CBR system, which uses the remaining 24 meta-cases. We then return it to the case base. We repeat, taking each meta-case in turn.

The advantage is that each query case base is now larger, since it was built from 60% of the original dataset, and it is less likely that it contains only cases of the same class.

The results are shown in Table 3. In these experiments, RC is less often one of

Table 3 Leave-one-out experiment

Algorithm	Error (%)	Harmonic Mean	Accuracy (%)	Deletion (%)
Best Possible	0	82.41	79.39	87.65
Meta-CBR	26.8	80.57	76.81	88.54
RC	35.2	80.30	76.24	88.71
ICF	70.0	74.41	74.69	78.38
CBE	94.4	62.56	77.96	54.88

the best algorithms and so always choosing it is not such a good strategy, resulting in 35.2% error. By contrast, the performance of the meta-CBR system is much improved. Its error, which was 43.2% in the holdout experiment, has fallen to 26.8%.

In these experiments, the highest possible harmonic mean value is 82.41. Our meta-CBR system comes closest to this with a harmonic mean value of 80.57, followed closely by RC with a value of 80.30. We also perform better than ICF and CBE, which have harmonic mean values of 74.41 and 62.56 respectively. Meta-CBR has post-maintenance accuracy that is just 2.6% off that achieved by using an oracle and second only to highly conservative CBE. It deletes a slightly greater proportion of the case base than the oracle achieves, and second only to very aggressive RC. This is a big improvement over our holdout experiments. This shows us that our complexity measures are more reliable and more predictive of the best maintenance algorithm to use when they are computed for case bases which have good coverage of the domain.

5 Related Work

The idea of meta-reasoning—reasoning about reasoning—has been explored in a number of different areas. For example, there is an amount of research into meta-planning [25, 27]. Within CBR, Fox and Leake [9] build a system that reasons about CBR: it uses introspection to improve indexing in a case-based planning system. They use a model to evaluate the performance of a case-based planner in comparison to its expected ideal performance, and they use this model to suggest a repair when the planner does not perform as it should.

Within machine learning and data mining, there has been an amount of research into meta-learning, in particular training meta-classifiers that predict the best classifier to use on a dataset. For example, Lindner & Studer take an approach similar to our own: they use a number of dataset complexity measures and other statistical measures as their meta-attributes [15]. But their system selects classifiers, not maintenance algorithms. Peng et al. also use a k-NN meta-classifier to choose between a number of classification algorithms (rather than maintenance algorithms) [20]. For their meta-attributes, they build decision trees on datasets and compute characteristics of the decision trees, such as the length of the longest branch. Bensusan et al., by contrast, use a representation of the decision tree itself as the description of the

dataset [2]. Pfahringer et al. take an approach that they call landmarking, whereby the meta-attributes come from measuring the performance of simple classifiers on the datasets [21]. Of course, some of our dataset complexity measures also have this character, e.g. N_3, which is the error rate of a 1NN classifier.

Within CBR also, Recio-García et al. use CBR to choose a template from a case base of templates to aid the design and implementation of CBR systems [22] . In particular, they describe a case-based recommender that recommends recommender system templates from a case base of twelve templates. Van Setten [23] compares decision-support systems built using CBR and built using decision trees that help the user to design a hybrid recommender system. Leake et al [14] use CBR to learn adaptation knowledge from a case base. This adaptation knowledge is stored as adaptation cases, which are then in turn used to help the CBR system in the future.

6 Conclusions and Future Work

We have presented a meta-case-based classifier that can form the basis of a decision-support system that assists case base administrators. It can choose a case base maintenance algorithm that is suited to the characteristics of a given case base at a given point in its lifetime. A key design decision was how to characterize case bases—both those that are described by meta-cases in our meta-case base, and incoming query case bases that are to undergo maintenance. We have used a number of measures of dataset complexity, which attempt to characterize the geometry of the case bases. The actual meta-attributes that we use are chosen by a feature selection algorithm from a large set of complexity measures.

The results of our first experiment, which used a holdout method, were promising. The meta-CBR system picked maintenance algorithms that produced case bases that achieved slightly higher classification accuracy than always picking the RC algorithm. However, always choosing RC resulted in a much larger proportion of cases being deleted, and hence a higher harmonic mean. Similarly, compared with selecting the best possible maintenance algorithm using an oracle, the meta-CBR system picked algorithms that produced case bases with comparable classification accuracy, but again was too conservative in the proportion of cases deleted.

Our second set of experiments used a leave-one-out method, enabling us to make better use of the available data. In particular, query case bases were three times larger than in the first experiment, and were much less likely to contain cases most or all of which were of the same class. In this experiment, the meta-CBR system outperformed the approach of always picking the same algorithm. For example, the algorithms chosen by meta-CBR deleted a slightly larger proportion of cases, and resulted in case bases with slightly higher classification accuracy, than always using RC. This makes the point that for meta-CBR to work, the case bases need to be large enough, and representative enough, that the dataset complexity measures are informative. In practice, of course, this is likely to be so, otherwise the case base administrator would not have deemed case base maintenance to be worthwhile.

An obvious line of future research is to perform more experiments. In particular, these could use a wider range of candidate maintenance algorithms. The meta-case base, and the incoming query case bases, could be based on a wider variety of datasets too. In this regard, it would be particularly interesting to create meta-cases from case bases at different points in their lifetimes, and similarly to use query case bases also at different points in their lifetimes. Now that the feasibility of using decision-support technology to choose a maintenance algorithm is established, a comparison with other decision-support technologies, such as neural nets or decision trees, would be of value too.

One concern is that current maintenance algorithms delete whole subsets of the cases in a case base. But as soon as so much as one case is deleted, it no longer follows that the same algorithm is the best to decide on the next case to delete. We are working on incremental versions of the case base maintenance algorithms, which recommend the deletion of only one case at a time. We are also working on incremental versions of some of the dataset complexity measures, whose values can be rapidly re-calculated for a case base following deletion of a case. This will allow us to build an incremental meta-CBR system, which will repeatedly select the best incremental case base maintenance algorithm, which will delete one case, and then return to the meta-CBR system to select an algorithm to delete the next case, and so on until the system predicts there to be no advantage in deleting a further case.

Acknowledgements This paper is based upon work partially supported by the Science Foundation Ireland under Grant Number 05/RFP/CMS0019.

References

1. Aha, D.W., Bankert, R.L.: A comparative evaluation of sequential feature selection algorithms. In: Procs. of the Fifth International Workshop on Artificial Intelligence and Statistics, pp. 1–7 (1994)
2. Bensusan, H., Giraud-Carrier, C., Kennedy, C.: A higher-order approach to meta-learning. In: Procs. of the Workshop on Meta-Learning at the European Conference on Machine Learning, pp. 109–117 (2000)
3. Brighton, H., Mellish, C.: On the consistency of information filters for lazy learning algorithms. In: J. Rauch, J. Zytkow (eds.) Proceedings of the Third European Conference on Principles of Data Mining and Knowledge Discovery, pp. 283–288. Springer-Verlag (1999)
4. Cummins, L.: Combining and choosing case base maintenance algorithms. Ph.D. thesis, Department of Computer Science, University College Cork, Ireland (2011 (forthcoming))
5. Cummins, L., Bridge, D.: Maintenance by a committee of experts: The MACE approach to case-base maintenance. In: L. McGinty, D.C. Wilson (eds.) Procs. of the 8th Intl. Conference on Case-Based Reasoning, pp. 120–134 (2009)
6. Delany, S., Cunningham, P.: An analysis of case-based editing in a spam filtering system. In: P. Funk, P. González-Calero (eds.) Procs. of the Seventh European Conference on Case-Based Reasoning, vol. LNAI 3155, pp. 128–141. Springer (2004)
7. Doyle, D., Cunningham, P., Bridge, D., Rahman, Y.: Explanation oriented retrieval. In: P. Funk, P. González-Calero (eds.) Procs. of the Seventh European Conference on Case-Based Reasoning, *Lecture Notes in Artificial Intelligence*, vol. 3155, pp. 157–168. Springer (2004)

8. Fornells, A., Recio-García, J., Díaz-Agudo, B., Golobardes, E., Fornells, E.: Integration of a methodology for cluster-based retrieval in jcolibri. In: L. McGinty, D.C. Wilson (eds.) Procs. of the Eighth International Conference on Case-Based Reasoning, vol. LNCS 5650, pp. 418–433. Springer (2009)
9. Fox, S., Leake, D.: Using introspective reasoning to refine indexing. In: C. Mellish (ed.) Proceedings of the Fourteenth International Joint Conference on Artificial Intelligence, pp. 391–397. IJCAI, Morgan Kaufmann, San Francisco, California (1995)
10. Frank, A., Asuncion, A.: UCI machine learning repository (2010). URL http:// archive.ics.uci.edu/ml
11. Guyon, I., Elisseeff, A.: An introduction to variable and feature selection. Journal of Machine Learning Research 3, 1157–1182 (2003)
12. Ho, T.K., Basu, M.: Measuring the complexity of classification problems. In: Proceedings of the Fifteenth International Conference on Pattern Recognition, pp. 43–47 (2000)
13. Ho, T.K., Basu, M.: Complexity measures of supervised classification problems. IEEE Transactions on Pattern Analysis and Machine Intelligence 24(3), 289–300 (2002)
14. Leake, D.B., Kinley, A., Wilson, D.C.: Learning to improve case adaption by introspective reasoning and CBR. In: M.M. Veloso, A. Aamodt (eds.) Proceedings of the First International Conference on Case-Based Reasoning, *Lecture Notes in Computer Science*, vol. 1010. ICCBR, Springer, Heidelberg, Germany (1995)
15. Lindner, G., Studer, R.: AST: Support for algorithm selection with a CBR approach. In: Procs. of the 3rd European Conference on Principles and Practice of Knowledge Discovery in Databases, pp. 418–423 (1999)
16. Liu, H., Yu, L.: Toward integrating feature selection algorithms for classification and clustering. IEEE Transactions on Knowledge and Data Engineering 17, 491–502 (2005)
17. Massie, S., Craw, S., Wiratunga, N.: Complexity profiling for informed case-base editing. In: T. Roth-Berghofer, M. Göker, H.A. Güvenir (eds.) Procs. of the Eighth European Conference on Case-Based Reasoning, pp. 325–339. Springer-Verlag (2006)
18. McKenna, E., Smyth, B.: Competence-guided case-base editing techniques. In: E. Blanzieri, L. Portinale (eds.) Proceedings of the Fifth European Workshop on Case-Based Reasoning, vol. LNCS 1898, pp. 186–197. Springer-Verlag (2000)
19. Orriols-Puig, A., Macià, N., Bernadó-Mansilla, E., Ho, T.K.: Documentation for the data complexity library in C++. Tech. Rep. GRSI Report No. 2009001, Universitat Ramon Llull (2009)
20. Peng, Y., Flach, P., Soares, C., Brazdil, P.: Improved data set characterisation for meta-learning. In: Procs. of the 5th International Conference on Discovery Science, pp. 141–152 (2002)
21. Pfahringer, B., Bensusan, H., Giraud-Carrier, C.: Meta-learning by landmarking various learning algorithms. In: Procs. of the Seventeenth International Conference on Machine Learning, pp. 743–750 (2000)
22. Recio-García, J.A., Bridge, D., Díaz-Agudo, B., González-Calero, P.A.: CBR for CBR: A case-based template recommender system for building case-based systems. In: K.D. Althoff, R. Bergmann, M. Minor, A. Hanft (eds.) Procs. of the Ninth European Conference on Case-Based Reasoning, vol. LNCS 5239, pp. 459–473. Springer-Verlag (2008)
23. van Setten, M.: Supporting people in finding information: Hybrid recommender systems and goal-based structuring. Ph.D. thesis, University of Twente (2005)
24. Smyth, B., McKenna, E.: Modelling the competence of case-bases. In: B. Smyth, P. Cunningham (eds.) Procs. of the Fourth European Workshop on Advances in Case-Based Reasoning, vol. LNCS 1488, pp. 208–220. Springer (1998)
25. Stefik, M.: Planning and meta-planning (MOLGEN: Part 2). Artificial Intelligence 16(2), 141–170 (1981)
26. Tomek, I.: An experiment with the edited nearest-neighbor rule. IEEE Transactions on Systems, Man, and Cybernetics 6(6), 448–452 (1976)
27. Wilensky, R.: Meta-planning: Representing and using knowledge about planning in problem solving and natural language understanding. Cognitive Science 5(3), 197–233 (1981)

Successive Reduction of Arms in Multi-Armed Bandits

Neha Gupta, Ole-Christoffer Granmo and Ashok Agrawala

Abstract The relevance of the multi-armed bandit problem has risen in the past few years with the need for online optimization techniques in Internet systems, such as online advertisement and news article recommendation. At the same time, these applications reveal that state-of-the-art solution schemes do not scale well with the number of bandit arms. In this paper, we present two types of Successive Reduction (SR) strategies - 1) Successive Reduction Hoeffding (SRH) and 2) Successive Reduction Order Statistics (SRO). Both use an Order Statistics based Thompson Sampling method for arm selection, and then successively eliminate bandit arms from consideration based on a confidence threshold. While SRH uses Hoeffding Bounds for elimination, SRO uses the probability of an arm being superior to the currently selected arm to measure confidence. A computationally efficient scheme for pairwise calculation of the latter probability is also presented in this paper. Using SR strategies, sampling resources and arm pulls are not wasted on arms that are unlikely to be the optimal one. To demonstrate the scalability of our proposed schemes, we compare them with two state-of-the-art approaches, namely pure Thompson Sampling and UCB-Tuned. The empirical results are truly conclusive, with the performance advantage of proposed SRO scheme *increasing* persistently with the number of bandit arms while the SRH scheme shows similar performance as pure Thompson Sampling. We thus believe that SR algorithms will open up for improved performance in Internet based on-line optimization, and tackling of larger problems.

Neha Gupta
University of Maryland, College Park, USA e-mail: neha@cs.umd.edu

Ole-Christoffer Granmo
University of Agder, Norway e-mail: ole.granmo@uia.no

Ashok Agrawala
University of Maryland, College Park, USA e-mail: agrawala@cs.umd.edu

M. Bramer et al. (eds.), *Research and Development in Intelligent Systems XXVIII*,
DOI 10.1007/978-1-4471-2318-7_13, © Springer-Verlag London Limited 2011

1 Introduction

Multi-armed bandit (MAB) problem is a classic example of the exploration vs. exploitation dilemma in which a collection of one armed bandits, each with unknown but fixed reward probability θ, is given. The key idea is to develop a strategy which results in the arm with the highest success probability to be played such that the total reward obtained is maximized. Although seemingly a simplistic problem, solution strategies are important because of their wide applicability in a myriad of areas such as adaptive routing, resource allocation, clinical trials, and more recently in online advertising and news article recommendation [4, 1], to name a few.

Thompson Sampling [19] based solution strategies have recently been established as top performers when it comes to solving MABs with Bernoulli distributed rewards [9, 18]. For every arm, there is a chance that exactly that arm is the one with the largest reward probability, and thus being the optimal choice. Thompson Sampling pulls the available arms with frequencies proportional to their probabilities of being optimal. By doing this, it gradually moves from exploration to exploitation, converging towards only selecting the optimal arm. Unfortunately, an inherent limitation of Thompson Sampling emerges when the number of arms grows large. In all brevity, in order for the optimal arm to be chosen in Thompson Sampling, it has to "beat" *all* of the inferior arms in a pair-wise manner. As the number of inferior arms grows, the probability of the superior arm winning deteriorates. The effect of this deterioration is easily seen in large scale real life applications, such as those found in the Internet domain, where it is common with several hundreds arms in a single MAB problem.

In this paper, we introduce a rather radical strategy — the Successive Reduction (SR) strategy — that addresses the above weakness directly. In brief, *Order Statistics* based on Thompson Sampling is used for arm selection, however, concurrently, bandit arms are successively eliminated from further consideration. Two elimination criteria are investigated, one based on so-called Hoeffding Bounds and another one based on Order Statistics. The purpose is to increase reward probability by not considering inferior arms, and at the same time reduce information storage and management needs.

2 Related Work

Seminal work on multi-armed bandit policies was done by Lai and Robbins [15]. They proved that for certain reward distributions, such as Bernoulli, Poisson, and uniform, there exists an asymptotic bound on regret (the loss experienced due to playing the suboptimal arms) that only depends on the logarithm of the number of trials and the Kullback-Leibler value of each reward distribution. The main idea behind the strategy is to calculate an upper confidence index for each arm, only dependent on the previous rewards of that arm. At each trial the arm which has the maximum upper confidence value is played, thus enabling deterministic play.

Agrawal [2] improved the results obtained by Lai and Robbins by proposing strategies that are independent of the reward distributions. Auer et al. [3] further proved that instead of an asymptotic logarithmic upper bound, an upper bound on the regret could be obtained in finite time for algorithms such as UCB-1, UCB-2 and some variants. In particular cases, even optimal performance is possible. The pioneering Gittins Index based strategy [7], for instance, performs a Bayesian look ahead at each step in order to decide which arm to play. This look ahead makes the Gittins technique intractable in practice. However, it enables optimal play for discounted rewards.

In our work we consider large-scale multi-armed bandit problems and formulate a Bayesian learning strategy based on *Order Statistics* [6, 12]. For Bayesian learning, knowledge about a reward probability takes the form of a distribution instead of a point estimate. The use of the Beta distribution for Bayesian reward probability learning was first considered in the 1933 paper by Thompson [19] for a different problem domain, in which main properties of this learning technique were identified. Recently, a new generation of Thompson Sampling based schemes have appeared, outperforming state-of-the-art algorithms in a plentitude of cases [18, 8, 20, 5]. The SR strategy suggested in this present paper is based on successive reduction of arms, selected based on Thompson Sampling. Our proposed scheme can thus be seen as a novel extension of the Thompson Sampling family of schemes.

In [14], an algorithm for best arm identification by successively rejecting arms has been proposed for the problem of pure exploitation. The problem of pure exploitation is different from our problem of online learning because we combine exploration and exploitation to maximize the total reward. In contrast, the optimization function for the pure exploitation case is the difference between the reward of the chosen arm and the optimal arm. We, on the other hand, aim to optimize the total reward obtained as the algorithm learns online.

In their paper, Maron et al. used Hoeffding Bounds to quickly discard bad models in order to accelerate model selection search for classification and function approximation [16]. In this paper, we apply Hoeffding Bounds as one of the measures for arm elimination in the Thompson Sampling based MAB strategy.

3 Multi-Armed Bandit Algorithms

In the MAB setting, each pull of an arm can be considered as a Bernoulli trial with output set $\{0,1\}$ — 0 denotes failure and 1 reward. The absence of a reward can also be considered as failure. A Bernoulli trial is specified by the means of a single parameter, θ, which is the probability of reward.

The probability distribution of the number of rewards obtained in n Bernoulli trials, denoted by S, have a Binomial distribution, $S \sim Binomial(n, \theta)$:

$$p(S = s|\theta) = \binom{n}{s}(1-\theta)^{n-s}\theta^s \tag{1}$$

It is well-known that the Beta distribution is a conjugate prior for the Binomial distribution [11]. Thus, when providing a Bayesian estimate for θ, it is natural to assume that it possesses a Beta distributed prior, fully specified by the parameters (α_0, β_0):

$$p(\theta; \alpha_0, \beta_0) = \frac{\theta^{\alpha_0-1}(1-\theta)^{\beta_0-1}}{B(\alpha_0, \beta_0)} \tag{2}$$

The parameters (α_n, β_n) after n trials can be defined recursively. If a reward is received at n^{th} trial, α becomes,

$$\alpha_n = \alpha_{n-1} + 1 \tag{3}$$

or if a failure is received at n^{th} trial, β is updated to,

$$\beta_n = \beta_{n-1} + 1 \tag{4}$$

Consequently, after s rewards and r failures, the parameters of Beta distribution become $(\alpha_0 + s, \beta_0 + r)$.

$$\theta \sim Beta(\alpha_0 + s, \beta_0 + r) \tag{5}$$

In the next subsections, we present multi armed bandit strategies for K arms where each arm i has a reward probability θ_i.

3.1 UCB Algorithms

The UCB-1 [3] algorithm computes an Upper Confidence Bound (UCB) for each arm: $(\theta_{in} + \sqrt{\frac{2\ln n}{n_i}})$. Here, θ_{in} is the average reward obtained from the arm i when the number of times arm i has been played is n_i and n is the overall number of plays so far. In this algorithm, the arm which has the maximum UCB value is played and the confidence bounds are updated at each trial.

UCB-2 is a similar strategy but the picked arm is played in epochs. The upper bounds of UCB-2 is calculated by the formula $\sqrt{\frac{(1+\varphi)\ln(en/\tau(r_i))}{\tau(r_i)}}$, where φ is a constant, r_i denotes the current epoch of arm i and $\tau(r_i) = \lceil (1+\varphi)^{r_i} \rceil$. UCB-tuned [3] is also a slight modification of UCB-1 that uses an upper bound of $\sqrt{\frac{\ln n \ min(1/4, V_i(n))}{n}}$, where $V_i(n)$ denotes the estimated variance of arm i. There are no theoretical proofs supporting UCB-tuned, but in empirical results, its performance turns out to be better than that of UCB-1, UCB-2. Hence, we will use UCB-Tuned for performing comparative analysis in this paper.

3.2 Successive Reduction (SR) Algorithm

3.2.1 Pure Thompson Sampling (TS)

Thompson Sampling is a randomized algorithm based on Bayesian modeling of the reward distributions of the arms in the MAB setting. The algorithm is shown in Alg. 1. The reward probabilities of each arm i, after n total trials, is modeled as a Beta distribution $Beta(\alpha_{in}, \beta_{in})$. In each trial any one of the values $\alpha_{1n}, \beta_{1n}, \alpha_{2n}, \beta_{2n}, ..., \beta_{Kn}$ can be increased, which leads to an infinitive state space of dimension $2K$: $\Phi_n = \{(\alpha_{1n}, \beta_{1n}), (\alpha_{2n}, \beta_{2n}), ..., (\alpha_{Kn}, \beta_{Kn})\}$.

For arm selection at each trial, one sample is drawn from the Beta distribution of each arm, and the arm with the largest sample value is played. Accordingly, the probability of an arm i being played is $P(\theta_i > \theta_1 \wedge \theta_i > \theta_2 \wedge \theta_i > \theta_3 ... \theta_i > \theta_{i-1} \wedge \theta_i > \theta_{i+1} ... \theta_i > \theta_K)$, but as can be seen from the algorithm there is no need to explicitly compute this value. Theoretical convergence proofs for this method have been discussed in [10, 17].

Algorithm 1 Thompson Sampling (TS)

Initialize $\alpha_{i0}=2$, $\beta_{i0} = 2$.
loop
    Draw a value π_i randomly from $Beta(\alpha_i, \beta_i) \forall i \in K$.
    Arrange the samples in decreasing order.
    Select the arm A s.t. $\pi_A = max_i(\pi_i)$, $\forall i \in K$.
    Pull arm A.
    if Arm A is successful **then**
        Update the values for $\alpha_{An} = \alpha_{An-1} + 1$.
    else
        Update the values for $\beta_{An} = \beta_{An-1} + 1$.
    end if
end loop

Although the traditional algorithms, such as Thompson Sampling and UCB-tuned, work well for smaller set of arms, they do not scale well — as the number of arms increases, performance drops. Our Successive Reduction (SR) algorithm aims to handle this problem of scalability in MABs. The SR algorithm works by carefully and persistently removing the non-performing arms based on a confidence measure. In the sections below, we suggest two methods for eliminating the non-performing arms, one based on Hoeffding Bounds, and another one based on Order Statistics.

3.2.2 Successive Reduction using Hoeffding Bounds (SRH)

Hoeffding Bounds [13] are important theoretical bounds and have been applied to a large number of areas such as algorithmic and learning theory, networking, and machine learning. In this paper, we use these bounds for successively eliminating

arms in the MAB problem, as shown in Alg. 2. Hoeffding Bounds provide an upper bound on the probability for the sum of random variables to deviate from its expected value by stating that for any $\theta_i \in [0, 1]$ with confidence δ,

$$P(|\theta_i^{true} - \theta_{in}| > \varepsilon_{in}) < 2e^{-2n_i\varepsilon_{in}^2}. \tag{6}$$

Hence, for the estimated mean to be within ε_{in} of the true mean with confidence $(1 - \delta)$, ε_{in} becomes

$$\varepsilon_{in} = \sqrt{\frac{log(2/\delta)}{2n_i}}. \tag{7}$$

In the SRH algorithm, we first do Thompson Sampling and select an arm to play. But at the end of each trial, we eliminate the arms whose upper Hoeffding bound is less than the lower Hoeffding bound of the best arm.

3.2.3 Successive Reduction using Order Statistics (SRO)

In order statistics based SRO algorithm, we select arm M according to Thompson Sampling but to reduce the arms, we compare each other arm, i, in the set with the selected arm M, and compute on a pairwise basis the probability of θ_M being greater than θ_i, i.e., $P(\theta_M > \theta_i)$. If this value is greater than a threshold value (γ), say 99%, then arm i is removed, as shown in Alg. 3. Next, we illustrate how given two arms with reward probabilities θ_1 and θ_2 we compute the $P(\theta_1 > \theta_2)$ efficiently.

Algorithm 2 Successive Reduction Method based on Hoeffding Bounds (SRH)

Initialize all $\alpha_{i0}=2$, $\beta_{i0} = 2$ and threshold δ.
loop
    Do Thompson Sampling as given in Alg. 1
    Identify the arm M which has the highest lower bound, $M = \{i : \max_i(\theta_{in} - \varepsilon_{in})\}$.
    for all arms i excluding arm M **do**
        if $(\theta_{Mn} - \varepsilon_{Mn}) > (\theta_{in} + \varepsilon_{in})$ **then**
            Remove arm i.
        end if
    end for
end loop

The value of $P(\theta_1 > \theta_2)$ depends on distance between the means of the two random distributions given by $\Delta_{12} = \theta_1 - \theta_2$ and the variance of the random distributions. We show that this function can be computed efficiently in real time by further simplification of the below formula (details are given in the appendix).

$$P(\theta_1 > \theta_2) \tag{8}$$

Algorithm 3 Successive Reduction Method based on Order Statistics (SRO)

Initialize all $\alpha_{i0}=2$, $\beta_{i0}=2$ and threshold γ.
loop
    Do Thompson Sampling as given in Alg. 1 and play arm M.
    for all arms i excluding arm M **do**
        Compute $p = P(\theta_M > \theta_i)$.
        if $p > \gamma$ **then**
            Remove arm i.
        end if
    end for
end loop

$$= \frac{\alpha_1+\beta_1-1}{\alpha_1+\beta_1+\alpha_2+\beta_2-2} \times \sum_{j=\alpha_2}^{\alpha_2+\beta_2-1} \frac{\binom{\alpha_2+\beta_2-1}{j}\binom{\alpha_1+\beta_1-2}{\alpha_1-1}}{\binom{\alpha_2+\beta_2+\alpha_1+\beta_1-3}{\alpha_1+j-1}} \qquad (9)$$

The solution of this formula can have applications outside the realm of multi-armed bandit problems [6].

Further, for larger α, β values, Beta distribution could be approximated to Normal distribution for calculating $P(\theta_1 > \theta_2)$. Fig. 1 shows the curves for Beta and Normal distributions for three different values of (α, β) parameters. For the first case, when $(\alpha = 2, \beta = 4)$, the two curves look slightly different, but for the case of $(\alpha = 10, \beta = 15)$ and $(\alpha = 30, \beta = 40)$, the curves are almost the same (overlapping). In case of Normal distribution, the incomplete integral can be easily computed using the error function (erf).

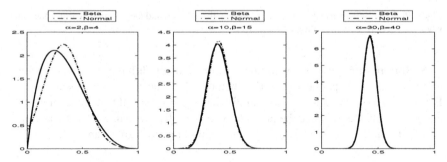

Fig. 1 Plot comparing Beta and Normal distributions for different parameter values. The curves are overlapping for large (α, β) values.

$$\int_0^{\theta_1} p(\theta_2)\mathrm{d}\theta_2 = \frac{1}{2}[1 + \mathrm{erf}(\frac{\theta_1 - \theta_{2n}}{\sigma_{2n}\sqrt{2}})] \qquad (10)$$

$$P(\theta_1 > \theta_2) = \int_0^1 \frac{1}{\sqrt{2\pi\sigma_{1n}^2}} e^{(\theta_1-\theta_{1n})/(2\sigma_{1n}^2)} \frac{1}{2}[1 + \mathrm{erf}(\frac{\theta_1 - \theta_{2n}}{\sigma_{2n}\sqrt{2}})]\mathrm{d}\theta_1 \qquad (11)$$

$$\theta_{1n} = \frac{\alpha_{1n}}{\alpha_{1n} + \beta_{1n}}, \theta_{2n} = \frac{\alpha_{2n}}{\alpha_{2n} + \beta_{2n}} \tag{12}$$

$$\sigma_{1n} = \sqrt{\frac{\alpha_{1n}\beta_{1n}}{(\alpha_{1n} + \beta_{1n})^2(\alpha_{1n} + \beta_{1n} + 1)}}, \sigma_{2n} = \sqrt{\frac{\alpha_{2n}\beta_{2n}}{(\alpha_{2n} + \beta_{2n})^2(\alpha_{2n} + \beta_{2n} + 1)}} \tag{13}$$

Also notice that Normal approximation becomes much more useful for the generalized case of computing $P(\theta_i > \theta_1 \wedge \theta_i > \theta_2 \wedge \theta_i > \theta_3...\theta_i > \theta_{i-1} \wedge \theta_i > \theta_{i+1}...\theta_i > \theta_K)$ since the incomplete integral is no longer a summation formula, as in the case of Beta distribution. But this is not the focus of the paper. Empirically, we have seen no difference in the results when either method is used since we use high values of thresholds ($> 95\%$) for cut-off. However, we avoid Normal approximations for the values of $\alpha_{in}, \beta_{in} < 5$.

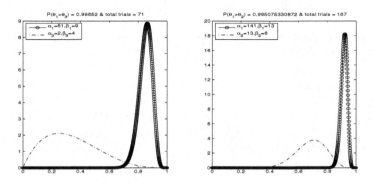

Fig. 2 Plots for Beta distribution curves comparing the selected and the suboptimal arm at the trial when the suboptimal arm is eliminated.

Setting the priors: Beta distribution can take many different forms depending on the values of the parameters α, β. When $\alpha, \beta \geq 2$, the curve becomes unimodal. For a better approximation to Normal distribution, it is desirable to have unimodal curves. Hence, we initialize the priors to be $\alpha_0 = 2, \beta_0 = 2$ and use exact computations until the constraints for using Normal approximations above are met.

3.2.4 Example SRO algorithm

To illustrate the working of the SRO algorithm, we take a case of 3 armed bandits with reward probabilities equal to ($\theta_1 = 0.9, \theta_2 = 0.6, \theta_3 = 0.3$) as an example. As per the algorithm, arms are selected according to Thompson Sampling, but are discarded based on the Order statistics method with a threshold value of 99.5%. Initially, the state of the system is $\Phi_0 = ((2,2),(2,2),(2,2))$. Fig. 2 represents probability distributions at the trials when the suboptimal arms are eliminated. The left graph shows the Beta distributions for $((\alpha_1 = 51, \beta_1 = 9), (\alpha_3 = 2, \beta_3 = 4))$

when θ_3 is eliminated at 71st trial at $\Phi_{71} = ((51,9),(12,5),(2,4))$. At this point, $P(\theta_1 > \theta_3) = 0.99652$. Since, the second arm has a higher value of the reward probability, it is removed much later at 167th trial when $\Phi_{167} = ((141,13),(13,6),(-,-))$ and $P(\theta_1 > \theta_2) = 0.995$ as shown in the right graph. So, at the end of 167th trial, only the optimal arm is left to be played and that is tried henceforth, thereby maximizing the rewards. Note that the simple case with three arms is presented here to graphically illustrate the probability distributions when an arm is eliminated.

4 Empirical Analysis

In this section, we evaluate the performance of SRO and SRH algorithms by comparing them with Thompson Method and UCB-Tuned algorithms. Though we performed significant experiments over several values of the reward distributions, we only report the most important and relevant experiments in this paper due to limited space. Each experiment is repeated 100 times from independent random streams and average values and standard deviations are reported in the results. We report the total reward obtained as the measure of performance of the MAB strategies.

4.1 Experiment 1: Varying Threshold

In the first experiment, we vary the threshold values for SRH and SRO algorithms to analyze their effect on the performance of the SR strategies. We consider a total of 50 arms, $\theta_{opt} = 0.6$, and all the other θ_i are generated from uniform distribution $U(0.6,0)$. Table 1 shows the reward obtained by using different thresholds for the SR method for 10,000 trials. The different values of threshold are 90%, 95%, 99%, 99.5%. We see that the SRH algorithm does not show any improvement over the Thompson Sampling algorithm for any value of the thresholds while the SRO algorithm gives a significant improvement over the Thompson Sampling and UCB-T algorithms.

In the variable threshold V_T experiment for SRO algorithm, we vary the threshold based on the number of times an arm considered for elimination has been played. The intuition behind the variable threshold is that the larger the number of plays of an arm, the lower is its variance and closer it is to its actual value, hence more risk could be taken while eliminating the arm. The values for variable threshold V_T are 99.5% when $n_i \leq 10$, 99% when n_i lies in range $(10,50)$ and 95% otherwise, where n_i is the number of times arm i has been tried. These values of n_i work well for Uniformly distributed reward probabilities $\theta_i \in [0,1]$.

Table 1 also reports the standard deviations in the total reward obtained and we see that the variable threshold has the least standard deviation. The standard deviation obtained in the SRO algorithm with threshold 90% is vey high while its reward is among the highest, hence it is a high risk threshold.

The number of arms left in the set at the end of the 10,000 trials is also shown in the column *Final Arms*. We see that out of 100 arms, less than 5 arms remain at the end of 10K trials for the case of SRO algorithm while for the case of SRO algorithm more than 20 arms remain. The average number of trials after which only a single optimal arm is left are also given in the column *Trial End*, if it is before 10000.

Table 1 The results obtained by varying threshold for a range of probabilities from (0.6,0) where $\theta_{opt} = 0.6$. for Experiment 1

Method	Threshold %	Reward	Std Dev	Final Arms	Trial End
SR -Order Stats.	90	5814.57	218.51	1.03	1242.86
SR -Order Stats.	95	**5861.82**	97.91	1.3	4487.06
SR -Order Stats.	99	5764.56	83.99	3.14	9663.09
SR -Order Stats.	99.5	5744.77	75.39	3.97	9945.72
SR -Order Stats.	V_T	5781.96	**58.23**	1.65	6867.33
SR -Hoeffding	90	5539.26	63.09	21.92	-
SR -Hoeffding	95	5534.59	69.08	26.93	-
SR -Hoeffding	99	5560.1	55.308	49.03	-
SR -Hoeffding	99.5	5541.78	70.22	49.98	-
Thompson	-	5540.22	63.76	-	-
UCB-T	-	5640.78	74.90	-	-

4.2 Experiment 2: Increasing Number of Arms

We perform this experiment to show the effect of increasing the number of arms on the reward obtained. We set $\theta_{opt} = 0.5$ and initially randomly generate a set of 9 θ_i with reward probabilities in interval $(0.5,0)$ using uniform distribution. For successive experiments, each consisting of 10,000 trials, the number of arms is increased by 4 using the same distribution $U(0.5,0)$. We use V_T threshold for SRO algorithm and 99% threshold for the SRH algorithm. As shown in Fig. 3, the SRO algorithm performs significantly better than the Thompson Sampling and UCB-Tuned algorithm. Also for the SRO algorithm, we notice that the total number of arms remaining at the end of 10K trials has an average value of < 5 even when the initial number of arms are > 100. SRH algorithm does not show any improvement in the reward values relative to Thompson Sampling and also the number of arms eliminated at the end of the experiment is almost zero.

4.3 Experiment 3: Increasing $\Delta_{opt-subopt}$

In this experiment, we systematically vary the difference in the optimal and the suboptimal arm and compare the performance of SR algorithms with UCB-Tuned

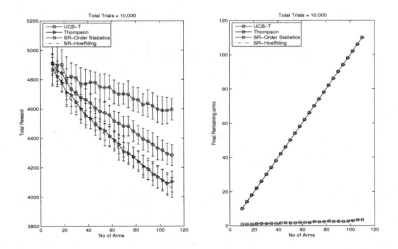

Fig. 3 Reward & remaining arms obtained when number of arms are varied for a total of 10K trials for Experiment 2. Remaining arms for all other algorithms except SR-Order Statistics overlap. Error bars represent one standard deviation.

and Thompson Sampling. We take a total of 100 arms and increase the difference in the optimal and sub-optimal arms denoted by $\Delta_{opt-subopt}$. The optimal arm is set to $\theta_{opt} = 0.9$ and different values of θ_{subopt} are chosen from the set $\{0.8, 0.7, 0.6, 0.5, 0.4, 0.3, 0.2\}$ such that $\Delta_{opt-subopt}$ varies from $[0.1 - 0.7]$. Rest of the θ_i are generated from a uniform random distribution between $U(\theta_{subopt}, 0)$. We use V_T as threshold for SRO algorithm and a constant 99% threshold for the SRH algorithm. The results in Fig. 4 show that the SRO algorithm performs significantly better than Thompson Sampling and UCB-T algorithms. SRH algorithm does not show any improvement over Thompson Sampling.

5 Conclusion and Future Work

From the experimental results and analysis done in this paper we conclude that state-of-the-art methods such as UCB, Thompson Sampling do not work well for large number of arms, hence new schemes need to be developed to handle the challenge of scalability in the Multi-Armed Bandit setting. Towards this direction, we presented Successive Reduction strategies, Successive Reduction Hoeffding (SRH) and Successive Reduction Order Statistics (SRO), for solving large scale multi-armed bandit problems in the scenario where no prior information was available about the arms. Our experiments reveal that SRO strategy significantly outperforms Thompson Sampling, UCB-Tuned and SRH algorithms and the performance increase is more significant with increasing number of arms. Arguably, Hoeffding Bounds are

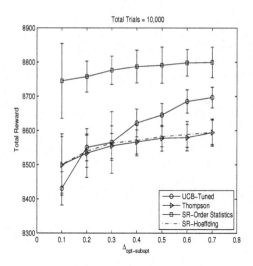

Fig. 4 Reward when $\Delta_{opt-subopt}$ is varied for Experiment 3. Error bars represent one standard deviation.

loose bounds which Thompson Sampling already takes care of, hence no improvement in performance is noticed in the SRH algorithm.

Although this paper discusses Bernoulli bandits with Beta distributions, the SR algorithms are applicable for all forms of random distributions. The SR strategy can be further extended to include variations such as finding the top-k arms, and immunity from elimination for some arms. We are working on proving the theoretical bounds for the SRO method and exploring the possibilities of extending it in other dimensions such as mortal bandits, and hierarchical bandits.

Appendix

We discuss the simplication of the Eqn. 9 below:

$$P(\theta_1 > \theta_2) = \int_0^1 p(\theta_1) \int_0^{\theta_1} p(\theta_2) d\theta_2 d\theta_1 \tag{14}$$

$$\int_0^{\theta_1} p(\theta_2) d\theta_2 \tag{15}$$

$$= \int_0^{\theta_1} \frac{\theta_2^{\alpha_2-1}(1-\theta_2)^{\beta_2-1} d\theta_2}{B(\alpha_2,\beta_2)} \tag{16}$$

$$= \Sigma_{j=\alpha_2}^{\alpha_2+\beta_2-1} \binom{\alpha_2+\beta_2-1}{j} \theta_1{}^j (1-\theta_1)^{\alpha_2+\beta_2-1-j} \tag{17}$$

$$\tag{18}$$

Hence,

$$P(\theta_1 > \theta_2) \tag{19}$$

$$= \frac{\alpha_1+\beta_1-1}{\alpha_1+\beta_1+\alpha_2+\beta_2-2} \times \Sigma_{j=\alpha_2}^{\alpha_2+\beta_2-1} \frac{\binom{\alpha_2+\beta_2-1}{j}\binom{\alpha_1+\beta_1-2}{\alpha_1-1}}{\binom{\alpha_2+\beta_2+\alpha_1+\beta_1-3}{\alpha_1+j-1}} \tag{20}$$

$$= \frac{\alpha_1+\beta_1-1}{\alpha_1+\beta_1+\alpha_2+\beta_2-2} \times \Sigma_j \frac{\binom{m}{j}\binom{p}{k}}{\binom{m+p}{j+k}} \tag{21}$$

$$m = \alpha_2+\beta_2-1, p = \alpha_1+\beta_1-2, k = \alpha_1-1 \tag{22}$$

Each term in the summation can be simplified as,

$$\frac{\binom{m}{j}\binom{p}{k}}{\binom{m+p}{j+k}} = \left(\prod_i \frac{j+k-i}{k-i}\right) \times A \times B \tag{23}$$

where

$$A = \frac{p}{(p+m)} \frac{(p-1)}{(p+m-1)} \cdots \frac{(p-k+1)}{(p+m-k+1)} \tag{24}$$

$$B = \frac{m}{(m+p-k)} \frac{(m-1)}{(m+p-k)} \cdots \frac{(m-j+1)}{(m+p-k-j+1)} \tag{25}$$

Further, each term in the summation can be computed from its previous term,

$$\frac{\binom{m}{j+1}\binom{p}{k}}{\binom{m+p}{j+k+1}} = \frac{m-j}{j+1} \times \frac{k+1}{m+p-j-k} \times \frac{\binom{m}{j}\binom{p}{k}}{\binom{m+p}{j+k}} \tag{26}$$

Simplifying the formula in the above manner ensures that the number of terms in the numerator and denominator are equal. Instead of multiplying the numerators and denominators separately, we first divide on a term by term basis and then multiply each result. Logarithms could be also be taken to prevent overflow. The above simplifications ensure an efficient computation of the quantity $P(\theta_1 > \theta_2)$, thereby eliminating the need of factorial look-up suggested in [20].

References

1. D. Agarwal, B.-C. Chen, and P. Elango. Explore/exploit schemes for web content optimization. In *ICDM*, 2009.
2. R. Agrawal. Sample mean based index policies with o(log n) regret for multi-armed bandit problem. *Advances in Applied Probability.*, 27:1054–1078, November 1995.
3. P. Auer, N. Cesa-Bianchi, and P. Fischer. Finite time analysis of multi-armed bandit problem. *Machine Learning*, 27(2-3):235–256, 2002.
4. D. Chakrabarti, R. Kumar, F. Radlinski, and E. Upfal. Mortal multi-armed bandits. In *NIPS*, 2008.
5. O. Chapelle and L. Li. An empirical evaluation of thompson sampling. In *ICML Workshop - Online Trading of Exploration and Exploitation 2*, 2011.
6. H. A. David. *Order Statistics*, volume 1 of *Wiley Series in Probability and Mathematical Statistics*, chapter 1, pages 1–32. John Wiley and Sons, Inc., second edition, 1981.
7. J. C. Gittins. Bandit processes and dynamic allocation indices. *Journal of Royal Statistical Society. Series B*, 41(2):148–177, 1979.
8. T. Graepel, J. Q. Candela, T. Borchert, and R. Herbrich. Web-scale bayesian click-through rate prediction for sponsored search advertising in microsofts bing search engine. In *ICML*, 2010.
9. O.-C. Granmo. The bayesian learning automaton empirical evaluation with two-armed bernoulli bandit problems. *Research and Development in Intelligent Systems XXV*, pages 235–248, 2009.
10. O.-C. Granmo. Solving two-armed bernoulli bandit problems using a bayesian learning automaton. *International Journal of Intelligent Computing and Cybernetics*, 2(3):207–234, 2010.
11. A. K. Gupta and S. Nadarajah. *Handbook of Beta Distribution and its applications*. Marcer Dekker Inc., New York, 2004.
12. S. S. Gupta and S. Panchapakesan. *Multiple Decision Procedures*, volume 1 of *Wiley Series in Probability and Mathematical Statistics*, chapter 4, pages 59–93. John Wiley and Sons, Inc., second edition, 1979.
13. W. Hoeffding. Probability inequalities for sums of bounded random variables. *Journal of the American Statistical Association*, 58(301):13–30, 1963.
14. Jean-Yves, S. Bubeck, and R. Munos. Best arm identification in multi-armed bandits. In *COLT*, 2010.
15. T. L. Lai and H. Robbins. Asymptotically efficient adaptive bandit rules. *Advances in Applied Mathemetics*, 1985.
16. O. Maron and A. W. Moore. Hoeffding races: Accelerating model selection search for classification and function approximation. In *NIPS*, 1994.
17. B. C. May, N. Korda, A. Lee, and D. S. Leslie. Optimistic bayesian sampling in contextual-bandit problems. *Submitted to the Annals of Applied Probability.*
18. T. Norheim, T. Brdland, O.-C. Granmo, and B. J. Oommen. A generic solution to multi-armed bernoulli bandit problems based on random sampling from sibling conjugate priors. In *ICAART*, 2010.
19. W. R. Thompson. On the likelihood that one unknown probability exceeds another in view of the the evidence of two samples. *Biometrika*, 1933.
20. J. Wyatt. Exploration and inference in learning from reinforcement. *Ph.D. thesis, University of Edinburgh*, 1997.

2D Mass-spring-like Model for Prediction of a Sponge's Behaviour upon Robotic Interaction

Veronica E. Arriola-Rios and Jeremy Wyatt

Abstract Deformable objects abound in nature, and future robots must be able to predict how they are going to behave in order to control them. In this paper we present a method capable of learning to predict the behaviour of deformable objects. We use a mass-spring-like model, which we extended to better suit our purposes, and apply it to the concrete scenario of robotic manipulation of an elastic deformable object. We describe a procedure for automatically calibrating the parameters for the model taking images and forces from a real sponge as ground truth. We use this ground truth to provide error measures that drive an evolutionary process that searches the parameter space of the model. The resulting calibrated model can make good predictions for 200 frames (6.667 seconds of real time video) even when tested with forces being applied in different positions to those trained.

1 Introduction

The objective of this research is the study of the process of physical modelling, prediction and evaluation of the predictive capabilities of a mass-spring-like model (as a prerequisite for planning), applied to the concrete scenario of robotic manipulation of an elastic deformable object (dish washing sponge). The robot identifies a region of the world, where its force sensor detects opposition to movement, and whose shape and behaviour can be modelled. This region can be better observed though a colour camera. A simple colour segmentation algorithm allows for the identification and tracking of the region's behaviour. A regular triangular mesh has been chosen as

Veronica E. Arriola-Rios
University of Birmingham, Edgbaston, Birmingham, B15 2TT, U.K. e-mail: veronica.esther@gmail.com

Jeremy Wyatt
University of Birmingham, Edgbaston, Birmingham, B15 2TT, U.K. e-mail: jlw@cs.bham.ac.uk

M. Bramer et al. (eds.), *Research and Development in Intelligent Systems XXVIII*,
DOI 10.1007/978-1-4471-2318-7_14, © Springer-Verlag London Limited 2011

the form of representation of this region, so that the mass-spring-like model can be applied to it. A search for the best set of parameters for the model is conducted by evaluating the similarity of the behaviour of the modelled sponge vs. the real sponge in the 2D sequence of images. The generalisability of the resulting set is tested on data gathered when the forces were applied on other parts of the sponge.

The aim of the robot is to find a way to calibrate a model, so that it can describe the behaviour of an occupied physical region (sponge), just with the help of the information it can receive from its sensors (a camera and a force sensor) during a few interactions with it (pushing it against an obstacle), and a set of basic knowledge of how to learn to calibrate those models (search algorithms). From here, the set of requirements for the representation of the deformable object are explained in Sect. 3.

For the simulation, we opted for what seemed to be a simple general physics based model proposed by Teschner[22]. However, in order to better reproduce the observed behaviours, some modifications and extensions where introduced, like a new force term that tends to preserve the angles between the springs in the mesh, as it is explained in Sect. 4.

Finally, Sect 5 presents the set of experiments where a Katana arm [14], equipped with a rigid finger, pushed a sponge against an obstacle (a pencil, fixed and perpendicular to the plane of the sponge). See Fig. 1. Given a good set of parameters, the program can take as inputs the position of the obstacles for every frame (finger and pencil), the initial position and shape of the sponge, and the sensed force in the direction of movement for every frame, and it will be able to predict the deformation of the sponge for the remaining frames in the video (200 frames, 6.667 seconds) with very good accuracy. Such good sets can be found though a systematic search of the space of parameters or by a simple genetic algorithm. Sect 6 summarises our conclusions.

2 Related Work

It is hard to catalogue the literature about deformable objects, because it covers a wide range of aspects which can be combined to obtain good simulations for different situations (we need to start as general as possible, but without loosing the other ones from sight), starting with computer vision (which covers: identification, representation [17, 15], classification, tracking [9]), simulation and manipulation (with applications mainly in robotics, medicine [12], computer graphics [16, 7] and industry [19]). Sometimes the technique involves manually characterising the behaviour of a family of materials [18], sometimes the main focus is in topological information [20], sometimes they overlap across fields or get combined for new applications, like the work by Luo and Nelson [10] where visual tracking can provide haptic information, after a calibration phase of a FEM model links vision and haptic feedback. The first aim of Computer Graphics is to provide with rich, general and flexible representations of deformable objects: meshes and splines cover these requirements in different ways [21], different behaviours can be attained by applying

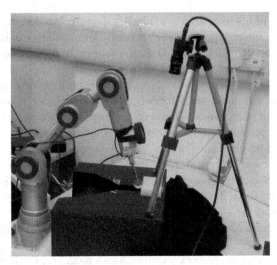

Fig. 1 Experimental setup. Viewing from a side, a one fingered Katana arm with a force sensor pushes a sponge. The transparent finger pushes the sponge away from it. On the other end, a pencil is used as an obstacle always opposed to the finger. A camera observes and records the action from the top.

transformations to vertices and control points, respectively, or by calculating its new possition individually, as it is done in this work.

Physics based models are commonly used either to reinforce tracking or to produce simulations. Two families of them pervade the scientific literature for deformable objects [4]:

Finite Element Methods (FEM): Objects are divided into unitary surface or volumetric elements joined at discrete node points where a continuous equilibrium equation is approximated over each element. To solve the system, large matrices connecting the elements must be solved. There are several variations of these: Non-linear FEM, Geometric Nonlinear FEM and Boundary Element Methods (which transforms the equations so that they have to be integrated at the border of the object instead of the whole volume). The Long Elements Method uses three mutually perpendicular reference planes that cross the object, and the relative positions of points inside the object with respect to these reference planes are simulated [1].

Mass-spring Methods: Objects are represented by meshes where masses are located at the nodes and the edges correspond to springs connecting them. It is possible to discretise and integrate the system of equations for each mass point separately, making the process easy and parallelisable. It can be easily applied to model volumes or 2D textiles [6].

In the area of predictive tracking, the work by Malassiotis [11] resembles the structure of our approach (even though the underlying model is different): a triangular mesh is calculated to cover the 2-D image of a textured deformable object of

interest. The aim of his technique is to identify the principal deformation modes in the mesh over the observed object, so that future deformations can be expressed as combinations of these modes. The 2-D shape of the object is modelled with an elastic membrane deformed by virtual forces, its strain energy is calculated by making use of the finite element theory, which causes it to be costly in time and complexity. This information will guide the deformations of the mesh, while trying to predict how the object will be deformed. However, the shapes it can describe are limited by what can be represented as combinations of the selected modes.

Among the most innovative works with mass-spring methods are: Burion et al. [3], who use a mass-spring skeleton model [4], where filling spheres are placed along the medial skeleton of the object and are connected together with elastic links, which model elongation, flexion and torsion properties. They use a particle filter algorithm to estimate the stiffness coefficients. Since we plan to extend our work to plasticine, the requirement of a skeleton make this approach unsuitable for our purposes.

Nevertheless, we chose to work with Teschner's model [22], following the experience of Morris [13] (in computer graphics), because it addresses the same issues but is easily implemented in 2D (the dimensionality of our ground truth). Here, additionally to the traditional damped springs at the edges, two new energy terms are devised to enforce preservation of area and volume, making this model more adequate to simulate a broad range of realistic behaviours. Also, the terms for distance, area and volume preservation have the same structure, this makes the model uniform and straightforward to implement and extend. Particularly, we added a term to consider preservation of angles, which considerably improved the stability of the simulation.

Also Barbara Frank works with learning of deformable objects, in colaboration with Teschner. Their work has the same general structure than ours, but they use a 3D FEM model for the simulation and search for calibration parameters using a gradient descent algorithm[5].

3 Representation of the Deformable Object

It is clear that it took centuries for humans to discover the molecular and atomic structure of matter, some time more to understand its interactions, how to control the creation of particular structures, and how the macroscopic attributes emerge from the underlying microscopic composition of the material [8]. Nevertheless, there was an intelligent process that allowed humans to handle materials even before they had this knowledge. Since in this work we are interested in the programming of cognitive robots, the model to be used does not have to be physically correct, but its behaviour must correspond with the observations, and it must be possible to apply it easily to a wide range of materials and shapes.

There is a set of simple requirements, given by the predictive task we have in mind:

1. The representation must be deformable, just as the original material.
2. Given that we are receiving visual information in 2D, we will try to keep things simple by having an internal representation also in 2D.
3. It must be possible to represent interactions between solids (rigid and deformable). Particularly, we need to detect contact.
4. The model must provide information beyond the points where data was collected [interpolation and extrapolation] e.g. beyond the points where testing forces were applied and deformations or displacements were registered. Observe that, in particular, the force sensor in our experiment only provides readings in one point, but the shape of the robotic finger is actually a sphere. Also, the initial shape and position of the mesh is given for the first frame, but the model must be able to deform the initial representation accordingly.

A very common representation of any object in computer graphics is a mesh. A mesh can be easily rendered, transformed (translated, rotated, resized, etc.) and deformed. It is also quite common to use meshes for physics based methods. Each node has a mass, and neighbour nodes are connected by edges. Since we are interested in real time modelling of dynamic behaviour, the evaluation of a mass-spring model is appealing, therefore, the mesh must be designed taking this into account. For mass-spring models, the shape of the mesh can lead to undesired anisotropic behaviours, since forces are applied only through the edges (which become springs) [2]. To attend this, to a certain extent, we opted for taking the simple approach of generating a symmetric triangular mesh.

4 Physics Model

4.1 Antecedents

To plan complex motions in AI a planner may find paths between keyframes and displacements of keypoints. It is thus an important task for learning algorithms to find these keypoints. In the case of deformable objects, the new shapes an object can take may be characterised by keypoints like points of high curvature. Nevertheless, they are still so varied that it is not possible to detect and remember them all in advance. Therefore, an algorithm that can predict the continuous or discontinuous transformations of key points in the deformation can help to explore the possible consequences of plans that include nove interactions whose key points are still unknown. In order to do that, the underlying representation of the model must not depend on those unknown keypoints. That is why a regular mesh has been proposed as the basis for the model we use. In future work, this mesh could be used to extract the keypoints mentioned.

This research approach is inspired by the work by Morris[13]. He works with a 3D finite element model as a ground truth to automatically calibrate an almost equivalent instance of the mass-spring model proposed by Teschner [22], which can

be used instead for real time simulations. Random sets of parameters are proposed and evaluated at equilibrium positions, an adaptive simulated annealing search is used to modify the best parameters of the springs and look for better candidates. Observe that only the final equilibrium positions are evaluated, the forces are applied on vertices of the mesh and the position of the objects is fixed.

4.2 Inputs

The katana arm has been equipped with a 6 degrees sensor (forces and torques), but for the experiments in this research only one direction is relevant. A colour camera with a resolution of 800x600 pixels is placed perpendicular to the direction of movement so that it can capture the movement of the finger and the deformation of the sponge. See Fig. 2.

KL:995.436, kd:8.336, KA:96.68, KFI:487.601

Fig. 2 Viewing from the top, a one fingered Katana arm with a force sensor pushes a sponge. The transparent finger pushes the sponge downwards. On the other end (below), a pencil (cap) is used as an obstacle always opposed to the finger. Both obstacles are represented by thin circles in the photo.

4.3 Graphical Constraints

Given that the main focus of this work is on the deformable object, the treatment of the rigid objects involved has been simplified as much as possible. Both, the finger and the pencil are represented as instances of hard circular obstacles. This implies that any element of the deformable mesh will not be allowed to enter or cross over the enclosed region. This constraint is enforced at every frame during the simulation through a standard set of collision detection subroutines. Also the

triangulation must remain without crossings. Whenever the displacemente of a node produces a crossing, the opposite ending of the affected triangle and the node itself get pushed in opposite directions to undo the error. If a set of parameters can not respect this constraints it is eliminated.

4.4 From Energy Constraints to Force terms

The core of the model is in the energy terms that enforce the preservation of three quantities: **length of the springs, area of each triangle** and **the internal angles of the triangles**. The first two terms are directly derived for the two dimensional case following Teschner's method and can be seen in [22]. The last term is our original contribution.

Equal masses are allocated at the nodes of the mesh and the edges correspond to the springs. The dynamics of the deformation of the objects are represented through dynamic constraints from which potential energies are obtained. The dynamics of the system are ruled by the forces that minimise these energies. Teschner indicates how to derive those forces and Morris [13] uses geometrical arguments to explain them. The following sections indicate the corresponding expressions.

4.4.1 Preservation of Distance:

The spring will tend to recover its original length. Strictly this is the only term that will force the triangles to recover their original shape. See Fig. 3.a.

Force:

$$F_D(p_i) = k_D \left(|p_j - p_i| - D_0 \right) \left(\frac{p_j - p_i}{|p_j - p_i|} \right) \tag{1}$$

Where p_i, p_j are the mass point positions, k_D the stiffness coefficient, E_D the potential energy based on the difference between the current distance of two points and the initial or rest distance D_0, with $D_0 \neq 0$. F_D is the force resulting from this energy and it will pull or push the masses in the direction of the line that joins them.

4.4.2 Preservation of Surface Area:

Every triangle in the mesh tries to recover its area. This term does not respect the original shape of the triangle, thus allowing the hole mesh to find a new equilibrium even if greatly deformed. See Fig. 3.b.

Force:

$$F_A(p_i) = k_A \cdot forcemag_A(p_i) \cdot forcedir_A(p_i) \tag{2}$$

$$forcemag_A(p_i) = \frac{\frac{1}{2}((p_k - p_i) \times (p_j - p_i)) - A_0}{A_0}$$

$$forcedir_A(p_i) = \frac{F_A(p_i)}{|F_A(p_i)|} = \frac{areagradient(p_i)}{|areagradient(p_i)|}$$

$$areagradient(p_i) = (p_i - p_j) - \left((p_k - p_j) \cdot \frac{(p_k - p_j) \cdot (p_i - p_j)}{(p_k - p_j) \cdot (p_k - p_j)}\right)$$

Where the energy E_A considers triples of mass points that build surface triangles. E_A represents energy based on the difference of the current area of a surface triangle and its initial area A_0 with $A_0 \neq 0$. Here k_A is an area stiffness coefficient. Each mass with move in the direction of the height of the triangle that passes through it, to increase or decrease its area.

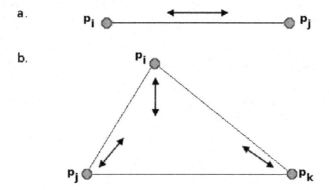

Fig. 3 a. The linear force of the spring pulls inside if the spring was elongated, or outside if it was compressed. b. The triangle tries to quickly recover its area by pulling all its vertices along its corresponding heights.

4.4.3 Preservation of Angles:

We added an extra term to enforce the preservation of angles. The energy depends on the difference of the angles between adjacent edges. The force emerging from this term is harder to visualize, it is a linear combinations of the vectors along the edges that form the angle of interest, it pretends to restore the original angle, but does not pay attention to the original size. See Fig. 4. Therefore, it helps recover a

similar triangle, but if used alone can collapse or explode the triangle. An additional line in the code also forces an inverted angle to recover its original orientation.

Energy:

$$E_\varphi(\varphi) = \frac{1}{2} k_\varphi (\varphi - \varphi_0) *$$ (3)

$$\varphi(p_i, p_j, p_k) = \arccos \left(\frac{(p_j - p_i) \cdot (p_k - p_i)}{\|p_j - p_i\| \, \|p_k - p_i\|} \right)^2$$

* It was also considered to multiply E_φ by the lengths of the edges, but it hasn't improved the performance of the model.

Where φ is the angle between adjacent edges, E_φ is the energy associated to changes in the angle and k_φ, the corresponding stiffness constant. Contrary to the previous cases, it is not so evident in which direction the force will act.

Force:

$$F_\varphi(p_i) = k_\varphi (\varphi - \varphi_0) \frac{\partial \varphi}{\partial p_i}$$ (4)

$$\frac{\partial \varphi}{\partial p_i}(p_i) = \frac{1}{d_{ji} d_{ki} \sqrt{1 - \left[\frac{pp}{(d_{ji})(d_{ki})} \right]^2}} \left\{ \left[1 - \frac{pp}{d_{ki}^2} \right] (p_k - p_i) + \left[1 - \frac{pp}{d_{ji}^2} \right] (p_j - p_i) \right\}$$

$$pp(p_i) = (p_j - p_i) \cdot (p_k - p_i)$$
$$d_{ji}(p_i) = \|p_j - p_i\|$$
$$d_{ki}(p_i) = \|p_k - p_i\|$$ (5)

The differential equations that rule the behaviour of the system are integrated with a numerical approach. Originally the acceleration of the masses is proportional to the force, the equation must be integrated twice to obtain the positions as a function of time. In this case, in order to compute the new state of the system ($x(t+h)$ position at time $t+h$, $v(t+h)$ velocity at time $t+h$) the Verlet integration scheme is used [6].

$$x(t+h) = 2x(t) - x(t-h) + h^2 \frac{F(t)}{m} + O(h^4)$$ (6)

$$v(t+h) = \frac{x(t+h) - x(t-h)}{2h} + O(h^2)$$ (7)

with $F(t) = F_D(t) + F_A(t) + F_\varphi(t)$, and m, the mass of the node.

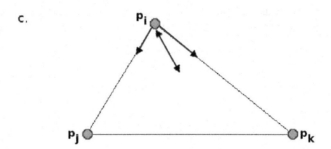

Fig. 4 The angular force displaces the vertex of interest in the direction of maximum change of the angle in order to recover its original value. This direction is a linear combination of the vectors that emerge from both edges forming the angle, and does not respect the original size of the triangle.

This will yield the typical oscillatory behaviour of springs. However, to simulate a heavily damped sponge we made the velocities proportional to the forces. Now, instead of having a second order set of equations, the set is first order. The simulations we obtained were closer to the observed behaviour. Also, for every frame in the simulation, there are 10 steps in the numerical integration.

$$x(t+h) = x(t) + h\frac{\mathbf{F(t)}}{m} \tag{8}$$

with $F(t) = F_D(t) + F_A(t) + F_\varphi(t)$.

However, to give stability to the numerical integration process it is necessary to add damping terms to the linear force. Teschner gives the following formula to calculate the force:

$$F^i(p_0, \ldots, p_{n-1}, v_0, \ldots, v_{n-1}) = \left(-kC - k_d \sum_{0 \leq j < n} \frac{\partial C}{\partial p_j} v_j \right) \frac{\partial C}{\partial p_i} \tag{9}$$

Given that F_D for every p_i only depends on p_i and p_j, the sum has two terms.

$$F_D(p_i, p_j) = \left(k_D \left(\frac{|p_j - p_i| - D_0}{D_0} \right) + k_d \frac{1}{D_0} \frac{p_j - p_i}{|p_j - p_i|} \cdot (v_j - v_i) \right) \frac{1}{D_0} \left(\frac{p_j - p_i}{|p_j - p_i|} \right) \tag{10}$$

Still these forces only represent the internal tension of the material that makes it tend to recover its shape. The external force applied by the finger and measured by the sensor is added to the forces acting on the nearest vertex to the finger in the mesh. Additionally, the mesh must respect the graphical constraint imposed by the finger, which greatly helps in shaping the sponge, and propagates the effect caused by the hole circular shape.

At the beginning we assumed that the spring terms would suffice even to reproduce the slight translation of the sponge as it is pushed by the finger, since pushing a spring should make this push its neighbours and so on. However, our first experi-

ments showed it not to be the case. The effect of pushing a spring get diluted among the deformation of the spring and the area and angular terms. In order to obtain the translation, we must add a solid propagation of the finger's force. This is, that part of the force is absorbed in deformation, while another amount affects all vertices and produces an even displacement. For the moment we just added an extra parameter to the model that fixes the amount of force that is invested in translation. There is an additional parameter f_t that represents a solid force that is constantly propagated to the entire sponge (to every vertex) and accounts for the overal solid translation of the object.

The algorithms where implemented in C++, making use of the GNU compiler gcc 4.4.4. The triangulations where managed with the CGAL library, and the vision part was handled with OpenCV.

5 Experiments

5.1 Evaluation: Difference of Areas

The function used to automate the decision of what makes a good set of parameters is quite simple, but provides a sufficient criterion to eliminate bad sets of parameters. It consists in measuring the difference between the area occupied by the image of the sponge and the area covered by the mesh of the model (this is done pixel by pixel). The bigger this difference, the worst the model. All the differences frame by frame are added up to assign a mark to the set of parameters during the hole duration of the video. See Fig. 5.

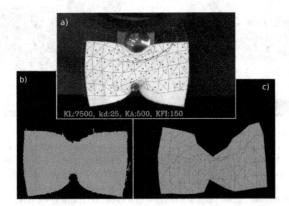

Fig. 5 a) Shows the original image with the mesh overlaid as the simulation is executed. b) The area occupied by the sponge. c) The area occupied by the mesh. The evaluation function counts the pixels in the difference: those in the sponge that are not in the mesh, and those in the mesh that are not in the sponge. The positions are absolute.

5.2 Results

The numerical value of the forces measured in the relevant direction of movement range from -3.8 N (due to noise in the sensor) to 170.3 N. We use a simple genetic algorithm to find good sets of parameters. Here, the first generation has only random values for every parameter, within the ranges: $k_D \in [0.001, 1000.0]$, $k_d \in [0.001, 100.0]$, $k_A \in [0.001, 200.0]$, $k_\varphi \in [0.001, 700.0]$ and $f_t \in [0.0, 200.0]$. After, for every generation, one third of the new elements are the best of the previous generation (they don't get evaluated again), one third are the previous ones plus Gaussian noise (the value of sigma gets reduced for every generation from 100 to 10), and the last third are new random elements. With the genetic algorithm, after the 8th generation the set of parameters with the best mark has been the same. It produced the videos summarized in Fig. 6, and the marks for the best sets are summarized in Table 1. However, other executions of the same algorithm have found other good sets of values (any of them would serve the purposes of the robot). Nevertheless we completed the analysis with a systematic run.

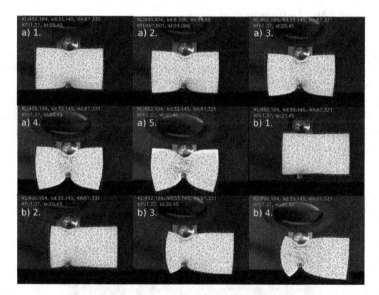

Fig. 6 Sequence taken from a simulation with the best set as evaluated by a genetic algorithm: $k_D = 492.184$, $k_d = 33.145$, $k_A = 67.331$, $k_\varphi = 1.37$ and $f_t = 20.45$. a) Over the video used for the evaluation of the parameters. a) 5. In the last frame an error remains due to the oversimplification of the translation function: the elements of the sponge keep being pushed down even after the finger has stopped moving (frame 300). b) Same model and parameters but with the forces acting on different positions. The predictions are fairly correct for 200 frames. We have another set where the forces are applied to the right side of the sponge, the results are symmetric, but are not shown for lack of space.

We noticed that big values for the preservation of areas create severe problems while trying to maintain the graphical constraints (T-test $t = 8.33$, for all the follow-

Table 1 Best sets of parameters for every generation.

Generation	Mark	k_D	k_d	k_A	k_φ	f_t
0	53,656,529	96.501	68.205	112.012	572.616	17.3
1	44,993,321	613.188	13.7061	85.1941	168.793	18.6731
3	42,767,941	249.164	23.855	145.933	276.542	19.326
8	41,291,354	492.184	33.145	67.331	1.37	20.45

For the generations not shown the values were repeated

ing: $df = 3274$, $p < 0.002$), large values of k_φ help (T-test $t = 9.32$) and $ft = 15$ is the best tested value (T-test $t = 246.6$). 53.5% of the sets of parameters in the range of values we considered ($k_D \in [600.0, 1000.0]$, $k_d \in [50.0, 100.0]$, $k_A \in [50.0, 200.0]$, $k_\varphi \in [50.0, 700.0]$ and $f_t \in [25.0, 200.0]$) got discarded. The best nine results have $k_D = 1000, k_d = 50, k_A \leq 50$, $f_t = 15$ and $k_\varphi \in [600.0, 700.0]$, with their marks around 52 million. There are also differences in magnitude depending on the number of elements in the mesh. Notice that the genetic algorithm was able to try values in a wider range, and in fact quickly found its best sets outside from what we had considered for the systematic search. If there are more elements in the mesh, the stiffness coefficients are smaller. Unfortunately the systematic search can take up to several weeks in a PC with an Intel(R) Core(TM)2 Quad CPU Q6600 @ 2.40GHz.

6 Conclusions

We managed to automatically calibrate a mass-spring-like model taking images and forces from a real sponge as ground truth. The discretisation of the equations of movement produce jumps whose effects are hard to control. The calibrated model works well until opposing forces make it difficult to respect all the graphical constraints. The simulation also fails at the end, when the translation term keeps acting even when the sponge is not moving any more (this requires a better function for the translation component). Furthermore, in order to consider new behaviours (plasticity, rotations, etc.) it is necessary to add new terms to the model and the search space is increased. This shows that, if we want to program a cognitive robot using physical models, it would be required to provide the robot with a big collection of components to consider, which leaves open the question of whether there is a simpler mechanism that can cover many behaviours on the same basis.

Acknowledgements Thank you to Dr. Helge Ritter and Matthias Schoepfer from the University of Bielefeld, Germany for their suggestions leading to the completion of this work. To Rustam Stolkin for his aid to make the experiments and Marek Kopicki for his software to control the arm. Also to Aaron Sloman for interesting discussions and suggestions for this research. To the CONACYT in Mexico and to the ORSAS scheme in the UK for sponsoring my PhD, also the research leading to these results has received funding from the European Community's Seventh Framework Programme [FP7/2007-2013] under grant agreement No. 215181, CogX.

References

1. Balaniuk, R., Salisbury, K.: Dynamic simulation of deformable objects using the long elements method. 10th Symposium On Haptic Interfaces For Virtual Environment And Teleoperator Systems, Proceedings pp. 58–65 (2002)
2. Bourguignon, D., Cani, M.P.: Controlling anisotropy in mass-spring systems. In: N. Magnenat-Thalmann, D. Thalmann, B. Arnaldi (eds.) 11th Eurographics Workshop on Computer Animation and Simulation, EGCAS 2000, August, 2000, Springer Computer Science, pp. 113–123. Springer-Verlag, Interlaken, Suisse (2000)
3. Burion, S., Conti, F., Petrovskaya, A., Baur, C., Khatib, O.: Identifying physical properties of deformable objects by using particle filters. 2008 Ieee International Conference On Robotics And Automation, Vols 1-9 pp. 1112–1117 (2008)
4. Conti, F., Khatib, O., Baur, C.: Interactive rendering of deformable objects based on a filling sphere modeling approach. In: Robotics and Automation, 2003. Proceedings. ICRA '03. IEEE International Conference on, vol. 3, pp. 3716 – 3721 (2003)
5. Frank, B., Schmedding, R., Stachniss, C., Teschner, M., Burgard, W.: Learning the elasticity parameters of deformable objects with a manipulation robot. In: Proc. of the IEEE/RSJ International Conference on Intelligent Robots and Systems (IROS) (2010)
6. Fuhrmann, A., Gro, C., Luckas, V.: Interactive animation of cloth including self collision detection. Journal of WSCG **11**(1), 141–148 (2003)
7. Gibson, S.F.F., Mirtich, B.: A survey of deformable modeling in computer graphics. Tech. rep., MERL (Mitsubishi Electric Research Laboratory) (1997)
8. Gonzlez-Vias, W., Mancini, H.L.: An Introduction To Materials Science. Princeton University Press, U.S.A. (2004). Translation of: Ciencia de los Materiales
9. Kass, M., Witkin, A., Terzopuolos, D.: Snakes: Active contour models. International Journal Of Computer Vision **1**(4), 321–331 (1988)
10. Luo, Y.H., Nelson, B.J.: Fusing force and vision feedback for manipulating deformable objects. Journal Of Robotic Systems **18**(3), 103–117 (2001)
11. Malassiotis, S., Strintzis, M.G.: Tracking textured deformable objects using a finite-element mesh. Ieee Transactions On Circuits And Systems For Video Technology **8**(6), 756–774 (1998)
12. McInerney, T., Terzopoulos, D.: Deformable models in medical image analysis: a survey. Med Image Anal **1**(2), 91–108 (1996)
13. Morris, D., Salisbury, K.: Automatic preparation, calibration, and simulation of deformable objects. Computer Methods In Biomechanics And Biomedical Engineering **11**(3), 263–279 (2008)
14. Neuronics: Katana user manual and technical description. http://www.neuronics.ch (2004)
15. Newcombe, R.A., Davison, A.J.: Live dense reconstruction with a single moving camera. In: CVPR (2010)
16. O'Brien, J.F., Bargteil, A.W., Hodgins, J.K.: Graphical modeling and animation of ductile fracture. ACM Trans. Graph. **21**(3), 291–294 (2002)
17. Ravishankar, S., Jain, A., Mittal, A.: Multi-stage contour based detection of deformable objects. Computer Vision - Eccv 2008, Pt I, Proceedings **5302**, 483–496 (2008)
18. Remde, A., Abegg, F., Worn, H.: Ein allgemainer ansatz zur montage deformierarbarer linearer objekte mit industrieroботern (a general approach for the assembly of deformable linear objects with industrial robots). In: Robotik'2000. Berlin, Germany (2000)
19. Saadat, M., Nan, P.: Industrial applications of automatic manipulation of flexible materials. Industrial Robot **29**(5), 434–442 (2002)
20. Saha, M., Isto, P.: Manipulation planning for deformable linear objects. Ieee Transactions On Robotics **23**(6), 1141–1150 (2007)
21. Song, Y., Bai, L.: 3d modeling for deformable objects. Articulated Motion And Deformable Objects, Proceedings **5098**, 175–187 (2008)
22. Teschner, M., Heidelberg, B., Muller, M., Gross, M.: A versatile and robust model for geometrically complex deformable solids. In: Proceedings of Computer Graphics International (CGI'04), pp. 312–319. Crete, Greece (2004)

SHORT PAPERS

Quality Management Using Electrical Capacitance Tomography and Genetic Programming: A new Framework

Alaa F. Sheta, Peter Rausch and Alaa Al–Afeef

Abstract Currently, many automotive companies struggle with expensive product recalls. To overcome these issues the need for quality management increases. Hence, we propose a monitoring and control framework for Lost Foam Casting (LFC) manufacturing processes using Electrical Capacitance Tomography (ECT) and an evolutionary Genetic Programming (GP) based system. The multi-tier framework simulates the process output, helps simulating a metal filling modeling part of the process and supports product quality control. The results are very promising.

1 Introduction

Currently, many automotive companies struggle with quality issues. To reinforce quality management and to reduce defects of parts or products, tomography can be deployed. Tomography is a method of producing a sectional image of the internal structures of an object using waves of energy [1, 2]. Technically, tomography involves taking direct sectional images (e.g. X-ray, infrared or ultrasound tomogram) or reconstructing indirect sectional images using boundary measurements based on the internal characteristics of the monitored object (e.g. electrical tomogram) [3]. It is one of the few feedback tools that gives information about what is actually happening inside an industrial process. This information is extremely important to support quality management, to develop processes efficiently and to reduce production costs. In this paper, we propose a general framework for monitoring and control of industrial manufacturing processes which supports quality management. Despite the fact, that the ideas discussed in this paper are focused on LFC processes in the automotive industry, it is important to notice, that the results of our research can be transferred to many fields of application as well.

LFC is a casting process that uses foam patterns as molds in which the molten metal decomposes the foam pattern and creates a casting in its shape [2, 4]. It is very simple and cheap to cast complex patterns. In order to ensure quality, imaging techniques can be used. ECT based approaches have become very popular. They have been applied successfully to study various industrial processes using capacitance measurements to generate images [1]. LFC uses the ECT technique to express

Alaa F. Sheta, Computer Science Department, The World Islamic Science and Education (WISE) University, Amman, Jordan, e-mail: asheta66@gmail.com
Peter Rausch, Computer Science Department, Georg Simon Ohm University of Applied Sciences, Nuremberg, Germany, e-mail: peter.rausch@ohm-hochschule.de
Alaa Al–Afeef, Image Technologies Inc. (ITEC), Amman, Jordan, e-mail: alaa.afeef@gmail.com

M. Bramer et al. (eds.), *Research and Development in Intelligent Systems XXVIII*,
DOI 10.1007/978-1-4471-2318-7_15, © Springer-Verlag London Limited 2011

the metal fill profile and to simulate the properties of molten metal inside the foam patterns during the casting process [4].

ECT is a method for the determination of the dielectric permittivity distribution in the interior of an object from external capacitance measurements and has a lot of advantages [5]. Compared to hard field tomography, it is fast and relatively in-expensive. However, the quality and accuracy of the reconstructed images of ECT measurement systems is often insufficient [6]. Especially in terms of the mentioned challenges concerning car parts' quality, this is an important issue. It can be man-aged with evolutionary software which is a component of the presented monitoring and control framework.

2 A Monitoring and Control Framework for Manufacturing

Figure 1 shows a block diagram of the proposed framework.

Fig. 1 Remote monitoring and control framework

A *Matlab* server is deployed to run the GP based evolutionary software which is used to simulate the metal filling modeling part of the process. Its models use sen-sor inputs and will be explained later. The software is used to simulate the process output. The underlying ECT system contains capacitance sensors which provide the necessary input (i.e. capacitance readings). Other components allow remote mobile access to communicate directly between the stationary server and mobile devices. So, users can keep track of the processes and have full capabilities to configure and (re)start execution remotely. Deploying the ECT approach in combination with the GP-based image representation, data from the manufacturing process execution layer can be monitored and analyzed using a controlling system on a regular base. The results produced by the Production Activity Control (PAC) component can be evaluated by quality and production managers. Like Figure 1 shows, it is also possi-ble to establish an ERP interface and to supply a Business Intelligence (BI)-system with data. So, analysis on the strategic level can be supported. The following sec-tions will provide more details of framework's components.

3 Image Reconstruction

There are two major computational problems in the ECT image reconstruction [7]: The first is *the forward problem* in which the capacitance measurement C_{ij} between electrodes i and j is determined from the permittivity distribution $\varepsilon(x,y)$: $C_{ij} = F(\varepsilon(x,y))$. Additionally, *the inverse problem* has to be solved which is the process of finding the inverse relationship such that the permittivity distribution is estimated using capacitance measurements and (as a result) constructing a visual image using a reconstructing algorithm. This process is also called *image reconstruction process*. The inverse relationship can be expressed as in Equation 1.

$$\varepsilon(x,y) = F^{-1}(C_{12}, C_{13}, C_{14}, \ldots, C_{ij}, \ldots, C_{N-1,N}) \tag{1}$$

There are a couple of issues making the implementation of ECT systems a challenge [5, 8]: Soft fields affect the sensors in which the electric field lines are dependent on the permittivity distribution in the imaging domain. Additionally, the ill-condition problem occurs. This means ill-posed response of the sensor due to a different location in the imaging domain. Also, the limited number of independent measurements affects the process. This is why usually very low resolution tomograms are produced [8]. Another issue is the ill-posed ECT problem. Getting worse, non-linearity of the relationship between the measured capacitance and permittivity distribution exits [8]. Furthermore, it is hard to establish an analytical and explicit expression which describes this relationship.

In order to master these challenges and to improve the imaging accuracy, more accurate reconstruction algorithms must be developed. So, in the following sections the idea of applying GP to the image reconstruction problem will be discussed. Our objective is to find a GP Inverse Solver that mathematically describes the nonlinear relationship F between the capacitance input variables C and the image pixel P of image vector G which represents the distribution of metal in the imaging area.

$$G_p = F(C_1, C_2, \ldots, C_{\frac{N(N-1)}{2}}) \tag{2}$$

In our case, the inverse solver consists of 64 GP models. Each model is responsible for deriving a relationship between capacitance measurements $[C_1 - C_{66}]$ and a specific pixel in an ECT image of 64 pixels. In another word, P in Equation 2 is ranging from 1 to 64 pixels, N is 12 electrodes. In Figure 2 the structure of the proposed system is shown. The number of measurements is 66 representing all the unique combinations of measurements between the 12 electrodes distributed around the measuring area. These measurements are represented by the symbols $C_1, \ldots, C_{66}$. One at a time, all the measurements are presented to each of the 64 GP systems.

To deploy the GP model, the *MatLab* toolbox was used. It was extended by a so-called ECTGP module which provides a Graphical User Interface (GUI) for solving the nonlinear inverse problems of ECT. By using another module of the ECTGP toolbox, the user is able to view capacitance measurements and ECT images, provided that he supplies the associated input. Supported by a GUI, the toolbox helps

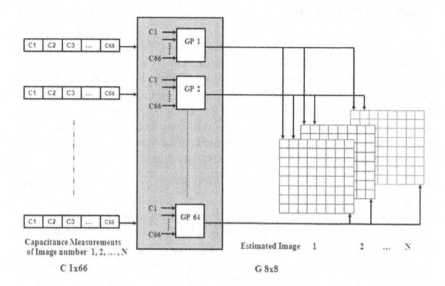

Fig. 2 Proposed GP Inverse Solver Model

setting up experiments (for instance to prepare training and testing data), executing a training session and loading resulted ECT images and the performance data. As a final step, the user can analyze and plot the GP performance over all runs using the *MatLab* extension. He can view the results, for instance estimated images, and analyze errors between original and estimated data according to many criteria.

The GP was trained using *lilgp* with ANSYS generated examples (see Figure 3).[1] A training set of 268 ECT images with the corresponding capacitance measurements was provided to the GP system. To test the performance of the GP models, a testing set of size 67 was used. A subset of these patterns and their corresponding GP estimated patterns are shown in Figure 3.

One of the major problems in GP is over-fitting in which the algorithm tends to follow a pattern based on the learning samples. To resolve this problem we used different data sets for testing and training in which the selected testing data set was different enough for testing the performance of the GP Inverse Solver.

The Best-so-far curve of the run is shown in Figure 4. It visualizes errors (y-axis) of the generations (x-axis) for all models (z-axis). The overall error percentage for the developed GP simulation in the training case was 2.53% and 2.63% in the testing case as given in Equation 3.

---

[1] The data was provided by Drs. Mohamed Abdelrahman and Wael Deabes, Tennessee Technological University. It was produced in conjunction with research project GO14228 supported by US Department of Energy (DOE), USA.

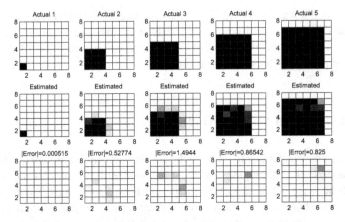

Fig. 3 A sample of actual and estimated patterns using GP: (1-3) training cases, (4-5) testing cases

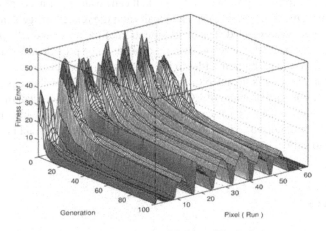

Fig. 4 Best-so-far curve of the GP Models accessible by mobile devices

$$EP_{set} = \frac{G^{set} - OAE}{G^{set}}, \quad \text{where} \quad OAE = \sum^{\alpha}\sum^{\beta} \left| G^{Actual} - G^{Estimated} \right| \tag{3}$$

set is either the training or testing set of the experiment. EP_{set} represents the error percentage of a given set. G^{set} denotes the total number of pixels of all images in that set. The Overall Absolute Error (OAE) is the summation of the absolute difference between the actual and the GP estimated image pixels of the complete image set. G^{Actual} and $G^{Estimated}$ are the actual and estimated pixel, respectively. α represents total number of images in the set. β denotes the image-size (i.e. the total number of a single image's pixels). In Equation 4, G_{64} is the estimated pixel number 64 of image G and C_n^e represents the corresponding capacitance measurement of the input variables n. e denotes an exponent.

$$G_{64} = C_{54} * C_{46}^3 (C_{46}^{38} * C_{52}^4 * C_{54} - C_{24} * C_{46}^{18} * C_{52}^2 - C_{54}) \tag{4}$$

In this model, it was found that G_{64} is mostly affected by the measurements C_{46}, C_{52}, C_{24} and C_{54}. The values of the input variables, for instance C_n, are in the range: $0 \leq C_n \leq 1$. This prevents the values of G from exceeding a range of $-1 \leq G \leq 1$ which is mapped using threshold levels into $\{0, 1\}$.

4 Conclusions and Future Work

In this paper, a new technique for solving the non-linear inverse problem of ECT has been introduced. The technique is based on GP to identify the models relating the sensors' capacitance measurements to the permittivity distributions. The presented technique showed promising results in terms of accuracy, the quality of reconstruction results and convergence rates. Furthermore, it could be shown that: companies can benefit a lot from the proposed framework. It can be an important contribution to quality management. Expensive product recalls and the related image damages can be avoided or at least reduced. The main limitation of the presented GP approach is the training time needed. Sufficient training data has to be provided, and data has to be expressive of the problem in order to have a successful prediction.

As a future work, it is intended to investigate other metal distributions and to apply GP to the forward problem of ECT. Additionally, the development of a process in order to improve the reconstructed images using look-up tables with all possibilities of grid formation to reduce the training time is needed. It would be also very interesting to extend the analysis and reporting components.

References

1. A. Al-Afeef. Image reconstructing in electrical capacitance tomography of manufacturing processes using genetic programming. Master's thesis, Al-Balqa Applied University, July 2010.
2. A. Al-Afeef, A. F. Sheta, and A. Al-Rabea. Image reconstruction of a metal fill industrial process using genetic programming. In *ISDA*, pages 12–17. IEEE, 2010.
3. M.S. Beck and R.A. Williams. Process tomography: a european innovation and its applications. *Measurement Science and Technology*, 7(3):215–224, 1996.
4. M. Abdelrahman, A. Sheta, and W. Deabes. Fuzzy mathematical modeling for reconstructing images in ect of manufacturing processes. In *Proc. Fuzzy Mathematical Modeling for Reconstructing Images in ECT of Manufacturing Processes*, December 2009.
5. J. Lei, S. Liu, Z. Li, and M. Sun. Image reconstruction algorithm based on the extended regularised total least squares method for electrical capacitance tomography. *IET Science, Measurement and Technology*, 2(5):326–336, September 2008.
6. S.M. Hoyle, B.S. Thorn, C. Lenn, C.G. Xie, S.M Huang, and M.S. Beck. Electrical capacitance tomography for flow imaging system model for development of image reconstruction algorithms and design of primary sensor. In *IEEE Proceedings G 139*, pages 89–98, 1992.
7. K. Alme and S. Mylvaganam. Electrical capacitance tomographysensor models, design, simulations, and experimental verification. *IEEE SENSORS*, 6(5), OCTOBER 2006.
8. O. Isaksen. A review of reconstruction techniques for capacitance tomography. *Sensors Journal, IEEE*, 7(3):325–337, March 1996.

MOEA/D with DE and PSO: MOEA/D-DE+PSO

Wali Khan Mashwani

Abstract: Hybridization is one of the important research area in evolutionary multi-objective optimization (EMO).It is a method that incorporate good merits of multiple techniques aim at to enhance the search ability of EMO algorithm. In this chapter, we combine two well-known search algorithms, DE and PSO, and developed algorithm known as MOEA/D-DE+PSO. We experimentally studied its performance on two types of continuous multi-objective optimization problems and found better improvement.

1 Introduction

In this paper, we interested in solving multiobjective optimization problem (MOP) of minimization type which is generally formulated as under:

$$\text{minimize } F(x) = (f_1(x), f_2(x) \ldots, f_m(x)) \tag{1}$$

Subject to $x \in \Omega$, where $\Omega \subseteq R^n$, $x = (x_1, \ldots, x_n)^T \in \Omega$ is an n-dimensional vector of the decision variables, Ω is the *decision (variable) space*, $F : \Omega \to R^m$ consist of m real-valued objectives function. Very often, the objectives of the problem (1) are in conflict with one another or incommensurable. Due this conflict among the objectives function, no solution in Ω can optimize all the objectives simultaneously. Instead, one has to find a set of good representative optimal solutions to the problem (1) in the form of best trade-off or compromises among the objectives in terms of Pareto optimality.

Wali Khan Mashwani is a PhD student in the Department of Mathematical Sciences, University of Essex, Wivenhoe Park, Colchester, CO4 3SQ, UK e-mail: wkhan@essex.ac.uk & a Faculty member of Kohat University of Science and Technology (KUST), PAKISTAN.

M. Bramer et al. (eds.), *Research and Development in Intelligent Systems XXVIII*, DOI 10.1007/978-1-4471-2318-7_16, © Springer-Verlag London Limited 2011

Since 1970*s*, numerous evolutionary multiobjective optimization (EMO) algorithms have been developed aim at finding a set optimal solutions to the problem 1. Among them, MOEA/D [1] is the novel developed paradigm which combines the decomposition strategies with evolutionary algorithm for solving problem (1) differently from existing Pareto dominance based EAs. Surprisingly, MOEA/D also used single algorithm for population evolution with exception [2].

In this paper, we study the combined effect of Differential evolution (DE) [3] and particle swarm optimization (PSO) [4] and developed hybrid version of the MOEA/D [1] known as MOEA/D-DE+PSO for continuous multiobjective optimization. We performed this study inspired by some recent reported work [5, 6, 2, 7].

The rest of this paper is organized as follows: **Section 2** explains the frameworks of MOEA/D-DE+PSO and the parameter settings in carried out experiments, **Section 3** provides a brief discussion on the experimental results, and finally **Section 4** concludes the paper.

2 MOEA/D with DE and PSO: MOEA/D-DE+PSO

The algorithmic steps of MOEA/D with DE and PSO, MOEA/D-DE+PSO is hereby outlined in **Algorithm 1**.

Table 1 Parameter Setting for solving ZDT [8] and CEC'09 Test Problems [9]. Here, N is the size of population, p_m is the mutation probability, η is the distribution index and T is the neighborhood size of subproblem in MOEA/D paradigm, r is a random number. The first column of the table represent the population size for the used test problems.

ZDT	100	$p_m = \frac{1}{n}, n = 10$	$\eta = 20$	25000	$T = 0.1N$
CEC'09	600(1000)	$p_m = \frac{1}{n}, n = 30$	$\eta = 20$	300,000	$T = 0.1N$
PSO & DE	$w = 0.3 + r/2$	$c_1 = c_2 = 0.4$	$\xi = 0.7$	$CR = 1$	$F = 0.5$

3 A Brief Discussion on obtained Experimental Results

We used Inverted generation distance (IGD)-metric [10] to compare and evaluate the performance of both versions of MOEA/D [1], namely, **MOEA/D-DE** and **MOEA/D-DE+PSO** on the ZDT test problems [8] and on the CEC'09 test instances [9]. To compute the IGD-metric values, we have chosen P^* of uniformly distributed points in the PF of size 1000 for all problems during 30 times simulation of each algorithm. We used the parameter setting as described in the **Table 1** in our experimental studies of both MOEA/D-DE and MOEA/D-DE+PSO to solve each test

Algorithm 1 Pseudocode of MOEA/D-DE+PSO

INPUT:

- MOP: the multiobjective optimization problem;
- N: population (i.e., the number of subproblems);
- F_{EVAL}: the maximal number of function evaluations;
- a uniform spread of N weight vectors, $\lambda_1, \ldots, \lambda_N$;
- T: the number of weight vectors in the neighborhood of each weight vector;

Output: $\{x^{(1)}, x^{(2)}, \ldots, x^{(N)}\}$ and $\{F(x^{(1)}), \ldots, F(x^{(N)})\}$;

Step 0 *Initialization:*

0.1:   Uniformly randomly generate a population of size N, $P = \{x^{(1)}, \ldots, x^{(N)}\}$ from the search space Ω;

0.2:   Initialize a set of N weight vectors, $\{\lambda^1, \lambda^2, \ldots, \lambda^N\}$;

0.3:   Compute the Euclidian distances between any two weight vectors and then find the T closest weight vectors to each weight vector. For the *ith* subproblem, set $B(i) = \{i_1, \ldots, i_T\}$, where $\lambda^{i1}, \ldots, \lambda^{iT}$ are the T closest weight vectors to λ^i;

0.4:   Compute the F-function value of each member in P, $F(x^i), i = 1, 2, \ldots, N$;

0.5:   Initialize $z = (z_1, \ldots, z_m)^T$ by problem-specific method;

0.6:   Set $\lceil \zeta_1 = 0.5N \rceil$; $\zeta_2 = N - \zeta_1$; where ζ_1, the number of subproblems deal by search algorithm A, and ζ_2, the number of new solutions deal by search algorithm B;

0.7:   Set $t = 0$;

Step 2: Updating Phase of the MOEA/D-DE+PSO:

1:   **while** $t < F_{EVAL}$ **do**
2:       Randomly divide $I = \{1, 2, \ldots, N\}$ into two sets, I_A and I_B, such that I_A has ζ_1 indices and I_B has ζ_2 indices at t ;
3:       **for** $i = 1 : N$ **do**
4:           **if** $i \in I_A$ **then**
5:               Apply search operator A to generate an offspring $\bar{x}^i$;
6:           **else**
7:               Apply search operator B to generate an offspring $\bar{x}^i$;
8:           **end if**
9:           Mutate $\bar{x}^i$ with probability p_m, to get $\bar{y}^i$;
10:          Repair $\bar{y}^i$ to produce an offspring y^i;
11:          Compute the F-function value of y^i, $F(y^i)$;
12:          **Update of z:** For each $j = 1, \ldots, m$, $f_j(y^i) < z_j$, then set $z_j = f_j(y^i)$;
13:          **Update of Neighboring Solutions:**
14:              For each index $k \in B(i) = \{i_1, \ldots, i_T\}$
15:              **if** $g^{te}(y^i | \lambda^k, z) \leq g(x^k | \lambda^k, z)$ **then**
16:                  $x^k = y^i$ and $F(x^k) = F(y^i)$
17:              **end if**
18:          **end for**
              Update ζ_1 and ζ_2 (Detail can found in Algorithm 2.)
19:          $t = t + 1$
20: **end while**

Algorithm 2 Updating Procedure of ζ_1 and ζ_2

Step 1: Compute the ζ_1, the number of subproblems deal by search algorithm A, and ζ_2 is number of subproblems deal by search algorithm B.

step 2: Compute the probability of success (i.e., τ_1) of the search algorithm A

$$\tau_1 = \frac{\frac{\kappa_1}{\zeta_1}}{\frac{\kappa_1}{\zeta_1} + \frac{\kappa_2}{\zeta_2}} \tag{2}$$

Where κ_1 is the total successful reward of search algorithm A out of ζ_1 subproblems.

Step 3: Replace $\zeta_1 = \lceil N \times \tau_1 \rceil$ and $\zeta_2 = N - \zeta_1$.

problem.

Table 2 and **Table 3** summarizes the IGD-metric values in terms of best (minimum), median, mean, standard deviation (std), worst (maximum), which are found by MOEA/D-DE and MOEA/D-DE+PSO, respectively. A bold data represent the best results for the corresponding algorithm on respective problem. This results show that MOEA/D-DE+PSO is more effective than MOEA/D-DE on most test problems. We didn't includes the plots of the Pareto front (PF) of the used test problems found by MOEA/D-DE and MOEA/D-DE+PSO due page limitation.

Table 2 *The IGD-metric value statistics found by MOEA/D-DE, MOEA/D-DE+PSO during 30times independent runs for ZDT test problems [8], ZDT1-ZDT4 and ZDT6.*

ZDT problems	MOEA/D, MOEA/D-DE+PSO					
	min	median	mean	std	max	Algorithms
ZDT1	0.00401	0.00419	0.00421	0.00018	0.00455	MOEA/D-DE
	0.00402	**0.00414**	**0.00415**	**0.000071**	**0.00436**	**MOEA/D-DE+PSO**
ZDT2	0.00383	0.00387	0.00388	0.000042	0.00403	MOEA/D-DE
	0.00381	**0.00385**	**0.00387**	**0.000052**	**0.0039**	**MOEA/D-DE+PSO**
ZDT3	**0.00848**	**0.00906**	**0.00914**	**0.000662**	**0.01252**	**MOEA/D-DE**
	0.00860	0.00908	0.0202	0.03753	0.19706	MOEA/D-DE+PSO
ZDT4	0.01196	0.03056	0.04258	0.03342	0.15796	MOEA/D-DE
	0.00414	**0.00709**	**0.0075**	**0.0019**	**0.01158**	**MOEA/D-DE+PSO**
ZDT6	0.00856	0.0151	0.01478	0.00405	0.0235	MOEA/D-DE
	0.0069	**0.0146**	**0.0145**	**0.0045**	**0.0246**	**MOEA/D-DE+PSO**

4 Conclusion

Different search algorithms suit different problems. It is natural way to use the desirable properties of multiple algorithms for population evolution self-adaptively

Table 3 *The IGD-metric value statistics found by MOEA/D-DE, MOEA/D-DE+PSO after 30times independent runs for the CEC,09 unconstrained test problems [9], UF1-UF10.*

IGD Statistical Results found by *MOEA/D-DE andMOEA/D-DE+PSO*					
CEC'09	min	median	mean	std	max	*Approach-Name*
UF1	0.004499	0.073061	0.078707	0.051734	0.193602	MOEA/D-DE
	0.004466	**0.018066**	**0.030952**	**0.023114**	**0.063822**	***MOEA/D-DE+PSO***
UF2	0.018233	0.057095	0.062814	0.032670	0.142833	*MOEA/D-DE*
	0.010218	**0.011671**	**0.011737**	**0.000756**	**0.013261**	***MOEA/D-DE+PSO***
UF3	0.027292	0.238281	0.220884	0.084442	0.319024	*MOEA/D-DE*
	0.003966	**0.006314**	**0.006529**	**0.002050**	**0.011023**	***MOEA/D-DE+PSO***
UF4	0.062797	0.070280	0.070560	0.004064	0.077784	*MOEA/D-DE*
	0.062322	**0.071080**	**0.070883**	**0.003396**	**0.076828**	*MOEA/D-DE+PSO*
UF5	**0.210113**	**0.428818**	**0.426645**	**0.131033**	**0.707106**	***MOEA/D-DE***
	0.282111	0.454364	0.490882	0.118561	0.708999	*MOEA/D-DE+PSO*
UF6	0.244165	0.456803	0.508164	0.142289	0.798462	***MOEA/D-DE***
	0.186140	0.823351	0.778214	0.157339	0.843885	*MOEA/D-DE+PSO*
UF7	0.007096	0.106932	0.239466	0.244556	0.648772	*MOEA/D-DE*
	0.006726	**0.008776**	0.245517	0.267355	0.674953	***MOEA/D-DE+PSO***
UF8	**0.057705**	**0.076824**	**0.079935**	**0.015975**	**0.138522**	***MOEA/D-DE***
	0.077700	0.087222	0.088455	0.006532	0.101902	*MOEA/D-DE+PSO*
UF9	0.047530	0.151860	0.139659	0.035320	0.160975	*MOEA/D-DE*
	0.035499	**0.038980**	**0.071131**	**0.051008**	**0.149478**	***MOEA/D-DE+PSO***
UF10	0.296028	0.427088	0.442905	0.067564	0.672801	*MOEA/D-DE*
	0.184050	**0.187033**	**0.187158**	**0.001552**	**0.190097**	***MOEA/D-DE+PSO***

for algorithmic improvement. In this paper, we have proposed the hybrid version of MOEA/D [1] known as MOEA/D-DE+PSO by incorporating DE [3] and PSO [4] for multiobjective optimization. Experimental results shows the improvement of the MOEA/D-DE+PSO over MOEA/D-DE on MOEA/D-DE almost all ZDT problems [8] and CEC'09 test instance [9].

References

1. Q. Zhang and H. Li, "MOEA/D," *IEEE Trans on EC*, vol. 11, no. 6, pp. 712–731, 2007.
2. W. Khan and Q. Zhang, " MOEA/D-DRA with Two Crossover Operators," in *Proceeding of the UKCI'10*, 2010, pp. 1–6.
3. R.Storn and K.V.Price, "Differential Evolution," *J.Global Opt*, vol. 11, no. 4, pp. 341–359, 1997.
4. R.Eberhart and J.Kennedy, "A New optimizer using Particle Swarm Theory," in *Proceedings of MHS'95*, pp. 39–43.
5. J. A. Vrugt et al., "AMALGAM," *IEEE Trans On EC*, vol. 13, no. 2, pp. 243–259, 09.
6. J. A. Vrugt et.al, "Improve AMALGAM," *PNAS'07*, vol. 104, no. 3, pp. 708–701.
7. W. Khan, "Integration of NSGA-II and MOEA/D in Multimethod Search Approach," in *GECCO'11 (Companion)*, 2011, pp. 75–76.
8. E. Zitzler et al., "Comparsion of MOEAs," *EC*, vol. 8, no. 2, pp. 173–195, 200.
9. Q. Zhang et al., "Test Instances for the CEC'09," Technical Report CES-487.
10. E. Zitzler et al, "Performance Assessment of Multiobjective Optimizers: An Analysis and Review," *IEEE Trans on EC*, vol. 7, pp. 117–132, 2003.

Cross Organisational Compatible Plans Generation Framework

Mohammad Saleem[1], Paul W.H. Chung[1], Shaheen Fatima[1], Wei Dai[2]

Abstract   In this modern era, organisations have to work in coordination with many other organisations in order to succeed in business. Interacting organisations can only proceed in business if they have compatible workflows. This paper proposes a framework to automatically generate compatible workflows for multiple interacting organisations from their process definitions and service descriptions. Existing systems can reconcile existing workflows only, and cannot generate compatible workflows for multiple organisations automatically.   The proposed system is different from existing systems since it targets workflow collaboration by generating workflows automatically. This allows the organisations to save the time that would otherwise be spent in modelling workflows and making them compatible with the workflows of interacting organisations.

1 Introduction

With the development of the Internet, there has been an increase in demand for business process automation. A business process is a set of ordered interlinked procedures and activities within the context of an organisational structure, which brings about an organisational goal [1]. When two or more organisations conduct business together, the need for cross organisational business process automation arises. Hence, there is a need for cross organisational workflow collaboration.

Business collaboration can only work if the workflows of the interacting organisations are compatible [2]. Interacting workflows are compatible when they have an agreed sequence of interface activities. An interface activity is a point where exchange of collaborative messages and information takes place between

---

[1] Computer Science Department, Loughborough University, Loughborough, LE11 3TU, UK
{M.Saleem, P.W.H.Chung, S.S.Fatima}@lboro.ac.uk

[2] School of Management and Information Systems, Victoria University, Melbourne, Victoria, Australia. Wei.Dai@vu.edu.au

M. Bramer et al. (eds.), *Research and Development in Intelligent Systems XXVIII*,
DOI 10.1007/978-1-4471-2318-7_17, © Springer-Verlag London Limited 2011

two interacting workflows [3]. Considerable effort is needed to ensure that workflows are compatible in the first place [4, 5].

Incompatibilities among workflows should be removed, through reconciliation, in order to proceed in business. If an organisation works with other organisations in coordination, this can be a highly time consuming task. To allow efficient use of time and resources, this paper proposes a new framework for cross organisational workflow generation and cross organisational workflow collaboration.

In the proposed framework, we treat the workflow generation problem as an AI planning problem [6]. The proposed system is implemented using Simple Hierarchical Ordered Planer 2 (SHOP2) [7, 8] for planning. SHOP2 requires domain description for planning. Domain description consists of operators and methods [9]. Operators are primitive tasks and methods are specifications for decomposing composite tasks. The proposed system translates process definitions of the interacting organisations to operators and methods, and uses the operators and methods to automatically create compatible plans for the interacting organisations. This enables the organisations to avoid the time consuming task of reconciliation.

Section 2 explains cross organisational domain compatible plans generation framework. Section 3 explains an example scenario for a customer and vendor, Section 4 summarizes related work. Conclusions are drawn in Section 5.

2 Cross Organisational Compatible Plans Generation Framework

Fig. 1 shows the proposed cross organizational compatible plans generation framework.

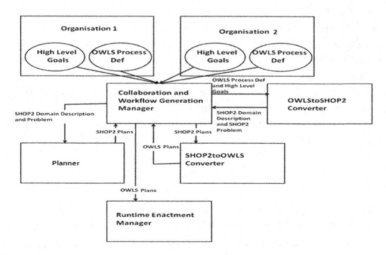

Fig. 1 Cross Organisational Compatible Plans Generation Framework.

Although the proposed framework works for any number of interacting organisations, for clarity, the figure only depicts two. Each organization models its OWLS process definitions and passes them to Collaboration and Workflow Generation Manager (CWGM). The organisations select their high level goals on the GUI. CWGM passes the process definitions to OWLStoSHOP2 translator, which translates them into SHOP2 domain descriptions. OWLStoSHOP2 translator also translates high level goals into a SHOP2 problem.

CWGM removes all those operators from the domain descriptions that are not used in planning. CWGM also collapses domain descriptions of all interacting organisations into a single joint domain, and SHOP2 problems of all interacting organisations into a single joint SHOP2 problem. Pre-planning analysis of the joint domain and joint problem is done so that operators, inputs (pre-conditions) and outputs of interacting organisations can be tracked. Operators in the domain that can form parallel plans are identified. Based on identified operators, sub-methods are inserted into the joint domain description. The inserted sub-methods are used by SHOP2 to create all possible plans. The original algorithm of SHOP2 is modified to suit this functionality.

The joint SHOP2 problem and the joint SHOP2 domain are passed to SHOP2 planner which creates all possible joint plans. A joint plan is a combined plan of all interacting organisations which achieves the combined goals of all the organisations. A joint plan is subdivided to create a set of interacting plans, one plan for each organisation, compatible with each other.

The set of compatible plans with the least number of activities is highlighted to the interacting organisations for execution. The highlighted or any other selected set of compatible SHOP2 plans is transferred to SHOP2toOWLS converter to convert the plans from SHOP2 format into OWL-S format. OWL-S plans are further passed to Runtime Enactment Manager which executes actual WSDL services in the OWLS plans.

3 Example

We generate compatible plans for a vendor and customer interacting with each other as an example. The vendor is an overseas exporter while the customer is an overseas importer. Based on the process definitions of vendor and customer, twenty possible set of compatible plans that can reach the goal states of the interacting organisations are generated. Fig. 2 shows processes of the vendor and customer and two of the twenty sets of compatible plans generated.

In this paper, an activity name followed by "_s" or "_r" depicts sending and receiving collaboration messages or collaboration information respectively.

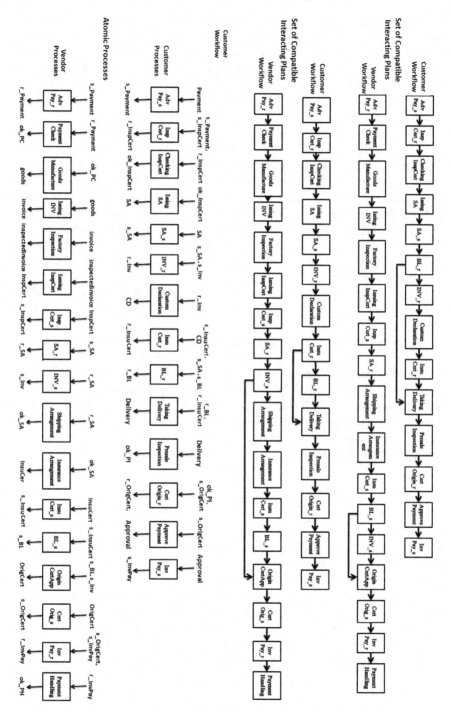

Fig. 2 Atomic Processes and Two Sets of Compatible Interacting Workflows.

4 Related Work

Existing research on workflow collaboration has mostly focused on coordination between existing workflows. Chen and Chung [3] proposed a framework for cross-organizational workflow collaboration. The framework proposed by Chen and Chung compares existing workflows of two organisations, detects incompatibilities between the workflows and gives offers and counter offers to the interacting organisations to reach reconciliation. This framework saves time and resources for the organisations by automatically creating offers and counteroffer for workflow reconciliation. The organisations still have to model their workflows initially in order to collaborate. The organisations also have to invest time by either accepting or rejecting the automatically generated offers, every time the organisations collaborate with new organisations.

Sirin *et al.* [10] initially presented a web service composition system to compose web services semi-automatically. Sirin *et al.* [9] later extended the semi-automatic system into a fully automated system. Their proposed system uses SHOP2 for web services composition. Sirin *et al.* also proposed a sound and complete algorithm for translating OWL-S processes into SHOP2 domain description. The system proposed by Sirin *et al.* is able to create plans from OWL-S processes of a single user or single organisation. It does not take cross organisational collaboration into account. The system also does not generate all possible plans.

Transplan [11] is another system based on SHOP2 planning algorithm to generate multiple plans from OWLS process definitions. Transplan uses the translation algorithm put forward by Sirin *et al.* [9]. Transplan does not guarantee to create all possible plans. Transplan also does not target collaboration among multiple organisations.

Work done by Sirin *et al.* is closely related to the work reported in this paper since they use OWLS process definitions of the interacting organisations, translate them to SHOP2 domain descriptions and create SHOP2 plans from the domain descriptions. All systems discussed above either target workflow collaboration between existing workflows, or they focus on automatic workflow generation for a single organisation. Framework presented in this paper targets automatic workflow generation and cross organizational collaboration at the same time.

5 Conclusion

This paper proposes a framework for the generation of compatible workflows for multiple interacting organisations. The proposed framework is different from existing systems since existing systems reconcile existing workflows. Other

systems generate workflows for single organisations only and do not take cross organisational collaboration into account. The proposed framework targets the integration of workflow generation and workflow collaboration.

The proposed system generates all possible sets of compatible workflows for interacting organisations and highlights the least costly set of compatible workflows to the interacting organisations for execution. The aim in future is to develop a runtime enactment mechanism that enacts the actual WSDL services in the plan and makes sure that the transfer of information and files among the interacting organisations occur smoothly.

Acknowledgments

This project is being funded by the UK Engineering and Physical Sciences Research Council (EPSRC) through the Innovative Manufacturing and Construction Research Centre (IMCRC) at Loughborough University.

References

1. Workflow Management Coalition: Terminology & Glossary. Technical Report WFMC-TC-1011 (1999).
2. Yang J., Papazoglou M.: Interoperation Support for Electronic Business. Communication of the ACM, Vol. 43, No. 6, pp. 39–47 (2000).
3. Chen X., Chung P.W.H.: Facilitating B2B E-Business by IT-Supported Business Process Negotiation Services. In: Proceedings of the 2008 IEEE International Conference on Service Operations and Logistics and Informatics, pp. 2800–2805 (2008).
4. Schulz K., Orlowska M.: Facilitating cross-organizational workflows with a workflow view approach. Data and Knowledge Engineering, Vol. 51, No.1, pp. 109–147 (2004).
5. Chiu D.K.W., Cheung S.C., Karlapalem K., Li Q., Till S., Kafeza E.: Workflow View Driven Cross-Organizational Interoperability in a Web-Services Environment. Information Technology and Management, Vol. 5, pp. 221–250 (2004).
6. Dong X., Wild D.: An Automatic Drug Discovery Workflow Generation Tool using Semantic Web Technologies. In: Proceedings of Fourth IEEE International Conference on eScience, pp. 652–657 (2008).
7. Nau D., Mu˜noz-Avila H., Cao Y., Lotem A., Mitchell S.: Total-order planning with partially ordered subtasks. In: IJCAI-2001, Seattle (2001).
8. Nau D., Au T., Ilghami O., Kuter U., Murdock J., Wu D., Yaman F.: SHOP2: An HTN planning system. Journal of Artificial Intelligence Research, pp. 379–404 (2003).
9. Sirin E., Parsia B., Wu D., Hendler J., Nau D.: HTN planning for web service composition using SHOP2. Journal of Web Semantics, Vol. 1, No. 4, pp. 377–396 (2004).
10. Sirin E., Hendler J., Parsia B.: Semi-automatic composition of Web services using semantic descriptions. In: Proceedings of Web Services: Modeling, Architecture and Infrastructure workshop in conjunction with ICEIS (2003).
11. Transplan. http://sourceforge.net/projects/transplan/

A Neural Network for Counter-Terrorism

S.J. Dixon, M.B. Dixon, J. Elliott, E. Guest and D. J. Mullier[1]

Abstract This article presents findings concerned with the use of neural networks in the identification of deceptive behaviour. A game designed by psychologists and criminologists was used for the generation of data used to test the appropriateness of different AI techniques in the quest for counter-terrorism. A feed forward back propagation network was developed and subsequent neural network experiments showed on average a 60% success rate and at best a 68% success rate for correctly identifying deceptive behaviour. These figures indicate that, as part of an investigator support system, a neural network would be a valuable tool in the identification of terrorists prior to an attack.

1 Introduction

DScent was a joint project between five UK universities combining research theories in the disciplines of computational inference, forensic psychology and expert decision-making in the area of counter-terrorism. This article discusses the findings of research and development around the role and the use of neural networks as a tool for identifying deception in the field of counter-terrorism.

For the purpose of data generation and system testing the project team devised a closed world game called "Cutting Corners". This game was used as a test-bed to allow development, application and validation of an artificial intelligence (AI) approach for identifying deceptive behaviour. Within the game participants acted as teams and traversed certain locations using GPS enabled devises to communicate, navigate and purchase items. The game participants either acted as *potentially dishonest*[2] builders who were constructing part of an Olympic stadium, or terrorists masquerading as builders with the aim of planting explosives. The game was divided into rounds with a certain number of dice throws per player and the winner was the first to accomplish their aim.

Each game consisted of four players with between one and three players acting as terrorists. During the game the players could visit three different types of virtual

---

[1] Leeds Metropolitan University, UK.
{s.j.dixon,m.dixon,j.elliott,e.guest,d.mullier}@leedsmet.ac.uk

[2] Participants taking on the role of builders during the game trials were encouraged to 'bend the rules' slightly, therefore concealing the deceptive behaviour of the terrorist data within a game.

M. Bramer et al. (eds.), *Research and Development in Intelligent Systems XXVIII*,
DOI 10.1007/978-1-4471-2318-7_18, © Springer-Verlag London Limited 2011

location: the Builders Yard, selling virtual construction blocks, soil and fertiliser; the Electronics Store, selling virtual wiring and dynamite and the Olympic Site, where virtual items could be unloaded. An initial amount of virtual cash and a virtual van was given to each player at the beginning of a game. During the game van searches and van weight checks were carried out where players displayed two items in their van and were weighed respectively. If the van exceeded the maximum weight allowance the player did not receive a cash reward. On completion of each round the sum of items sold from each shop was calculated.

An investigator support system, known as DScentTrail [1], was developed that presented graphical *scent trails*[3] of a suspect over time. This support system was underpinned by a neural network to help identify and highlight deceptive behaviour. Preliminary work was carried out on a behavioural based AI module which would work separately alongside the neural network, with both identifying deception before integrating their results to update DScentTrail.

2 AI Techniques for Counter-Terrorism

The use of various AI techniques, such as data mining, artificial neural networks, symbolic AI and Case Based Reasoning for counter-terrorism have been advocated by Markman [2] and Marappan [3]. Schneier [4] however, in his article on *Why Data Mining Won't Stop Terror*, writes that data mining works best when you're searching for a well-defined profile, a reasonable number of attacks per year and a low cost of false alarms. Rudmin [5] is also sceptical regarding the use of data mining techniques and disregards them completely as in order to make a Bayesian computation, he estimates that at best in the USA there would be a base-rate of 1 terrorist per 300,000 people and that if a surveillance monitoring system had an accuracy rate of 40% positive identification of real terrorists then according to Bayes' Theorem the misidentification rate would be .01%, or 30,000 innocent people. Rudmin stresses that these numbers are simply examples based on one particular technology. Jonas and Harper [6] in their report on *Effective Counterterrorism and the Limited Role of Predictive Data Mining* agree with Rudmin regarding the unacceptable number of likely false positives, they state that it would be a waste of resources and a threat to civil liberties. In addition to the high number of false positives, they argue against the usefulness of predictive data mining for counterterrorism due to the absence of terrorism patterns, leaving it impossible to develop useful algorithms.

Data mining was not used on the DScent project since it is generally used for extracting information from large quantities of data that is collected for reasons other than for the purpose of mining itself. The DScent data was explicitly designed and collected for identifying suspicious behaviour. DScent would not encounter the problems outlined by Rudmin, Jonas or Harper of having to

---

[3] A scent trail within the project is a collection of ordered, relevant behavioural information over time for a suspect.

potentially question a huge number of innocent people as the set did not contain the entire population, it was merely a well established sub-set. Ware [7] states that neural networks do not lend themselves easily to real-time updated information, and has concerns regarding the limited availability of historical data. Although Ware's observations may be valid, by identifying the key input factors to the neural network and keeping these to an absolute minimum, the amount of historical data required for training will be far less. Furthermore, if the neural network can identify deception amongst humans from a small amount of inputs then we are getting closer to that *well-defined profile* of which Schneier speaks.

The choice of a neural network was made as it is the most likely technique that will work with a non-polynomial problem such as behavioural patterns of humans. Jonas and Harper are correct when they state that it is impossible to design algorithms if no differences exist in terrorist and non-terrorist behaviours, though the project team believe that differences may exist. A neural network was chosen at this stage to identify whether these differences did occur. Preliminary work within DScent has paved the way for further research into this area which, providing differences in behaviour can be identified, will include the development of a hybrid AI system including both a neural network and a behavioural based AI module.

3 Development

Feed forward back-propagation neural networks were developed using the JOONE toolset [8] which is an object based neural network framework with a graphical user interface. EasyNN-plus [9] was used to validate the output from Joone. The neural network architecture took the input data from an Excel spreadsheet entering the input layer containing 122 neurons, the data progressed to a hidden layer containing 10 neurons, before it finally reached the output layer which contained a single neuron. The output value was in the range zero to one and was passed into an Excel spreadsheet, all three layers utilised the sigmoid activation function [10]. The Teacher layer trained the network by presenting it with complete examples, including whether the example was a terrorist or not (this is known as supervised learning). The training was then presented graphically via a Root Mean Square Error chart (RMSE) [11] examples of which are presented within the DScent Final Report [1].

The data from the Cutting Corners board game was collated into an Excel spread sheet. The spread sheet contained 144 rows of game data which resulted from playing 36 games. This game data was divided into separate training and test files with a ratio of 4:1 respectively. Three types of training and three types of test files, each containing varying numbers of terrorists, were created for each variation on the input file.

The effectiveness of a neural network is greatly reduced when the number of variables (horizontal), do not have adequate training pattern examples (vertical), as the network does not have the opportunity to explore a large proportion of the

possibilities. It is therefore necessary to prune the input file of unnecessary variables prior to training. It is apparent that by knowing which variables are contributing to the neural network [12] the developer has not only improved the effectiveness of the networks ability to generalise but also gains a better understanding of the problem. Experiments were performed excluding different variables within the import file to enable the ultimate level of accuracy given the number of training patterns available.

Due to the severe lack of training data the results were predictably inaccurate, though much better than anticipated. This did not however present a problem, as the purpose of phase one was to experiment with different tools, architectures, input variables, the ratio of positive and negative patterns presented within the training and test files and to identify the optimal classification threshold within the output. A total of 55 neural network experiments were. A threshold of 0.5 was used as the cut-off point, where a value of 0 indicated 'builder' and a value of 1 indicated 'terrorist', therefore any result greater than or equal to 0.5 was deemed to be a terrorist. The RMSE was plotted for each experiment during training to establish the optimum number of times the neural network was presented with the entire training set, known as an epoch. It is crucial not to over train the network as it has then the potential to memorise the training data and therefore looses the ability to generalise with different data.

The Mann Whitney U test [13] was used to ascertain whether differences between two sets of result data could not have occurred by chance alone. Firstly, the least successful set of neural network results were compared against the most successful set. Secondly, the most successful set were compared against a random set of 28 zeros and ones. An online automated calculation tool [14] was used to perform the final part of the tests, as significance lookup tables do not have U values beyond 30; these results are shown below:

- Test 1: The two samples are not significantly different ($P >= 0.05$, two-tailed test).
- Test 2: The difference between the two samples is highly significant ($P < 0.001$, two-tailed test).

These tests prove the value of the neural network even with such small amounts of training data. Altering the threshold to determine whether an output was positive or negative had a direct effect on the success rate of the network. If the initial threshold value of 0.5 was shifted down to a value of 0.13 the number of true positives was increased from 53% to 60%. This had a slightly negative effect on the total number of correct classifications within the test files, taking the percentage down from 64% to 60%. This percentage loss was deemed acceptable, as it was not identifying terrorists from the entire population, but identifying individuals who merited further investigation from a preselected subset who where under suspicion. This was identified as a suitable capability by the stakeholders[4] when consulted regarding functionality for the system.

---

[4] The project was funded by the EPSRC, grant number: EP/F014112/1. Stakeholders included a number of interested personnel from the CPNI and the MoD.

4 Results and Conclusions

The experiments showed on average a 60% success rate (68% peek) for correctly identifying terrorist behaviour. The winning architecture consisted of all three layers; input, hidden and output using the sigmoid activation function. The hidden layer contained 10 neurons which resulted in 11% of the number of variables contained within the input file. The information variables which proved to be of importance were 'locations', 'Stock Items' and 'Stock Take'. Excluded variables were 'Game Number', 'Colour' and 'Van Weight'. The patterns within the training file were presented to the neural network randomly rather than in sequence using over 1500 epochs.

Certain rows within the input file were consistently classified either correctly or incorrectly, obtaining either a minimum of a 90 percent success rate or a maximum of 10 percent success rate throughout all 50 neural network experiments. The proportion of these successful and unsuccessful rows that were terrorist patterns of behaviour was 14% and 71% respectively. After analysing these rows it was apparent that the neural network had generalised much better for the builders, this was as expected given there were more builder examples in the training files. From the correctly identified terrorist rows, the neural network performed far better for those who used dynamite to carry out the tasks rather than those using fertiliser, again due to more terrorists using dynamite. Not all games were played in full; they ended when a player won, which is another reason for the neural network incorrectly classifying records. The next stage of development would have been to introduce the concept of pattern completeness; this would be to train and refine the neural network on patterns with varying degrees of completeness and identify chunks of behaviour which were deceptive in isolation. This type of discrete deception identification would be far more valuable in reality.

Problem domains such as counter-terrorism intrinsically contain many information variables. Each time a variable is added, the number of possible pattern combinations increases exponentially. Therefore, with 100 variables within the input file, a vast number of rows would be required to cover just a small number of possible combinations of data. Take for example the winning neural network where only location information, stock items and stock take information was used (92 variables), each variable had an average of four possible values, i.e. 4^{92}, resulting in 2.45 x 10^{55} rows of training data required to cover every possible combination. This poses a problem, as large numbers of historical patterns of terrorist behaviour are not available.

Overall the neural network showed extremely promising results taking into account the sparse amount of training data. Future work is underway to develop a method for generating behavioural data, building on the rules of the board game. This is planned to be done by combining intelligent agents [15] with gene expression programming [16] and the use of an Emdros database [17].

A neural network has great potential in the quest to aid counter-terrorism, though certain pre-requisites must be met. These include providing an adequate set

of training data; identification of an optimal results classification threshold; and performing pre-processing to undertake tasks with which neural networks have difficulty, such as cross referencing rows against column data.

References

1. Dixon, S., Guest, E., Dixon, M., Elliott, J., Mullier, D.: DScent Final Report (2011). Available from: http://www.leedsmet.ac.uk/aet/computing/Computing_DScentFinalReport v2_0_2011.pdf Accessed 8 March 2011.
2. Markman, A., Rachkovskij, D., Misuno, I., Revunova, E.: Analogical Reasoning Techniques in Intelligent Counterterrorism Systems. International Journal "Information Theories & Applications" Volume 10 (2) (2003).
3. Marappan, K., Nallaperumal, K., Kannan, S., Bensujin, B.: A Soft Computing Model to Counter Terrorism. IJCSNS International Journal of Computer Science and Network Security, Volume 8 May 2008, p.141. (2008).
4. Schneier, B.: Why Data Mining Won't Stop Terror. Wired (2006). Available from: http://www.wired.com/politics/security/commentary/securitymatters/2006/03/70357 Accessed 28 October 2010.
5. Rudmin, F.: Why Does the NSA Engage in Mass Surveillance of Americans When It's Statistically Impossible for Such Spying to Detect Terrorists? Counterpunch (2006). Available from:http://www.counterpunch.org/rudmin05242006.html Accessed 1 Aug 2011.
6. Jonas, J., Harper, J.: Effective counterterrorism and the limited role of predictive data mining. CATO Institute (2006) Available from: http://www.cato.org/pubs/pas/pa584.pdf Accessed 27 October 2010.
7. Ware, B.S., Beverina, A., Gong, L., Colder, B.: A Risk-Based Decision Support System for Antiterrorism (2002). Available from: http://www.dsbox.com/Documents/MSS_A_Risk-Based_Decision_Support_System_for_Antiterrorism.pdf Accessed 30 Jan 2009
8. Marrone, P.: An Object Oriented Neural Engine. SourceForge (2010). Available from: http://www.jooneworld.com Accessed 26 October 2010.
9. Neural Planner Software: EasyNN-plus - Neural Network Software. (2010). Available from: http://www.easynn.com Accessed 26 October 2010.
10. Mitchell, T.M.: Machine Learning, WCB-McGraw-Hill (1997).
11. Levinson, N.: The Wiener RMS (ROOT MEAN SQUARE) ERROR Criterion in Filter Design and Prediction. Journal of Mathematics and Physics (1946).
12. Sexton, R.S., Sikander, N.A.: Data mining using a genetic algorithm-trained neural network. Intelligent Systems in Accounting, Finance and Management 10(4):201-210. doi:10.1002/isaf.205 (2002).
13. Mann, H.B., Whitney, D.R.:On a test of whether one of two random variables is stochastically larger than the other. Annals of Mathematical Statistics Volume 18 March 1947, p.50–60 (1947)
14. Avery, L.: Mann-Whitney U Test (2007). Available from: http://elegans.swmed.edu/~leon/stats/utest.html Accessed 27 October 2010.
15. Evertsz, R.: Populating VBS2 with Realistic Virtual Actors. Proceedings of the 18th Conference on Behavior Representation in Modeling and Simulation, p.1–8. (2009).
16. Ferreira, C.: Gene Expression Programming: Mathematical Modeling by an Artificial Intelligence (Studies in Computational Intelligence). 2nd ed. Springer (2006).
17. Petersen, U.: Emdros: a text database engine for analyzed or annotated text. Proceedings of the 20th international conference on Computational Linguistics (2004). Available from: http://emdros.org/petersen-emdros-COLING-2004.pdf Accessed 24 January 2011.

Applications and Innovations
in Intelligent Systems XIX

BEST APPLICATION PAPER

Web Community Knowledge Extraction for *myCBR 3*

Christian Sauer and Thomas Roth-Berghofer

Abstract The current development of web communities and the Web 2.0 provide a huge amount of experiences. Making these experiences available as knowledge to be used in CBR systems is a current research effort. The process of extracting such knowledge from the diverse data types used in web communities and formalising it for CBR is not an easy task. In this paper we present the knowledge extraction workbench prototype *KEWo* and also review some of the challenges we were facing while integrating it into the case-based reasoning tool *myCBR 3*.

1 Introduction

One of the kinds of data with the fastest grow in volume on the Web is user generated content, mostly in the form of semi-structured texts. This user generated content often contains artefacts of user experiences, expressed explicitly or implicitly [15]. Accessing this information is still a task not easily accomplished by a machine, mainly because most of it is unsystematic and thereby hard to retrieve efficiently and thus not easily available to be reused [4]. By becoming more user-friendly more and more users participate in one of the many forms of web communities Web 2.0 offers [6]. This development further increases the amount of data, again very often as semi-structured texts, like, for example the 140 character messages in the popular web service Twitter.

Following the idea of the Experience Web [23] one has to ask how experience based technologies such as Case-Based Reasoning (CBR) might be able to bene-

Christian Sauer
Explanation-aware Computing Systems, Institute of Computer Science, University of Hildesheim, Germany, e-mail: christian.sauer@uni-hildesheim.de

Thomas Roth-Berghofer
Explanation-aware Computing Systems, Institute of Computer Science, University of Hildesheim, Germany e-mail: thomas.roth-berghofer@uni-hildesheim.de

M. Bramer et al. (eds.), *Research and Development in Intelligent Systems XXVIII*,
DOI 10.1007/978-1-4471-2318-7_19, © Springer-Verlag London Limited 2011

fit from the experience contained in semi-structured texts, generated by the users of web communities and social networks. According to Richter [18], the knowledge of CBR systems comprises four knowledge containers: vocabulary, similarity measures, transformational (or adaptation) knowledge and cases. An approach to extract a controlled vocabulary and similarity knowledge in the form of taxonomies from semi-structured texts provided by a web community is described in [2]. The respective tool is called 'Knowledge Extraction Workbench' (*KEWo*). In this paper we show how integrating *KEWo* into the open-source case-based reasoning tool *my-CBR 3* [25, 19] supports the knowledge modelling of vocabularies and similarity measures.

myCBR focuses on the similarity-based retrieval step of the CBR cycle [1]. A popular class of such retrieval-only systems comprises case-based product recommender systems [7]. *myCBR* allows to model and use highly sophisticated, knowledge-intensive similarity measures [24]. Such domain specific similarity measures can improve the retrieval quality substantially. However, they also increase the development effort significantly.

In contrast to earlier versions of *myCBR* (Versions 1.x and 2.x), which were a plug-in for the Open Source ontology editor Protégé[1] [12], *myCBR 3* is a completely new and OSGi-based tool. *myCBR 3* still focuses on ease-of-use regarding the creation of the case model, modelling of similarity measures and testing the similarity-based retrieval by offering an easy-to-use graphical user interface. In order to reduce also the effort of the preceding step of defining an appropriate case representation, it includes tools for generating the case representation automatically from existing raw data.

We believe that the initially proved abilities of *KEWo* to extract elements of a controlled vocabulary and to build similarity measures in the form of taxonomies of terms plus the ability to generate at least limited amounts of adaptation-knowledge from the taxonomies form a useful addition to *myCBR*. This belief is further strengthened by the (semi-)automatic extraction of such vocabularies and their according similarity measures from semi-structured and, to a certain extent, even unstructured texts that *KEWo* supports [2].

A desirable next step for the extraction of data from the web, to be used in CBR systems, is it to enable the access to Linked Data, especially to Linked Open Data (LOD). Linked open data is provided without charge and contains comprehensive ontologies based on Semantic Web standards. The complex knowledge repository DBpedia is a prominent example of an LOD repository. It is generated from the online encyclopedia Wikipedia. The terms are organised in an ontology and are being enriched with further information. Currently, the DBpedia ontology contains 1.67 million instances.[2]

Accessing LOD has the potential to further ease the development of Web CBR systems. *KEWo* was successfully transformed in another prototype that is able to extract a vocabulary and similarity measure from Linked Open Data [22]. The abil-

---

[1] http://protege.stanford.edu/
[2] http://dbpedia.org/About [Last access: 8 June 2011]

ity to adapt *KEWo* with a relatively small amount of effort to new data types from which it extracts knowledge for CBR systems further adds to the idea of integrating *KEWo* into *myCBR 3* to enable knowledge and system engineers to benefit from the knowledge extraction capabilities of *KEWo*.

The rest of the paper is structured as follos: In Section 2 we give an overview about related work in the field of knowledge extraction from web-data for CBR systems. The process model for knowledge extraction used by *KEWo* is described in Section 3, and *KEWo* itself and its functionalities are detailed in Section 4. After introducing *KEWo* and its approaches to knowledge extraction we take a brief look at the performance of *KEWo* in Section 5. In Section 6 we give a detailed view of the challenges we met during the integration of *KEWo* into *myCBR 3*. The last Section summarises our approach and gives an outlook on two future goals for the extension of the abilities of *KEWo*.

2 Related Work

The knowledge of Case-Based Reasoning systems comprises the four knowledge containers vocabulary, similarity measures, transformational (or adaptation) knowledge and case base [18]. The task one must accomplish, if data from the Web 2.0, respectively from a web community, is to be extracted for use in an CBR system, is to properly formalise the extracted data to meet the formal needs of the chosen knowledge container it is extracted for.

The wide variety of web communities can be classified into certain archetypes and prevalent forms of data types used in this communities [6, 21]. One, then, faces a multitude of possible combinations. Combinations consists of the possible forms the source-data types used in a web community and the formal structure of a target knowledge container for which to extract knowledge from the community data are designed. However, with respect to the fast growing amount of very diverse data, containing a rich amount of experiences from the users of web communities, the task of extracting knowledge from this data to use in CBR systems seems worth the effort. Given the fact that the underlying methodology of CBR traditionally works upon previously recorded experiences, the development of Web CBR was the next logical step (see, e.g., [16]). An issue yet to be solved is the already mentioned problem of numerous possible combinations of source data and targeted knowledge container(s) to extract knowledge for.

In contrast to *myCBR*, jCOLIBRI[3] is a framework for developing CBR systems in Java and for modelling knowledge for such systems [3, 17]. As Recio-García et al. point out there is a variety of opportunities if web-based data sources can be integrated into a development framework for CBR systems such as jCOLIBRI [16]. Their approach is similar to the approach described in this paper. However, *myCBR 3*

---

[3] http://gaia.fdi.ucm.es/projects/jcolibri/

follows a tool approach[4] with a rich graphical user interface, providing ease-of-use by itself. Considering that the *KEWo* prototype itself also offers a variety of easy to use GUI features makes them a perfect match.

KEWo focuses on the extraction of knowledge from semi-structured texts plus, in a further developed version, from LOD, for the knowledge containers vocabulary and similarity measure [2, 22]. During the development of this approach it was found that, due to the formal needs of the knowledge containers, it was only possible to extract knowledge from web data in a highly customised process. There are plenty of similar approaches for certain combinations of web community data and knowledge containers to extract knowledge from that web community data, e.g. [23, 14, 15, 13]. All of these approaches prove the benefits of extracting knowledge from web community data but they also have in common the need for highly tailored processes to fit the formal needs of the knowledge representation in the knowledge containers.

The Integration of *KEWo* into such a tool as *myCBR* provides a starting point for using standard techniques for knowledge extraction from community data and for just trying out initial tests. *KEWo* already enables the extraction from varying forms of source data types for already two of the four knowledge containers, thus sparing developers of CBR systems the work of designing customised ways to extract, formalise and integrate knowledge from web sources into their CBR systems.

3 Knowledge Extraction Process

The knowledge extraction approach utilised by *KEWo* is to extract relevant terms out of a previously specified domain from text data retrieved from web communities. Upon the extracted terms a taxonomy is built by assigning the terms in a hierarchy according to an analysis of the term frequency in a given text.

As already mentioned *KEWo* provides a, yet limited, amount of adaption knowledge by constructing taxonomies of symbols in a given domain. The approach to exploit the taxonomies as a source of adaption knowledge can be described as follows. The nodes in the taxonomy are assigned with similarity values according to their distance in the taxonomy. This approach allows *KEWo* to derive also a limited amount of adaptation knowledge from the structure of the taxonomy by offering the possibility to choose between different siblings, sharing the same level and parent node in the taxonomy [2].

A possible example for such an adaption: A case describing a headache contains an attribute 'medicamentation' meaning the medication best used and the best choice offered by the case base is the instance 'Aspirin' for the attribute medicamentation. The user now states to the system that Aspirin is not available in his context. The system than could access the taxonomy of medicaments and adapt the case, namely the attribute 'medicamentation' with the instance 'Ibuprofen' which it

---

[4] Please note that *myCBR 3* is a complete reimplementation comprising a software development kit (SDK) and an eclipse-like GUI.

would find as another sibling of the parent node of Aspirin, which might be 'Painre-liefers' as an abstraction of 'Aspirin' and 'Ibuprofen'. Thus an adaption is realised using substitutional knowledge from the taxonomies.

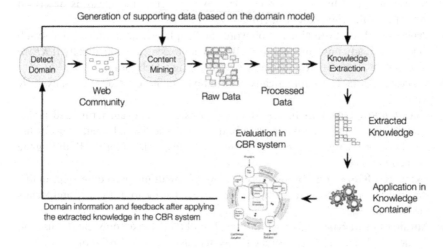

Fig. 1 Knowledge Extraction Process Model for CBR Systems [2]

The *KEWo* knowledge extraction approach [2] follows a process model based on the knowledge discovery in databases (KDD) process [10]. This process model can be seen as a valid approach in all possible combinations of source data to extract knowledge from and target knowledge containers for which knowledge is extracted.

The process model described in Figure 1 shows a knowledge extraction for a CBR system with the aim to extract knowledge for two of the CBR systems knowledge containers namely the vocabulary and the similarity measure. The extracted knowledge is than used and evaluated in the CBR system itself for which it is extracted.

Also the extraction of knowledge in the form of symbols for the vocabulary and the construction of taxonomies itself is already implemented as a fully automatic process the last step of the process model, the evaluation still has to be done manually.

Referring to the process model we will now inspect each step of the process closer and give a brief insight into how the step in question is implemented within *KEWo*.

1. **Domain Detection** This first step describes the identification of the domain properties and results in the assignment of what kind of information can be extracted and in which knowledge container it should be integrated. For *KEWo* this can be almost any domain. Targeted knowledge containers are the vocabulary, the similarity measures and to a certain extent the adaptation knowledge.

2. **Web Community Selection** In this step a web community is identified from which data should be used for extraction. With regards to *KEWo* currently text based communities, e.g., forums are preferred.
3. **Content Mining** This describes the process of acquiring the raw data. This can be accomplished by, e.g., web crawlers. A more convenient way is described in [11] with the approach of intelligent web forums.
4. **Processing Raw Data** Noise, stop words and duplicates are removed. These sub steps are already implemented in *KEWo* and are executed automatically if *KEWo* accesses raw text data from a database underlying a web forum.
5. **Processed Data** The automatically refined text data is now ready for analysis by *KEWo*.
6. **Knowledge Extraction** In this step *KEWo* extracts relevant terms and builds a taxonomy of these terms as already described. Additional input data for the extraction process, e.g., gazetteers, is automatically updated by *KEWo* during the extraction process.
7. **Extracted Knowledge** Being closely woven in with the preceding step, in this step the taxonomy generated by *KEWo* is saved back to a *myCBR* and stands ready to be used.
8. **Application in Knowledge Container** The obtained taxonomy can be used in the development and testing of a CBR system using the *myCBR* tool.
9. **Evaluation** Evaluating the generated taxonomy may delivers hints on how to optimise the auxiliary data and preferences for the ANNIE application [9] (see next section) used in the extraction process. The evaluation may result in performance gains and/or gains in quality of the extracted taxonomies. These steps still have to be done manually within *KEWo*.

KEWo offers the user a high degree of interactivity, ranging in modes of operation from fully automatic to manual. The degree of useful automatic analysis strongly depends on the quality of the data to be analysed and the quality of the auxiliary data, e.g., the gazetteers and rule sets, used by the ANNIE application within *KEWo*.

The degree of interactivity can be increased from fully automatic by enabling dialogues with the knowledge engineer, questioning her if either a found symbol is valid and/or if a newly found symbol, not yet part of the used ANNIE gazetteer should be integrated in the gazetteer in use. Furthermore the knowledge engineer can at any time of the extraction process interact with the taxonomy currently build to make adjustments if so desired.

KEWo itself is a Java-based middleware for the extraction of knowledge for CBR systems. Currently *KEWo* relies on *myCBR* for the data type of the taxonomies and the calculation of distance-based similarity measures between the symbols of the taxonomies. The main purpose of *KEWo* is to extract symbols from a given domain and construct taxonomies usable in *myCBR* from the extracted symbols. The process underlying the extraction of symbols is mainly provided by the text engineering tool set GATE [9], specifically by the ANNIE application (A Nearly-New Information Extraction System), which has been customised for *KEWo* by using specific gazetteers and rule sets that identify terms from a given domain. Thus *KEWo* relies

on a customised ANNIE application to extract symbols from unstructured texts and either build completely new or expand existing taxonomies of symbols to be used in *myCBR*.

4 Knowledge Extraction Workbench

Figures 2 and 3 show screenshots of *KEWo*. The knowledge extraction workbench in its first version offers the ability to either start the generation of a taxonomy of symbols from scratch or import one from a *myCBR* project to work on. After creating or importing a taxonomy *KEWo* offers a variety of functions to improve the taxonomy. Besides the automatic extraction and addition of further symbols to the taxonomy from analysed source text, *KEWo* offers the abilities to recalculate the similarity measures of the symbols with almost any given formula and the possibility to edit the taxonomy symbols manually to refine the taxonomy [2].

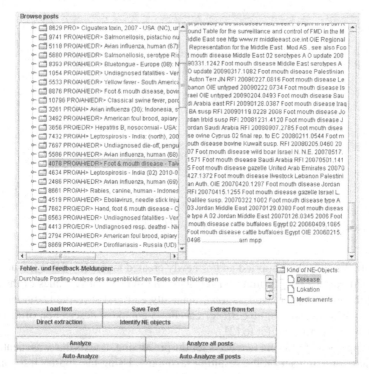

Fig. 2 Screenshot of the Knowledge Extraction Workbench

Figure 2 shows a minimalistic browser with which the user can navigate a web forum targeted for extraction. The user can choose between two different analysis

methods that define the strategy in which the symbols are added to the taxonomy. Further the user can decide if she either wants to run a fully automatic analysis or an interactive one, in which she can decide if extracted symbols are added to the taxonomy and/or added to support data used by the extraction techniques, e.g., gazetteers. A third option is given to the user by the decision to extract from a given thread posting by posting or from the whole thread as one text.

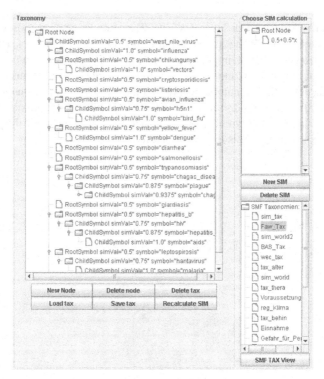

Fig. 3 Screenshot of the Knowledge Extraction Workbench

Figure 3 shows the imported and/or newly created taxonomy. Here the user can define and apply a new formula for recalculating the similarity values of the symbols in the taxonomy as well as load, manually edit and save the taxonomy. The taxonomy can be saved in *myCBR* format. For a complete description of the functionalities of *KEWo* we refer to [21].

The approach of offering two ways for the processing of texts that was mentioned above has some impact on the resulting taxonomy. Using the approach to analyse each posting of a thread as a singular text *KEWo* tends to generate deeper taxonomies whilst using the approach to analyse a thread as a whole text generates a shallow taxonomy. The described effects on the depth of the taxonomies generated originates from the numerical approach used by *KEWo* to build the taxonomies. Upon the extracted terms a taxonomy is build by assigning the terms in a hierarchy according

to an analysis of the term frequency in a given text, assuming that two similar terms appear together more often [8].

The basic requirements, regarding a tool for a first step in the direction of standardised knowledge extraction from the web for specific knowledge containers of a CBR system, are met by *KEWo*. In the next section it is our aim to show that the performance requirements are also met.

5 *KEWo* Experiment and Results

In order to show the effectiveness of the knowledge extraction process experiments were performed on text data provided by a forum of experts in the field of travel medicine (in German). *KEWo* was used to extract taxonomies of terms out of the three domains diseases, medicaments, and geographical locations from the 6500 postings in that forum.

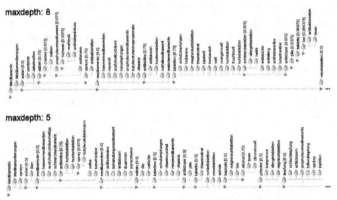

Fig. 4 Taxonomy depth comparison (overview)

Both of the approaches, to analyse posting by posting or whole threads as a single text, were evaluated and delivered the already mentioned different kinds of taxonomies, regarding the depth of the taxonomies (see section above). Figure 4 shows two of the generated taxonomies with the result of the thread analysis in the upper half and the post-by-post analysis in the lower half.

Please note the difference in term chain length due to the two different approaches causing the differences in the depths of the generated taxonomies.

All generated taxonomies were of acceptable quality with regard to making sense in the hierarchy of extracted terms. Figure 5 shows two snippets of a taxonomy of German terms from the domain of diseases. The taxonomy was built fully automatic by *KEWo*. While processing text data the F1-score of the term extraction gained by *KEWo* ranged between 68,7 and several numbers in the 80ies range, depending on the domain and the degree of auxiliary data provided for the extraction [21].

Fig. 5 Snippets of a taxonomy generated by *KEWo*

For each domain: diseases, locations and medicaments, a gazetteer and a jape transducer consisting of a set of jape rules to identify word composite was designed in the ANNIE application used by *KEWo* for term extraction from the postings. The gazetteers for the three domains contained a randomly chosen set of terms from the given domain. The gazetteer for diseases contained 717 terms, for locations there were 331 terms and 32 terms for medicaments were present at the start of the experiment [21].

To test *KEWo*'s and its underlying ANNIE applications abilities to extract terms from the forum postings a set of experiments were done. During these experiments *KEWo* together with its underlying ANNIE application was able to automatically expand the gazetteers by identifying word composite. The additions were: 74 terms for diseases, 47 terms for locations and 123 terms for medicaments. The high number of composites found for the domain of medicaments was partly due to the deliberately low initial population of the gazetteer for the domain medicaments to explicitly test *KEWo*'s ability to work with sparse gazetteers and rely on the rule based jape transducers the ANNIE application provided [21].

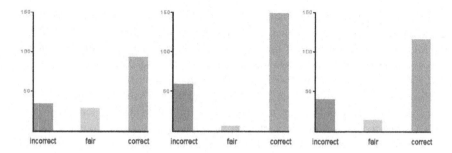

Fig. 6 Number of symbols found and integrated into taxonomies by *KEWo* for the domains 'diseases', 'locations' and 'medicaments'

In another experiment the first 100 postings of the forum from which the knowledge was extracted from were analysed manually. All occurrences of terms from the domain of medicaments were identified and counted manually, resulting into 38 manually identified terms from the domain medicaments. Of these 38 terms *KEWo* was able to automatically identify 22 terms correctly and 4 terms were incorrectly identified as medicaments [21].

The maximum depth the taxonomies reached was 8. Figure 6 shows the total numbers of symbols *KEWo* identified and integrated into the taxonomies. The numbers are given from left to right for the domains: diseases, locations and medicaments. Please note that the category 'fair' refers to symbols which were correct from their syntactic structure but didn't had a correct semantic meaning in the domain they were extracted for. Most of these symbols were synonyms.

The ability of *KEWo* to also process retrieved data sets from LOD sources had no negative influence on the quality of the generated taxonomies [22] thus *KEWo* also proved to be useful to enable CBR developers to use LOD as a source of knowledge for their CBR systems.

6 Challenges of Integrating the Knowledge Extraction Workbench with *myCBR 3*

As we have shown the knowledge extraction workbench is a reliable and useful tool for extracting experience from web community knowledge to be used in the development of CBR systems. Now we want to focus on some challenges we faced when integrating *KEWo* into *myCBR 3*and some challenges we foresee for the integration of further features into the *KEWo*being embedded in myCBR 3.0 now.

Making the data types used by *KEWo* compatible with *myCBR* data types is an already solved problem as *KEWo* was specifically developed for *myCBR 2*. A point more challenging was the extension of *KEWo*'s ability to extract knowledge for the two containers not yet covered by *KEWo*: adaptation knowledge and case base. For the adaptation knowledge we added the capability to browse in the taxonomy in order to derive adaptation knowledge from the structure of the taxonomy. For the extraction of cases we had to implement an extension to *KEWo* aiming at structural cases, due to the ease such cases may be extracted with techniques derived from the well researched field of template completion.

Currently we provide a taxonomy of terms annotated with a similarity value for each term derived from its position in the taxonomy. Bringing together the variety of data types given for web data and the strict formalisms of adaptation knowledge and cases, we aimed at first focusing on certain types of at least semi-structured data sources such as annotated documents for the extraction of cases or fully structured data such as RDF-based sources of Linked (Open) Data to extract structural information, e.g. hierarchies from this kind of data to be directly used in the generation of adaptation knowledge.

To access more data sources we will integrate more flexible interfaces into *KEWo* allowing it to better parse and thus preprocess the raw data from a wider variety of web sources. Tasks involved in acquiring this goal are the addition of more flexible text and XML parsers, a flexible interface to connect to MySQL-databases and an option to use a crawler on a web source, e.g. a forum, from which data is to be extracted.

We already included into the *KEWo* the ability to connect to any given online repository of Linked Data. After this prototypical inclusion the *KEWo* is able to query the repository it has connected using SPARQL queries which are handled by use of the open sourced Sesame-Framework.[5] We are currently working on exploiting this connectivity to further facilitate the retrieval from highly structured data repositories which to a high degree will help reducing the effort currently invested in knowledge extraction due to the, at best, semi-structured format data is currently mostly available on the net.

7 Summary and Outlook

In this paper we tried to emphasise the benefits of integrating a capability for extracting knowledge from web-sources for the development of CBR systems into one of the available tools for such developments, namely the tool *myCBR*.

We examined the performance and limitations of the *KEWo* prototype by examining it's abilities to extract and correctly formalise knowledge from semi-structured texts and Linked Data for the CBR knowledge containers vocabulary and similarity measure. The ability to tap into such highly structured sources as, e.g., LOD, was successfully tested in a second *KEWo* prototype.

A future goal, after integrating *KEWo* into *myCBR 3*, is given by the shifting of the extraction approach now implemented in *KEWo* in the direction of Linked Open Data retrieval. This goal will be followed to benefit from the rapidly growing amount of highly structured data available on the web and at the same time reduce the costly process of extracting knowledge from less structured data [5].

As another future goal we see the possibility of adding explanation capabilities to the than integrated *KEWo*. The *myCBR*tool already possesses some explanation capabilities, namely conceptualisation of symbols from a vocabulary and explaining the similarity calculation [20]. We aim at an automatic extraction of both of these sources of conceptualising information from the web and at adding provenance information.

---

[5] http://www.openrdf.org/ [Last access: 8 June 2011]

References

1. Aamodt, A., Plaza, E.: Case-based reasoning : Foundational issues, methodological variations, and system approaches. AI Communications 1(7) (Mar 1994), `ftp://ftp.ifi.ntnu.no/pub/Publikasjoner/vitenskaplige-artikler/aicom-94.pdf`; letzte Verifikation 11. Juni 2007
2. Bach, K., Sauer, C.S., Althoff, K.D.: Deriving case base vocabulary from web community data. In: Marling, C. (ed.) ICCBR-2010 Workshop Proceedings: Workshop on Reasonng From Experiences On The Web. pp. 111–120 (2010)
3. Bello-Tomás, J., González-Calero, P.A., Díaz-Agudo, B.: JColibri: An Object-Oriented Framework for Building CBR Systems. In: Calero, P.A.G., Funk, P. (eds.) Proceedings of the 7th European Conference on Case-Based Reasoning. Lecture Notes in Artificial Intelligence LNAI, Springer (2004)
4. Bergmann, R.: Experience Management: Foundations, Development Methodology, and Internet-Based Applications, LNCS, vol. 2432. Springer (2002)
5. Bizer, C., Heath, T., Berners-Lee, T.: Linked data-the story so far. Int. J. Semantic Web Inf. Syst. 5(3), 1–22 (2009)
6. Boyd, D.M., Ellison, N.B.: Social network sites: Definition, history, and scholarship. Journal of Computer-Mediated Communication 13(1), 210–230 (October 2007)
7. Bridge, D., Göker, M.H., McGinty, L., Smyth, B.: Case-based recommender systems. Knowledge Engineering Review 20(3) (2006)
8. Church, K.W., Hanks, P.: Word association norms, mutual information, and lexicography. Computational Linguistics 16(1), 22–29 (1990)
9. Cunningham, H., Maynard, D., Bontcheva, K., Tablan, V.: Gate: A framework and graphical development environment for robust nlp tools and applications. In: Proc. of the 40th Anniv.Meeting of the Assoc. for Comp. Linguistics (ACL'02) (2002)
10. Fayyad, U., Piatetsky-Shapiro, G., Smyth, P.: The kdd process for extracting useful knowledge from volumes of data. Commun. ACM 39(11), 27–34 (1996)
11. Feng, D., Shaw, E., Kim, J., Hovy, E.: An intelligent discussion-bot for answering student queries in threaded discussions. In: IUI '06: Proc. of the 11th Intl Conf. on Intelligent user interfaces. pp. 171–177. ACM Press, New York, NY, USA (2006)
12. Gennari, J.H., Musen, M.A., Fergerson, R.W., Grosso, W.E., Crubézy, M., Eriksson, H., Noy, N.F., Tu, S.W.: The evolution of Protégé an environment for knowledge-based systems development. Int. J. Hum.-Comput. Stud. 58(1), 89–123 (2003)
13. Ihle, N., Hanft, A., Althoff, K.D.: Extraction of adaptation knowledge from internet communities. In: Delany, S.J. (ed.) ICCBR 2009 Workshop Proc., Workshop Reasoning from Experiences on the Web. pp. 269–278 (July 2009)
14. Milne, P., Wiratunga, N., Lothian, R., Song, D.: Reuse of search experience for resource transformation. In: Delany, S.J. (ed.) ICCBR 2009 Workshop Proc., Workshop Reasoning from Experiences on the Web. pp. 45–54 (July 2009)
15. Plaza, E., Baccigalupo, C.: Principle and praxis in the experience web: A case study in social music. In: Delany, S.J. (ed.) ICCBR 2009 Workshop Proc., Workshop Reasoning from Experiences on the Web. pp. 55–63 (July 2009)
16. Recio-García, J.A., Casado-Hernández, M., Díaz-Agudo, B.: Extending cbr with multiple knowledge sources from web. In: Bichindaritz, I., Montani, S. (eds.) Case-Based Reasoning. Research and Development, Lecture Notes in Computer Science, vol. 6176, pp. 287–301. Springer Berlin / Heidelberg (2010), 10.1007/978-3-642-14274-1_22
17. Recio-García, J.A., Díaz-Agudo, B., Gómez-Martín, M.A., Wiratunga, N.: Extending jcolibri for textual cbr. In: Muñoz-Avila, H., Ricci, F. (eds.) Case-Based Reasoning, Research and Development, 6th International Conference, on Case-Based Reasoning, ICCBR 2005, Chicago, IL, USA, August 23-26, 2005, Proceedings. Lecture Notes in Computer Science, vol. 3620, pp. 421–435. Springer (2005), `http://dblp.uni-trier.de/db/conf/iccbr/iccbr2005.html#RecioDGW05`

18. Richter, M.M.: Introduction. In: Lenz, M., Bartsch-Spörl, B., Burkhard, H.D., Wess, S. (eds.) Case-Based Reasoning Technology – From Foundations to Applications. LNAI 1400, Springer-Verlag, Berlin (1998)
19. Roth-Berghofer, T., Adrian, B., Dengel, A.: Case acquisition from text: Ontology-based information extraction with SCOOBIE for myCBR. In: Bichindaritz, I., Montani, S. (eds.) Case-Based Reasoning Research and Development: 18th International Conference on Case-Based Reasoning, ICCBR 2010. No. 6176 in LNAI, Springer, Alessandria, Italy (2010)
20. Roth-Berghofer, T.R., Bahls, D.: Explanation capabilities of the open source case-based reasoning tool mycbr. In: Petridis, M., Wiratunga, N. (eds.) Proceedings of the thirteenth UK workshop on Case-Based Reasoning UKCBR 2008. pp. 23–34. University of Greenwich, London, UK (2008)
21. Sauer, C.S.: Analyse von Webcommunities und Extraktion von Wissen aus Communitydaten für Case-Based Reasoning Systeme. Master's thesis, Institute of Computer Science, University of Hildesheim (2010)
22. Sauer, C.S., Bach, K., Althoff, K.D.: Integration of linked open data in case-based reasoning systems. In: Atzmüller, M., Benz, D., Hotho, A., Stumme, G. (eds.) Proceedings of LWA2010 - Workshop-Woche: Lernen, Wissen & Adaptivitaet. Kassel, Germany (October 2010)
23. Smyth, B., Champin, P.A., Briggs, P., Coyle, M.: The case-based experience web. In: Delany, S.J. (ed.) ICCBR 2009 Workshop Proc., Workshop Reasoning from Experiences on the Web. pp. 74–82 (July 2009)
24. Stahl, A.: Learning of Knowledge-Intensive Similarity Measures in Case-Based Reasoning. Ph.D. thesis, University of Kaiserslautern (2003)
25. Stahl, A., Roth-Berghofer, T.R.: Rapid prototyping of cbr applications with the open source tool mycbr. In: ECCBR '08: Proc. of the 9th European conference on Advances in Case-Based Reasoning. pp. 615–629. Springer, Heidelberg (2008)

KNOWLEDGE DISCOVERY AND DATA MINING

Web-Site Boundary Detection Using Incremental Random Walk Clustering

Ayesh Alshukri, Frans Coenen and Michele Zito

Abstract In this paper we describe a random walk clustering technique to address the Website Boundary Detection (WBD) problem. The technique is fully described and compared with alternative (breadth and depth first) approaches. The reported evaluation demonstrates that the random walk technique produces comparable or better results than those produced by these alternative techniques, while at the same time visiting fewer 'noise' pages. To demonstrate that the good results are not simply a consequence of a randomisation of the input data we also compare with a random ordering technique.

1 Introduction

There have been numerous studies that perform analysis of the web at the web-page level [8, 2, 6]. A web page can be considered as a low level element on the web. There is potential benefit to studying the web on a higher level, that level being the level of a website. A website can be considered as a single high level entity that is made up of a collection of lower level resources. These resources can include text/html web pages, images, video etc, which together collectively represent a website. Studying the web at this abstract level can have many possible applications, including; web archiving [21, 1], web search and information retrieval [20] and web analysis [7, 10, 17, 8]. The Web-site Boundary Detection (WBD) problem is concerned with discovering all web resources within the boundary of a particular website given some "seed(s)" resources from that website. WBD is an open problem [7] and can be difficult to solve [14].

In this work we follow [5] in postulating that a set of resources contained in a website is, by definition, 'intended' by the author/publisher of the content to be

Ayesh Alshukri · Frans Coenen · Michele Zito
The University of Liverpool, Department of Computer Science, Ashton Building, Ashton Street, Liverpool, L69 3BX, UK. e-mail: {a.alshukri, coenen, michele}@liverpool.ac.uk

M. Bramer et al. (eds.), *Research and Development in Intelligent Systems XXVIII*,
DOI 10.1007/978-1-4471-2318-7_20, © Springer-Verlag London Limited 2011

deemed related using the high level notion of a website. It is this concept of intention that is used in this paper to define a website, in that the resources featured in the website share similar attributes, and also they are more highly connected.

The WBD problem can be addressed in a static manner by first collecting all pages connected to a given seed page up to a certain distance (depth) from the seed page. If the depth is sufficiently large the resulting collection can be expected to contain both pages belonging to the target web site and noise pages. Typically, so as to ensure that the entire target web site is included in the collection the distance moved from the seed page has to be substantial, hence a significant number of noise pages will be included in the collection. The task is then to differentiate the target pages from the noise pages, i.e. identify the web site boundary. The static WBD problem can thus be argued to be a binary clustering problem where we wish to divide the collection of web pages into a web site cluster and a noise cluster.

An alternative approach, which aims to limit the number of noise pages visited, is to proceed in a dynamic manner and attempt to identify the web site boundary using some form of incremental clustering. There are a number of ways whereby this may be achieved. For example we can proceed in a Breadth First (BF) or Depth First (DF) manner, stopping whenever it is determined that the web site boundary has been identified. In this paper we advocate a random walk based approach. As will be demonstrated the Random Walk (RW) technique produces comparable or better performance than the BF or DF approaches, while at the same time visiting far fewer nodes.

The evaluation is conducted using synthetic data sets generated using the web modelling technique proposed in [15] and [16]. The reason that we elected to use artificial data sets is that, for experimental purposes, we have much greater control over the ratio of web pages against noise pages. We compared the operation of the RW approach with the BF and DF approaches. We also compare the operation of RW with an alternative random walk approach, Random Ordering (RO), to demonstrate that the effectiveness of RW is not simply a result of the randomisation of the input data (which has been shown to have a positive effect with respect to K-means [23, 19]).

2 Preliminaries

The RW approach advocated in this paper is directed at a portion of the world-wide web. We may think of this as a graph $G = (V, E)$, where V is a collection of web-pages, and the set E keeps track of all directed links between pairs of elements of V. Without loss of generality assume that G is connected. Each page has a numerical feature vector associated with it. Technically this can be determined once the page has been downloaded from the internet. Thus, there exists a function $f : V \to \mathbb{R}^k$, for some fixed integer $k \geq 1$, such that for any $P \in V$, $f(P)$ is an ordered sequence of k real numbers characterising the page P. In what follows we will denote the elements of V using italicised capital letters. We will use the terms page, web-page,

node, and vertex interchangeably, but in all cases we will actually be referring to the pair formed by an element of V and its corresponding feature vector. Given a specified web-page $P \in V(G)$, our purpose is to define a set $\mathscr{W} = \mathscr{W}(P) \subseteq V(G)$ called the *web-site* of P, containing all pages of G that are similar to P.

In the work described in this paper we focus on iterative clustering processes founded on the template presented in Table 1. The graph G is assumed to model a portion of the web. For the purpose of our experiments (see Section 3.1) we may assume that it resides on some secondary memory storage device and bits of it are retrieved as needed. If the algorithms were to be used on the real web, G would be distributed at different sites across the internet and its content would have to be downloaded through http requests. Note that the well known k-means [11, 13, 22, 24] clustering method fits this template, however the template can equally be used to represent a host of different algorithms. In the forthcoming sections we provide details concerning the proposed iterative clustering processes proposed in this paper.

Algorithm clustering_template (P)
$W = \{P\}; N = \{\};$
set up the process internal state;
repeat
    select a page Q from G;
    add Q to W or N;
    update the process state;
until convergence;
return W;

Table 1 Clustering algorithm template.

2.1 k-means clustering

The classical k-means clustering algorithm is obtained from the template given in Table 1 by assuming that the state of the process contains information about the (two) clusters centroids, that the pages in G are inspected one at a time in some given order (which may vary over subsequent iterations) and that the state update is only performed after a complete sweep of the data has been performed. Also, it is assumed that the graph $G = (V, E)$ is not initially available. It is retrieved from the web incrementally as different pages get requested inside the process main loop. The loop is then further repeated until the system state does not change from one sweep of the graph to the next one.

This paper considers two variants of this process, named Breadth-First (BF) and Depth-First (DF) clustering. They are obtained by assuming that the order in which the pages of G are examined is determined by the way in which they are retrieved from the web, and is given by a fixed and bound breadth-first (resp. depth-first)

traversal of the web starting at P, including all pages up to a certain bounded distance from P.

2.2 Clustering based on random crawling

Many different processes fit the template described above. The order in which the pages are considered needn't be fixed or deterministic. The way in which the web-graph is explored can be quite arbitrary. Furthermore the process state may be updated every time a new page is considered, rather than at the end of a whole sweep of the given dataset. Finally the periodical state update might include major modification of the retrieved web-graph content. In the remainder of this section we describe two possible processes of this type: Random Walk (RW) clustering and Random Ordering (RO) clustering. The first is appealing because of its simplicity, the second will be used to critically analyse the other processes. Other variants, not reported in this paper, were tested but the results were found not to be significantly different from those of the two methods considered.

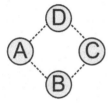

Fig. 1 Example web dataset displayed as a graph; vertices's indicate web pages, dashed edges indicate hyperlinks (directions omitted so as to maintain clarity)

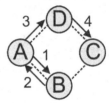

Fig. 2 Sample run of RW (numbered directed edges indicate progress of the random walk)

2.3 Random Walk (RW) Clustering.

Given an arbitrary graph G, the sequence of vertices visited by starting at a vertex and then repeatedly moving from one vertex to the next by selecting a neighbour of the current vertex at random is termed a *random walk* on the graph G (see for instance [18]). Random walks arise in many settings (e.g. the shuffling of a deck of cards, or the motion of a dust particle in the air) and there's a vast literature related to them (the interested reader is referred to the classical [12], or the very recent [3] and references therein). In particular they can be used [4] as a means for exploring a graph.

The process RW is the variant of the clustering_process in Table 1 based on the idea of performing a random walk on G. A pure random walk is not easily simulated

(at least initially) if we want to keep the constraint that the process does not require access to the full dataset to start off with. The sequence of pages to be (re-)clustered is thus given by the order in which they are visited by performing a random walk on the *known portion* of G. Initially the walk has to choose a neighbour of P. In general, given the current page Q, the page to be visited next is selected at random among those pointed at by a link of Q and the set of pages seen so far that point to Q. For example, with reference to the example graph given in Figure 1, the first four steps of the process might be as shown in Figure 2, with clustering performed at every step. Note that the walk can revisit nodes multiple times, even before having completed a full sweep of G. It is therefore convenient to re-compute the centroids after each step of the walk, rather than at the end of a sweep. It is well-known [4] that any random walk on a finite connected graph eventually visits all vertices in it. Thus, in principle, the process could run until convergence as in the standard k-means algorithm. It will turn out, however, that stopping the process after a given maximum number of "steps" (MAXITERATIONS) is more effective and still results in good quality clusters. Some pseudo code describing the RW technique is presented in Table 2. The decision on whether to add Q to W or the *noise cluster N* is based on the computation of the Euclidean distance between Q's feature vector and the centroids of the two clusters $W \setminus \{Q\}$ and $N \setminus \{Q\}$.

Algorithm RW (P)

  $W = \{P\}; N = \{\}$;
  set Q to P; set a counter to one;
  set up the process internal state;
  repeat
    redefine Q to be a random neighbour of Q in G;
    add Q to W or N;
    increase the counter;
    update the process state;
  until counter goes past MAXITERATIONS;
  return W;

Table 2 Pseudo code for RW

2.4 Random Ordering (RO) clustering.

Random walks, as defined above, are examples of so called Markov stochastic processes [12]. The evolution of a process of this type is fully determined by its current state: in the example in Figure 1, and assuming perfect information, every time we visit vertex A we have a 50-50 chance of moving to B or D and no chance at all to visit vertex C next.

The process RW, strictly speaking, already breaks this framework. In this section we describe a simpler process (RO) that moves even further from a pure random walk process. The process traverses the graph vertices in a random order in a similar manner as in the case of RW. However in the case of RO, all vertices are picked with

equal chance, irrespective of edges. In Figure 1, again assuming perfect knowledge (In reality a deterministic crawl can identify all nodes in the structure to a certain depth). Every time we visit vertex A, there is a 1 in 4 chance of visiting either vertex A,B,C or D. In this process edges are disregarded, and thus we produce a complete random ordering of the graph.

```
Algorithm RO (P)
    W = {P}; N = {};
    set Q to P; set a counter to one;
    set up the process internal state;
    repeat
        redefine Q to be a random vertex in G;
        add Q to W or N;
        increase the counter;
        update the process state;
    until counter goes past MAXITERATIONS;
    return W;
```

Table 3 Pseudo code for RO

It is this selection of nodes, chosen in a random order that is the key difference between RO and RW. The traversal of RW is influenced by the graph based on its structural properties. For instance if a graph contains a highly connected sub set of nodes, then RW is more likely to re-visit this locality, in contrast to less connected nodes. The RO method would visit vertices of the graph at random, and would not be effected by any structural properties of the graph.

3 Experimentation and Evaluation

To assess the quality of RW we tested it on a number of artificial data sets. Graphs $G = (V, E)$ containing a particular set of pages similar to some chosen element of V were put together by first creating artificial host graphs using the well established web-graph model proposed by Kumar *et al.* [15]. One of the generated host graphs was then selected to be the target graph (web site). The graphs were then represented using a standard feature vector representation that included noise words randomly selected from a "bag" of noise words. The generation of the experimental data is described in further detail in Section 3.1. To evaluate the operation of RW we used a number of measures, these are given in Section 3.2. The results are presented in Section 3.3.

3.1 Experimental Data

As noted above, for experimental purposes, we modelled a collection of web pages using the process described in [15], but with case 3 (see below) derived from [16]. Given a positive integer m, the process generates a synthetic model of the world

wide web starting from a graph $G_0^{K,m}$ having a single vertex with m links pointing to itself. Then, for $t \geq 1$, $G_t^{K,m}$ is derived from $G_{t-1}^{K,m}$ according to the following procedure (here α, β, and v are real numbers between zero and one):

1. With probability $\alpha \times \beta$ add a new vertex to $G_{t-1}^{K,m}$ with m links pointing to itself.
2. With probability $\alpha \times (1 - \beta)$ choose a random edge in $G_{t-1}^{K,m}$ and make its source point to P.
3. With probability $(1 - \alpha) \times \beta$, pick a random copying vertex Q_c; a new vertex P will point to m vertices chosen as follows:

   Uniformly At Random - with probability v, choose a random vertex Q and add (P, Q) to the graph.
   Preferential Attachment - with probability $1 - v$, add (P, R) to the graph, where R is a random neighbour of Q_c.

4. With the remaining probability $(1 - \alpha) \times (1 - \beta)$ no new vertex is generated and a random edge is added to $G_{t-1}^{K,m}$.

In our experiments we used values of m mirroring the fact that the average page on the world wide web contains some 40-50 links [9]. Also $\alpha = 0.01$, $\beta = 0.9$ and $v = 0.2$. So, most of the time, new vertices will be generated to which 50 neighbours will be linked according to the procedure described in 3 above. The resulting graph shared many features with the real web, in particular: (i) in and out degree distribution, (ii) the diameter, and (iii) the presence of small bipartite "cliques". For the purpose of our experiments, we generate $G_T^{K,m}$ and then remove $G_0^{K,m}$ from it. Because of the copy mechanism by which we add edges to $G_{t-1}^{K,m}$, the single page in $G_0^{K,m}$ contains a large number of links and is linked by a large number of "younger" pages. Removing it from the graph used for our experiments makes the resulting graph, which we denote by K_T more realistic.

The use of a synthetic version of the web has many advantages. However Kumar's graphs have one disadvantage: the lack of the "clustery" nature of the real web. To complete the definition of our artificial data we need to identify a web-site $\mathcal{W}$ within K_T (and then complete the definition of G by adding some noise cluster, $\mathcal{N}$). To this end we performed the following steps:

1. Given K_T, we picked a random node X from this graph. Such node will represent the home-page in $\mathcal{W}$.
2. To create the set of pages in $\mathcal{W}$ we then performed a breadth-first crawl of K_T starting from X, up to a certain maximum depth. The nodes visited by such process are then added to $\mathcal{W}$ with some fixed probability p.
3. The noise cluster $\mathcal{N}$ is created by continuing the breadth-first crawl until a further maximum depth, it contains all nodes reachable from X that have not been added to $\mathcal{W}$ in the previous step.
4. The graph G is then defined as the subgraph of K_T induced by the set $\mathcal{W} \cup \mathcal{N}$.

For the experiments reported in this paper we generated datasets of four types, which we identify as sets A, B, C and D. In each case the data set included 10 distinct

graphs G. All sets were generated from copies of K_T using $m = 40$ and $p = 0.8$. Sets of type A were derived from graphs that included in $\mathscr{W}$ all nodes (pages) at a distance of at most three links (with $p = 0.8$) from the seed page X, while continuing to a distance of 5 links from the initial page so as to define the noise cluster $\mathscr{N}$. Sets B, C, and D used the same distance of three links for set $\mathscr{W}$, and distance six, eight and nine links respectively to define $\mathscr{N}$. In Table 4 some graph-theoretic statistics are presented the values reported in the table are averages over the 10 graphs included in each set. From the table it can be observed that the size of noise clusters steadily increases from set A to D, while the size of the target cluster $\mathscr{W}$ remains fairly constant. Also $\mathscr{W}$ has many more internal links than links to $\mathscr{N}$ (modelling the fact that the elements of $\mathscr{W}$ represent homogeneous web-pages). Furthermore $\mathscr{W}$ is *popular* in the sense that many links from the noise cluster $\mathscr{N}$ point back to $\mathscr{W}$.

Given a particular graph structure G, we may generate several instances of this structure by changing the feature vectors that we associate with the various pages (vertices). In general, for any page $P \in \mathscr{W}$ (resp. in $\mathscr{N}$, the feature vector $f(P)$ can be chosen from the superposition of two k-dimensional normal multivariate distributions, having different means, $\mu_{\mathscr{W}}$ and $\mu_{\mathscr{N}}$, and equal deviations σ. The vectors associated with the elements of $\mathscr{W}$ may be chosen from the $N_k(\mu_{\mathscr{W}}, \sigma)$ distribution, those for $\mathscr{N}$ from $N_k(\mu_{\mathscr{N}}, \sigma)$. Varying the relative position of the means results in datasets of differing complexity.

For our experiments we simulated such process in a very simple way. Given P in $V(K_T)$, $f(P)$ contains $k = 20$ integer numbers, corresponding to the number of occurrences of the elements of a pool of words S in a bag associated with P. The pool S is split in two disjoint groups of equal size, $S_{\mathscr{W}}$ and $S_{\mathscr{N}}$. The bag of P is defined by sampling, independently, k elements of S. If P is in $\mathscr{W}$, each chosen word has a chance $\pi = 0.7$ (resp. $1 - \pi$) of belonging to $S_{\mathscr{W}}$ (resp. $S_{\mathscr{N}}$), and is selected uniformly at random with replacement, from the chosen group. If $P \in \mathscr{N}$, the selection is symmetrically biased towards $S_{\mathscr{N}}$.

Set	Cluster $\mathscr{W}$			Cluster $\mathscr{N}$		
-----	Average nodes	# Intra edges	Inter edges	Average nodes	# Intra edges	Inter edges
A	100	389.5	128.2	198.8	224.2	260.7
B	100.8	409.3	159.6	405.4	729.6	692
C	102.1	422.6	145.8	405.4	2015.3	1702.1
D	103.1	392.6	188.4	1440.4	4329.1	2734.4

Table 4 Data set graph-theoretic statistics. *Intra edges* are links connecting two pages in the same cluster. *Inter edges* are links connecting pages in different clusters.

For experimental purposes, using the above described mechanism, 40 graphs were generated and divided into four sets as shown in Table 4. The distinction between the four sets is that they feature an increasing amount of noise. The scenario created by a set reflects a portion of the web containing a particular website, which also contains an amount of noise. In a perfect scenario, this portion of the web would contain only pages from a single website. Then the task of identifying this website would trivially be the whole set. In reality the amount of noise that can be collected

is substantial, as a website that resides on the www is surrounded by a large amount of pages that are not part of the website itself. Therefore each of the four data sets must contain a restricted amount of noise. Set A simulates a scenario where the portion of the web graph is restricted to a noise to class ratio of 1:2, for each set there after the amount of noise is double that of the previous set.

An ever increasing amount of noise in the data to be clustered, has the effect of increasing the complexity of the clustering process in that large numbers of noise items increases the likelihood of outliers thus blurring the distinction between $\mathcal{W}$ and $\mathcal{N}$. Also, in the deterministic BF and DF processes, each of the sets simulates an increasing uncertainty in the amount of the web to collect to ensure all class items are contained.

3.2 Evaluation Criteria

We used a number of measures to compare the performance of the various clustering methods considered in this paper. Given an instance (G, f) generated as described in Section 3.1, the output (W, N) of a particular clustering algorithm $\mathcal{A}$ on (G, f) can be expressed as:

$$W = W_t \cup W_f \qquad N = N_t \cup N_f$$

where W_t (resp. W_f) is the collection of class items (noise items) that are correctly (resp. incorrectly) identified as being within the target web site, and, similarly, N_t (resp. N_f) is the collection of noise items (resp. items in W) that are correctly (resp. incorrectly) identified as noise. The *accuracy* $\gamma = \gamma(\mathcal{A}, (G, f))$ of algorithm $\mathcal{A}$ on input (G, f) is given by the expression:

$$\frac{|W_t| + |N_t|}{|\mathcal{W}| + |\mathcal{N}|}$$

which measure the proportion of correctly classified items.

For completeness we will also track two obvious *coverage* parameters:

$$\chi_{\mathcal{W}} = \frac{|W_t| + |N_f|}{|\mathcal{W}|} \qquad \chi_{\mathcal{N}} = \frac{|W_f| + |N_t|}{|\mathcal{N}|},$$

the number of steps $\varsigma = \varsigma(\mathcal{A}, (G, f))$ (i.e. iterations of the main algorithm loop) performed and the average CPU time to complete a single step, denoted by $\theta = \theta(\mathcal{A}, (G, f))$ calculated as the total execution time to terminate a particular run divided by how many steps the algorithm took to terminate.

3.3 Results

Table 5 shows the performance of RW, in comparison with DF, BF and RO, using data generated as described in Section 3.1. The results show the performance of each method with respect to the test data SetA to SetD. Each of the methods were run 50 times on each group of graphs in each test set.

Table 5 Table shows the average performance of each method (RW, RO, BF and DF) run 50 times on each graph in sets *A* to *D*. Accuracies and coverages are reported as percentages

	Algorithm	Accuracy	Class Coverage	Noise Coverage	Execution	End Steps
	BF	77.21	100	100	0.89	1001
	DF	93.77	100	100	0.85	1001
SetA	RO 10k	94.02	100	100	0.16	10k
	RW 10k	94.66	89.85	66.84	0.12	10k
	BF	81.24	100	100	1.41	1600
	DF	92.12	100	100	1.48	1600
SetB	RO 10k	84.53	99.92	99.93	0.28	10k
	RW 10k	94.04	83.42	48.12	0.15	10k
	BF	74.97	100	100	3.66	5290
	DF	77.08	100	100	3.46	5290
SetC	RO 10k	69.59	97.05	95.96	1.92	10k
	RW 10k	92.04	79.38	19.68	0.21	10k
	BF	51.17	100	100	6.24	11266
	DF	51.55	100	100	6.21	11266
SetD	RO 10k	66.32	79.36	77.76	7.03	10k
	RW 10k	91.75	84.16	08.64	0.24	10k

The effect of an incremental increase in noise on the performance of each of the techniques can be seen in the plots given in Figures 3, 5 and 4. In the accuracy plots (Figure 3) we can observe a sharp decrease in the accuracy of the BF and DF techniques as the noise increases. This is due to the fact that both the BF and DF methods consider all nodes in the graph (Figures 5 and 4) and thus as the amount of noise is increased the performance decreases. RO also displays a decreasing accuracy trend, but is much more resilient to the increasing presence of noise than BF and DF. This is due to the fact that RO effectively randomises the ordering of nodes. This produces a clustering that is much less susceptible to a "bad" initial starting conditions than in the case of the BF and DF methods. As shown in the accuracy plot given in Figures 3, RO has a much more subtle decrease in accuracy. RO also covers slightly less noise nodes than BF and DF (Figure 5), but displays a decreasing trend with respect to the amount of class items that are covered (Figure 5).

The accuracy of RW is only slightly effected by the increasing amount of noise. RW achieves a consistently better accuracy than the RO, BF and DF methods. The reasons for this improved accuracy are: (i) RW has the advantages of covering a smaller percentage of noise nodes, which can make it easier for the clustering algorithm to determine clusters; and (ii) RW randomises the ordering of nodes, which

serves to improve the clustering accuracy by over-coming a possible bad initial conditions.

RW tends not to cover the entire graph (in reasonable time). It is also slower than the DF and BF which both cover all nodes. The performance of RW is relative to its run time. However we argue that, in the context of web-site boundary detection (where the aim is to identify all pages belonging to a website), it is satisfactory to correctly classify 95% of the website page if 40% of noise is not accessed at all. It should also be noted that the overall run time is not a very meaningful measure; the average running time per step is a better comparative measure of the effectiveness of the methods considered.

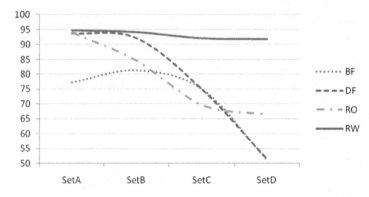

Fig. 3 Accuracy

In summary RW offers the following advantages: (i) it does not need to be re-run several times to overcome a bad initial clustering condition, because it randomises the nodes while traversing the hyperlink structure of the graph; (ii) it visits fewer noise pages thus reducing the resources used for downloading, parsing and pre-processing of web pages; and (iii) produces comparable or better accuracy in relation to the website boundary detection problem.

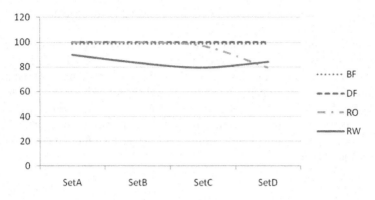

Fig. 4 Class coverage

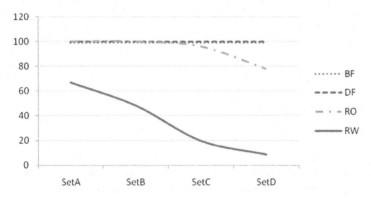

Fig. 5 Noise coverage

4 Conclusion

In this paper we have described a random walk approach (RW) as a solution for the
Website Boundary Detection (WBD) problem. The operation of RW was evaluated
with respect to three comparator approaches: BF, DF and RO. The main findings are
as follows:

The BF and DF methods give accuracies that decrease when the amount of noise
increases. This is due to the fact that the inclusion of an increasing amount of noise
items make clustering more difficult as noise items blur the distinction between the
target web site cluster and the noise cluster.

The RO method covers the elements of a graph in a random ordering, irrespective of previously selected nodes or the link structure. This method does have the

advantage of randomising the node ordering so as to enhance the clustering process. As demonstrated by the results obtained, randomising the node ordering can improve the clustering, thus RO has consistently improved accuracy over BF and DF. However the RO method is also susceptible to noise, as the accuracy decreases when more noise is included in the graph. The RO method could, of course, not realistically be used for the dynamic resolution of the WBD problem.

The RW method offers the advantage of improved clustering accuracy (obtained by randomising the ordering of nodes) over the other methods included in the evaluation. However, because RW utilises the link structure of the graph, it also reduce the number of noise nodes visited. Thus requiring less resources in the context of the WBD problem, while giving the best performance over RO, BF and DF.

References

1. S. Abiteboul, G. Cobena, J. Masanès, and G. Sedrati. A First Experience in Archiving the French Web. In *ECDL '02 Proceedings of the 6th European Conference on Research and Advanced Technology for Digital Libraries*, volume 2458 of *Lecture Notes in Computer Science*, pages 1–15. Springer, 2002.
2. R. Albert, H. Jeong, and A-l. Barabási. Diameter of the world wide web. *Computing Research Repository*, 1999.
3. D. Aldous and J. Fill. Reversible Markov chains and random walks on graphs. *Monograph in preparation*, 2002.
4. R. Aleliunas, R.M. Karp, R.J. Lipton, L. Lovasz, and C. Rackoff. Random walks, universal traversal sequences, and the complexity of maze problems. *20th Annual Symp. on Foundations of Computer Science*, pages 218–223, 1979.
5. A Alshukri, F. Coenen, and M. Zito. Web-Site Boundary Detection. In *Proceedings of the 10th Industrial Conference on Data Mining*, pages 529–543, Berlin, Germany, 2010. Springer.
6. Albert-Laszloand Barabasi and Reka Albert. Emergence of scaling in random networks. *Science*, 1999.
7. K. Bharat, B-W. Chang, M. Henzinger, and M. Ruhl. Who links to whom: mining linkage between Web sites. In *Proceedings 2001 IEEE International Conference on Data Mining*, pages 51–58, Washington, DC, USA, 2001. IEEE Computer Society.
8. A. Z Broder. Graph structure in the Web. *Computer Networks*, 33(1-6):309–320, June 2000.
9. A. Z Broder, M Najork, and J. L Wiener. Efficient URL caching for world wide web crawling. In *WWW'03 Proceedings of the 12th international conference on World Wide Web*, pages 679–689, Budapest, Hungary., 2003. ACM.
10. P. Dmitriev. As we may perceive: finding the boundaries of compound documents on the web. In *WWW'08 Proceeding of the 17th international conference on World Wide Web*, pages 1029–1030, Beijing, China, 2008. ACM.
11. M. H. Dunham. *Data Mining: Introductory and Advanced Topics*. Prentice Hall PTR Upper Saddle River, NJ, USA, 2002.
12. W. Feller. Introduction to probability theory and its applications. *WSS*, vol. 1, 1968.
13. J. Han and M. Kamber. *Data Mining: Concepts and Techniques*. Morgan Kaufmann, 2001.
14. M. Henzinger. Finding near-duplicate web pages: a large-scale evaluation of algorithms. In *Proceedings of the 29th annual international ACM SIGIR conference on Research and development in information retrieval*, pages 284–291. ACM, 2006.
15. R. Kumar. Trawling the Web for emerging cyber-communities. *Computer Networks*, 31(11-16):1481–1493, May 1999.

16. R. Kumar, P. Raghavan, S. Rajagopalan, D. Sivakumar, A. Tomkins, and E. Upfal. Stochastic models for the Web graph. In *Proceedings 41st Annual Symposium on Foundations of Computer Science*, pages 57–65, Washington, DC, USA, 2000. IEEE Computer Society.

17. B. Liu. *Web Data Mining: Exploring Hyperlinks, Contents, and Usage Data.* Springer, Springer-Verlag New York, Inc., 2007.

18. L. Lovász. Random walks on graphs: A survey. *YaleU/DCS/TR-1029*, 2:1–46, 1994.

19. J.M Peña, J.A Lozano, and P Larrañaga. An empirical comparison of four initialization methods for the K-Means algorithm. *Pattern Recognition Letters*, 20(10):1027–1040, October 1999.

20. J. Pokorn. Web Searching and Information Retrieval. *Computing in Science and Engineering*, 6(4):43–48, 2004.

21. P. Senellart. Identifying Websites with Flow Simulation. In David Lowe and Martin Gaedke, editors, *ICWE*, volume 3579 of *Lecture Notes in Computer Science*, Orsay, France., 2005. Gemo, INRIA Futurs., Springer.

22. P. N. Tan, M. Steinbach, and V. Kumar. *Introduction to Data Mining*. Pearson International Edition, 2006.

23. B. Meck Thiesson, C. Chickering, and D. Heckerman. Learning mixtures of Bayesian networks. Technical report, Microsoft Research Technical Report TR-97-30, Redmond, WA, 1997.

24. I. H. Witten and E. Frank. *Data Mining: practical machine learning tools and techniques.* Morgan Kaufman, 2005.

Trend Mining and Visualisation in Social Networks

Puteri N.E. Nohuddin[1], Wataru Sunayama [2], Rob Christley[3], Frans Coenen[1]
and Christian Setzkorn[3]

Abstract A framework, the IGCV (Identification, Grouping, Clustering and Visualisation) framework, is described to support the temporal analysis of social network data. More specifically the identification and visualisation of "traffic movement" of patterns in such networks, and how such patterns change over time. A full description of the operation of IGCV is presented, together with an evaluation of its operation using a cattle movement network.

1 Introduction

Trend mining is concerned with the application of data mining techniques to extract trends from time stamped data collections [11, 12]. Likewise, social network mining is normally directed at finding communities but in this work we are interested in the "traffic" flow in such networks. The work described in this paper is directed at trend mining of social networks. The trends of interest are "traffic movement" patterns in which trends are defined in terms of the fluctuations of traffic between nodes in the networks. The main issues associated with social network trend mining are: (i) the large amount of data that has to be processed (social network datasets tend to be substantial); and (ii) trend mining techniques typically generate large numbers of trends which are consequently difficult to analyse.

To address these two issues we present an end-to-end social network trend mining framework that takes as input a time stamped data set, describing the activity in a

1 Department of Computer Science, University of Liverpool, UK,
puteri, frans@liverpool.ac.uk

2 Graduate School of Information Sciences, Hiroshima City University, Japan,
sunayama@sys.info.hiroshima-cu.ac.jp

3 Dept. of Epidemiology & Population Health, University of Liverpool and National
Centre for Zoonosis Research, Leahurst, Neston, UK,
robc, c.setzkorn@liverpool.ac.uk

M. Bramer et al. (eds.), *Research and Development in Intelligent Systems XXVIII*,
DOI 10.1007/978-1-4471-2318-7_21, © Springer-Verlag London Limited 2011

given social network; and, as an end result, produces a visualisation of the most significant trends. The process is predicated on the assumption that end users are interested in the manner in which frequent patterns and trends change over time. We refer to this framework as the IGCV (Identification, Grouping, Clustering and Visualisation) framework. IGCV comprises four stages (Figure 1):

1. **Trend Identification**: The application of frequent itemset mining techniques to define and identify frequent patterns and trends within social network data.
2. **Trend Grouping**: The grouping, using a Self Organising Map (SOM) approach, of the large number of trends that are typically identified.
3. **Pattern Migration Clustering**: Identification of "communities" of pattern migrations, within the SOM groupings, using a hierarchical clustering mechanism based on the Newman method.
4. **Pattern Migration Visualisation**: Visualisation of the pattern migrations using a *spring model* to display, what are considered to be the most significant, pattern migrations.

To evaluate the operation of IGCV a social network extracted from the Cattle Tracing System (CTS) in operation in Great Britain has been used. CTS includes a database that records cattle movements through out Great Britain. By considering the *holding areas* (farms, markets, abattoirs, etc.) as nodes, and the cattle movement between holding areas as the traffic, a large scale social network can be derived.

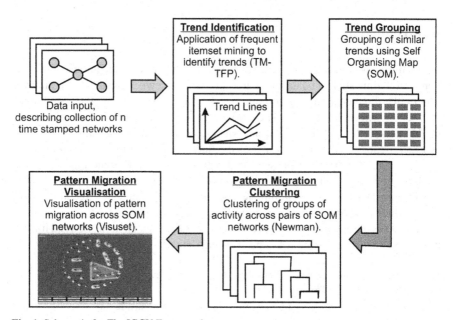

Fig. 1 Schematic for The IGCV Framework

2 Related Work

Social networks are communities of interacting entities. Well known examples include web-based applications such as Facebook, Bebo and Flickr. Social network mining is typically directed at identifying patterns and sub-communities (clusters) within network data [21, 23]. The mining of social networks is usually conducted in the static context whereby data mining techniques are applied to a "snap shot" of the network of interest. Little work has been directed at applying data mining techniques to social network data in the dynamic context so as to discover, for example, trends in the network data. The problem domain, which is the focus of the work described is this paper, is therefore the identification of trends in dynamic social networks. There has been some previous work on social networks trend analysis. For example, Gloor *et al.* introduced a trend analysis algorithm to generate trends from Web resources [8]. There has also been some work on the identification of trends in social networks in the context of online viral marketing [19] and stock market activities [2]. However these systems do not define trends in terms of traffic movement frequency, and do not include any visualisation.

The IGCV framework provides for the visualisation of pattern and trend changes using Visuset, software specifically developed for this purpose. There has been some previous work on network trend visualisation. For example Havre *et al.* [9] described a technique for displaying thematic changes as *river flows* so that changes of topics can be observed. Chen [6] describes a system to visualise a network so as to identify *emerging trends*. However, the network is displayed with respect to a specific time stamp, therefore changes in trends cannot be easily observed. Visuset can display trend transitions as an animation so as to demonstrate how trends change over a given period. Robertson et al. [20] also introduced a system to illustrate trends by animation in the form of *traces*, however in this system trend changes are considered independently. In Visuset trends are correlated against one another so that observers can see how groups of trends change with time.

3 Formalism and Definitions

The input to IGCV comprises a sequence of n time stamped data sets, $D = \{d_1, d_2, \ldots, d_n\}$. Each data set comprises a binary valued table such that each record represents the traffic between a node pair in the social network of interest. The level of detail provided may vary between applications, nodes may be described in terms of a single attribute or a number of attributes. For example nodes may include information about the entity they represent. In the case of the CTS application a number of node categories are identified (farms, markets, abattoirs, etc.). The traffic is defined in terms of a sequence of ranges. Additional traffic information may also be provided, for example in the case of the CTS application information concerning the nature of the cattle moved is included (breed type, gender, etc.). Thus, each record,

in each dataset d_1 to d_n, comprise a subset of a global set of binary valued attributes $A = \{a_1, a_2, \ldots, a_m\}$.

A pattern trend t is then defined in terms of the frequency of occurrence, over time, of discovered patterns within the input data. The trends are conceptualised as *trend lines*, one per pattern, representing a mapping of frequency of occurrence against time. Similar trends (time series), which are mapped by the trained SOM, can still belong to very different patterns. To identify changes in frequent patterns (or lack of them), the number of time stamps is subdivided into e *episodes*, each of equal length m, thus $n = e \times m$. The size of m, and hence the number of episodes e, will be application dependent. However, with respect to the CTS application a granularity of one month was used and hence m was set at 12; consequently each episode represented a year. Thus, a trend t comprises a set of values $\{v_1, v_2, \ldots, v_n\}$ where each value represents an occurrence count. The collection of trends, T, that we wish to analyse thus comprise a sequence of sub-collections $\{T_1, T_2, \ldots, T_e\}$ (where e is the number of episodes).

4 Pattern and Trend Identification

The first stage in the IGCV framework is to identify the traffic movement trends of interest. In the work described in this paper, we define trends in terms of the changing frequency of traffic movement patterns found in social network data. Frequent patterns are sets of attributes that "frequently" co-occur within data according to some user specified *frequency threshold* [1]. To mine pattern trends an extended version of the TFP (Total From Partial) algorithm [3, 4] was used, TM-TFP (Trend Mining TFP). TFP is an established frequent pattern mining algorithm distinguished by its use of two data structures: (i) a P-tree used to both encapsulate the input data and record a *partial* frequency count for each pattern, and (ii) a T-tree to store the identified patterns together with their *total* frequency counts. The T-tree is essentially a reverse *set enumeration tree* that allows fast *look up*. TFP follows an *apriori* style of operation, founded on the well documented *support framework*, whereby a frequency count threshold (the *support threshold*) defines a frequent pattern. TM-TFP incorporates a TM-T-tree to store the desired patterns. Further details of the TM-TFP can be found in [16] and [17]. The output from the TM-TFP algorithm is a collection of trends $T = \{T_1, T_2, \ldots, T_e\}$. Typically, a large number of trends are identified. In the case of the CTS network, Table 1 presents the number of patterns discovered using three different support thresholds (the first column gives the episode identifier). The large number of discovered trends, and the consequent difficulty in analysing the trends, was one of the main motivations for the IGCV framework.

Episode	Support Threshold		
(year)	0.5%	0.8%	1.00%
2003	63,117	34,858	25,738
2004	66,870	36,489	27,055
2005	65,154	35,626	25,954
2006	62,713	33,795	24,740

Table 1. Number of patterns identified using TM-TFP for a sequence of four CTS network episodes and a range of support threshold values.

5 Trend Grouping

The second stage in the IGCV process is to group the discovered trends. The intuition here is that end users are expected to be interested in particular types of trends, for example increasing or decreasing trends. To perform the grouping Self Organising Map (SOM) technology was adopted [10]. SOMs may be viewed as a type of feed-forward, back propagation, neural network that comprises an input layer and an output layer (the $i \times j$ grid). Each output node is connected to every input node. The SOM is "trained" using a training set. Each record in the training set is presented to the SOM in turn and the output nodes compete for the record. For each record, once it has been assigned to a node, the network's weightings are adjusted to reflect the new position. A feature of the network is that adjacent nodes hold similar records, the greatest dissimilarity is thus between nodes at opposite corners of the grid. In the case of the CTS network the authors experimented with different mechanisms for training the SOM. The most effective was found to be training the SOM using trends associated with one of the episodes. The resulting *proto-type map* was then populated with data from the remaining $e - 1$ episodes, to produce a sequence of e maps $M = \{M_1, M_2, \ldots, M_e\}$.

SOMs are often described as a visualisation technique. However, given a large and/or complex data set the number of items within each group (map node) may still be large. This was found to be the case with respect to the CTS application. One potential solution was to increase the size of the grid, however this would have resulted in an undesirable computational overhead and was found not to resolve the situation as many of the map *nodes* remain empty (i.e. the items are consistently held in a small number of map nodes such that increasing the size of i and j has little or no effect). In the case of the CTS network a 10×10 node SOM was found to be the most effective as this gave a good decomposition while still ensuring computational tractability. There is no certain scientific method [5] to specify the optimum value for $n \times m$ for how many clusters should be presented in SOM. A 10×10 node SOM was chosen as a result of earlier experiments repeated in [16, 18].

6 Pattern Migration Clustering

The next stage in the IGCV process provides for further analysis of the trend data contained in the generated SOMs (one per episode). The motivation here was that, at least in the context of the CTS network, consultation with end users indicated that it would be of interest to know how trends associated with individual patterns changed, or did not change, with time. Thus whether patterns associated with a trend in an a given episode remained associated with that trend in following episodes, or whether patterns move from one trend to another. Thus we are also interested in how patterns *migrate* across the collection of SOMs from a SOM (map) M_{e_k} to a SOM $M_{e_{k+1}}$ (where e_k and e_{k+1} are "episode stamps"). For this purpose, pairs of SOMs were represented using a second network, a "SOM network" (containing potentially $i \times j$ nodes and $(i \times j)^2$ links, including "self links"). The nodes in the SOM network represent nodes in the SOM maps, and the links the migration of trends from M_{e_k} to $M_{e_{k+1}}$. It was also considered desirable to display "communities" within these networks, i.e. clusters of SOM network nodes which were "strongly" connected, i.e. where substantial migration had taken place. To this end a hierarchical clustering mechanism, founded on the Newman method [13] for identifying clusters in network data, was applied. Newman proceeds in the standard iterative manner on which hierarchical clustering algorithms are founded. The process starts with a number of clusters equivalent to the number of nodes. The two clusters (nodes) with the greatest "similarity" are then combined to form a merged cluster. The process continues until a "best" cluster configuration is arrived at or all nodes are merged into a single cluster. Best similarity is defined in terms of a *Q-value* (a "modularity" value). Experimentation conducted by Newman and Girvan [14] indicates that if the Q-value is above 0.3 then communities can be said to exist within the target network; a value of 0.3 was thus adopted with respect to IGCV. Note that if all nodes are placed in one group the Q-value will be 0.0 (i.e. a very poor clustering).

7 Pattern Migration Visualisation and Animation using Visuset

IGCV provides two forms of visualisation (integrated into a single software system called Visuset):

1. Visualisation of pattern migration between two successive SOMs.
2. Animation of the pattern migration between three successive SOMs.

In each case the visualisation (animation) includes the pattern migration clusters discovered, using Newman, as described above. The clusters are depicted as "islands" demarcated by a "shoreline" (for aesthetic purposes the islands are also contoured, although no meaning should be attached to these contours). The visualisation process is described in Sub-section 7.1, and the animation in Sub-section 7.2.

7.1 Visualisation of Trend Migration

For the visualisation, IGCV locates nodes in a 2-D "drawing area" using the *Spring Model* [22]. The spring model for drawing graphs in 2-D space is designed to locate nodes in the space in a manner that is both aesthetically pleasing and limits the number of edges that cross over one another. The graph to be depicted is conceptualised in terms of a physical system where the edges represent springs and the nodes objects connected by the springs. Nodes connected by "strong springs" therefore attract one another while nodes connected by "weak springs" repulse one another. The graphs are drawn following an iterative process. Nodes are initially located within the 2D space using a set of (random) default locations (defined in terms of an x and y coordinate system) and, as the process proceeds, pairs of nodes connected by strong springs are "pulled" together. In the context of IGCV the spring value was defined in terms of a *correlation coefficient* (C):

$$C_{ij} = \frac{X}{\sqrt{(|M_{e_k i}| \times |M_{e_{k+1} j}|)}} \qquad (1)$$

where C_{ij} is the correlation coefficient between a node i in SOM M_{e_k} and a node j in SOM $M_{e_{k+1}}$ (note that i and j can represent the same node but in two different maps), X is the number of trends that have moved from node i to j and $|M_{e_k i}|$ ($|M_{e_{k+1} j}|$) is the number trends at node i (j) in SOM M_{e_k} ($M_{e_{k+1}}$). A migration is considered "interesting", and thus highlighted by Visuset, if C is above a specified minimum relationship threshold (Min-Rel). With respect to the CTS network we have discovered that a threshold of 0.2 is a good working Min-Rel value; although Visuset does allow users to specify, and experiment with, whatever Min-Rel value they like. The Min-Rel value is also used to prune links and nodes; any link whose C value is below the Min-Rel value is not depicted in the visualisation, similarly any node that has no links with a C value above Min-Rel is not depicted.

The Visuset spring model algorithm (a simplified version) proceeds as follows:

1. Set drawing area size constants, *SIZEX* and *SIZEY*.
2. For all pair of nodes, allocate an *ideal distance*, $IDIST_{ij}$, where i and j are node numbers. In the current implementation: if a pair has a link, the distance is set as 200 pixels; otherwise it is set to 500 pixels.
3. Set initial coordinates for all nodes. All nodes are "queued" in sequence, according to their node number, from the top-left of the drawing area to the bottom-right.
4. For all node pairs determine the actual pixel distance $RDIST_{ij}$ (where i and j are node numbers).
5. For all nodes, recalculate the coordinates using equations 2 and 3 where: $node_{i_x}$ ($node_{i_y}$) is the x (y) coordinate of $Node_i$, n is the number of nodes to be depicted, K is the *spring constant*, and dx_{ij} (dy_{ij}) is the absolute value of $Node_{i_x} - Node_{j_x}$ ($Node_{i_y} - Node_{j_y}$).
6. If $dx_{ij} + dy_{ij}$ is below a specified threshold (in terms of a number of pixels), or if some maximal number of iterations is reached, exit.

7. Go to Step 4.

$$node_{i_x} = node_{i_x} + \sum_{j=1}^{j=n} \left(dx_{i_j} \times K \times \left(1 - \frac{IDIST_{i_j}}{RDIST_{i_j}} \right) \right) \qquad (2)$$

$$node_{i_y} = node_{i_y} + \sum_{j=1}^{j=n} \left(dy_{i_j} \times K \times \left(1 - \frac{IDIST_{i_j}}{RDIST_{i_j}} \right) \right) \qquad (3)$$

For the current version of Visuset $SIZEX = 1280\ pixels$ and $SIZEY = 880\ pixels$, and the spring constant was set to 0.2. These values were chosen, as result of sequence of experiments, because they tended to give the most desirable end result. The stopping threshold can be set to any value, but from experimentation we have found that the number of nodes (as a pixel value) provides good operational results. Using Visuset it is also possible to disable the spring model so that the user can manually position nodes (and, if applicable, also change the size of individual islands at the same time). Further details concerning the background and development of Visuset can be found in [15].

In the current implementation of Visuset nodes are depicted as: single nodes (i.e. self links where the "migration" is to the same node), node pairs linked by an edge, chains of nodes linked by a sequence of edges, or node clusters (islands). The size (diameter) of the nodes indicates the number of elements represented by that node in M_{e_k} (the size of nodes at $M_{e_{k+1}}$ could equally well have been used, or some interpolation between M_{e_k} and $M_{e_{k+1}}$).

7.2 Animation of Pattern Migration

The animation mechanism, provided by Visuset, can be applied to pairs of visualisations (as described above) to illustrate the migration of patterns over three episodes (SOMs). We refer to each visualisation as a mapping of the nodes in a SOM M_{e_i} to a SOM M_{e_j}. At the start of an animation the display will be identical to the first visualisation (Map 1) and will move to a configuration similar to the second visualisation (Map 2), although nodes will not necessarily be in the same display location. Thus the animations show how subsequent mappings change. As the animation progresses the correlation coefficient (C-values) are linearly incremented or decremented from the value for the first map to that of the second map. Thus as the animation progresses the links, nature of the islands, and overall number of nodes will change. For example if the correlation coefficient for a node in Map 1 is 0.3 and in Map 2 is 0.1 (assuming a threshold of 0.2) the node will "disappear" half way through the animation. Alternatively, if the correlation coefficient for a node in Map 1 is 0.1 and in Map 2 is 0.5 (again assuming a threshold of 0.2) the node will "appear" a quarter of the way through the animation. Nodes that disappear and appear are highlighted in white and pink respectively (nodes that persist are coloured yellow). The example

presented here focuses on three subsequent maps, however the same technique can be applied to a series of N maps.

8 Demonstration

In this section the operation of the ICGV framework is presented in terms of the CTS network introduced earlier. Some further detail concerning the CTS network is first presented in Sub-section 8.1. Then, in the following sections, the operation of IGCV is illustrated in terms of its four component stages as described above.

8.1 Cattle Movement Database

The Cattle Tracing System (CTS) in operation in Great Britain records all the movements of cattle registered within or imported into Great Britain. The database is maintained by the Department for Environment, Food and Rural Affairs (DEFRA) [7]. Cattle movements can be "one-of" movements to final destinations, or movements between intermediate locations. Movement types include: (i) cattle imports, (ii) movements between locations, (iii) movements in terms of births and (iv) movements in terms of deaths. Currently the CTS database holds some 155 Gbytes of data.

The CTS database comprises a number of tables, the most significant of which are the animal, location and movement tables. For the demonstration reported in this section the data from 2003 to 2006 was extracted to make up 4 episodes (2003, 2004, 2005 and 2006) each comprising 12 (one month) time stamps. The data was stored in a single data warehouse such that each record represented a single cattle movement instance associated with a particular year (episode) and month (time stamp). The number of CTS records represented in each data episode was about 400,000. The maximum number of cattle moved (traffic value) between any pair of locations for a single time stamp was approximately 40 animals.

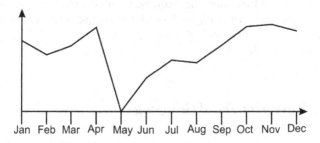

Fig. 2 Example frequent pattern trends associated with a single episode

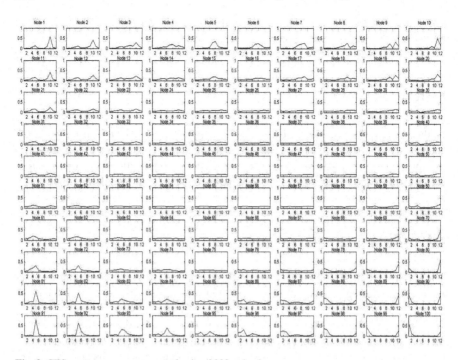

Fig. 3 CTS prototype map generated using 2003 episode

8.2 Cattle Movement Trend Mining

IGCV commences with the identification of trends using the TM-TFP algorithm. For the experiments reported here, a support threshold values of 0.5% was used. The number of identified frequent patterns discovered over the four episodes (2003, 2004, 2005 and 2006) were 63117, 66870, 65154 and 62713 respectively. Each pattern is attached with a trend line, the frequencies of occurrences in an episode. An example trend line is shown in Figure 2 for the the frequent pattern {*AnimalAge = 2_to_5_years, Breed = Friesian, BreedType = dairy, ReceiverLocationType = SlaughterHouse(RedMeat)*}.

8.3 Cattle Movement Trend Grouping

To identify groupings within the collection of trends identified using TM-TFP the SOM software was initialising with a 10×10 node map, and trained using the fre-

quent pattern trends produced for the (earliest) 2003 episode. The resulting proto-type map is shown in Figure 3. The prototype map groups similar trends occurring in the 2003 episode so that (say) seasonal variations can be identified. For example: node 3, node 4, node 13 and node 14 describe trends where the number of cattle movements increases slightly in March, June and October; nodes 95 and 96 both describe trends where the number of cattle movement is considerably higher in spring and summer; and so on. Once the initial prototype map had been generated a sequence of trend line maps was produced, one for each episode.

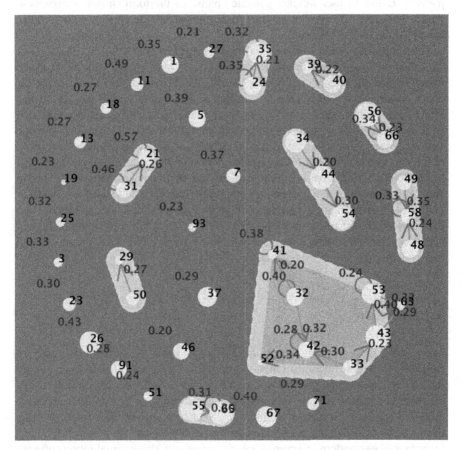

Fig. 4 Visuset visualisation (map) indicating movement of trends from episode 2003 to episode 2004

8.4 Cattle Movement Pattern Migration Visualisation and Animation

Using the IGCV framework, once we have generated a sequence of SOM maps, we can perform some further analysis. With respect to the CTS application we were particularly interested in how patterns associated with trends change with time (from one episode to the next), i.e. we wish to determine how patterns move from one map to another. As noted above, we are also interested in identifying clusters of migrating patterns. Using Visuset we can generate "plots" of the form shown in Figures 4, which shows the migration of patterns from episode 2003 to episode 2004 (A Min-Rel threshold of 2.0 was used).

Inspection of Figure 4 shows that the plot displays 45 nodes out of a total of 100, thus only 45 nodes included links with a C-value greater than 2.0 (and are therefore deemed interesting). Several islands are displayed, determined using the Newman method described above, including a large island comprising eight nodes. The islands indicate communities of pattern migrations. The nodes are annotated with an identifier (the "from" SOM node number) and the arcs with their C-value number. From the map we can see that there are a relatively large number, 30 in all, of self-links; excluding self-links there are only 18 links indicating that, with respect to the 2003 and 2004 episodes, the patterns are fairly constant. However, we can deduce that (for example) patterns are migrating from node 34 to node 44, and from node 44 to 54 (thus indicating a trend change). From Figure 3, we can observe that the nodes hold a fairly similar shape of trend line which has consistent numbers of cattle movement throughout the 12 month time stamps and thus migration between these three trends is understandable.

9 Conclusion

The IGCV trend mining framework has been described. The framework comprises four distinct stages: Identification, Grouping, Clustering and Visualisation. During the identification stage, patterns and trends are identified and extracted. To facilitate interpretation, during the grouping stage trends that display similar features are collected together. To further facilitate interpretation, during the clustering stage, the migration of patterns is considered and "communities" of pattern migrations identified. These pattern migrations are then presented, using visualisation software (Visuset), in the final visualisation stage. Detail concerning each of these four stages has been presented. The operation of the framework was illustrated using a sequence of networks extracted form the Cattle Tracing System (CTS) in operation in Great Britain.

References

1. Agrawal, R., Imielinski, T., and Swami, A. Mining Association Rules between Sets of Items in Large Databases. Proc ACM SIGMOD International Conference on Knowledge Discovery and Data Mining (KDD'93), ACM, pp 207–216 (1993)
2. Choudhury, M.D., Sundaram, H., John, A. and Seligmann D.D. Can blog communication dynamics be correlated with stock market activity? Proc of the 19th ACM Conference on Hypertext and hypermedia, ACM, pp 55–60 (2008)
3. Coenen, F.P., Goulbourne, G. and Leng, P. Computing Association Rules Using Partial Totals. Proc. PKDD, LNCS 2168, Springer, pp 54–66 (2001)
4. Coenen, F., Leng, P. and Ahmed, S. Data Structures for Association Rule Mining: T-trees and P- trees. IEEE Transactions on Data and Knowledge Engineering, 16(6), pp 774–778 (2004)
5. Cottrell, M., Rousset, P. A powerful Tool for Analyzing and Representing Multidimensional Quantitative and Qualitative Data. In Proceedings of IWANN 97. LNCS, Springer Berlin / Heidelberg, vol. 1240, pp 861-871 (2006)
6. Chen, C. CiteSpace II: Detecting and visualizing emerging trends and transient patterns in scientific literature. Journal of the American Society for Information Science and Technology, 57(3), pp 359–377 (2006)
7. Defra. Livestock movements, identification and tracing: Cattle Tracing System. http://www.defra.gov.uk/foodfarm/farmanimal/movements/cattle/cts.htm
8. Gloor, P.A., Krauss, J.S., Nann, S., Fischbach, K. and Schoder, D. Web Science 2.0: Identifying Trends Through Semantic Social Network Analysis. Social Science Research Network. (2008)
9. Havre, S., Hetzler, E., Whitney, P. and Nowell, L. ThemeRiver: Visualizing Thematic Changes in Large Document Collections. IEEE Transactions on Visualization and Computer Graphics, 8(1), pp 9–20 (2002)
10. Kohonen, T. The Self Organizing Maps. Series in Information Sciences, vol. 30. Springer, Heidelberg. (1995)
11. Kohavi, R., Rothleder, N.J. and Simoudis, E. Emerging trends in business analytics, Commun. ACM, 45(8), pp 45–48 (2002)
12. Lent, B., Agrawal, R. and Srikant, R. Discovering Trends in Text Databases Proc ACM SIGMOD International Conference on Knowledge Discovery and Data Mining (KDD'93), ACM, pp 227–230 (1997)
13. Newman, M.E.J. Fast Algorithms for Detecting Community Structure in Networks. Phys. Rev. E 69, 066113, pp 1–5 (2004)
14. Newman, M.E.J. and Girvan, M. Finding and evaluating community structure in networks. Phys. Rev. E 69, 026113, pp 1–15 (2004)
15. Nishikido, T., Sunayama W. and Nishihara, Y. Valuable Change Detection in Keyword Map Animation. Proc. 22nd Canadian Conference on Artificial Intelligence, Springer-Verlag, LNCS 5549, pp 233–236 (2009)
16. Nohuddin, P.N.E., Coenen, F., Christley, R. and Setzkorn, C. Trend Mining in Social Networks: A Study Using A Large Cattle Movement Database. Proc. 10th Ind. Conf. on Data Mining, Springer LNAI 6171, pp 464–475 (2010)
17. Nohuddin, P.N.E., Christley, B., Coenen, F. and Setzkorn, C. Detecting Temporal Pattern and Cluster Changes in Social Networks: A study focusing UK Cattle Movement Database. Proc. 6th Int. Conf. on Intelligent Information Processing (IIP'10), IFIP, pp 163–172 (2010)
18. Nohuddin, P.N.E., Christley, R., Coenen, F., Patel, Y., Setzkorn, C. and Williams, S. Social Network Trend Analysis Using Frequent Pattern Mining and Self Organizing Maps. Research and Development in Intelligent Systems XXVII, Springer-Verlag London Limited, pp 311 (2011)
19. Richardson, M. and Domingos, P. Mining Knowledge Sharing Sites for Viral Marketing, Proc ACM SIGKDD International Conference on Knowledge Discovery and Data Mining (KDD'02), ACM, pp 61–70 (2002)

20. Robertson, G., Fernandez, R., Fisher, D., Lee, B. and Stasko, J. Effectiveness of Animation in Trend Visualization. Transactions on Visualization and Computer Graphics, 14(6), pp 1325–1332 (2008)
21. Safaei, M., Sahan, M. and Ilkan, M. Social Graph Generation and Forecasting Using Social Network Mining. 33rd Annual IEEE International Computer Software and Applications Conference, Compsac, vol. 2, pp 31–35 (2009)
22. Sugiyama K. and Misue, K. Graph Drawing by the Magnetic Spring Model, Journal of Visual Languages and Computing, Vol. 6, No. 3, pp 217–231 (1995)
23. Xu Z., Tresp, V., Achim, R. and Kersting, K. Social Network Mining with Nonparametric Relational Models. Advances in Social Network Mining and Analysis - the Second SNA-KDD Workshop at KDD 2008, LNCS Vol. 5498 (2010), pp 77–96 (2008)

DenGraph-HO: Density-based Hierarchical Community Detection for Explorative Visual Network Analysis

Nico Schlitter, Tanja Falkowski and Jörg Lässig

Abstract For the analysis of communities in social networks several data mining techniques have been developed such as the DenGraph algorithm to study the dynamics of groups in graph structures. The here proposed DenGraph-HO algorithm is an extension of the density-based graph clusterer DenGraph. It produces a cluster hierarchy that can be used to implement a zooming operation for visual social network analysis. The clusterings in the hierarchy fulfill the DenGraph-O paradigms and can be efficiently computed. We apply DenGraph-HO on a data set obtained from the music platform Last.fm and demonstrate its usability.

1 Introduction

DenGraph-HO was developed in order to fulfill the special needs of social network analysts. In most cases, the visual inspection of a network is the first step of the analytical process and helps to determine the basic graph characteristics and further actions. DenGraph-HO supports this early stage by providing a quick visual analysis of the network structure. It provides the ability of zooming into network clusterings and has proven its usefulness for our practical work.

The zooming feature is based on a cluster hierarchy that is computed by applying DenGraph-HO. Our approach differs from traditional hierarchical clustering methods in that DenGraph is a non partioning cluster algorithm. We consider the fact

Nico Schlitter
University of Applied Sciences Zittau/Görlitz, Group for Enterprise Application
Development, e-mail: NSchlitter@hs-zigr.de

Tanja Falkowski
University of Göttingen, Göttingen International, e-mail: Tanja.Falkowski@zvw.uni-goettingen.de

Jörg Lässig
University of Applied Sciences Zittau/Görlitz, Group for Enterprise Application
Development, e-mail: JLaessig@hs-zigr.de

M. Bramer et al. (eds.), *Research and Development in Intelligent Systems XXVIII*,
DOI 10.1007/978-1-4471-2318-7_22, © Springer-Verlag London Limited 2011

that not all nodes are necessarily member of clusters. In addition, the proposed hierarchy is not strictly build up by the classic divisive or agglomerative approach that is known from literature. We generalize these methods and propose a top-down and bottom-up approach by extending the hierarchy paradigms. The proposed hierarchy supports superordinate clusters that contain subclusters and nodes which are not assigned to clusters due to their distance.

Each level of the hierarchy represents a clustering that fulfills the DenGraph paradigms which are described below. The levels, respectively the clusterings, differ in the density that is required to form a cluster. While lower level clusterings aggregate nodes with a lower similarity, higher level clusterings require a higher similarity between nodes. The density-based cluster criteria are controlled by the parameters η and ε which are iteratively applied for each level of the hierarchy. Thereby, an existing clustering is used to compute the clustering of the next level. The efficiency of our algorithm is based on this iterative sequence of cluster adaption instead of recalculating each cluster.

The remainder of this paper is organized as follows. Section 2 introduces the original DenGraph algorithm and its variations DenGraph-O and DenGraph-IO. Section 3 covers the proposed approaches of the DenGraph-HO algorithm. Its usability is demonstrated in Section 4 by applying DenGraph-HO on a dataset obtained from the online music platform Last.fm. Finally, a conclusion and an outlook are given in Section 5.

2 Related Work

DenGraph [5] is a density-based graph clustering algorithm developed in 2007 for community detection in social networks. It is inspired by DBSCAN [2], a well known clustering algorithm for spatial data, and applies a similar local cluster criterion. In the following, we briefly introduce the original DenGraph algorithm and its variations DenGraph-O and DenGraph-IO.

2.1 DenGraph

Given a graph $G = (V, E)$ consisting of a set of nodes V and a set of weighted, undirect edges E, the DenGraph algorithm produces a clustering $\zeta = \{C_1, \ldots, C_k\}$ whereas each cluster C_i ($i = 1 \ldots k$) consists of nodes $V_{C_i} \subseteq V$. Since DenGraph is a non-partitioning clustering algorithm there can be *noise nodes* $V_N = \{u \in V \mid u \notin C_i\}$ that are not part of the clustering ζ. The remaining non-noise nodes are either *core nodes* or *border nodes* of a cluster. A node $u \in V$ is considered as core node if it has an ε-neighborhood $N_\varepsilon(u) = \{v \in V \mid \exists (u, v) \in E \land dist(u, v) \leq \varepsilon\}$ (where $dist(u, v)$ is the distance between u and v) of at least η neighbor nodes ($|N_\varepsilon(u)| \geq \eta$). Nodes

which are in the ε-neighborhood of a core node but have not an own ε-neighborhood are called border nodes.

The actual cluster criterion is based on the concepts *directly density-reachable*, *density-reachable* and *density-connected* which are defined below according to [3] and illustrated in Fig. 1.

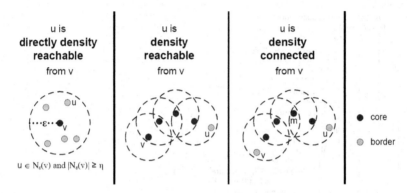

Fig. 1 The concepts *directly density reachability*, *density reachability* and *density connectedness* to determine whether nodes are density connected. (cf. [3])

Definition 1. Let $u, v \in V$ be two nodes. u is *directly density-reachable* from v within V with respect to ε and η if and only if v is a core node and u is in its ε-neighborhood, i.e. $u \in N_\varepsilon(v)$.

Definition 2. Let $u, v \in V$ be two nodes. u is *density-reachable* from v within V with respect to ε and η if there is a chain of nodes $p_1, \ldots, p_n$ such that $p_1 = v, p_n = u$ and for each $i = 2, \ldots, n$ it holds that p_i is directly density-reachable from p_{i-1} within V with respect to ε and η.

Definition 3. Let $u, v \in V$ be two nodes. u is *density-connected* to v within V with respect to ε and η if and only if there is a node $m \in V$ such that u is density-reachable from m and v is density-reachable from m.

In general, a set of core and border nodes V_C forms a cluster C if each node $u \in V_C$ is density-connected to each node $v \in V_C$.

The DenGraph algorithm itself is described in Alg. 1. It uses a stack in order to process the graph nodes. In a first step, all nodes V are marked as noise. Afterwards, each so far unprocessed node v is visited and checked if it has an ε-neighborhood. If the neighborhood contains at least η nodes ($|N(v)| \geq \eta$) v is marked as core and a new cluster is founded. Each of v's neighbors is marked as border, becomes a member of the new cluster and is pushed on the stack. After handling all neighbors, each node u from the stack is checked regarding having an ε-neighborhood and marked correspondingly. If u became core node, all of it's neighbors are marked as

border and pushed on the stack. This procedure is repeated until all nodes of the graph are processed.

Algorithm 1: DenGraph (cf. [3])

input : Graph,η,ε
output: ClusterModel

begin

    foreach $r \in V$ **do** r.state=noise;
    foreach $(u \in V | u.state = noise)$ **do**
        if $(|N_\varepsilon(u)| \geq \eta)$ **then**
            Cluster=CreateNewCluster();
            Cluster.addNode(u);
            u.state=core;
            foreach $n \in N_\varepsilon(u)$ **do**
                Cluster.addNode(n);
                n.state=border;
                stack.push(n);
            repeat
                v=stack.pop();
                if $(|N_\varepsilon(v)| \geq \eta)$ **then**
                    v.state=core;
                    foreach $n \in N_\varepsilon(v) | n.state \neq core$ **do**
                        Cluster.addNode(n);
                        n.state=border;
                        stack.push(n);
            until *stack is empty*;
    return ClusterModel;

2.2 DenGraph-O

Practical work with DenGraph in the field of Social Network Analysis revealed a minor drawback: While in real world applications nodes - respectively human beings - might be part of more than one community, the DenGraph algorithm does not allow for clusters to overlap. This issue was addressed in [6] and the extended version DenGraph-O[1] allows border nodes that are part of more than one cluster.

Figure 2(a) shows an exemplary graph visualization of the Enron dataset, which encodes the communication frequency of Enron employees [8]. The graph was clustered by applying the original DenGraph. Core nodes are blue, border nodes are green and noise nodes are drawn in red color. An example for overlapping clusters is illustrated in Fig. 2(b).

---

[1] O stands for **O**verlapping

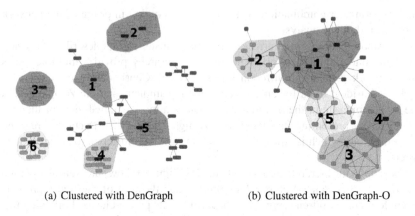

(a) Clustered with DenGraph   (b) Clustered with DenGraph-O

Fig. 2 Visualization of the Enron graphs clustered with DenGraph and DenGraph-O (cf. [3])

2.3 DenGraph-IO

Falkowski et al. propose [4, 6] to analyze the dynamics of communities over time by comparing the changes between clusterings that are obtained in different time points. For this, it is necessary to compute the graph clusterings that are observed over time. A huge computational effort would be necessary if the original DenGraph was used to process multiple consecutive snapshots of social networks. However, as social structures often change slowly, the graphs G_t and G_{t+1} differ just slightly. Therefore, a total re-clustering, as the use of the original DenGraph would demand, would be quite inefficient. The incremental cluster algorithm DenGraph-IO[2] addresses this issue and updates an existing clustering based on the changes of the underlaying graph. Since the DenGraph-IO algorithm deals exclusively with the parts of the graph that changed from one point in time to the other, the computational complexity is dramatical reduced and even huge networks can be processed in reasonable time.

3 DenGraph-HO

One challenge of the DenGraph algorithm is the choice of the parameters epsilon (ε) and eta (η). Several heuristics have been developed, however, the "right" parameter combination mainly depends on the aim of the analysis. If the analyst is for example interested in observing strongly connected nodes rather than in clusterings that show the overall structure, the parameters need to be chosen accordingly. DenGraph-HO addresses this issue and allows for a quick visual representation of the clustering for

---

[2] IO stands for **I**ncremental and **O**verlapping

a chosen parameter combination. The process of zooming in or out of the network can be steered by the analyst.

The proposed algorithm returns a hierarchical clustering that describes the structure of the underlaying network. Thereby, the hierarchy provides multiple views of the network structure in different levels of detail. Consequently, the cluster hierarchy is an ideal basis for an efficient zooming implementation. Zooming-in is done by stepping up in the hierarchy. It provides a more detailed view of the current cluster by presenting its subclusters. A higher level of abstraction is reached by zooming-out, which is equivalent to merging similar clusters into superordinate clusters.

In principle, the hierarchy is a tree of clusters. Figure 3 shows an exemplary graph clustering and the related cluster hierarchy. Since the root of the tree represents the whole graph, children represent subclusters of its parent cluster. Following this definition, the leaves of the tree correspond to the smallest clusters.

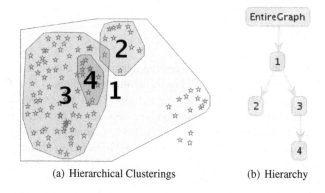

(a) Hierarchical Clusterings   (b) Hierarchy

Fig. 3 Visualization of the Enron graph clustered with DenGraph-HO

Here, we are proposing a hierarchy that is based on the concepts of the DenGraph algorithm. Each level of the tree (besides the root) represents a valid clustering that fulfills the DenGraph-O paradigms. The hierarchy could be built by repeatedly applying DenGraph-O while using specific parameter settings for each level of the tree. Thereby, the choice of the parameters η and ε is limited by constraints in order to ensure that lower level clusters are subclusters of the parent cluster.

Let us assume that the clustering ζ_l forms level l of the hierarchy and is computed by applying DenGraph-O with the parameters ε_l and η_l. Level $l+1$ represents a clustering that is based on ε_{l+1} and η_{l+1} and guarantees a higher similarity of nodes in the cluster. According to the description above, ζ_{l+1} has to contain subclusters of clusters that are element of ζ_l. In order to preserve this parent-child relation we have to ensure the following constraints:

1. The parameter ε_l that is used to generate the clustering ζ_l has to be bigger or equal than ε_{l+1} which is used to compute the clustering ζ_{l+1}:

$$\varepsilon_l \geq \varepsilon_{l+1}$$

2. The parameter η_l that is used to generate the clustering ζ_l has to be lower or equal than η_{l+1} which is used to compute the clustering ζ_{l+1}:

$$\eta_l \leq \eta_{l+1}$$

Increasing ε might lead to a transition of a node state from noise or border to core or from noise to border. By increasing ε a core node can not loose its state. This explains why increasing ε might create a new or expand an existing cluster and why it surely avoids cluster reductions or removals. The same argument holds for decreasing η and shows why the demanded cluster-subcluster relation can be guaranteed by the given constraints.

In the following, we discuss how the proposed cluster hierarchy can be efficiently generated based on a list of parameter settings that fulfill the discussed constraints. An obvious approach would be to perform multiple re-clusterings until each parameter setting is processed. However, this is very inefficient and would be a huge computational effort because for a re-clustering the whole graph needs to be traversed again.

The proposed DenGraph-HO algorithm addresses this issue and uses incremental parameter changes to generate the cluster hierarchy. Instead of computing a complete new clustering for each level, an existing clustering is used and adapted. In the following, we discuss how an existing clustering of level l can be used to compute the clusterings of level $l+1$ and $l-1$. We propose a bottom-up and top-down approach and analyze their efficiency depending on the graph structure. The input for both approaches is a graph $G = (V,E)$ and an existing clustering $\zeta_l = \{C_1^l, \ldots, C_k^l\}$ that fulfills the DenGraph paradigms.

3.1 Top-down Approach: Cluster Reduction, Split or Removal

The top-down approach performs a zoom-in operation and generates a new clustering for level $l+1$ of the hierarchy. Where in level $l+1$, nodes are clustered which have a higher similarity than clusters in level l. Thereby, clusters of level l might be reduced, split or removed. By decreasing ε and increasing η the state of nodes within a cluster might change. A former border node might become noise (Cluster Reduction). Former core nodes might get border state (possible Cluster Splitting) or noise state (Cluster Reduction, possible Cluster Splitting or Removal).

Due to the DenGraph paradigms, it is guaranteed that noise nodes can not reach border or core state by decreasing ε or increasing η. Thus, noise nodes will not change their state and do not need to be processed.

Consequently, the top-down approach traverses just border and core nodes and performs a reclustering for each existing cluster. For this purpose, we use a modified DenGraph-O that is shown in Alg. 2. Each cluster C of level l is reclustered by applying the parameters of level $l+1$. Regarding the cluster hierarchy, if new clusters emerge, they are subclusters of C.

Algorithm 2: TopDown

---

input : Graph,Clustering,ε,η
output: Clustering

foreach $(C \in \zeta)$ **do**
    foreach $r \in C$ **do** r.state=noise;
    foreach $(u \in C | u.state = noise)$ **do**
        if $(|N_\varepsilon(u)| \geq \eta)$ **then**
            Cluster=CreateNewCluster();
            C.addCluster(Cluster);
            Cluster.addNode(u);
            u.state=core;
            foreach $n \in N_\varepsilon(u)$ **do**
                Cluster.addNode(n);
                n.state=border;
                stack.push(n);

    repeat
        v=stack.pop();
        if $(|N_\varepsilon(v)| \geq \eta)$ **then**
            v.state=core;
            foreach $n \in N_\varepsilon(v) | n.state \neq core$ **do**
                Cluster.addNode(n);
                n.state=border;
                stack.push(n);
    until *stack is empty*;

return Clustering;

3.2 Bottom-up Approach: Cluster Creation, Absorption and Merging

Figuratively, the bottom-up approach performs a zoom-out operation and generates a new clustering for level $l - 1$. Thereby, new clusters may be created, existing clusters of ζ_l might absorb new members or get merged with other clusters.

As discussed above, by increasing ε and decreasing η, the state of a core node remains unchanged. A former noise node may become core node (cluster creation) or border node (absorption). A former border node could become core node (absorption). In case a former border node is member of multiple clusters (overlapping clusters), its transition to core state leads to a merge of those clusters.

Since core nodes keep their state, there is no need to consider them in the bottom-up approach. Consequently, the proposed procedure processes only noise and border nodes in order to determine their new state and to adapt the clustering accordingly. Following this argumentation, the procedure's efficiency is based on the saved time that the original DenGraph-O would have spent for processing core nodes.

Algorithm 3 describes the procedure that performs the bottom-up step by dealing with the changes of η and ε. First, the algorithm iterates over all existing clusters in order to expand them. Therefore it traverses all border nodes and updates their state based on the number of nodes in the ε-neighborhood and η. In case a former border node becomes core, this new core node is pushed on the stack for further processing. After dealing with all border nodes, the procedure *Cascade_Expand* checks if new

core nodes absorb their neighbors into the cluster. In case an absorbed neighbor has no own ε-neighborhood of cardinality η it becomes border node, otherwise it becomes a core node. The newly discovered core nodes are pushed on the stack and the procedure is repeated until no further nodes are absorbed into the cluster. Since we allow for clusters to overlap, a new core node might have been a member of multiple clusters before. Due to its new core state, the affected clusters are merged into a superordinate cluster.

After dealing with all border nodes the existing clusters are maximal expanded with respect to the changed η and ε. Now, the remaining noise nodes are processed to check whether their state has changed. In case a former noise node becomes core, a new cluster is created and the procedure *Cascade_Create* absorbs the ε-neighbors according to the DenGraph-O paradigms. If these neighbors become core nodes, this cascade is repeated until no new ε-neighbors are found. During the handling of noise nodes a newly created cluster will not merge with an existing one. If the new cluster would be in ε-distance to an other cluster, the nodes of the new cluster would have been already absorbed into the existing cluster during handling the border nodes.

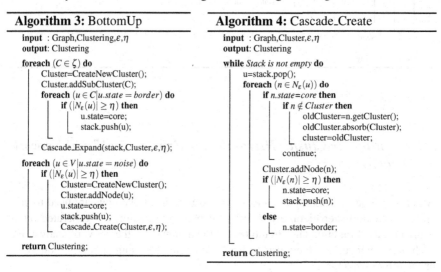

Algorithm 3: BottomUp

input : Graph,Clustering,ε,η
output: Clustering

foreach $(C \in \zeta)$ **do**
  Cluster=CreateNewCluster();
  Cluster.addSubCluster(C);
  foreach $(u \in C | u.state = border)$ **do**
    if $(|N_\varepsilon(u)| \geq \eta)$ **then**
      u.state=core;
      stack.push(u);
  Cascade_Expand(stack,Cluster,ε,η);

foreach $(u \in V | u.state = noise)$ **do**
  if $(|N_\varepsilon(u)| \geq \eta)$ **then**
    Cluster=CreateNewCluster();
    Cluster.addNode(u);
    u.state=core;
    stack.push(u);
    Cascade_Create(Cluster,ε,η);

return Clustering;

Algorithm 4: Cascade_Create

input : Graph,Cluster,ε,η
output: Clustering

while *Stack is not empty* **do**
  u=stack.pop();
  foreach $(n \in N_\varepsilon(u))$ **do**
    if *n.state=core* **then**
      if $n \notin Cluster$ **then**
        oldCluster=n.getCluster();
        oldCluster.absorb(Cluster);
        cluster=oldCluster;
      continue;
    Cluster.addNode(n);
    if $(|N_\varepsilon(n)| \geq \eta)$ **then**
      n.state=core;
      stack.push(n);
    else
      n.state=border;

return Clustering;

Algorithm 5: Cascade_Expand

---

input : Graph,Clustering,Cluster,ε,η
output: Clustering

```
while Stack is not empty do
    u=stack.pop();
    foreach (n ∈ Nε(u)|n.state ∈ {noise,border}) do
        Cluster.addNode(n);
        if (|Nε(n)| ≥ η) then
            if n.state = noise then
                n.state=core;
                stack.push(n);
            else
                n.state=core;
                //Cluster Merge
                foreach (C ∈ ζ|n ∈ C) do
                    Cluster.addSubCluster(C);
                    foreach (p ∈ C|p.state = border) do
                        if (|Nε(p)| ≥ η) then
                            p.state=core;
                            stack.push(p);
                        else
                            p.state=border;
        else n.state=border;
return Clustering;
```

3.3 Creating the Cluster Hierarchy for Explorative Visual Network Analysis

Algorithm 6 describes how the top-down and bottom-up methods are used to generate the final cluster hierarchy. The list of parameter settings is generated by an heuristic-based function and should reflect the demands of the network analyst. For each parameter setting, the clusterings are computed by using either the bottom-up or the top-down approach.

4 Application

Last.fm[3] is a music community with over 20 million active users based in more than 200 countries. After a user signs up, a plugin is installed and all tracks a user listens to are submitted to a database.

From the *Last.fm* Website we obtained the user listening behavior of 1,209 users over an interval of 130 weeks (from March 2005 to May 2008). *Last.fm* provides

---

[3] http://www.last.fm/

Algorithm 6: CreateClusterHierarchy

---

input : Graph
output: Clustering

PS=CreateParameterSettingList();
Direction=DecideDirection();
if *Direction=BottomUp* **then**
    ClusterHierarchy=DenGraph(Graph,PS[0].η,PS[0].ε);
    for $i \leftarrow 1$ **to** $(size(PS) - 1)$ **do**
        ClusterHierarchy=BottomUp(ClusterHierarchy,PS[i].η,PS[i].ε);

else
    ClusterModel=DenGraph(Graph,PS[$size(PS)$].η,PS[$size(PS)$].ε);
    for $i \leftarrow (size(PS) - 1)$ **to** $size(0)$ **do**
        ClusterHierarchy=TopDown(ClusterHierarchy,PS[i].η,PS[i].ε);

return Clustering;

---

for each user and interval (here one week) a list of the most frequently listened artists and the number of times the artist was played. Based on this information we determine user profiles for each interval and calculate the similarity of music preferences between users. Based on these similarities, we generate a graph in which the nodes represent the users and the edge weights code the distance between users based on the similarity of their music listening behavior [7].

For our analysis we used a Last.fm graph consisting of 1,209 nodes and 12,612 edges. The graph has an average degree of 20.8 and a density of 0.017. We applied DenGraph-HO and obtained the cluster hierarchy shown in Figure 4. The calculated cluster labels are based on the profiles of the users in the same cluster. Table 1 gives more details about the clustering of each hierarchy level. Shown are the parameters ε and η, the cluster label and the number of nodes in each cluster.

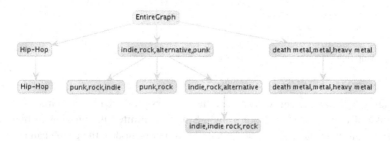

Fig. 4 DenGraph-HO: Hierarchy

The plausibility of the relation between a cluster and its subclusters is demonstrated by the *(indie, rock, alternative, punk)*-cluster that is divided in the clusters *(punk, rock, indie)*, *(punk, rock)* and *(indie, rock, alternative)*. Obviously, music gen-

Table 1 Overview about the cluster hierarchy

Level	ε	η	Cluster Labels	# Nodes
0	-	-	Entire Graph	1209
1	0.05	22	hip-hop	35
			indie, rock, alternative, punk	631
			death metal, metal, heavy metal	85
2	0.037	24	hip-hop	31
			punk, rock, indie	86
			punk, rock	33
			indie, rock, alternative	316
			death metal, metal, heavy metal	37
3	0.025	26	indie, indie rock, rock	120

res that are similar but separated in level 2 of the hierarchy are merged into one cluster in level 1.

The number of nodes per cluster increases, when going from a leave to the root of the cluster hierarchy. Due to the parameter setting of ε and η the clusters grow either through cluster merging or absorption of new nodes. These properties of DenGraph-HO and the efficient calculation of the cluster hierarchy are the base for the proposed zooming purpose.

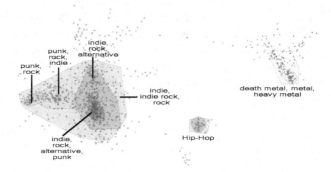

Fig. 5 DenGraph-HO: Graph and Clustering

Figure 5 shows the entire graph and the clusters produced by DenGraph-HO. For the sake of clarity edges are not drawn. Since we limited the number of hierarchy levels in our example and due to the small number of nodes, the graph can be easily understood. However, graphs with millions of nodes and a hierarchy depth greater than ten ask for appropriate tools.

The ability of zooming through the graph enriches our tool set and is an important step for studying the graph structure. Figure 6 shows the three zooming steps that are provided by DenGraph-HO for the given example. Each level of the hierarchy is shown as a single clustering.

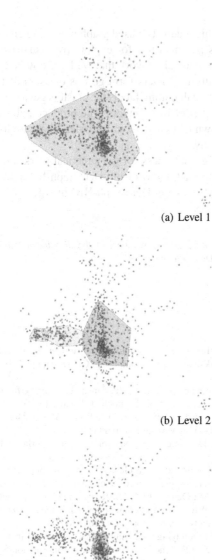

(a) Level 1

(b) Level 2

(c) Level 3

Fig. 6 Zoom-in Operation

5 Conclusion

In this paper we proposed the hierarchical density-based graph clustering algorithm DenGraph-HO. We demonstrated its practical use for explorative visual network analysis by applying the algorithm to a social network that we have obtained from the Last.fm music platform. The resulting clusters form groups of users that have similar music listening preferences. By calculating labels the clusters get a semantic meaning based on the music preferences of its members. The produced cluster hierarchy and clustered graph have shown that clusters with similar labels are located closely in the graph and the in hierarchy.

Since DenGraph-HO has proven its usefulness for our practical work, our next step is to integrate the incremental approach known from DenGraph-IO in a hierarchical incremental density-based graph clusterer DenGraph-HIO in order to analyze clusters over time.

Acknowledgements This work was supported by the members of the *distributedDataMining* BOINC [1] project (http://www.distributedDataMining.org).

References

1. Anderson, D.P.: Boinc: A system for public-resource computing and storage. In: Proceedings of the 5th IEEE/ACM International Workshop on Grid Computing, GRID '04, pp. 4–10. IEEE Computer Society, Washington, DC, USA (2004)
2. Ester, M., Kriegel, H.P., Sander, J., Wimmer, M., Xu, X.: Incremental clustering for mining in a data warehousing environment. In: A. Gupta, O. Shmueli, J. Widom (eds.) VLDB'98, Proceedings of 24rd International Conference on Very Large Data Bases, August 24-27, 1998, New York City, New York, USA, pp. 323–333. Morgan Kaufmann (1998)
3. Falkowski, T.: Community Analysis in Dynamic Social Networks. Sierke Verlag, Gttingen (2009)
4. Falkowski, T., Barth, A.: Density-based temporal graph clustering for subgroup detection in social networks. Presented at Conference on Applications of Social Network Analysis (2007)
5. Falkowski, T., Barth, A., Spiliopoulou, M.: Dengraph: A density-based community detection algorithm. In: Proc. of the 2007 IEEE / WIC / ACM International Conference on Web Intelligence, pp. 112–115. IEEE Computer Society, Washington, DC, USA (2007)
6. Falkowski, T., Barth, A., Spiliopoulou, M.: Studying community dynamics with an incremental graph mining algorithm. In: Proc. of the 14 th Americas Conference on Information Systems (AMCIS 2008). Toronto, Canada (2008)
7. Schlitter, N., Falkowski, T.: Mining the dynamics of music preferences from a social networking site. In: Proceedings of the 2009 International Conference on Advances in Social Network Analysis and Mining, pp. 243–248. IEEE Computer Society, Washington, DC, USA (2009)
8. Shetty, J., Adibi, J.: Enron email dataset. Tech. rep. (2004). URL http://www.isi.edu/adibi/Enron/Enron.htm

MACHINE LEARNING

Using the Gamma Test in the Analysis of Classification Models for Time-Series Events in Urodynamics Investigations

Steve Hogan, Paul Jarvis, Ian Wilson[1]

Abstract   Urodynamics is a clinical test in which time series data is recorded measuring internal pressure readings as the bladder is filled and emptied. Two sets of descriptive statistics based on various pressure events from urodynamics tests have been derived from time series data. The suitability of these statistics for use as inputs for event classification through neural networks is investigated by means of the gamma test. BFGS neural network models are constructed and their classification accuracy measured. Through a comparison of the results, it is shown that the gamma test can be used to predict the reliability of models before the neural network training phase begins.

1 Introduction

Urodynamics is a clinical used to diagnose the pathophysiological reason behind lower urinary tract symptoms with which a patient presents.

The test is carried out by taking pressure measurements inside the bladder and rectum and observing how pressure changes during bladder filling and voiding. The data recorded in urodynamics is usually in the form of a time series containing three pressure traces (the two measured pressures, in the bladder and rectum, and the difference between them which is assumed to be bladder muscle activity) The flow rate of any fluid voided and the amount of fluid that has been pumped into the bladder during the test is also recorded. Occasionally X-ray video is used to aid in diagnosis but in most cases the presence of certain pressure events and key values taken during the bladder voiding cycle are used to make a diagnosis.

The pressure events in urodynamics can be thought of as deviations from a resting pressure or baseline value. A comprehensive explanation of urodynamics

[1] University of Glamorgan, Pontypridd, CF37 1DL, UK
{sbhogan,psjarvis,idwilson}@glam.ac.uk

M. Bramer et al. (eds.), *Research and Development in Intelligent Systems XXVIII*,
DOI 10.1007/978-1-4471-2318-7_23, © Springer-Verlag London Limited 2011

and a full description of the equipment and methods involved and its clinical significance can be found in [1].

An algorithm has been written to generate the baseline or resting pressure for urodynamic tests. Significant deviations from the baseline have been extracted from the time series and are considered separate pressure events. A significant deviation is considered to be any pressure change that deviates from baseline pressure levels by more than 10cmH$_2$O.

The pressure events recorded during urodynamics which are present in this study are:

- Coughs
- Descending pressure (due to a tube leak)
- Bladder muscle contractions
- Abdominal straining
- Rectal contractions
- Incorrect positioning of three way taps
- Movement or tube knock artefacts
- Line flush
- Expelled catheter
- Patient position change

The difficulty in classifying the pressure events stems from their variability in size and duration both within examples from a single patient and in examples of each event between patients.

Two sets of indicators which, it is thought can be used to classify the pressure events have been derived from the data. A library of these indicators has been recorded for all pressure events found in 200 patient files, in total this represents over ten thousand significant pressure events all of which have been classified by eye. The aim of the investigation in this paper is to find out whether the set of indicators are likely to produce a reliable and robust model for classifying pressure events using an Artificial Neural Network (ANN) which can then be used in automated classification. Potential indicators have been identified and analysed using the Gamma Test [2] and neural network models have been created using the Broyden-Fletcher-Goldfarb-Shanno (BFGS) training algorithm [3]. The success of these models is then assessed and an interpretation of the results is presented.

Although it may be possible to ascertain the correct classification for a pressure event by the appropriate selection of key indicators, a common problem in this sort of investigation is identifying indicators that are relevant and necessary for producing reliable classification results. For dimensionality reduction it is desirable to use as few indicators as possible, whilst maintaining the reliability of the model. Choosing the smallest possible set of indicators to produce a reliable model reduces complexity of the problem.

When using urodynamics data, the indicators chosen can be based on what a trained clinician would look for when interpreting the pressure signals. Indicators representative of what a urodynamicist would routinely look for, are measures of

the size and shape of the pressure deviation coupled with information about concurrent pressure changes in the other traces. Data has been collected on all relevant indicators which may be of use. These indicators can be added to an ANN model as inputs and the success measured against the desired classification output [4]. Some indicators may have little or no impact on the final classification and the exclusion of these inputs can result in a more robust model. It may also be the case that some indicators are only useful in determining one class of pressure event whilst others are important in all assigning classes. Further problems may arise if some indicators are susceptible to noise.

In this paper the gamma test is used to assess the suitability of indicators chosen and to investigate the reliability of fitting an ANN to predict the classification of events based on the indicator set.

2 The Gamma Test

This section contains an overview of the Gamma test and its relevance in selecting appropriate indicators for the classification of urodynamic pressure event data.

The gamma test can be used to help identify whether a data set is likely to produce reliable results when generating an ANN based on the Mean Square Error (MSE) of connections between a set of inputs and a single classification output. If the relationship between a set of inputs, vector v , and an output y based on some function $y = f(v) + \varepsilon$, where ε represents noise, then the gamma test can be used to estimate variance of ε provided:

- the training and testing data are separate sets;
- the training set inputs are not sparse input spaces;
- each output is determined from the inputs by same process;
- each output is subjected to statistical noise with finite variance whose distribution may be different for different output, but is the same in both training and testing data sets for each output [5].

In order to ensure the above criteria were met some pre-processing to the recorded indicators was needed to avoid sparse input spaces.

The gamma test was developed to combat the three drawbacks of backpropagation neural networks, [6] namely:

- overfitting,
- need for cross validation data sets and
- choosing optimum inputs

The Gamma test provides a guide to the potential reliability of a model built with a given combination of inputs at the fraction of the computational cost of

implementing a full neural network model. An assumption is made that a similar set of inputs should result in a similar output, differences in the relationship between inputs and outputs are attributed to noise. The Gamma test returns a score based on the mean squared error (MSE) between inputs and outputs of the proposed model. A high MSE results in a high Gamma score a low MSE results in a low Gamma score. The Gamma score can be used to anticipate the likely success of an ANN in advance of training the network. Only models with the lowest Gamma score need be fully constructed. If an input is not truly related to the output then it will carry with it a high MSE and its omission will result in a model with a lower overall MSE. Therefore, the Gamma test can provide a more efficient way of establishing whether the chosen set of inputs are the most appropriate, without the necessity of training multiple networks for comparison purposes. Furthermore, the results of the Gamma test can be used to identify a set of indicators which can be used for developing a robust and reliable model regardless of modelling technique used.

The gamma test uses the statistics

$$\gamma M(k) = \frac{1}{2M} \sum_{i=1}^{M} (y_{N[i,k]} - y_i)^2$$

Where $y_{N[i,k]}$ represents the kth nearest neighbour to output y_i, and

$$\delta M(k) = \frac{1}{M} \sum_{i=1}^{M} (x_{N[i,k]} - x_i)^2$$

where $x_{N[i,k]}$ represents the kth nearest neighbour to the set of inputs x_i

The Gamma statistic, used to assess the suitability of the inputs for the desired output, Γ, is calculated as the intercept of the vertical $\delta = 0$ axis of the least squared error regression line constructed for the points $(\delta M(k), \gamma M(k))$. Obviously the choice of how many near neighbours is used will influence the results and this can be investigated while using all available inputs, prior to testing combinations of inputs. [7] recommends using 10 near neighbours, the suitability of this suggestion will be tested and if there is no evidence to reject this value, 10 near neighbours will be used in all models.

A more detailed and thorough description of the Gamma test can be found in [2, 5].

3 Classification using artificial neural networks

ANNs have been applied to many areas of medicine and have even been used to aid medical diagnosis [8, 9]. In this section the architecture of the neural network

is described along with the method to be used for measuring the performance of neural network models.

In this study the aim is to investigate the suitability of using the gamma test to inform the selection of input parameters for use in ANNs and so the training algorithm is of less importance. Chai carried out a comparison of many training algorithms [10] and found the BFGS training algorithm returned the lowest root mean squared error for classification accuracy. The BFGS algorithm also has the advantage of reducing training time by approximating the hessian matrix required by a conventional backpropagation algorithm [11]. In this study the training algorithm will remain unchanged and the BFGS training algorithm has been selected to create the ANN due to its reliability and speed.

Sections 3.1 to 3.4 describe the network architecture of the ANN used in the experiments.

3.1 Network architecture

The ANN consists of an input layer which is the length of the input vector, an output layer which produces the classifications and two hidden layers in which the number of nodes can be varied. Although a single hidden layer can approximate any complex non-linear function, it has been shown that two hidden layers result in a more compact architecture that is also more efficient and this is the reason two hidden layers have been used.[12, 13]. The result of changing the number of nodes in each of the hidden layers has been experimented with. Classification accuracy results of using 5, 10 and 15 nodes in each hidden layer are presented in section 4.2.

3.2 Nodes in the input layer

The number of nodes in the input layer corresponds to the number of inputs used in classification. The number of inputs is consistent for all pressure events in each data set. However, since input set A has 30 data points and set B has 41 data points for each pressure events, the number of nodes in the input layer varies between data sets. It is possible to estimate the impact of any input by excluding it and observing any change in classification accuracy and this may be carried out in the future. A change in the number of inputs used in the creation of an ANN will result in an equal change in the number of nodes in the input layer.

3.3 Nodes in the output layer

For the classification problem there is a single output node for each of the input vectors tested. Ideally, the value of the output node will match the desired classification value. Due its nature ANN output nodes are continuous and in most cases the output value will need to be rounded to the nearest classification value to test classification accuracy.

3.4 Performance measure

The predicted class from the output node for each set of inputs will be rounded to the nearest exact class value. This value is then compared to the actual class for each set of inputs and will score a one if correct and zero otherwise. The overall performance of the ANN will be measured in the form of a percentage score calculated from the count of correct classifications divided by the number of input vectors tested.

4 Experiments

In this section the number of optimum near neighbours is discussed and identified. A comparison of two possible input sets is made based on the gamma test results and classification accuracy of the neural networks is assessed.

It is suggested that 10 near neighbours produce reasonable results for most data sets [7]. To investigate the suitability of this value the Gamma statistic was created for all nearest neighbour values from 1 to 100. As an heuristic the gamma value for the optimum number of near neighbours for the data should be close to the origin and in a relatively stable part of the graph.

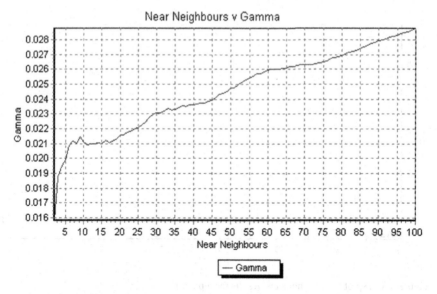

Figure 1 Increasing near neighbours.

As can be seen from Figure 1, the graph stabilises at 10 near neighbours with very little change in the Gamma value until after 15 nearest neighbours. This result supports previously published findings and 10 near neighbours will be used for future experiments with this data set.

4.1 Comparison of input sets

Two separate sets of input indicators, (input set A and input set B) have been recorded each of which can be thought to describe the changes in the time series data during a pressure event. The gamma test will be used to identify the set of indicators that is most likely to produce a reliable model. Both models will then be formally constructed and tested to check that the results of the gamma are an effective guide in model constriction.

The gamma statistic is calculated for all input vectors. Set A contains 30 inputs and input set B contains 41. For 10 nearest neighbours the gamma statistic is 0.021 for input set A and 0.006 for input set B. Both values indicate that reasonably reliable classification results should be obtained from a model using either set of inputs but the difference in gamma test statistic implies that the alternative set of inputs should produce a superior model.

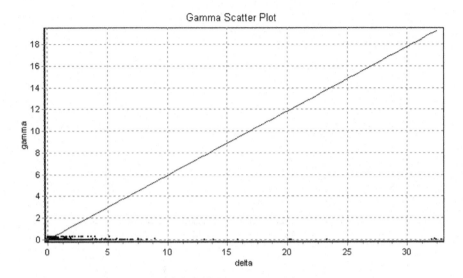

Figure 2 A 2D plot of the gamma test results for input set A.

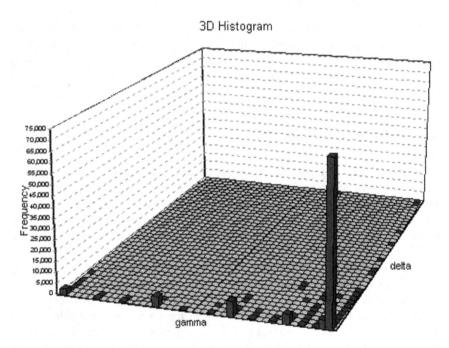

Figure 3 A 3D histogram of gamma test results for input set A.

The graphs indicate that similar inputs will consistently provide similar outputs, as low gamma values tend to equate to low delta values. The 3D graph (Figure 3) highlights these similarities with the tall spike at the origin providing a clearer visual representation of the overlapping points shown on the 2D graph (Figure 2).

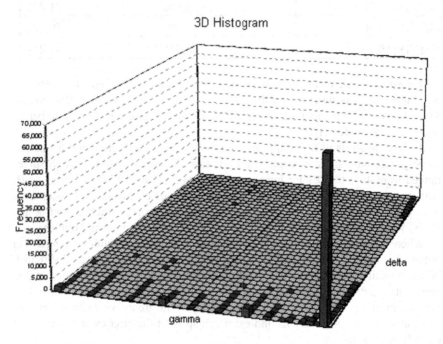

Figure 4 A 3D histogram of gamma test results for input set B.

Both Figure 3and Figure 4 have the desired high peak near the origin but input set B has smaller peaks along the gamma axis and this is further evidence that set B should produce better classification accuracy than set A.

4.2 *Results of fitting the BFGS model*

In this section 4000 data points were used in model fitting and 6000 used for testing. BFGS models were used with a varying number of nodes in the two hidden layers. The number of nodes experimented with were (5,5), (10,10) and (15,15) in each of the hidden layers.

Table 1 A comparison of classification success rates between input sets A and B.

Neural Network Architecture	Classification Performance of Input Set A	Classification Performance of Input Set B
BFGS (5,5)	55.6%	81.8%
BFGS (10,10)	58.0%	79.6%
BFGS(15,15)	64.5%	81.4%

The success rate of the models created using input set A ranges from 55% to 65%, input set B is superior and the success rate increases to around 80% overall. The success rate for input set B remains consistent regardless of the number of nodes in each hidden layer.

A closer analysis of the results showed that some events were more difficult to classify than others, for example, the classification success rate for cough spikes ranged from 40% to 50% for input set A but hovered around 55% in input set B. Although input set B outperformed set A in terms of overall performance, there were some event types in which set A proved more accurate such as with a line flush –where fluid is forced through a catheter to remove trapped air bubbles.

Where classification accuracy is low, the inclusion of suitable inputs can potentially rectify the problem by giving additional information to distinguish between similar event types. The number of examples of each event, found in 200 consecutive patient files, varied widely from 1700 examples in some cases to less than 10 in others. The success rate for smaller event groups was either 100% or 0% and it may be necessary to find extra examples of the rarer events to improve classification accuracy.

4.3 Discussion of results

The gamma test results suggested that input set B would create the best neural network for event classification and the results obtained when full models are created show this prediction to be true.

The fact that one set of inputs did not out perform another in all event classes suggests that a mix of the inputs from the two sets could lead to a new hybrid input set capable of delivering further improvements in classification accuracy.

These results have indicated the potential for improvement in classification accuracy through more appropriate selection of input indicators. With further work focusing upon the selection of even more suitable inputs then it is likely that the classification accuracy can be improved to an even greater extent. Further analysis may show that there is a pattern to the misclassifications, i.e. one event is

regularly misclassified as a certain other event type. If a pattern in misclassifications can be identified then it may be possible to find additional indicators that would be capable of separating these classes before the inputs are sent to a neural network reducing the likelihood of such a misclassification. The neural network can then work alongside other techniques in order to maximise the classification success rate of an integrated model.

It is clear from the results that the selection of inputs needed to produce a reliable neural network for urodynamic signal classification needs to be refined, but the gamma test will allow the usefulness of a selection of indicators to be assessed without formally constructing and testing a model.

5 Conclusion

Descriptive statistics of pressure events recorded during urodynamic investigations can be used in event classification. The gamma test can be used to indicate which set of inputs is more likely to produce a reliable classification model where multiple input sets are possible. Although the results of using neural networks in event classification have not been consistently high for all event types the likely effect of additional or alternative sets of inputs can be investigated using the gamma test. A significant drop in the gamma statistic will result in significantly higher classification accuracy.

6 Future work

An analysis of the results can be carried out to ascertain the incorrect mappings of inputs to output classifications. The results of this analysis will be useful in identifying the need for additional inputs that may improve the classification results.

Combinations of the existing inputs can be altered experimentally through the use of partial masks where some inputs are excluded from the model. The process of running the gamma test with various input masks may result in the identification of some inputs which do not contribute to event classification and could even be hindering the classification process.

References

1. Abrams, P., *Urodynamics*. 2006: Springer Verlag.
2. Evans, D. and A.J. Jones, *A proof of the Gamma test*. Proceedings of the Royal Society of London. Series A: Mathematical, Physical and Engineering Sciences, 2002. **458**(2027): p. 2759.
3. Broyden, C., et al., *BFGS method*. Journal of the Institute of Mathematics and Its Applications, 1970. **6**: p. 76-90.
4. Zurada, J.M., *Introduction to artificial neural systems*. 1992.
5. Stefánsson, A., N. Končar, and A.J. Jones, *A note on the Gamma test*. Neural Computing & Applications, 1997. **5**(3): p. 131-133.
6. Kemp, S., I. Wilson, and J. Ware, *A tutorial on the gamma test*. International Journal of Simulation: Systems, Science and Technology, 2004. **6**(1-2): p. 67–75.
7. Evans, D., *Data-derived estimates of noise for known smooth models using near-neighbour asymptotics*, in *Department of Computer Science*. 2002, Cardiff University Cardiff.
8. Dreiseitl, S. and L. Ohno-Machado, *Logistic regression and artificial neural network classification models: a methodology review*. Journal of Biomedical Informatics, 2002. **35**(5-6): p. 352-359.
9. Baxt, W.G., *Application of artificial neural networks to clinical medicine*. The lancet, 1995. **346**(8983): p. 1135-1138.
10. Chai, S.S., et al., *Backpropagation neural network for soil moisture retrieval using NAFE'05 data: a comparison of different training algorithms*. Int Archives Photogramm, Remote Sens Spatial Inf Sci (China), 2008. **37**: p. 1345.
11. Xia, J.H. and A. Kumta, *Feedforward Neural Network Trained by BFGS Algorithm for Modeling Plasma Etching of Silicon Carbide*. Plasma Science, IEEE Transactions on, 2010. **38**(2): p. 142-148.
12. Chester, D.L. *Why two hidden layers are better than one*. 1990.
13. Cybenko, G., *Continuous valued neural networks with two hidden layers are sufficient*. Mathematics of Control, Signal and Systems, 1989. **2**: p. 303-314.

DScentTrail: A New Way of Viewing Deception

S.J. Dixon, M.B. Dixon, J. Elliott, E. Guest and D. J. Mullier[1]

Abstract   The DScentTrail System has been created to support and demonstrate research theories in the joint disciplines of computational inference, forensic psychology and expert decision-making in the area of counter-terrorism. DScentTrail is a decision support system, incorporating artificial intelligence, and is intended to be used by investigators. The investigator is presented with a visual representation of a suspect's behaviour over time, allowing them to present multiple challenges from which they may prove the suspect guilty outright or receive cognitive or emotional clues of deception. There are links into a neural network, which attempts to identify deceptive behaviour of individuals; the results are fed back into DScentTrail hence giving further enrichment to the information available to the investigator.

1 Introduction

DScent was a joint project between five UK universities combining research theories in the disciplines of computational inference, forensic psychology and expert decision-making in the area of counter-terrorism. This paper concentrates on phase two of the project and discusses DScentTrail which is an investigator decision support system. A neural network links into DScentTrail and attempts to identify deceptive behavioural patterns. Preliminary work was carried out on a behavioural based AI module that would work separately alongside the neural network with both AI modules identifying deception before updating DScentTrail with their integrated results. For the purpose of data generation along with hypothesis and system testing, the project team devised a closed world game; the Location Based Game.

The Location Based Game was an extension of a board game; the Cutting Corners Board game [1] created within phase one of the project. Phase one consisted of the development of a feed-forward back-propagation neural network used to identify deceptive behavioural patterns within the game data. Due to extra complexities introduced with the location based game a feed-forward back-

[1] Leeds Metropolitan University, LS6 3QS, UK

{s.j.dixon, m.dixon, j.elliott, e.guest, d.mullier}@leedsmet.ac.uk

M. Bramer et al. (eds.), *Research and Development in Intelligent Systems XXVIII*,
DOI 10.1007/978-1-4471-2318-7_24, © Springer-Verlag London Limited 2011

propagation architecture was no longer suitable, therefore research into alternative architectures was required, this is further discussed in the Neural Network section.

2 The Location Based Game

Participants from a variety of different backgrounds were recruited to partake in the game trials. These participants traversed set locations (see figure 1) using GPS enabled devises to communicate, navigate and purchase items. Each participant took either the role of a builder attempting to construct part of an Olympic stadium, or a terrorist masquerading as a builder with the aim of planting explosives. For reasons discussed in the conclusions, only 2 games worth of data was available for testing purposes.

Each game comprised of four teams, and each team comprised of three players, a foreman, and two of the following tradesmen: an electrician; an explosives expert; or a builder. The games were divided into four tasks with the winning team being the first to complete all four. Virtual cash rewards were given to teams upon completion of tasks. Each task involved specific team members being in certain locations at certain times. They involved participants purchasing specific items and unloading these at their site. One team member was given the role of van driver and could purchase items. Vans were virtual and could be transferred between team members via the mobile device.

The GPS locations consisted of four shops; four sections of the Olympic site, one per team; and three fixed checkpoints where players would be checked by investigators and either given a cash reward or penalty. Police investigators performed random checks on players who they suspected to be behaving suspiciously, the same rules applied as with the fixed checkpoints. The four shops consisted of a local and a national electrical store selling dynamite sticks and wiring looms, and a local and a national builder's yard selling construction blocks, soil and fertiliser. Both local stores only stocked one item type at any given time whilst the national stores carried full stock.

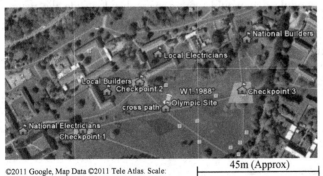

©2011 Google, Map Data ©2011 Tele Atlas. Scale: 45m (Approx)

Figure 1 Map of Location Based Game Playing Area showing the four stores; three fixed checkpoints and the four areas of the Olympics Site.

To complete the game all three types of tradesmen were required, therefore, the foremen were required to sub-contract players between teams to perform specific tasks. The GPS enabled devices recorded all player movements within the game area. The same devices were used to store and transfer money, transfer vans between team members and to purchase, reveal and drop off virtual items at the sites. Before each game all teams were given a short amount of time, approximately 30 minutes, to devise their strategies. The terrorist teams would need to be deceptive in order to cover up their overall objective of causing an explosion, whereas the building teams would devise strategies which were not based on deception, rather maybe slightly bending the rules to gain an advantage. On completion of a game all team members were interviewed separately by police investigators.

3 AI techniques for counter-terrorism

The use of various AI techniques, such as data mining, artificial neural networks, symbolic AI and Case Based Reasoning for counter-terrorism has been advocated by Markman [2] and Marappan [3]. Projects which consider such techniques are discussed below.

Schneier [4] in his article on *Why Data Mining Won't Stop Terror*, writes that data mining works best when you are searching for a well-defined profile, a reasonable number of attacks per year and a low cost of false alarms. Rudmin [5], Professor of Psychology at the University of Tromso, Norway, is also sceptical regarding data mining techniques used for counter-terrorism and disregards them completely. Rudmin states that in order to make a Bayesian computation, he estimates that at best in the USA there would be a base-rate of one terrorist per 300,000 people and that if a surveillance monitoring system had an accuracy rate of 40% positive identification of real terrorists then according to Bayes' Theorem [6] the misidentification rate would be 0.01%, or 30,000 innocent people. Rudmin stresses that these numbers are simply examples based on one particular technology.

Data mining was not used on the DScent project since it is generally used for extracting information from large quantities of data that is collected for reasons other than for the purpose of mining itself, the purpose of the mining being to find extra, useful information. The DScent data was explicitly designed and collated for identifying suspicious behaviour. DScent would not encounter the problems outlined by Professor Rudmin of having to potentially question 30,000 innocent people as the set did not contain the entire population, it is merely a well established sub-set. Ware [7] in his paper on antiterrorism states that neural networks do not lend themselves easily to real-time updated information and has concerns regarding the limited historical data on terrorist attacks, he further comments on how terrorist tactics are not static and change over time. These issues have been carefully considered during the project and are discussed in

further detail below. The reason for choosing a neural network as an AI application within DScentTrail, was that a neural network is the most likely type of computer system that will work with a non-polynomial problem such as behavioural patterns of humans. Although Ware's observations may be valid, by identifying the key input factors to the neural network and keeping these to an absolute minimum, then the amount of historical data required for training will be far less. Furthermore, if the neural network can identify deception amongst humans from a small amount of inputs then we are getting closer to that "well-defined profile" of which Schneier speaks.

4 DScentTrail System

A graphically based software product was developed to help visualise game data. Extensive research was carried out to ensure that the interface was designed in such a way that it would benefit investigators in an interview situation and not only serve as a visualisation tool within the project. Various types of information were collated, processed and then presented by means of a 'scent trail'. A scent trail within the project is a collection of ordered, relevant behavioural information over time for a suspect. Viewing this information graphically would allow an investigator to present multiple challenges from which they may prove the suspect guilty outright or receive cognitive or emotional clues of deception [8]. DScentTrail has links into a neural network that attempts to identify deceptive behavioural patterns of individuals, giving further enrichment to the information available to the investigator, not only by supplying them with related information that may not have been possible to find manually but also by reducing their cognitive load, allowing them to concentrate on their interviewing techniques.

4.1 User Interface Design

Various screen designs were created, figure 2 shows the primary suspect screen with two secondary suspects selected. The primary suspect window is located to the left and stays constant throughout the investigation, whereas various secondary suspect windows may be activated as and when required.

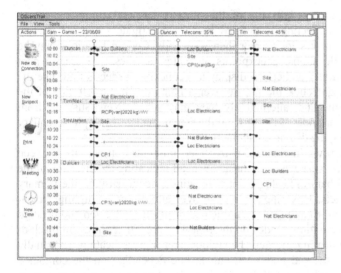

Figure 2 DScentTrail screen design showing both primary and secondary suspects movements and actions through time with their associated communication and location links.

For all windows within the DScentTrail system, time is displayed down the y axis and suspect information along the x axis, both of which are scrollable. All suspect windows display a time-line. A time-line represents the 'scent trail' and shows a series of events for a participant, the name of the suspect is displayed at the top of the window. A time-ordered list of locations and police checks is displayed down the right side of the time-line, these locations are listed in the 'The Location Based Game' section above. If a participant driving a van enters a fixed or has an investigator initiated checkpoint additional information is displayed, consisting of the weight of the van and up to two items which must be revealed. In figure 2 above, Sam at 10.16am had an investigator initiated *random* checkpoint, had a van weight of 2020kg and revealed two wiring looms. At 10.26am Sam entered checkpoint1 but as she was not driving a van, no additional information was displayed. Table 1 shows the codes used for the various stock items.

Table 1. The Stock Item Code Cross Reference Table showing the codes which would be displayed against the checkpoint events whenever the primary or secondary suspects revealed one or two stock items.

Stock Item	Code
Dynamite	D
Wiring Loom	W
Construct ion Block	B
Fertiliser	F
Soil	S

The information down the left side of the primary suspect's time-line shows potential meetings. A meeting is defined by the investigator; it is where two players are within x meters for greater than y seconds. Certain locations may be excluded, for example shops, checkpoints and sites, as these are areas where participants may naturally gather. To display a secondary suspect's time-line the investigator would right click the mouse over a name down the left side of the primary suspect's time-line, alternatively they may select 'New Suspect' from either the top menu bar under 'File' or from the side menu bar. Multiple secondary suspect time-lines may be displayed at one time.

The horizontal arrows in figure 2 show telecommunication activity between primary and secondary suspects with the arrow head indicating the direction of the call. The horizontal bars indicate potential meetings, again between the primary and secondary suspects. Hovering the mouse over either type of highlighter bar provides additional information, for example call or meeting duration and detailed meeting location information. Nodes on the time-line are either shown in black or red, with black indicating normal behaviour and red indicating potentially deceptive behaviour; the red nodes varying in hue depending on the combined certainty factor generated from the AI modules, drawing the investigators attention to a potential terrorist.

The investigator has the option to highlight alerts for all movements into locations which have taken greater than the calculated maximum travel time; figure 3 displays a detailed trajectory view. Here the dotted arrow shows the player leaving the local electrical store at 10.28am, stopping for two minutes, continuing, stopping for a further three minutes before arriving at checkpoint1 at 10.38am. The investigator may choose to hover their pointer over the rest events to view all other participants within a close proximity from the primary suspect during that rest period, which may indicate a reason for the rest period.

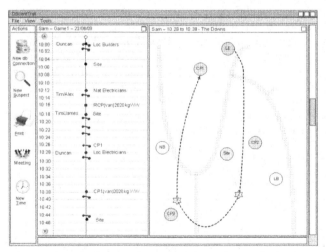

Figure 3 DScentTrail screen design detailing the trajectory of a slowly walked route between two points; the *local electrical store* and *checkpoint1* including a rest event of two minutes followed by a second rest event of three.

Various reporting screens are available to the investigator. Figure 4 shows a telecommunications bar chart for a primary suspect within a game. Other participants who have either made or received calls from the primary suspect during a game are represented along the x axis and the number of calls is displayed along the y axis. A similar chart is available for meetings behaviour during a game. These reporting summary screens may be accessed via the View menu. In addition, the telecommunications chart may be accessed by right clicking the mouse on any of the handset icons down the primary suspect's time-line then selecting 'view summary report'. The meetings chart may be selected by right clicking the mouse on any of the names down the left side of the primary suspect's time-line and selecting 'view summary report'.

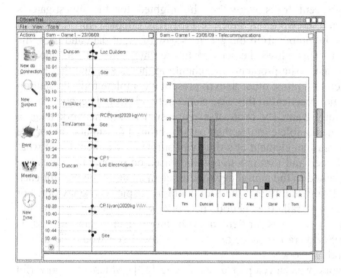

Figure 4 DScentTrail screen design showing the summary of all telecommunication activities for a participant. This chart divides the communications into calls made and calls received.

4.2 Technical System Design

DScentTrail is an Object Oriented [9] (OO) system, designed and specified using various techniques from the Unified Modelling Language [10] (UML), such as class and object modelling within the QSEE Superlite Development Environment [11]. All user interface design was created using Microsoft Visio and was written in the Java programming language [12] within the Eclipse Integrated Development Environment [13] (IDE). The game data was captured and stored in an Oracle Spatial database [14]. The DScentTrail system connects to this Oracle database using the Java Database Connectivity (JDBC) application programmer's interface (API) [15]. It was never the intention to implement the entire design for

DScentTrail as this would not have been achievable within the timeframe and with the allocated resources. However, all major areas were implemented, this allowed for the data to be imported from an external non-tailored database and a dynamic class model [2] built, from this meaningful information could be drawn.

5 Neural Network

A neural network was built which attempted to identify deceptive behaviour for a suspect. This neural network was integrated with the DScentTrail system, potentially deceptive scent trails were then highlighted for the investigator's attention. A regression network architecture [16] was adopted for the neural network which takes the output from the previous row of input data and uses this as input with the next. This allows the network to see time series data as opposed to discrete chunks of data. The problem with chunking the data is that there is no distinct point at which to do this, other than to present a complete trail. Presenting a complete trail was not practical in this case as the network would become far too complex to successfully train. By contrast a regression neural network takes a subset of inputs and the complete trail is then passed through the inputs, rather like a person viewing the trail an element at a time whilst retaining a memory of what they have previously seen and forming an opinion based on potentially increasing evidence. A trail is passed to the neural network an element at a time and for each presentation it outputs a certainty that the trail contains suspicious behaviour. For a genuinely suspicious trail the neural network would output a steadily strengthening certainty as it is presented with more data. This process is transparent to the DScentTrail system, all the user would see would be a final output from the neural network.

The neural network was developed using Encog [17], which is a powerful neural network and artificial intelligence application programmer's interface. The neural network architecture used was an Elman Recurrent Network [18], see figure 5 for a graphical representation of the network architecture.

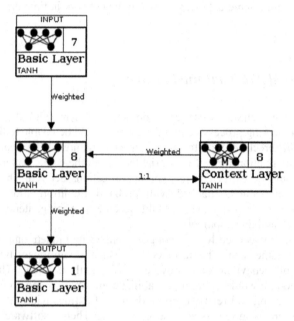

Figure 5 Neural Network Architecture for DScentTrail.

Due to the severe lack of data available, it proved impossible to train the network. Though a regression neural network was implemented and integrated into the DScentTrail system. Future work[2] is underway to develop a method for automatically generating behavioural data, building on the rules of the location based game [19]. This will be done by combining intelligent agents [20] with gene expression programming [21] and the use of an Emdros database [22]. The intention is to train and fully test the neural network on the receipt of this game data. To allow the network a chance of generalising, the number of columns in the input file were reduced to a bare minimum. The resulting columns were 'event'; 'time'; 'items'; 'award'; 'call duration'; 'call location'; 'call count' and 'close players'. The 'game Id', 'player Id' and 'time' were present for all rows, but not

---

[2] An EPSRC Standard Proposal is currently being reviewed to continue the work of DScent. This proposal has the following main objectives: 1) Incrementally develop techniques for generating deceptive behavioural data starting with the DScent board game, extending to the location based game, and finally making the data more closely model everyday life. This will include developing methods for generating new deceptive behavioural patterns, as we cannot assume that all past and future patterns are present in the data. 2) Incrementally extend DScentTrail so that it can handle more types of data and more complexity bringing it away from the constraints of the game towards real life. Develop a hybrid AI module consisting of the existing neural network and a (yet to be decided on) behavioural based AI module. 3) Validate the automatically generated data against existing data obtained from the DScent project and against real-life criminal datasets. The DScent system including the hybrid AI module will be fully tested at the end of each development phase with the automatically generated data.

presented. A player's worth of game data was shown to the network in time order; see [2] for more details.

5.1 Behavioural Based Artificial Intelligence

Phase two incorporated the preliminary stages of design for a symbolic AI [23] system, here the decision making process behind the output would be visible to the investigators; this was in direct contrast to the 'black box' nature of the neural network. By analysing the relationships of the variables within the game, patterns and behavioural rules could be extracted and type classifications derived. These models would then be embedded, attached with probabilistic information to identify emergent deceptive behaviour. This would become a refining, iterative process for future research and development.

Theme 5.0 software [24] was used for detecting and analysing hidden patterns of behaviour within the game data. Theme detects statistically significant time patterns in sequences of behaviour and provides basic analysis tools. This behavioural based AI module would contain probabilistic information and would be centred on pattern matching and relationship modelling of entities within their environment. Two files are required to analyse data using Theme software; a category table and a data file [2]. The category table contains coded metadata used to record the subject (participants); the behaviours (events) and the modifiers (variables). Mutual exclusivity between the three is enforced within this file. The data file contains behavioural data, scored according to the codes defined in the category table. Separate data files were required for each participant resulting in 21 for analysis purposes.

Analysis was performed on full game and individual team game data. When entire game data was analysed Theme detected over 170 patterns. Due to the nature of the game; each player being part of a three person team there was no disadvantage in splitting the analysis down into teams, this resulted in more manageable data sets and subsequently a simplified analysis process. The results were analysed using both temporal and event based analysis.

5.1.1 Temporal Analysis of Results

Theme detected a total of 329 patterns over the two games by setting the following search parameters: "Minimum Occurrences = 3"; "Significance Level = 0.0005" and "Exclude Frequent Event Types = Yes". Due to the simplicity of the game rules, Theme did not identify any patterns which the development team were not already aware, though it did serve as verification. It was apparent that by identifying these patterns Theme recognised the individual teams, which would be extremely significant in a more complex system outside the constraints of the game. Theme provides various ways of viewing pattern information; figure 6

shows a Pattern Length Distribution graph giving an overview of patterns grouped by their number of internal elements.

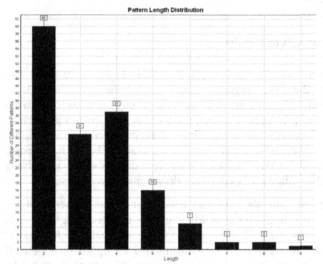

Figure 6 Theme pattern length distribution graph showing the number of different patterns containing various lengths.

From here analysis was carried out within the individual length categories by viewing the separate pattern breakdown diagrams, an example of which can be seen in figure 7 below:

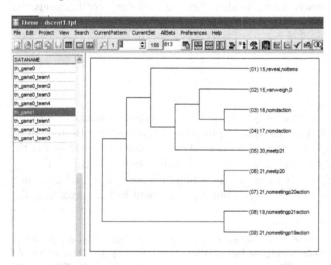

Figure 7 Theme pattern breakdown diagram showing the structure of patterns found within the data.

Once relevant patterns had been identified, it was then important to know how many of each specific relevant pattern had been identified, this was done by viewing the data using the Current Pattern Statistics view.

5.1.2 Event Based Analysis of Results

Key events with their average number of occurrences were identified and calculated for each of the three players within a team, before calculating team averages. The totals were then considered to see whether any teams were behaving differently to others, i.e. differences between the building and the terrorist teams. Numbers were highlighted to indicate significant variants which required further analysis [2]. Alternative categorisation scenarios were analysed but with the sparse amount of data available, no significant patterns were detectable for identifying deceptive behaviour. The following results were drawn from this analysis:

1. Visits to Checkpoint1 and the National Electricians were higher with the terrorist team, this was because the building teams were spreading their visits between the electrical and building stores to purchase what they needed for their building tasks, whereas the terrorist teams had the option of buying all their items from just the electrical stores. Checkpoint1 was on route to the National Electricians; see figure 1 for details.
2. The National Builders and Checkpoint3 were visited much less with the terrorist team, this again was because the terrorist teams did not need to visit the building stores. Checkpoint3 was on route to the National Builders and therefore was visited far less by the terrorist team.

By performing the above analysis process; particularly with more complex data, key events and combinations could be identified and from these combinations, the rules and intelligence of the system could start to be derived.

6 Conclusion

DScentTrail presents a new way of viewing deceptive behaviour both by individuals and by groups. The system proved to be extremely effective when studied by psychologists and experts in the field of interrogation and serious crime investigation[3]. The AI modules working to identify deception would provide DScentTrail with intelligent information attracting the investigator's attention to a subset of potential terrorist suspects. Future work would include separating the

---

[3] Presentations were given to the stakeholders, including personnel from CPNI and the MoD, showing screen designs and discussing the functionality of the DScent system along with its AI modules. Discussions were had with criminologists to arrive at the optimal visualisation of scent trail information, taking into account different interviewing techniques.

scent trail information into chunks and training the neural network to identify deceptive patterns within a scent trail; which would be necessary when used in the real world.

Meeting the dual requirement of making the location based game playable while enabling it to generate suitable data for all the various analysis required on the project proved not possible within the timeframe. The cognitive load placed on the participants for the location based game was much higher than for the original board game. In addition the participants had less time to think because with the location based game participants played continuously rather than waiting for their throw of a dice. This resulted in the data from the board game being much richer than the location based game, by which is meant containing greater variations in strategies of play. The software development effort required for programming the mobile devices was greatly underestimated resulting in incomplete and unreliable data for system testing purposes.

The observations above suggest that it is very difficult, if not impossible to generate suitably complex data via game playing. Future plans are underway to complete and extend the work of the DScent project. These plans include continuing the work started with Theme and developing a behavioural based AI module to work alongside the neural network in identifying deception; creating a method for automatically generating behavioural data, building on the rules of the location based game and incrementally bringing it in line with reality. This automatically generated data would then be used to fully test the DScent system.

A tentative conclusion drawn from the analysis is that the deceptive behaviour of terrorists is camouflaged by the dishonest behaviour of much of the general population. Artificial intelligence is a powerful tool and can be extremely useful in today's mass of information, though the results generated by AI techniques are difficult for regular users to interpret without an effective method of visualisation such as DScentTrail.

Acknowledgements
The DScent project was funded by the EPSRC, grant number: EP/F014112/1
Project partners included Lancaster University, University of Nottingham, University of St. Andrews and University of Leicester.

References

1. Dixon, S., Dixon, M., Elliott, J., Guest, E., Mullier, D.: DScent Final Report (2011). Available via: http://www.leedsmet.ac.uk/aet/computing/Computing_DScentFinalReport v2_0_2011.pdf Accessed 8 March 2011.
2. Markman, A., Rachkovskij, D., Misuno, I., Revunova, E.: Analogical Reasoning Techniques in Intelligent Counterterrorism APNN. International Journal ITA Vol. 10, (2)

(2003). Available via: http://www.foibg.com/ijita/vol10/ijita10-2.pdf#page=19 Accessed 27 November 2010.

3. Marappan, K., Nallaperumal, K., Kannan, S., Bensujin, B.: A Soft Computing Model to Counter Terrorism. International Journal of Computer Science and Network Security Vol. 8, May 2008, pp.141, (2008).

4. Schneier, B.: Why Data Mining Won't Stop Terror. Wired (2006). Available via: http://www.wired.com/politics/security/commentary/securitymatters/2006/03/70357 Accessed 23 August 2011.

5. Rudmin, F.: Why Does the NSA Engage in Mass Surveillance of Americans When It's Statistically Impossible for Such Spying to Detect Terrorists? Counterpunch (2006). Available via: http://www.counterpunch.org/rudmin05242006.html Accessed 30 October 2010.

6. Joyce, J.: Bayes' Theorem. In: The Stanford Encyclopedia of Philosophy, Fall 2008 Edition. Edward (2008). Available via: http://plato.stanford.edu/archives/fall2008/entries/bayes-theorem/ Accessed 09 June 2011.

7. Ware, B.S., Beverina, A., Gong, L., Colder, B.: A Risk-Based Decision Support System for Antiterrorism (2002). Available via: http://www.dsbox.com/Documents/MSS_A_Risk-Based_Decision_Support_System_for_Antiterrorism.pdf Accessed 30 January 2009.

8. Ekman, P.: Telling lies: Clues to deceit in the marketplace, marriage, and politics. New York, Norton (2001).

9. Ambler, S.W.: Introduction to Object-Orientation and the UML (2009). Available via: http://www.agiledata.org/essays/objectOrientation101.html Accessed 26 January 2011.

10. Booch, G., Jacobson, I., Rumbaugh, J.: The Unified Modeling Language User Guide. Object Technology Series. 2nd Ed., Addison Wesley (2005).

11. Dixon, M.: QSEE Superlite home. QSEE Technologies (2004). Available via: http://www.leedsmet.ac.uk/qsee Accessed 26 October 2010.

12. Flanagan, D.: Java In a Nutshell, 4th Ed., O'Reilly Media (2002).

13. The Eclipse Foundation: Eclipse.org home (2004). Available via: http://www.eclipse.org/ Accessed 14 October 2010.

14. Oracle Corporation: Oracle Spatial and Oracle Locator (2010). Available via: http://www.oracle.com/us/products/database/options/spatial Accessed 26 October 2010.

15. Reece, G.: Database Programming with JDBC and Java, 2nd Ed., Sebastopol, CA, USA, O'Reilly & Associates, Inc. (2000).

16. Ripley, B.D.: Pattern Recognition and Neural Networks. New York, Cambridge University Press (2008).

17. Heaton, J.: Programming Neural Networks with Encog2 in Java. Heaton Research (2010).

18. Elman, J.L.: Distributed representations, simple recurrent networks, and grammatical structure. Machine Learning Vol. 7, no. 2-3 pp.195-224, doi: 10.1007/BF00114844 (1991).

19. Guest, E., Bolotov, A., Dixon, S., Sandham, A.: Realistic Deceptive Data Generation for Counter Terrorism (2011). EPSRC Standard Proposal. Wiltshire, UK. Ref: M1504908 July 2011.

20. Evertsz, R., Pedrotti, M., Busetta, P., Acar, H.: Populating VBS2 with Realistic Virtual Actors. Proceedings of the 18th Conference on Behavior Representation in Modeling and Simulation pp.1–8, (2009).

21. Ferreira, C.: Gene Expression Programming: Mathematical Modeling by an Artificial Intelligence (Studies in Computational Intelligence), 2nd Ed., Springer (2006).

22. Petersen, U.: Emdros: a text database engine for analyzed or annotated text. Proceedings of the 20th international conference on Computational Linguistics (2004). Available via: http://emdros.org/petersen-emdros-COLING-2004.pdf Accessed 24 January 2011.

23. Haugeland, J.: Artificial Intelligence: The Very Idea. Cambridge, MA, MIT Press (1985).

24. Noldus Information Technology: Theme. Noldus Information Technology (2004). Available via: http://www.noldus.com/content/theme-0 Accessed 27 October 2010.

Semi-Automatic Analysis of Traditional Media with Machine Learning

Daoud Clarke, Peter C.R. Lane and Paul Hender

Abstract The analysis of traditional and social media is a non-trivial task, requiring the input of human analysts for quality. However, the ready availability of electronic resources has led to a large increase in the amounts of such data to be analysed: the quantities of data (tens of thousands of documents per day) mean that the task becomes too substantial for human analysts to perform in reasonable time frames and with good quality control. In this project, we have explored the use of machine-learning techniques to automate elements of this analysis process in a large media-analysis company. Our classifiers perform in the range of 60%–90%, where an average agreement between human analysts is around 80%. In this paper, we examine the effect of using active-learning techniques to attempt to reduce the amount of data requiring manual analysis, whilst preserving overall accuracy of the system.

1 Introduction

Media analysis is a discipline closely related to content analysis [6], with an emphasis on analysing content with respect to *favourability* and *key messages*. Favourability records to what degree coverage relating to an organisation is positive (favourable) or negative (unfavourable). Coverage may also be entirely neutral, or contain both favourable and unfavourable elements (mixed favourability). It is an important metric for organisations and PR firms since it reflects the current image of the organisation or brand as it is portrayed in the media or online.

Daoud Clarke
University of Hertfordshire, Hatfield, UK e-mail: daoud@metrica.net

Peter C.R. Lane
University of Hertfordshire, Hatfield, UK e-mail: peter.lane@bcs.org.uk

Paul Hender
Metrica, 140 Old Street, London, UK e-mail: paul@metrica.net

M. Bramer et al. (eds.), *Research and Development in Intelligent Systems XXVIII*,
DOI 10.1007/978-1-4471-2318-7_25, © Springer-Verlag London Limited 2011

The identification of key messages is to select documents relating to topics or areas that a client is interested in: for example, to obtain feedback on the success of a public-relations campaign. Media analysis has traditionally been done manually, however the explosion of content on the world-wide web, in particular social media, has led to the introduction of automatic techniques for performing media analysis, e.g. [15]: an important set of techniques for this application are drawn from machine learning.

There are a number of practical and technical problems in the application of machine learning to media analysis. The first is the source of classified data to use for training: any supervised machine-learning approach will depend on the availability of a representative sample of pre-labelled data. All documents come into the company unclassified, and, traditionally, a human analyst must view each document and decide on its label. In a commercial setting, human analysts cost a lot of money, and their time is valuable. As the number of documents to be labelled increases, the number of required analysts, or overall time for analysis, must also increase.

The problem of obtaining these data is compounded by the imbalanced class distribution, as many more of one class may need to be seen before obtaining a suitable number of the minority class. In media analysis, it frequently happens that desirable documents fall into a minority group. In previous work [3], we tackled the imbalanced data problem in two ways. First, we explored the value of training our models with datasets formed by balancing the class distribution in the training data. Second, we evaluated our models using the geometric mean [7], to produce a numeric figure which balances the contributions of both classes.

However, the imbalanced data problem also has another effect. To get a representative sample of the minority group, many more documents must be analysed from the majority group than perhaps are needed. As the class imbalance increases, this 'cost' of analysing additional documents becomes more important. For example, if there is an imbalance of three times as many documents in one class, and it is decided to use undersampling to balance the training sets, then twice as many documents are being labelled by the analysts than are required for training the classification system.

One promising alternative to the staged process of constructing classified data is to use the partially-trained machine learning system to select or request the next documents from an unlabelled pool, with only these selected documents passed to human analysts for classification. This process is known as *active learning*, and is related to theoretical studies of providing a learning algorithm with an oracle, or query-based learning.

In this paper, we describe our approach to the document-labelling problem, which uses a combination of heuristic information from a support-vector machine model and some random exploration. We perform some comparative experiments between alternative active learning systems based on support-vector machines and a naïve Bayes algorithm.

2 Background to Favourability Analysis

The Gorkana Group[1] consists of three companies servicing the public relations (PR) industry:

- **Gorkana** provide a media database, giving PR workers information and insights into journalists and bloggers and their expertise.
- **Durrants** provides a media monitoring service, covering print, online, broadcast and social media.
- **Metrica** provides a media analysis service, giving in-depth analysis and insight into the current perception of an organisation in the media.

Our experiments are based on documents supplied by Durrants and analysed by Metrica. Although we ultimately expect to apply our findings to social media, our data are taken from traditional media (mainly newspapers and magazines) since at the time of starting the experiment there was more manually analysed content available.

The task of determining favourability is very similar to the tasks of sentiment analysis and opinion mining, however there is an important semantic distinction: favourability records how positive the coverage is with respect to the client *overall*, whereas sentiment relates only to the subjective opinion of the speaker. Thus good news about an organisation reported objectively would be considered as favourable; since it is reported objectively, the writer's sentiment would be considered neutral.

Favourability of documents is recorded as two non-negative integers indicating "favourability" and "unfavourability". A completely neutral document would have zero for both of these numbers. A document containing a single positive mention of an organisation would have a score of 1 for favourability. If this mention is very positive or prominent, then the score would be 2, and similarly for unfavourability. Repeated favourable or unfavourable mentions increase this score.

2.1 Description of Data

We assign each document a class based on its favourability f and unfavourability u scores. Favourability is typically reported to a client on a three or five point scale, and the exact mapping from scores depends on the client brief. For the purposes of our experiments, documents are categorised as follows:

$f > 0$ and $u > 0$: **mixed**
$f = 0$ and $u > 1$: **very negative**
$f = 0$ and $u = 1$: **negative**
$f = 0$ and $u = 0$: **neutral**
$f = 1$ and $u = 0$: **positive**
$f > 1$ and $u = 0$: **very positive**

---

[1] http://gorkana.com/group

Table 1 shows the number of documents in each category for three datasets A, C and S, which are anonymised to protect the clients' privacy. A and S are datasets for high-tech companies, whereas C is for a charity. This is reflected in the low occurence of negative favourability with dataset C. Datasets A and C contain only articles that are relevant to the client, whereas S contains articles for the client's competitors. We only make use of favourability judgments with respect to the client, however, so those that are irrelevant to the client we simply treat as neutral. This explains the overwhelming bias towards neutral sentiment in dataset S.

Dataset	Mixed	V. Neg.	Negative	Neutral	Positive	V. Pos.
A	472	86	138	1610	1506	1664
C	7	0	5	2824	852	50
S	522	94	344	9580	2057	937

Table 1 Number of documents in each class for the datasets A, C and S.

In our experiments, we consider only those documents which have been manually analysed and for which the raw text is available. Duplicates were removed from the dataset. Duplicate detection was performed using a modified version of Ferret [8] which compares occurrences of character trigrams between documents. We considered two documents to be duplicates if they had a similarity score higher than 0.75.

This paper describes experiments for two tasks:
Neutrality identification — detecting the presence or absence of favourability. This is thus a two-class problem with **neutral** documents in one class, and all other documents in the other. The equivalent task with respect to sentiment is *subjectivity analysis*. See Table 2 for details.

Dataset	Neutral	Non-neutral
A	1610	3866
C	2824	914
S	9580	3954

Table 2 Class distributions for the neutrality identification task

Favourability polarity — distinguishing between documents with generally positive and negative favourability. In our experiments, we treat this as a two class problem, with **negative** and **very negative** documents in one class and **positive** and **very positive** documents in the other (ignoring mixed sentiment). This task is similar to that of *sentiment analysis*. See Table 3 for details.

Dataset	Positive	Negative
A	3170	224
C	902	5
S	2994	438

Table 3 Class distributions for the favourability polarity task

3 Semi-Automated Media Analysis System

Our proposed system is semi-automated, as it relies on the input from human analysts. There are five main components, as shown in Figure 1. First, there is the source of documents. Second a sample of these documents is given to human analysts for labelling. Third, the documents are converted into feature sets. Fourth, these feature sets and labels are used to train a classification model. Fifth, the model is applied to the incoming documents to add labels, and also selects a sample of these documents for the human analysts, and the cycle repeats.

We now briefly discuss the process of representing and selecting feature sets for the classification algorithms, and also the training and evaluation process used. More information on these stages can be found in [3]. The more interesting stage for this paper is the construction of the training set using an active learning process based in part on the output from the learning algorithm.

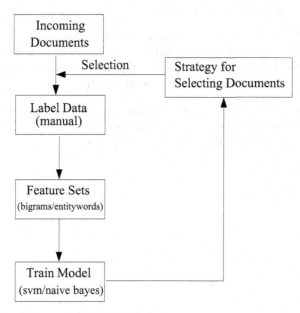

Fig. 1 Overview of document classification / selection process.

3.1 Feature Sets

There are many kinds of features that can be used for text classification, including a variety of n-grams, entity words or other kind of dependencies. We currently focus on just two types of features: bigrams and entity words. A bigram is simply a pair of adjacent words in the text. An entity word is a word occurring within a sentence containing a mention of the organisation in question. Manually-constructed regular expressions, based on datasets and results used elsewhere in the company, were used for identifying organisations, with sentence boundary detection achieved using an OpenNLP[2] tool.

Training time with classifiers is an issue when there are many features. We use attribute selection using a chi-squared measure to select 250 features from the sets of bigrams or entity words, in each case.

3.2 Strategies for Constructing the Training Set

We adopt the following procedure for constructing a training set. We begin with two examples, one example of each of the two classes. For each training cycle, we construct two classifiers, one support-vector machine (SVM) and one naïve Bayes (NB). In each cycle, we select a new document from the pool of unused training examples. We use the following heuristics:

1. random selection: the next example is selected at random
2. svm probability: the SVM is queried with each document, and the document which is classified with the least confidence (the lowest probability) is selected
3. hybrid strategy: on alternate steps, we use (1) or (2).

These strategies combine elements of active-learning, based on the SVM's probability estimates, and random exploration. We discuss the relation of these strategies with active learning and similar ideas in the Discussion.

---

[2] http://opennlp.sourceforge.net

4 Experiments

The experiments presented here consider the alternate strategies for constructing the training set by incrementally selecting the next training instance.

4.1 Method

The experiments are conducted in five settings: we have three datasets, and two tasks (although one task is not applicable to one dataset, as described earlier). In all five cases, we train two classification algorithms in three different ways, using the heuristics above. We also repeat the experiment for two kinds of feature sets: bigrams and entity words.

We order each dataset by time, and split it in two, reserving the newest third of the documents as a **held out set**, and using the oldest two-thirds as an **experiment set**. We use the held out set to verify the performance of the trained classifiers on new data.

We perform thirty runs of the experiment; for each aspect of the experiment that involves a pseudo-random number sequence, we use a different seed on each run. For each run:

1. We randomize the order of the experiment set, and remove a third of this set as a **test set**. The remainder forms the **pool** from which the active learning strategies will choose documents.
2. Remove three documents from the pool, and put these in a **learning set**.
3. Train each classifier (naïve Bayes and SVM) on the learning set and evaluate it on the test and held out sets.
4. Ask each the active learning strategy to choose a document from the pool.
5. Remove the chosen document from the pool and place it in the learning set.
6. Go back to step 3, and repeat until n iterations have been performed, where n is the maximum of 500 and one fifth of the number of documents in the experiment set.

For the SVM classifier, we used the radial-basis kernel, and performed parameter search every 10 iterations. We varied gamma exponentially between 10^{-5} and 10^5 in multiples of 100, and cost between 1 and 15 in increments of 2. We used the geometric mean of the accuracies on the two classes under consideration to optimise the parameters. We also performed attribute selection every 10 iterations, using chi-squared to determine the optimal 250 features given the current state of the learning set. This was necessary since there were too many features to perform the SVM learning efficiently using all the features. We initially started performing feature selection and parameter search on every iteration but this was prohibitively costly in computation time.

The active learning strategies we employed were as follows:

- **random**, a baseline stragegy, which chooses from the pool at random;
- **SVM probability**, which chooses the element from the pool for which the classification probability is the lowest
- **hybrid**, which alternates between the previous two strategies, choosing one at random and then one using the SVM probability.

The classification probability is an estimate of the probability that the SVM has chosen the correct class. We use the LibSVM classifier [1] which provides such an estimate; a description of the algorithm used is given in [17].

4.2 Results

Table 4 shows the average number of iterations to get to 90% of the accuracy obtained when training on a large sample of the complete dataset. This value is calculated by giving runs that don't reach this level of accuracy a value of the total number of iterations performed for this dataset, and is thus an underestimate of the true average number of iterations that would be needed.

Data	Features	Task	Classf.	Rand. ± Err.	SVM ± Err.	Hybrid ± Err.	RSVM	RHyb
S	B	DS	SVM	460 ± 22.3	259 ± 15.9	380 ± 26.5	201	80.4
S	B	DS	NB	723 ± 49.3	656 ± 31.2	558 ± 23.2	66.8	165
S	EW	DS	SVM	23.2 ± 2.8	16.9 ± 2.29	22.1 ± 4.11	6.38	1.17
S	EW	DS	NB	4.7 ± 0.75	304 ± 66.8	9.17 ± 3.23	-300	-4.5
S	B	DPN	SVM	291 ± 31.3	486 ± 11.1	493 ± 3.93	-190	-200
S	B	DPN	NB	428 ± 23.4	327 ± 24.6	466 ± 21.3	101	-38
S	EW	DPN	SVM	379 ± 32.4	497 ± 0	482 ± 14.4	-120	-100
S	EW	DPN	NB	354 ± 34.5	438 ± 27.8	445 ± 26.3	-85	-91
A	B	DPN	SVM	447 ± 22.5	481 ± 16.1	481 ± 15.4	-34	-35
A	B	DPN	NB	243 ± 32.3	326 ± 39.1	297 ± 39.8	-83	-53
A	EW	DPN	SVM	388 ± 22.5	363 ± 24.7	420 ± 24.6	24.4	-32
A	EW	DPN	NB	114 ± 16.8	76.6 ± 11.9	68.6 ± 6.88	37.6	45.6
A	B	DS	SVM	365 ± 29.5	415 ± 21.4	397 ± 30.5	-51	-32
A	B	DS	NB	381 ± 19.9	375 ± 20.4	398 ± 21.5	5.77	-17
A	EW	DS	SVM	113 ± 21.2	221 ± 34.1	136 ± 25.1	-110	-22
A	EW	DS	NB	497 ± 0	497 ± 0	481 ± 15.7	0	16
C	B	DS	SVM	245 ± 23.1	376 ± 24.6	330 ± 27	-130	-85
C	B	DS	NB	469 ± 15.3	294 ± 19.1	425 ± 18.3	175	44.5
C	EW	DS	SVM	252 ± 37.8	232 ± 32.7	251 ± 33.1	19.8	0.07
C	EW	DS	NB	134 ± 19.7	87.8 ± 13.1	103 ± 19.3	46.5	31.5

Table 4 The average number of iterations to reach 90% of the maximum accuracy achieved over all runs and classifiers. (Features EW – EntityWords, B – Bigrams. Task DS – DetectSentiment, DPN – DetectPosNeg.) RSVM is the reduction in the SVM, RHyb is the reduction in the hybrid.

Figures 2–5 show a selection of results over time for the sample dataset; in general the results on the held out set are similar, although the accuracies are lower, as discussed in [3]. The number of iterations is shown on the x axis, and the arithmetic mean of the accuracy on the two classes is shown on the y axis, averaged over the thirty runs. The error bars show the estimate of the error in the mean. The results are selected to highlight the wide variations in behaviour we found.

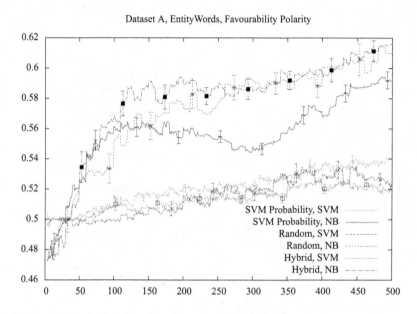

Fig. 2 Example showing hybrid and random strategies with naïve bayes performing best.

4.3 Summary

The results show a varying impact of the active-learning strategies. In some cases, active learning gives a large reduction in the amount of manual analysis, for example, dataset S with bigrams for the neutrality identification task (Figure 4) reduces from 460 ± 22 iterations using random sampling to 259 ± 16 iterations using the SVM probability strategy.

However, in some cases, the SVM probability strategy has a large negative impact, for example dataset S with Entity Words for the neutrality identification task (Figure 5) quickly falls below 50% accuracy and stays there, with the naïve Bayes classifier. We hypothesise that in this case, the strategy constantly fails to pick out documents that are needed by the naïve Bayes classifier, while still benefitting the

Dataset S, Bigrams, Favourability Polarity

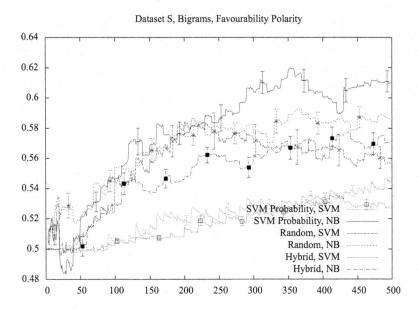

Fig. 3 Example showing probability strategy for naïve bayes performing best.

Dataset S, Bigrams, Neutrality

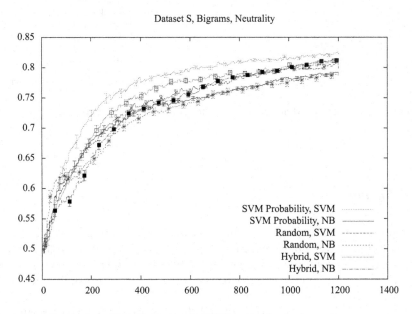

Fig. 4 Example showing probability strategy for SVM performing best.

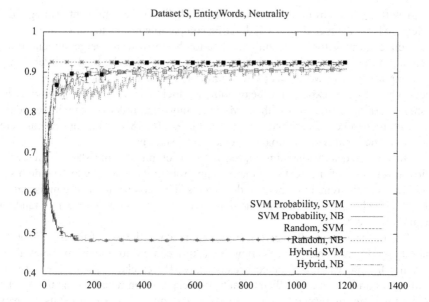

Fig. 5 Example showing poor performance of probability strategy for naïve bayes.

SVM classifier. Conversely, random sampling was the fastest strategy on this dataset with naïve Bayes.

Sometimes, the active-learning leads to unpredictable behaviour: in Figure 3 the probability strategy with naïve Bayes begins badly, but ends up producing clearly superior performance after 300 instances.

This observation lead us to try the hybrid strategy. This generally mitigates the failings of the SVM strategy, yielding good performance for dataset A with entity words for the favourability task (Figure 2), but also reduces its effectiveness on the whole.

On average over all datasets, classifiers and tasks, both strategies give an *increase* in analysed data. The average increase is 21 for SVM probability and 17 for the hybrid strategy. This is clearly disappointing, however, it may be possible to find ways to identify beforehand which datasets are likely to be amenable to an active learning strategy.

5 Discussion

Naïve Bayes and support-vector machine algorithms are perhaps the two most popular algorithms for document classification. Interestingly from our results here and in [3], we find that naïve bayes performs well without any special treatment, in con-

trast with findings from authors such as [4, 5]. From the sentiment mining side, Melville [10], Pang et al. [13, 12] describe comparable results to our own.

Active learning for document classification has also seen a large amount of attention in the literature, due to the importance of reducing the burden of labelling. An important early work was by McCallum [9], where training examples are selected based on the expected value of obtaining their class examples. In some cases, active-learning approaches with SVMs have shown an order of magnitude reduction in the number of required training examples [16, 18]), but as our results here indicate, these gains are not to be expected in all settings.

Our preferred active-learning approach uses a combination of a standard heuristic-driven selection of the next document using probability scores, with a random selection from the remaining pool of documents. This combination is reminiscent of learning techniques which combine deliberate search with an element of random exploration, e.g. [11].

Another feature of our active-learning approach is the use of the SVM's probability output as a basis for selecting the next document for the naïve Bayes algorithm. This process was adopted because naïve Bayes classifiers are poor at providing confidence levels on their outputs, especially when wrong, while the SVM's output is better motivated. The combination, as shown in our experiments, appears to work reasonably, and is an interesting contrast to approaches such as expectation-maximisation [9] or query-by-committee [14].

Alternative approaches to active learning include those under the heading of semi-supervised learning, which has become an increasingly popular topic recently (e.g. see [2] for a survey). The difference between active and semi-supervised learning is that in the latter the unlabelled examples are used to help inform decisions made on new data, whereas in active learning an oracle is requested to provide labels for selected data, but only labelled data are used in developing the model.

6 Conclusion

We have described a document classification system currently used in a commercial setting. The main features of this system are its reliance on machine-learning techniques to identify documents for manual analysis and use these documents to further refine the classifiers. In an attempt to reduce the burden of manual labelling, we have implemented and compared active-learning approaches for two classifier systems, and we have described a novel use of the SVM's probability output to select training instances for a naïve Bayes classifer. We have demonstrated that in some datasets an approach combining this active-learning output with a random selection reduces the required amount of labelled training data. In future work, we will explore further active-learning techniques, and test our system on new sources of data.

References

1. Chang, C.C., Lin, C.J.: LIBSVM: A library for support vector machines. ACM Transactions on Intelligent Systems and Technology **2**, 27:1–27:27 (2011). Software available at http://www.csie.ntu.edu.tw/~cjlin/libsvm
2. Chapelle, O., Schölkopf, B., Zien, A. (eds.): Semi-Supervised Learning. MIT Press (2006)
3. Clarke, D., Lane, P., Hender, P.: Developing robust models for favourability analysis. In: A. Balahur, E. Boldrini, A. Montoyo, P. Martinez-Barco (eds.) Proceedings of the Second Workshop on Computational Approaches to Subjectivity and Sentiment Analysis (WASSA 2.011), pp. 44–52. Association for Computational Linguistics, Portland, Oregon (2011)
4. Joachims, T.: Text categorization with support vector machines: Learning with many relevant features. In: C. Ndellec, C. Rouveirol (eds.) Machine Learning: ECML-98, *Lecture Notes in Computer Science*, vol. 1398, pp. 137–142. Springer Berlin / Heidelberg (1998)
5. Kim, S., Han, K., Rim, H., Myaeng, S.: Some effective techniques for naive bayes text classification. IEEE Transactions on Knowledge and Data Engineering **18**, 1457–1466 (2006)
6. Krippendorff, K.: Content analysis: An introduction to its methodology. Sage Publications, Inc (2004)
7. Kubat, M., Holte, R., Matwin, S.: Machine learning for the detection of oil spills in satellite radar images. Machine learning **30**(2), 195–215 (1998)
8. Lane, P.C.R., Lyon, C.M., Malcolm, J.A.: Demonstration of the Ferret plagiarism detector. In: Proceedings of the Second International Plagiarism Conference (2006)
9. McCallum, A., Nigam, K.: Employing em in pool-based active learning for text classification. In: Proceedings of the 15th International Conference on Machine Learning, pp. 350–358. Madison, US (1998)
10. Melville, P., Gryc, W., Lawrence, R.D.: Sentiment analysis of blogs by combining lexical knowledge with text classification. In: Proceedings of the 15th ACM SIGKDD international conference on Knowledge discovery and data mining, KDD '09, pp. 1275–1284. ACM, New York, NY, USA (2009)
11. Osugi, T., Kun, D., Scott, S.: Balancing exploration and exploitation: A new algorithm for active machine learning. In: Proceedings of the Fifth IEEE International Conference on Data Mining (ICDM'05), pp. 330–335 (2005)
12. Pang, B., Lee, L.: Opinion mining and sentiment analysis. Foundations and Trends in Information Retrieval **2**(1-2), 1–135 (2008)
13. Pang, B., Lee, L., Vaithyanathan, S.: Thumbs up?: sentiment classification using machine learning techniques. In: Proceedings of the ACL-02 conference on Empirical methods in natural language processing-Volume 10, pp. 79–86. Association for Computational Linguistics (2002)
14. Seung, H., Opper, M., Sompolinsky, H.: Query by committee. In: Proceedings of the fifth annual workshop on Computational learning theory, pp. 287–294 (1992)
15. Tatzl, G., Waldhauser, C.: Aggregating opinions: Explorations into Graphs and Media Content Analysis. ACL 2010 p. 93 (2010)
16. Tong, S., Koller, D.: Support vector machine active learning with applications to text classification. Journal of Machine Learning Research **2**, 45–66 (2001)
17. Wu, T., Lin, C., Weng, R.: Probability estimates for multi-class classification by pairwise coupling. The Journal of Machine Learning Research **5**, 975–1005 (2004)
18. Yang, B., Sun, J.T., Wang, T., Chen, Z.: Effective multi-label active learning for text classification. In: The 15th ACM SIGKDD Conference On Knowledge Discovery and Data Mining (KDD) (2009)

AI IN ACTION

Design of Robust Space Trajectories

Giovanni Stracquadanio, Angelo La Ferla, Matteo De Felice and Giuseppe Nicosia

Abstract In this paper we apply a novel black-box optimisation algorithm to the Global Trajectory optimisation Problem provided by the European Space Agency (ESA). The proposed algorithm, called SAGES, has been applied to instances of seven trajectory design problems, comparing it with the known best solutions. The numerical results show clear improvements on the majority of the problems and, in order to investigate deeply the problems, a sensitivity and solutions robustness analysis has been performed, measuring the influence of each single variable to the objective function.

1 Introduction

A crucial problem in mission analysis is planning interplanetary trajectories, which consist in launching a spacecraft from a given astronomical body (usually the Earth) along a trajectory which leads to an other; the goal of the optimisation is to provide the best trajectory, in terms of starting date, necessary fuel, mission temporal length, in order to obtain a cost-effective mission. Thus, space missions can be tackled as global optimisation problems, which are characterized by a huge search space and large plateau regions in the search landscape.

Giovanni Stracquadanio
Dept. of Biomedical Engineering - Johns Hopkins University, USA e-mail: `stracquadanio@jhu.edu`

Angelo La Ferla
Dept. of Mathematics & Computer Science - University of Catania, Italy e-mail: `laferla@dmi.unict.it`

Matteo De Felice
Energy and Environment Modelling Unit, ENEA, Italy e-mail: `matteo.defelice@enea.it`

Giuseppe Nicosia Dept. of Mathematics & Computer Science - University of Catania, Italy e-mail: `nicosia@dmi.unict.it`

M. Bramer et al. (eds.), *Research and Development in Intelligent Systems XXVIII*, DOI 10.1007/978-1-4471-2318-7_26, © Springer-Verlag London Limited 2011

Many approaches have been proposed for this task, combining several modelling and optimisation techniques. In 2005 ESA ACT (Advanced Concept Team) proposed the Global Trajectory optimisation Competition (GTOC) and since then it has created the Global Trajectory optimisation Problems (GTOP) database. It contains the models, the constraints, the bounds and the current optimal solutions of a large number of famous ESA missions, which are modelled using various Multiple Gravity Assist (MGA) models [6]. Various optimisation algorithms and meta-heuristics have been used, e.g. Machine Learning techniques [4], Evolutionary Algorithms such as Genetic Algorithms [11, 1] and Differential Evolution [7].

We propose a new black-box optimisation algorithm, called *Self-Adaptive Gaussian Evolutionary Strategy* (SAGES), tailored for space trajectory optimisation; we test our algorithm on the first five MGA-1DSM problems of the ESA GTOP database. The experimental results show that this new algorithm is able to locate new minima for the Cassini2, Messenger, Messenger Full, SAGAS problems and some instances for TandEM problem. Moreover, a Sensitivity and Robustness analysis has been performed, leading to an interesting analysis on the influence of single variables to the overall objective function.

The paper is structured as follows: Section 2 introduces the trajectory optimisation problem, describing the specific problems we tackle in this paper. Successively, Section 3 proposes the SAGES algorithm. Sensitivity and Robustness Analysis are introduced in Sections 4 and 5. Experimental results are presented in Section 6. Finally, Section 7 concludes the paper.

2 Problem Description

The general problem tackled in this paper is a trajectory design problem, which can be modelled as a global optimisation problem. Each space mission requires the choice of one or more optimal trajectories with respect to the energy (fuel) and/or the time needed for the mission accomplishment.

In this work we compare a black-box optimisation algorithm on seven optimisation problems proposed by ESA ACT, for all of them objective functions are available in MATLAB and C++ programming languages[1].

In order to move from an astronomical body to another, the spacecraft needs to provide a single impulse, that leads a single change of velocity Δv_i. In the initial trajectory section (usually called 'leg'), the spacecraft will have to provide a single impulse v_0 to leave the Earth and reach the starting velocity at the initial leg. Each impulse causes a mass consumption proportional to the modulus of the change of velocity and, hence, it is required to minimize the overall mass consumption. Formally, we have to find the minimum of the following objective function:

---

[1] Available at http://www.esa.int/gsp/ACT/inf/op/globopt.htm

$$\Delta V = \sum_{i=1}^{n} ||\Delta v_i|| \qquad (1)$$

where n is the number of astronomical bodies in the fly-by sequence and Δv_i is the i-th change of velocity

The objective of each problem is a set of parameter values $\mathbf{x} \in \mathbb{R}^N$ used to determine a trajectory for a spacecraft in order to minimize or maximize the objective function. The difficulty of such problems is given by the large amount of local optima and the absence of information about error gradients.

Given the high complexity of the problem, usually a simplified model is used during the optimisation phase, refining the best solution with a more accurate ones. The problems are modelled using Multiple Gravity Assist (MGA) models, which refers to a system of Lambert equations describing the move of a spacecraft equipped with high thrust engines. However, in order to balance the complexity and the accuracy of the model, ESA missions are described using an MGA model one Deep Space Maneveur (MGA-1DSM) [17]. This model describes an interplanetary trajectory of a space vehicle with chemical propulsion, which is able to thrust engines once for each trajectory section (usually called 'leg').

The difference between this model and the previous one (MGA model [6]) is the capability to perform more than one manoeuvre in order to have a realistic simulation of the interplanetary trajectory. In fact, the MGA model allows to the spacecraft to thrust only during its planetocentric phase leading to small dimensional problems but also unrealistic trajectories.

We coped with a total of seven different global trajectory optimisation problems (GTOPs):

1. Messenger: representing a rendezvous mission to Mercury;
2. Messenger-full: a more difficult version of the previous problem;
3. Cassini 2: the trajectory sequence with DSMs to reach Saturn;
4. Rosetta: relative to the mission to reach the comet 67P/Churyumov-Gerasimenko;
5. SAGAS: the mission to reach Jupiter;
6. GTOC1: benchmarking problem based on the first Global Trajectory optimisation Competion (GTOC, see [8]);
7. TandEM-Atlas1: 24 unconstrained problem instances based on ESA mission named TandEM with the objective of reaching Titan and Enceladus.

In Table 1 we provide the typology of the model used for each problem and its number of variables. All the above problems have a bounded parameter space, given the physical meaning for each variable. The problem TandEM-Atlas1 has the same dimension for all the 24 instances.

Table 1: Summary of the model used, optimisation type and problem dimension for the GTOP problems considered in this paper.

Problem	Model used	Min/Max	No. of variables
Messenger	MGA-1DSM	Min	18
Messenger-full	MGA-1DSM	Min	26
Cassini 2	MGA-1DSM	Min	22
Rosetta	MGA-1DSM	Min	22
SAGAS	MGA-1DSM	Min	12
GTOC1	MGA	Max	8
TandEM-Atlas1	MGA-1DSM	Max	18

Algorithm 1 SAGES main procedure

1: **procedure** $SAGES(M, B)$ ▷ M is the max. number of fitness evaluations
2:     $x_{\text{start}} \leftarrow UniformRandomPoints(B)$
3:     $x_0 \leftarrow UseRandomAlgorithm(x_{\text{start}})$ ▷ Generate N point with a random selected procedure
4:     $f \leftarrow N$
5:     $t \leftarrow 0$
6:     **while** $f < M$ **do**   ▷ While number of fitness evaluations is below M
7:         $x_t \leftarrow Discard(x_t, 0.2)$
8:         $C \leftarrow AGNES(x_t)$
9:         $C_{\text{best}} \leftarrow getClusterBest(C)$
10:        $x_{t+1} \leftarrow UseRandomAlgorithm(C_{\text{best}})$
11:        $t \leftarrow t + 1$
12:        $f \leftarrow update(f)$
13:    **end while**
14:    **return** x_t
15: **end procedure**

---

3 SAGES Algorithm

In this work, we propose an algorithm called SAGES (Self-Adaptive Gaussian Evolution Strategies), is an extended Evolutionary Algorithm that uses a multivariate normal distribution to generate new candidate solutions; these solutions are exploited by combining other state-of-the-art optimisation algorithms. Three algorithms are employed during the optimisation process; the Covariance Matrix Adaptation Evolutionary Strategy (CMA-ES, [5]), Differential Evolution (DE, [12]) and Divide RECTangle (DiRECT, [9]). DE and CMA-ES are state-of-the-art evolutionary algorithms; the first relies on a weighted recombination of individuals, instead the second uses an adaptive multi-variate Gaussian distribution to generate new solutions. DIRECT is a derivative-free global optimisation algorithm for bounded problems. DIRECT exploits the principle of Lipschitzian optimisation algorithms removing the necessity of the knowledge of the Lipschitz constant, increasing the speed of convergence and reducing the computational complexity for higher dimensions.

The algorithm is iterative; at each iteration, it generates an offspring population according with a Gaussian multivariate distribution. Successively, the offspring are

evaluated and the distribution updated according to the maximum-likelihood princi-ple; it updates the distribution such that the likelihood of previously successful steps to appear again is increased. At the end of each iteration a traditional $\mu + \lambda$ selection is performed, in this implementation we put $\mu = 1000$ and $\lambda = 2000$.

SAGES has been designed to handle both inequality and equality constraints, and it does not make any assumption on the constraint functions. The algorithm consider the constraints values during the selection procedure; given two individuals p_1, p_2, if both are feasible the one with the lowest objective function value is picked; if p_1 is feasible and the p_2 is unfeasible, p_1 is picked, otherwise if p_1 and p_2 are unfeasible the one with the lowest constraints violation is picked.

The algorithm starts with B random points (sampled uniformly between the pa-rameter space) and then it uses an algorithm chosen randomly between Differential Evolution (DE) and CMA-ES to obtain the initial set of N points used for the main iteration. Then, the algorithm iterates until it has reached the maximum number of function evaluations M performing an initial discard of the 20% of solutions with the worst fitness value and a hierarchical clustering with AGNES (AGglomerative NESting) algorithm (see [10]). Consequently, a search procedure with an algorithm selected among DE, CMA-ES and DIRECT is performed starting from the best point in each cluster. In our experimentations, we set M equals to $2 \cdot 10^6$.

4 Sensitivity Analysis: the Morris Algorithm

The sensitivity analysis (SA) concerns the study of how uncertainty in the output of a model can be apportioned to different sources of uncertainty in the model in-put. In particular, SA tries to identify the most influential parameters of a given model; understanding which are the most important parameters of a model could be extremely difficult since it is common to deal with non-linear, highly noisy and computational expensive models. In our research work, we want to assess which variables are crucial for the space trajectory optimisation problem; in order to per-form this analysis, we used the Morris algorithm, which is particularly suited when the number of uncertain variables, called factors, is high and the model could be expensive to compute. The Morris algorithm belongs to the class of the *one-factor-a-time* (OAT) methods [13, 14]; OAT means that a factor is perturbed in turn while keeping all other factors fixed at their nominal value. In particular, the Morris algo-rithm varies one factor at time across a certain number of levels selected in the space of the input factors; this grid-like sampling makes the algorithm easily adaptable for discrete and continuous variables. For each variation, a factor elementary effect is computed as follows:

$$u_i = (Y(x_1, x_2, \ldots, x_i + \Delta x_i, \ldots, x_k) - $$
$$- Y(x_1, x_2, \ldots, x_i, \ldots, x_k)) / \Delta x_i \qquad (2)$$

where Y is the model output,

$$x_1, x_2, \ldots, x_i + \Delta x_i, \ldots, x_k \qquad (3)$$

is the perturbed parameters vector and $x_1, x_2, \ldots, x_i, \ldots, x_k$ is the nominal parameters vector. For each factor, at different levels, various estimates of the elementary effect u_i are performed. In order to study the importance of the variables, the mean μ_i and the standard deviation σ_i are computed over the elementary effects u_i of the i−th parameter. A high value of μ_i denotes a high linear effect for a given factor, while a high value of σ_i denotes either non-linear or non-additive behaviour. In our experiments, we use the modulus version of μ_i^* since it is better than μ_i in ranking factors in order of importance; for each variable we use 100 levels perturbed 10 times (10^4 trials); the noise is 1%. As bounds of the variables we set the lower and upper bounds using the $\pm 100\%$ of the nominal value of each variable.

5 Robustness Analysis

The robustness is a dimensionless metric that assesses the yield of a given system, model, solution, it is the property of the system itself to undergo to mutations remaining in a reference state and continuing to perform its tasks in a reliable way. In engineering, robustness is generally regarded as a crucial feature. The ability of a system to survive to changes in the environment and the system itself is important to build and produce manufacturable solution.

By inspecting the space trajectory optimisation problem, it is extremely important to evaluate how the objective function changes due to perturbations in the variable values. It is obvious that it is important to find the variable values that maximize or minimize the objective function, and that assure a reliable behaviour also in presence of noise. In our research work, we define $\Omega = \{\{p_i\}_{i=1}^m, \{\phi_i\}_{i=1}^n\}$ as a system with m parameters (variables) and n properties. We called *nominal value* (N_v) the value of a property for a given parameter set. A *trial* τ is a perturbed system generated by an α function, also called α-perturbation, such that $\tau = \alpha(\Omega, \sigma)$. The α function applies a stochastic noise σ on the reference system Ω; without loss of generality, we assume that the noise is normally distributed. In order to simulate a statistically meaningful perturbation phenomenon, we generate an ensemble, T, of perturbed systems. A trial $\tau \in T$ is considered *robust* to a perturbation (mutation) of the stochastic noise σ for a given property ϕ, if the following *robustness condition* is verified:

$$\rho(\Omega, \tau, \phi, \varepsilon) = \begin{cases} 1 \ if \ \mid \phi(\Omega) - \phi(\tau) \mid \leq \varepsilon \\ 0 \qquad otherwise \end{cases} \qquad (4)$$

where Ω is the *reference system* and ε is a *robustness threshold*. The robustness of a system Ω is the number of *robust trials* of T respect the property ϕ over the total number of trials ($\mid T \mid$); we denote this measure as the *robustness* of the system. Formally, we define a *robustness function* Γ as follows:

$$\Gamma(\Omega, T, \phi, \varepsilon) = \frac{\sum_{\tau \in T} \rho(\Omega, \tau, \phi, \varepsilon)}{|T|} \tag{5}$$

The function Γ is a dimensionless quantity that assesses the probability that the nominal value of a property changes at most ε due to perturbations; high Γ values means high system robustness. Local robustness analysis has been performed: differently from global robustness, where a stochastic noise is applied to all the variables of the system, the *local robustness* analysis applies the noise one variable at time (the *single robustness* of an variable). While the global robustness analysis studies global changes of the system, instead the local robustness analysis studies the relative robustness of a single variable.

It is crucial to estimate how changes in the starting date, planetocentral velocity, mission duration alter the final δV mass consumption. In this sense, the *robustness of trajectory denotes the probability of consuming a prefixed amount of propellant.*

The ensemble T has been generated using a Monte Carlo algorithm; we generate an ensemble of 10^3 trials for each variable for the local robustness, the noise is 1%, and the threshold is fixed to 5% of the nominal value of the objective function.

It is important to remark the differences between Robustness (RA) and SA; RA aims to evaluate which is the probability of a system to remain in a reference state under perturbations, instead, SA perturbs a system in order to find which is the aspect that mainly affects its behaviour and to detect the dependencies among input parameters and between input and output.

6 Experimental Results

In this section, we analyse the optimisation and SA/RA results for the Messenger, Messenger Full, Cassini2, Rosetta, SAGAS, TandEM-Atlas1 and GTOC1 problems.

6.1 Optimisation

In Table 2, we compare the results that we have obtained after 30 runs with the current best-known solutions. It is important to note that for the Messenger Full problem we achieve an improvement of the 4.13% while for the other problems we obtain three refinements and an ex-aequo, unless for the case GTOC1 where our best solution is slightly lower (as depicted in Table 1 GTOC1 is a maximization problem) than the already known one.

Results for all the TandEM-Atlas501 problem instances are shown instead in Table 3.

In this case our approach leads to better results in five instances on 24 and, more in general, the difference from the best known results is under the 1%, unless for instance 4 where it is about 2.6%.

Table 2: Summary Results for SAGES Algorithm. For each problem we report mean, standard deviation and best-found solutions after 30 independent runs. In **bold face** new optima found compared to known best values (with references).

Problem	μ	σ	Best	Best Known with Ref.
Messenger	13.094	9.761	**8.629 km/s**	8.630 km/s [3]
Messenger Full	5.203	12.432	**2.970 km/s**	4.254 km/s [3]
Cassini 2	11.402	5.379	**8.382 kg km/s**	8.383 $kg\ km/s$ [15]
Rosetta	1.918	0.549	1.343 km/s	1.343 km/s [16]
SAGAS	23.368	14.408	**18.18 year**	18.19 $year$ [18]
GTOC1	1414998.982	16971.391	1581948 $kg\ km^2/s^2$	1581950 $kg\ km^2/s^2$ [15]

We can compare the differences between standard deviations of the various problems we tackled in this paper. For all the TandEM instances we have a percentage ratio of σ/μ below the 2% while for the other problems we have values drastically higher, from the 28% of Rosetta to the 238% of Messenger Full. Although the ratio between standard deviation and mean (called coefficient of variation) does not describe completely the algorithm behaviour, it can give an idea of its variance and reliability with respect to a specific optimisation problem.

6.2 Robustness and Sensitivity Analysis

For five of the trajectory optimisation problems we tackled on Section 6.1 we propose here a sensitivity analysis. For each solution, we perform a robustness analysis and a Morris sensitivity analysis; these analysis aims to estimate the importance parameters of the problems.

Table 3: Summary Results for TandEM-Atlas501 unconstrained instances with SAGES Algorithm (unit of measurement is kg). For each instance we report mean, standard deviation and best-found solutions after 30 independent runs. In **bold face** new optima found compared to known best values. All the known best values refer to [2].

Inst.	μ	σ	Best	Best Known	Inst.	μ	σ	Best	Best Known
1	1139.63	6.90	1231.53	1233.49	13	714.65	6.22	759.32	764.74
2	1395.42	4.52	1409.84	1412.28	14	902.56	8.93	943.85	945.40
3	742.96	7.49	769.210	772.53	15	699.98	4.69	723.61	726.81
4	932.95	3.92	950.126	976.18	16	801.39	11.96	834.91	836.46
5	1128.40	6.93	1132.67	1142.6	17	849.49	4.67	889.63	896.96
6	1654.94	2.18	**1673.88**	1637.99	18	1159.04	12.36	1234.71	1242.61
7	1148.30	3.98	1158.58	1163.60	19	1150.00	9.53	1186.93	1192.62
8	1547.90	5.01	1589.056	1603.4	20	1307.36	6.93	1342.31	1351.53
9	631.90	4.28	648.712	657.84	21	799.31	4.56	**812.216**	804.49
10	1056.02	5.80	1097.349	1104.51	22	1150.42	21.41	**1265.44**	1252.62
11	439.68	3.35	468.45	471.99	23	1015.43	11.51	**1077.95**	1077.51
12	576.09	8.91	601.09	603.76	24	1151.76	2.43	**1209.26**	1198.54

In Tables 4-8, we report the parameters vector of each solution and the results obtained by the robustness and Morris analysis.

Table 4: Messenger: for each parameter, we report the robustness, the mean and standard deviation of the Morris analysis.

Variable	Value	Units	Local Robustness (%)	μ_S	σ_S^2
t_0	1.171e+03	MJD2000	0.10	120.03	56.39
V_{inf}	1.420e+00	km/sec	2.90	56.34	35.47
u	3.781e-01	n/a	2.80	79.78	57.38
v	5.000e-01	n/a	31.00	133.81	51.40
T_1	4.000e+02	days	0.00	128.70	70.16
T_2	1.789e+02	days	0.50	146.68	73.26
T_3	2.993e+02	days	0.10	105.34	56.25
T_4	1.807e+02	days	1.70	65.66	37.35
η_1	2.365e-01	days	100.00	108.39	240.11
η_2	4.014e-02	n/a	100.00	8.72	0.35
η_3	8.330e-01	n/a	4.60	105.30	50.98
η_4	3.127e-01	n/a	55.70	69.42	93.97
r_{p1}	1.744e+00	n/a	4.40	51.82	40.86
r_{p2}	3.030e+00	n/a	0.10	90.86	34.07
r_{p3}	1.100e+00	n/a	7.00	93.59	31.04
b_{incl1}	1.351e+00	n/a	10.10	102.33	56.29
b_{incl2}	1.093e+00	n/a	0.00	91.97	33.05
b_{incl3}	1.345e+00	n/a	2.54	116.36	21.62

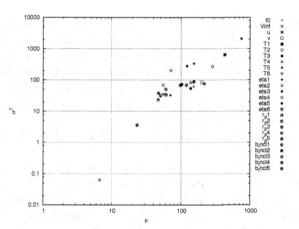

Fig. 1: Morris Analysis for the Messenger Full Problem

Table 5: Messenger-full: for each parameter, we report the robustness, the mean and standard deviation of the Morris analysis.

Variable	Value	Units	Local Robustness (%)	μ_S	σ_S^2
t_0	1.951e+03	MJD2000	0.00	151.74	60.59
V_{inf}	4.050e+00	km/sec	0.20	71.36	200.14
u	7.325e-01	n/a	1.70	217.27	75.57
v	5.192e-01	n/a	0.00	199.96	83.23
T_1	2.364e+02	days	0.00	430.56	640.93
T_2	1.117e+02	days	0.00	285.42	267.94
T_3	2.061e+02	days	0.00	137.64	53.52
T_4	2.639e+02	days	0.00	137.49	82.34
T_5	2.564e+02	days	16.80	70.01	32.25
T_6	4.491e+02	days	88.80	55.66	35.75
η_1	4.418e-01	days	2.10	153.41	332.20
η_2	2.717e-01	n/a	100.00	6.69	0.06
η_3	5.899e-01	n/a	0.30	751.35	2087.87
η_4	7.398e-01	n/a	92.40	55.15	68.27
η_5	5.112e-01	n/a	20.50	121.94	275.42
η_6	8.708e-01	n/a	100.00	60.32	50.10
r_{p1}	1.100e+00	n/a	0.70	46.66	23.35
r_{p2}	1.100e+00	n/a	0.10	102.50	71.74
r_{p3}	1.050e+00	n/a	0.30	60.74	33.48
r_{p4}	1.050e+00	n/a	0.40	50.91	31.51
r_{p5}	1.050e+00	n/a	100.00	23.28	3.61
b_{incl1}	3.350e-01	n/a	0.40	100.28	69.86
b_{incl2}	1.404e+00	n/a	21.80	153.28	86.99
b_{incl3}	-3.013e-01	n/a	93.90	119.24	68.69
b_{incl4}	-4.635e-01	n/a	98.90	97.65	67.72
b_{incl5}	1.566e+00	n/a	0.60	47.32	37.99

As described in Section 4, Sensitivity Analysis may help to know how each single variable affects the objective function and where its effect is linear or non-linear. Both the μ_S and σ_S^2 parameters have an interesting meaning for optimisation purposes, the first parameter describes the magnitude of objective function change with respect to the variation of the selected variable, on the other hand σ_S^2 describes how this variation is affected by the value of the other variables, also with non-linear effects. This means that parameters with low σ^2 are more suitable for local search while parameters with higher values need a global search due to the non-linear relations with other variables.

We can observe in Figure 1 a plot with both the Sensitivity Analysis parameters (μ and σ) for Messenger Full problem (we omitted the same plot for the other problems due to space reasons). The figure can give a sort of ranking of variables' criticality, given the effect of their variation on the objective function, e.g. the parameter η_3 seems to be the most influential; on the other hand the parameter η_2 shows a particularly low impact on the objective function.

The RA tries to explain how much a single variable may be perturbed without causing any drastic change (in this case a variation above the 5%, as explained in Section 5) observed in the objective function. A high value of local robustness means

Table 6: Cassini 2: for each parameter, we report the robustness, the mean and standard deviation of the Morris analysis.

Variable	Value	Units	Local Robustness (%)	μ_S	σ_S^2
t_0	-7.801e+02	MJD2000	1.40	223.91	81.50
V_{inf}	3.275e+00	km/sec	8.50	71.75	39.24
u	5.306e-01	n/a	2.90	231.24	119.03
v	3.821e-01	n/a	37.20	79.43	63.06
T_1	1.685e+02	days	5.20	140.34	58.46
T_2	4.240e+02	days	8.70	130.03	64.48
T_3	5.331e+01	days	50.90	52.46	14.68
T_4	5.898e+02	days	100.00	27.92	12.94
T_5	2.200e+03	days	100.00	12.91	3.52
η_1	7.745e-01	n/a	100.00	19.05	8.01
η_2	5.332e-01	n/a	100.00	9.89	1.71
η_3	1.093e-01	n/a	100.00	8.38	0.00
η_4	8.166e-02	n/a	100.00	8.38	0.00
η_5	8.781e-02	n/a	100.00	8.38	0.00
r_{p1}	1.361e+00	n/a	100.00	21.55	9.61
r_{p2}	1.050e+00	n/a	100.00	13.45	1.81
r_{p3}	1.307e+00	n/a	100.00	11.31	1.15
r_{p4}	6.981e+01	n/a	100.00	11.27	2.29
b_{incl1}	-1.594e+00	rad	100.00	40.82	33.41
b_{incl2}	-1.960e+00	rad	100.00	18.77	5.25
b_{incl3}	-1.555e+00	rad	100.00	15.39	3.85
b_{incl4}	-1.513e+00	rad	100.00	14.77	3.46

that a variation of the specific variable does not affect severely the optimality of the solution, obviously a relation between this value and the results obtained from the SA can exist: in fact, we can notice that all the parameters with the lowest μ_S and σ_S display a local robustness of 100%, further underlining their low influence on the objective function.

7 Conclusions

Space missions offer continuous challenges to the computational design community, since many astrophysical problems are intrinsically optimisation problems. This kind of missions is extremely complex since they require a rendezvous with an astronomical body, which is moving in space. Optimizing the trajectory of this kind of missions is a challenge and it represents an ideal field for assessing the fitness of the proposed design principles.

This work proposes a novel Evolutionary Computation algorithm for global optimisation, focusing on its application on a particularly hard problem, spacecrafts trajectory optimisation. Numerical results on the benchmark problems released by ESA ACT in the last years show an improvement on many instances with an achievement of the best solutions found so far. With the aim of a further investigation of the

Table 7: Rosetta: for each parameter, we report the robustness, the mean and standard deviation of the Morris analysis.

Variable	Value	Units	Local Robustness (%)	μ_S	σ_S^2
t_0	1.542e+03	MJD2000	1.50	49.80	26.64
V_{inf}	4.453e+00	km/sec	5.10	21.60	13.34
u	2.771e-01	n/a	3.50	58.67	32.90
v	9.488e-01	n/a	4.10	37.38	19.69
T_1	3.652e+02	days	0.30	72.08	19.14
T_2	7.081e+02	days	3.70	109.49	71.04
T_3	2.574e+02	days	14.30	40.79	17.61
T_4	7.305e+02	days	6.20	37.14	24.53
T_5	1.850e+03	days	100.00	3.15	1.83
η_1	4.264e-01	n/a	100.00	1.35	0.00
η_2	8.097e-01	n/a	100.00	14.49	29.53
η_3	2.149e-02	n/a	100.00	1.34	0.00
η_4	1.393e-01	n/a	100.00	1.34	0.00
η_5	4.353e-01	n/a	100.00	2.69	2.27
r_{p1}	1.050e+00	n/a	93.20	39.44	18.43
r_{p2}	1.050e+00	n/a	100.00	3.01	0.47
r_{p3}	2.637e+00	n/a	100.00	8.79	8.72
r_{p4}	1.209e+00	n/a	100.00	18.95	10.84
b_{incl1}	-9.873e-01	rad	8.80	33.61	15.21
b_{incl2}	1.789e+00	rad	100.00	4.28	1.45
b_{incl3}	-2.101e+00	rad	82.70	19.54	15.75
b_{incl4}	-1.871e+00	rad	100.00	25.76	17.36

Table 8: SAGAS: for each parameter, we report the robustness, the mean and standard deviation of the Morris analysis.

Variable	Value	Units	Local Robustness (%)	μ_S	σ_S^2
t_0	7.020e+03	MJD2000	53.50	1772.02	13119.31
V_{inf}	5.345e+00	km/sec	100.00	18.29	0.15
u	4.000e-04	n/a	100.00	18.34	0.11
v	5.003e-01	n/a	100.00	18.25	0.07
T_1	7.894e+02	days	100.00	2872.70	16640.62
T_2	4.840e+02	days	100.00	17202.73	37708.87
η_1	4.946e-01	n/a	100.00	33.02	1218.38
η_2	1.000e-02	n/a	100.00	17.72	0.76
r_{p1}	1.050e+00	n/a	100.00	18.14	0.02
r_{p2}	1.085e+01	n/a	100.00	93071.16	25391.38
b_{incl1}	-1.572e+00	pi	100.00	57757.56	49385.61
b_{incl2}	-7.003e-01	pi	100.00	18.19	0.00

global trajectory optimisation problems (GTOPs) we performed an accurate sensitivity and robustness analysis, two tools that are able to examine deeply black-box optimisation problems but nonetheless not commonly used in Evolutionary Computation field.

Although the results show that the proposed approach performs well with proposed optimisation problems, in our opinion a deeper analysis of the cases where it did not succeed in improving the known best might help to improve the knowl-

edge the GTOP problems. This analysis may be performed also with Sensitivity and Robustness Analysis, which, as future work, we would like to extend for multiple variables.

In conclusion, we think that our approach has a great potential for GTOP problems and moreover we think that Sensitivity and Robustness Analysis are powerful tools in Evolutionary Computation, which might lead to an improved algorithms design.

References

1. O. Abdelkhalik and D. Mortari. N-impulse orbit transfer using genetic algorithms. *Journal of Spacecraft and Rockets*, 44(2):456, 2007.
2. Bernardetta Addis, Andrea Cassioli, Marco Locatelli, and Fabio Schoen. A global optimization method for the design of space trajectories. *Computational Optimization and Applications*, pages 1–18, 2009. 10.1007/s10589-009-9261-6.
3. F. Biscani, D. Izzo, and C.H. Yam. A global optimisation toolbox for massively parallel engineering optimisation. *Arxiv preprint arXiv:1004.3824*, 2010.
4. A. Cassioli, D. Di Lorenzo, M. Locatelli, F. Schoen, and M. Sciandrone. Machine learning for global optimization. *Computational Optimization and Applications*, pages 1–25, 2010. 10.1007/s10589-010-9330-x.
5. N. Hansen, S.D. Müller, and P. Koumoutsakos. Reducing the time complexity of the derandomized evolution strategy with covariance matrix adaptation (cma-es). *Evolutionary Computation*, 11(1):1–18, 2003.
6. D. Izzo, VM Becerra, DR Myatt, SJ Nasuto, and JM Bishop. Search space pruning and global optimisation of multiple gravity assist spacecraft trajectories. *Journal of Global Optimization*, 38(2):283–296, 2007.
7. D. Izzo, M. Rucinski, and C. Ampatzis. Parallel global optimisation meta-heuristics using an asynchronous island-model. In *Evolutionary Computation, 2009. CEC'09. IEEE Congress on*, pages 2301–2308. IEEE, 2009.
8. Dario Izzo. 1st act global trajectory optimisation competition: Problem description and summary of the results. *Acta Astronautica*, 61(9):731 – 734, 2007. Global Trajectory Optimization. Results of the First Competition Organised by the Advanced Concept Team (ACT) of the European Space Agency (ESA).
9. D.R. Jones, C.D. Perttunen, and B.E. Stuckman. Lipschitzian optimization without the lipschitz constant. *Journal of Optimization Theory and Applications*, 79(1):157–181, 1993.
10. L. Kaufman, P.J. Rousseeuw, and Ebooks Corporation. *Finding groups in data: an introduction to cluster analysis*, volume 39. Wiley Online Library, 1990.
11. S. Li, R. Mehra, R. Smith, and R. Beard. Multi-spacecraft trajectory optimization and control using genetic algorithm techniques. In *Aerospace Conference Proceedings, 2000 IEEE*, volume 7, pages 99–108. IEEE, 2000.
12. K.V. Price, R.M. Storn, and J.A. Lampinen. *Differential evolution: a practical approach to global optimization*. Springer Verlag, 2005.
13. A. Saltelli. *Sensitivity analysis in practice: a guide to assessing scientific models*. John Wiley & Sons Inc, 2004.
14. A. Saltelli, M. Ratto, T. Andres, and Ebooks Corporation. *Global sensitivity analysis: the primer*. Wiley Online Library, 2008.
15. M. Schlüter, M. Gerdts, and J.J. Rückmann. Midaco: New global optimization software for minlp. 2011.
16. M. Vasile, E. Minisci, and M. Locatelli. A dynamical system perspective on evolutionary heuristics applied to space trajectory optimization problems. In *Evolutionary Computation, 2009. CEC'09. IEEE Congress on*, pages 2340–2347. IEEE, 2009.

17. T. Vinkó and D. Izzo. Global optimisation heuristics and test problems for preliminary space-craft trajectory design. Technical report, GOHTPPSTD, European Space Agency, the Advanced Concepts Team, 2008.

18. T. Vinkó, D. Izzo, and C. Bombardelli. Benchmarking different global optimisation techniques for preliminary space trajectory design. In *58th International Astronautical Congress, International Astronautical Federation (IAF)*, 2007.

Intelligent Tuning of a Dynamic Business Simulation Environment

Thierry Mamer, Sid Shakya, John McCall and Gilbert Owusu

Abstract One important use of simulation tools is to use an existing base-model of a business, representing the systems of interest, and then modelling and testing alternative scenarios by making changes to this base-model. This way, business managers can estimate the consequences of policy changes without having to actually introduce them into the business. The act of ensuring the continuous validity of a base model in a continuously changing business is called *Tuning*. In this paper, we investigate how heuristic based optimisation algorithms like Evolutionary Algorithms can be used to improve the tuning of a dynamic business simulation environment, within the framework of a software called WDS. We test a number of different algorithms on this problem, using two different encoding-schemes and evaluate the results.

Thierry Mamer
IDEAS Research Institute, The Robert Gordon University, St. Andrew Street, Aberdeen AB25 1HG, Scotland, Research Internship at BT Innovate and Design, e-mail: thierry@doheem.com

Siddhartha Shakya
Business Modelling & Operational Transformation Practice, BT Innovate and Design, Adastral Park, Ipswich, IP53RE, UK, e-mail: sid.shakya@bt.com

John McCall
IDEAS Research Institute, The Robert Gordon University, St. Andrew Street, Aberdeen AB25 1HG, Scotland, e-mail: j.mccall@rgu.ac.uk

Gilbert Owusu
Business Modelling & Operational Transformation Practice, BT Innovate and Design, Adastral Park, Ipswich, IP53RE, UK, e-mail: gilbert.owusu@bt.com

M. Bramer et al. (eds.), *Research and Development in Intelligent Systems XXVIII*,
DOI 10.1007/978-1-4471-2318-7_27, © Springer-Verlag London Limited 2011

1 Introduction

Workforce Dynamics Simulator (WDS) [1] [2] [3] [4] is a simulation environment which enables large scale simulation of workforces and notable resources. It uses historical or generated data to investigate the execution of work plans.

WDS takes detailed input data on geographical locations, tasks to be completed each day and engineers available on each day. The task details include among other things their type and location, what skills are required to complete these tasks and details of any existing appointments. The engineer details include among other things their rosters, skills, preferred working areas and starting locations.

WDS uses this input data to simulate the completion of tasks over a number of days. The process starts with the time at which the task is reported and enters into the system, continues with the tasks being allocated to a engineer which then travels to the task's location, completes the task (or fails to do so). The allocation of tasks to engineers is done through a scheduler which uses a rule-based allocation system to decide which task is allocated to an available engineer. This scheduler takes into account geographical domains and locations, technical skills which are available and required, importance of tasks as well as their appointments and committed times.

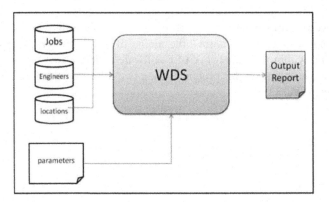

Fig. 1 WDS dataflow

After a simulation is run, WDS provides a detailed report, containing daily expected numbers on productivity, volume of jobs completed, volume of jobs failed, volume of jobs carried over to the next day, and the percentage of successes (See Figure 1 for a dataflow diagram of WDS). This can then be used to support decision making in the business.

1.1 Tuning WDS

To be able to predict the consequences of policy changes in the real world, before they are actually implemented, the key is to have a good base-scenario. However, as the real world periodically changes, the base scenarios have to be revised periodically as well, making sure that they still reflect the real world. This process is called *Tuning*.

The process of Tuning WDS aims to bring simulated results and the current real world observed values (Actuals) closer together. To achieve this, there are five variables in WDS which we are allowed to change:

Average Speed (AS)   : reflects the average speed at which the engineers travel towards the location of the task which was assigned to them.

Inefficiency Factor (IF)   : reflects a number of minutes which engineers are idle after each job completion. No jobs can be assigned to them during this time.

Overtime Allowed (OA)   : reflects the additional time which engineers are allowed to spend completing the task, after the rostered time has ran out.

Lateness Allowed (LA)   : reflects the amount of time engineers can use to complete a task when they have arrived on location too late.

Distribution of Reassigned Tasks (RT)   : reflects the percentage of jobs which have a strong probability of failure after the first assignment. These tasks will then be reassigned.

Tweaking these values often gives a dramatic change in the output of WDS simulations. The challenge is to find the best combination of these values enabling WDS to run a base-scenario with results closest to the Actuals. Once the base-scenario is tuned, it can be used to simulate the effect of changes in other setups such as the effect of adding more technicians to the workforce or adding more jobs to the workstack.

Thus far, WDS Tuning entails testing a large number of combinations of the possible values for these tuning variables and simulating all of them extensively. If this is done manually, it involves the following steps:

```
1. Determine a list of parameters to be tested.
2. For each set of parameters:
2.1. Set up WDS to run the simulation
2.2. Start the simulation and wait until it is finished
2.3. Open the report and extract required information
2.4. Compare that information against the Actuals
2.5. Decide on the quality of the results
3. Choose the best set of parameters
```

A *WDS Tuning Tool* tool is available which automates the above series of steps. It enables the user to set a number of options, including testing ranges for the five tuning variables AS, IF, OA, LA and RT as well as a *step-size*. The step-size defines how many values in between these ranges will be tested. For example, a step-size

of k for tuning variable v_i indicates that from $min(v_i)$ to $max(v_i)$, each kth value will be tested, including $min(v_i)$ and $max(v_i)$ themselves. The WDS Tuning Tool runs all the simulations requested and provides a detailed analysis, including a proposed best set of tuning variables (the set with the highest score). Even though this tool significantly simplifies WDS Tuning, it is not ideal, as it relies on the user to decide on a meaningful setup. The process is also quite limited in its search by the use of the step-sizes, as no value between the steps will be tested. Another downside is that once the process has started, a considerable amount of time will pass until the results can be analysed, without a guarantee to find a good result.

In this work, we set out to develop an intelligent system, able to decide autonomously which tuning variables should be tested and go ahead and run the required simulations, without any interaction with the user. As simulations return their results, it should be able to dynamically react to them and decide which simulations to run next. At the end of the process, the system should report the best set of tuning variables found.

2 Tuning Optimisation Problem

The Tuning optimisation problem is defined as the problem to find the set of WDS tuning variables $V = \{v_1, v_2, \ldots v_n\}$ which, when passed to the simulation engine, result in the daily simulated values closest to the Actuals both in terms of values and trend. In our case, V contains $n = 5$ variables: $v_1 = AS$, $v_2 = IF$, $v_3 = OA$, $v_4 = LA$ and $v_5 = RT$ and $V = \{AS, IF, OA, LA, RT\}$. Because any possible combination of these values is allowed, it is impossible to test all the possible combinations through simulations. Consider that the total number of possible simulations to test (Ω) is the product of all the ranges of the tuning variables v_i. If the range of a tuning variable v_i is noted as $\Delta v_i = max(v_i) - min(v_i)$, then: [1]

$$\Omega = \Delta AS \times \Delta IF \times \Delta OA \times \Delta LA \times \Delta RT$$
$$= 32 \times 64 \times 64 \times 16 \times 16$$
$$= 33,554,432$$

To run one simulation of one week (7 days) takes on average 105 seconds [2]. So if we were to test each of these possible combinations for one week simulations, it would take around 3,500,000,000 seconds, which would amount to almost 111 years. On top of that, WDS is usually tuned for 90 days and not for 7, which would make the time intractable. It is clear that extensive search through all possible variations is not an appropriate method to find the best set of parameters. An intelligent algorithm guiding this search is required.

---

[1] The ranges used here are typical ranges, also shown in Table 1

[2] This time was measured on a Intel(R) Core(TM) i5 CPU M 520 @ 2.40GHZ, 2GB of RAM

2.1 Methodology

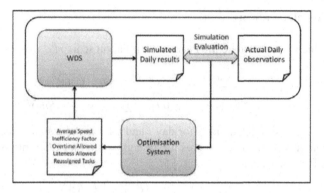

Fig. 2 Optimisation system dataflow

We developed a specialised instance of WDS (see Figure 2), which can run the simulation using a set of given tuning variables $V = \{AS, IF, OA, LA, RT\}$ and return a score based on the match between the simulated values and the Actuals (observed in the past). This score is a combination between the Pearson Correlation [5] (measuring the correlation between two variables over time) and the Mean Absolute Percentage Error MAPE [6] (measuring accuracy in a fitted time series) calculated between the Actuals and the daily simulated values over a period of d days.

The Actuals used in this work contain the real world observations on tasks belonging to two different categories: *Provision* and *Repair*. Provision tasks deal with proactively installing some part of the infrastructure needed for future services, whereas Repair tasks deal with the customers immediate needs, reacting to their requests.

For each day i, the Actuals include the following values (x):

Provision Performance (PP_i): a performance percentage for Provision tasks.

Repair Performance (PR_i): a performance percentage for Repair tasks.

Provision Failures (PF_i): the number of Provision tasks which have failed on day i (completed but after its committed time).

Provision Successes (PS_i): the number of Provision tasks which were completed successfully on day i.

Provision Totals (PT_i): the total number of Provision tasks which have been completed on day i (usually $PF_i + PS_i$).

Repair Failures (RF_i): the number of Repair tasks which have failed on day i (completed but after its committed time)

Repair Successes (RS_i): the number of Repair tasks which were completed successfully on day i.

Repair Totals (RT_i): the total number of Repair tasks which have been completed on day i (usually $RF_i + RS_i$).

For each simulation result, we will compare these daily Actual values with their simulated counterparts to compute a score.

Pearson Correlation Score

For each value x, we calculate the Pearson Correlation score $r(x)$ over the period of d days:

$$r(x) = \frac{\sum_{i=1}^{d}(xAct_i - \overline{xAct})(xSim_i - \overline{xSim})}{\sqrt{\sum_{i=1}^{d}(xAct_i - \overline{xAct})^2}\sqrt{\sum_{i=1}^{d}(xSim_i - \overline{xSim})^2}} \qquad (1)$$

where $xSim$ is the simulated value for day i and $xAct$ is the actual value for day i. Then we combine the Pearson Scores for all eight values together into one Overall Simulation Pearson Score:

$$Pearson(sim) = \left(\alpha \times \frac{|r(PP)| + |r(PR)|}{2}\right) +$$

$$\left((1-\alpha) \times \frac{|r(PS)| + |r(PF)| + |r(PT)| + |r(RS)| + |r(RF)| + |r(RT)|}{6}\right) \qquad (2)$$

where correlation weight α is a parameter provided to the function in order to balance the weight of the performance percentages (PP and PR) and the values counting tasks. In this work, $\alpha = 0.7$, assigning more weight to performance percentages than to the counts of tasks.

Mean Absolute Percentage Error (MAPE)

For each value x, we calculate the Mean Absolute Percentage Error (MAPE) as $\varepsilon(x)$ over the period of d days:

$$\varepsilon(x) = \frac{1}{d}\sum_{i=1}^{d}\left|\frac{xSim - xAct}{xSim}\right| \qquad (3)$$

Then we combine the MAPE scores for all eight values together into one Overall Simulation MAPE Score:

$$MAPE(sim) = \left(\beta \times \frac{|\varepsilon(PP)| + |\varepsilon(PR)|}{2}\right) +$$

$$\left((1-\beta) \times \frac{|\varepsilon(PS)| + |\varepsilon(PF)| + |\varepsilon(PT)| + |\varepsilon(RS)| + |\varepsilon(RF)| + |\varepsilon(RT)|}{6}\right) \qquad (4)$$

where error weight β, similar to α above, is a parameter provided to the function in order to balance the weight of the performance percentages (PP and PR) and the values counting tasks. In this work, $\beta = 0.7$.

Overall Simulation Score

Finally, *Pearson(sim)* and *MAPE(sim)* are combined to compute one overall Simulation Score *simScore* for each simulation:

$$simScore(sim) = (\gamma \times Pearson(sim) + ((1 - \gamma) \times (1 - MAPE(sim)))) \quad (5)$$

where γ allows the balancing between *Pearson(sim)* and MAPE(sim). In this work, we set $\gamma = 0.5$, assigning equal weight to both scores. As this final score aims to maximise the correlation while minimising the errors, $(1 - MAPE(sim))$ was used. The simulation result with the highest overall simulation score *simScore* is considered to be the best simulation.

The optimisation system can now use a number of different algorithms to find *solutions* which consist of (or can be converted to) sets of tuning variables V and use WDS to calculate their fitness:

$$fit(V) = simScore(sim) \quad (6)$$

The optimisation problem is to find the set of variables V that maximise $fit(V)$.

2.2 Representation of the Tuning Variables

Here we consider the use of heuristic based optimisation algorithms for the WDS Tuning problem. Particularly, we are interested in Evolutionary Algorithms (EA). EAs can encode a solution in many ways. Here we test *binary-coding* and *real-coding*. There is a trade-off between using these two methods. Using binary-coding, the methods to manipulate the solutions are easier to design and it is a rather simple process to transform a binary string into real numbers later. The downside of binary-coding is that with a higher number of variables, the length of the binary string increases. Using real-coding, the solutions are much shorter, however the design of the methods to manipulate the solutions are more difficult. Also, in some algorithms real-coding can lead to premature convergence [7].

Some optimisation algorithms do prefer one encoding method over the other by the nature of their design. In our experiments, we have used both encoding methods. Using real-encoded solutions, we get our five tuning variables almost straight from the algorithm. In the case of binary-coded solutions, we have transformed the binary string into five numbers.

The total bit-size we need for one set of variables V is:

$$\begin{aligned} bit(V) &= bit(AS) + bit(OA) + bit(LA) + bit(IF) + bit(RT) \\ &= 5 + 6 + 6 + 4 + 4 \quad \text{(values taken from Table 1)} \\ &= 25 \end{aligned}$$

where $bit(v_i)$ is the bit-size of one variable v_i.

Each solution generated by the optimisation algorithm consists of 25 bits and is converted into a set of five natural numbers by the WDS fitness function. The first five bits are converted into a natural number between 0 and 31. Then the minimum value for AS, $min(AS) = 10$, is added, which gives us a number between 10 and 41, corresponding to the range given in Table 1. This process is then repeated for OA, LA, IF and RT respectively.

	Average Speed	Overtime Allowed	Lateness Allowed	Inefficiency Factor	Reassigned Tasks Dist.
Minimum	10	0	60	2	2
Maximum	41	63	123	17	17
No. of values	32	64	64	16	16
bits required	5	6	6	4	4

Table 1 The five Decision Variables, their ranges and the number of bits allocated to them.

2.3 Optimisation algorithms applied

We have built our optimisation system with a number of evolutionary optimisation algorithms (OA). They include several population-based Evolutionary algorithms (EA) [8] [9] and Estimation of Distribution Algorithms (EDA) [10] [11] [12] as well as one non-population based algorithm. These algorithms are listed below.

Genetic Algorithm (GA)[8] [13], a population based EA, which generates solutions using techniques inspired by natural evolution, such as selection, crossover and mutation. We have used both binary-encoding and real-encoding to represent solutions for GA.

Population-based incremental learning (PBIL) [14] [15], a population based EDA. PBIL is similar to GA, however instead of using crossover and mutation it estimates univariate marginal probability of each solution variable and samples it to generate new solutions. We have used binary-encoding to represent solutions for PBIL.

Distribution Estimation using Markov Random Field with direct sampling (DEUM$_d$) [16] [17] [18], a population based EDA which is similar to PBIL, however it builds a model of the fitness function for estimated marginal probabilities. We have used binary-encoding to represent solutions for DEUM$_d$.

Univariate Marginal Distribution Algorithm for continuous domains (UM-DAc) [19] [20], a population based EDA where the solution variations are continuous (real-valued). The main idea of UMDAc is to represent each variable as a Gaussian. New solutions are generated by estimation and sampling from this Gaussian. We have used real-encoding to represent solutions for UMDAc.

Simulated Annealing (SA) [21] [22], a non-population based algorithm which evolves just one single solution. We have used both binary-encoding and real-encoding to represent solutions for SA.

Because of the limit in available space, we were not able to give the workflows for each of these algorithms in this paper. Interested readers are referred to the respective references. A workflow of GA, PBIL, SA and DEUM$_d$ can be also found in [23] and [24].

2.4 Objective

To evaluate the results achieved, we did not only compare the different OAs with each other, but we also used a benchmark which we aimed to outperform. This benchmark is the performance of the *WDS Tuning Tool* which was mentioned earlier, in Section 1.1. We ran this tool using the standard step-sizes and providing it with same ranges as all other optimisation algorithms in this work:

	min	max	step-size	No of values
AS	10	40	10	4
OA	0	60	30	3
LA	60	120	10	7
IF	2	16	2	8
RT	2	16	2	8

Total number of simulations : $ns = 4 \times 3 \times 7 \times 8 \times 8 = 5376$

Using this setup, the tool ran 5376 simulations. The best result found had a fitness of 0.8077 (see Equation 6). During our experiments, our objective was to address the two following challenges:

1. Surpass this benchmark (e.g. consistently find a set of tuning variables which result in a better fitness than the current tool).
2. Find results in reasonable proximity to the benchmark (tuning variables resulting in a similar fitness), but running significantly less simulations.

3 Experiments and Results

3.1 Algorithm specific settings

We ran each of the presented OAs on our WDS Tuning Optimisation problem using a number of different algorithm settings. Because simulations in WDS are very time

consuming to run, most OAs ran for almost a whole day before results could be analysed, some even ran over several days (e.g. DEUM$_d$ and SA using real-encoding). Because of these long execution times, we were not able to run every possible setup multiple times extensively. Instead, we ran our experiments in two stages. In a first stage, we tested a wide range of parameter setups for each algorithm by running each of them two times. Based on the results achieved from those, we estimated which would be the most promising setup for each OA. In a second stage of experiments, we ran the chosen setups six times and collected the results.

Our solution size was 25 for bit-encoding (see Section 2.2) and 5 for real encoding. For population-based algorithms (all except SA), we set a population size of 50 solutions. We also allowed for the 2 best solutions of each generation to pass over to the next generation unaltered. As it was our aim to outperform our benchmark, we did not allow any of our algorithms to run more evaluations than our benchmark (5376). To determine an appropriate maximum number of generations, we investigated at what point the OA converged in our first stage experiments. We ran the GA and UMDAc allowing for a maximum of 50 generations, PBIL for 60 generations and DEUM$_d$ for 100 generations. We allowed SA to go through a maximum of 3000 generations. In light of this rather small amount of evaluations, we set an accordingly large SA cooling rate of 0.05 in both real- and bit-encoding experiments. We set PBIL to use a selection size of 20 and a learning rate of 0.3. We used GA with one-point crossover, a crossover probability of 0.7 and a tournament selection operator. Our first stage experiments indicated that using a real-encoding, GAs find the best solutions using a mutation rate of 0.1, while a mutation rate of 0.05 worked best when using a bit-encoding. DEUM$_d$'s cooling rate was set to 6.0. Please see referenced literature for more details on these algorithm parameters.

3.2 Fitness Set

Often, OAs will generate solutions which have been tested for fitness previously in the same execution, especially when the search converges into one area of the search space. As our WDS Tuning objective function is so expensive to run, we avoided multiple simulations using identical decision variables. We have implemented a *Fitness Set*, a table in the working memory, storing each solution which has already been evaluated in the current execution, and its fitness. Each time a solution is tested for fitness, it is checked whether it is already stored in the Fitness Set. If it is, the previously calculated fitness is reused and no new simulations are run.

3.3 Results

Each of the presented OAs has been executed six times using identical setups. The fitness mean and standard deviation (stDev) of the best solutions from each of the

Optimisation Algorithm	Mean	StDev.	Best Fitness	Dist. from BM Mean	Best	Evals Mean
UMDAc (real)	0.8312	0.0054	0.8389	0.0235	0.0312	1462
PBIL (bit)	0.8209	0.0028	0.8252	0.0132	0.0175	1283
GA (real)	0.8226	0.0053	0.8284	0.0149	0.0207	1090
GA (bit)	0.8140	0.0058	0.8230	0.0063	0.0153	334
SA (real)	0.8240	0.0036	0.8293	0.0147	0.0179	2733
SA (bit)	0.8232	0.0054	0.8321	0.0155	0.0244	1410
DEUM$_d$ (bit)	0.8236	0.0025	0.8279	0.0163	0.0216	2926

Table 2 Results

six executions, as well as the fitness of the overall best solution found, is given in Table 2. It also gives the mean of the distances between the benchmark (BM) and the best solutions found as well as the distance between the BM and the overall best solution found (where: $distance = Fitness - BM$). Finally, Table 2 also gives the mean number of total simulations (Evals. Mean) which were run during the six executions. This value is different from the maximum number of allowed evaluations due to our Fitness Set feature, which prevents multiple identical simulations to be executed. Figure 3 plots the mean best fitness achieved for each OA over all six executions as well as the fitness of the overall best solution over all six executions. For a better graphical comparison, we also included the benchmark fitness in Figure 3. Finally, Figure 4 plots the mean number of total simulations run over all six executions for each OA.

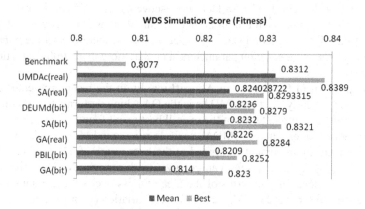

Fig. 3 Mean Fitness (over six executions) and maximum fitness achieved with each Optimisation Algorithm applied. They are ordered in descending order with respect to the mean fitness.

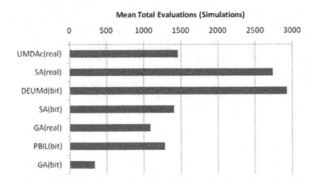

Fig. 4 Mean total number of simulations run (over six executions) for each Optimisation Algorithm applied.

4 Discussion

In this work, we set two different challenges. The first challenge was to find better solutions than can be found by a standard setup of the current WDS Tuning Tool, which was set as the benchmark (0.8077). This challenge was met by all of the tested OAs.

The second challenge was to find solutions of a similarly fitness compared to our benchmark, but using significantly less evaluations. This challenge was also met by all of the tested OAs. In fact, we discovered early on, in the first stage of our experiments, that such a high number of simulations is never required to find good results. For our second stage of experiments, we therefore set the *population size* and *maximum generation* parameters such that more than 3000 simulations are unlikely to be run.

Comparison of Optimisation Algorithms. From the results presented in Figure 3, we can clearly see that UMDAc is the OA which performs best on our WDS Tuning problem, both in terms of the overall best result found in six executions and in each individual execution. UMDAc needs to run around 1500 simulations, which is a significant improvement compared to the benchmark of 5376, however as we can see on Figure 4, some OAs can get away with running even less simulations. $DEUM_d$ is a close third in terms of the mean fitness over six executions. Also, in Table 2 we can see that $DEUM_d$ has the lowest variation (with a standard deviation of 0.0025), therefore finding good solutions consistently, however it runs a comparatively large number of simulations during its execution; at least twice as many as all the other OAs tested in this work. SA(bit), SA(real), PBIL and GA(real) behave comparably in terms of the fitness of solutions found, however SA(real) has to run a much larger number of simulations during its execution. Finally, GA(bit) is the worst in terms of the fitness of the solutions found, however in most cases it is still finding solutions which are better than the benchmark. It is also worth pointing out that it runs a remarkably small amount of simulations during its execution, less

than half the amount of the next lowest OA we tested, GA(real), less than a third compared to UMDAc and less than a tenth compared to our benchmark.

Trade-off between best fitness and least evaluations. Taking into account the results presented in Figures 3 and 4, there might be an acceptable trade-off between finding the best overall solution and the number of evaluations required to get there. For example, UMDAc does indeed consistently find the best solution, however it needs to process almost 1500 simulations to get there. On the other hand, GA (bit) does not quite find the best solution out there, but nevertheless, it finds a better solution than the benchmark while executing less than 500 simulations (which is less than 10% comparing to the benchmark). Considering that WDS simulations take a long time to run, using an OA which converges faster might be more beneficial in the end.

Encoding scheme. The results presented in this work suggest that for our WDS Tuning problem, better solutions are found when they are encoded as real numbers. UMDAc, the OA which scored highest, is using real-encoding. What is more, we can see from the experiments with GA and SA, which used both encoding schemes, that the real encoding always delivers better solutions compared to the bit-encoding.

5 Conclusion

We have shown in this work that heuristic Optimisation Algorithms like population-based Evolutionary algorithms or Simulated Annealing can be used to automate the Tuning of a complex simulation software. Our experiments showed that on our WDS simulation package, not only do OAs find better tuning variables than the existing automated WDS Tuning Tool, but they also do so in a significantly shorter period of time.

We found that real-encoding schemes worked better on our real value WDS Tuning problem than bit-encoding. We also discussed an optional trade-off between the fitness of the best solution found and the time which is needed to reach it. When dealing with very expensive evaluation processes such as our WDS Tuning problem, it might be worth settling for solutions which are good enough, but not the best, considering that they can be found three times faster.

The proposed intelligent approach to tuning is being incorporated in the WDS framework and is expected to significantly improve the tuning time as well as its accuracy. This will result in better field workforce simulations for the business.

References

1. A. Liret, J. Shepherdson, Y. Borenstein, C. Voudouris, and E. Tsang, "Workforce dynamics simulator in service operations scheduling systems," *Conference on Enterprise Information Systems, Ofir, Portugal*, October 2009.

2. N. Shah, E. P. K. Tsang, Y. Borenstein, R. Dorne, A. Liret, and C. Voudouris, "Intelligent agent based workforce empowerment.," in *KES-AMSTA'09*, pp. 163–172, 2009.
3. Y. Borenstein, N. Shah, E. Tsang, R. Dorne, A. Alsheddy, and C. Voudouris, "On the partitioning of dynamic workforce scheduling problems," *Journal of Scheduling*, vol. 13, pp. 411–425, 2010.
4. A. Liret and R. Dorne, "Work allocation and scheduling," in *Service Chain Management: Technology Innovation for the Service Business*, CENTERIS 2009 Conference on ENTERprise Information Systems, pp. 159–176, Springer-Verlag Berlin, 2008.
5. J. L. Rodgers and W. A. Nicewander, "Thirteen ways to look at the correlation coefficient," *The American Statistician*, vol. 42, no. 1, pp. 59–66, 1988. http://www.jstor.org/stable/2685263.
6. S. Makridakis and M. Hibon, "The m3-competition: results, conclusions and implications," *International Journal of Forecasting*, vol. 16, no. 4, pp. 451–476, 2000.
7. T. K. Paul and H. Iba, "Design and application of hybrid intelligent systems," ch. Optimization in continuous domain by real-coded estimation of distribution algorithm, pp. 262–271, Amsterdam, The Netherlands, The Netherlands: IOS Press, 2003.
8. D. E. Goldberg, *Genetic Algorithms in Search, Optimization and Machine Learning*. Boston, MA, USA: Addison-Wesley Longman Publishing Co., Inc., 1st ed., 1989.
9. T. Davis, "The handbook of genetic algorithms," *Artificial Intelligence*, 1991.
10. P. Larrañaga and J. A. Lozano, eds., *Estimation of Distribution Algorithms: A New Tool for Evolutionary Computation*. Springer, Oct. 2002.
11. S. Shakya and J. McCall, "Optimization by estimation of distribution with deum framework based on markov random fields," *International Journal of Automation and Computing*, vol. 4, pp. 262–272, 2007.
12. H. Mhlenbein and G. Paa, "From recombination of genes to the estimation of distributions i. binary parameters," pp. 178–187, Springer-Verlag, 1996.
13. M. Mitchell, *GA An introduction to genetic algorithms*. MIT Press, Cambridge, Massachusets, 1997.
14. S. Baluja, "Population-based incremental learning: A method for integrating genetic search based function optimization and competitive learning," tech. rep., 1994.
15. S. Baluja, "An empirical comparison of seven iterative and evolutionary function optimization heuristics," tech. rep., Carnegie Mellon University, 1995.
16. S. Shakya, *DEUM: A framework for an estimation of distribution algorithm based on markov random fields*. PhD in Computing, The Robert Gordon University, Aberdeen, UK, April 2006.
17. A. Petrovski, S. Shakya, and J. McCall, "Optimising cancer chemotherapy using an estimation of distribution algorithm and genetic algorithms," in *Proceedings of the 8th annual conference on Genetic and evolutionary computation*, GECCO '06, (New York, NY, USA), pp. 413–418, ACM, 2006.
18. S. Shakya, A. Brownlee, J. McCall, F. Fournier, and G. Owusu, "DEUM a fully multivariate EDA based on markov networks," in *Exploitation of Linkage Learning in Evolutionary Algorithms* (L. M. Hiot, Y. S. Ong, and Y.-p. Chen, eds.), vol. 3 of *Adaptation, Learning, and Optimization*, pp. 71–93, Springer Berlin Heidelberg, 2010.
19. C. Gonzlez, J. A. Lozano, and P. Larraaga, "Mathematical modelling of umdac algorithm with tournament selection. behaviour on linear and quadratic functions," 2002.
20. B. Yuan and M. Gallagher, "Convergence analysis of UMDAC with finite populations: a case study on flat landscapes," in *Genetic and Evolutionary Computation Conference*, pp. 477–482, 2009.
21. S. Kirkpatrick, C. D. Gelatt, and M. P. Vecchi, "Optimization by simulated annealing," *Science, Number 4598, 13 May 1983*, vol. 220, 4598, pp. 671–680, 1983.
22. R. H. J. M. Otten and L. P. P. P. van Ginneken, *The Annealing Algorithm*. Boston, MA: Kluwer, 1989.
23. S. Shakya and F. O. G. Owusu, "Analysing the effect of demand uncertainty in dynamic pricing with EAs," in *Research and Development in Intelligent Systems XXV*, p. 77, Springer-Verlag London, 2009.
24. S. Shakya, F. Oliveira, and G. Owusu, "An application of EDA and GA to dynamic pricing," in *Proceedings of the 9th annual conference on Genetic and evolutionary computation*, GECCO '07, (New York, NY, USA), pp. 585–592, ACM, 2007.

Towards Large-Scale Multi-Agent Based Rodent Simulation: The "Mice In A Box" Scenario

E. Agiriga, F. Coenen, J. Hurst, R. Beynon, D. Kowalski

Abstract Some initial research concerning the provision of a Multi-Agent Based Simulation (MABS) frameworks, to support rodent simulation, is presented. The issues discussed include the representation of: (i) the environment and the characters that interact with the environment, (ii) the nature of the "intelligence" that these characters might posses and (iii) the mechanisms whereby characters interact with environments and each other. Two categories of character are identified: "dumb characters" and "smart characters", the obvious distinction being that the first posses no intelligence while the second have at least some sort of reasoning capability. The focus of the discussion is the provision of a simple "mice in a box" scenario simulation.

1 Introduction

Multi-Agent Based Simulation (MABS) is concerned with the harnessing of Multi-Agent System (MAS) technology to enable large scale simulations. The challenge is the mechanisms and representations required to build frameworks to support the desired simulation. Using MABS the *characters* that play a part in the simulation, and the environment(s) in which they exist, are conceptualised as agents. MABS has been applied in many domains such as: the monitoring and control of intelligent

E. Agiriga, F. Coenen, D. Kowalski
Dept. of Computer Science, University of Liverpool, Liverpool L69 3BX, UK. e-mail: {grigs,coenen,darek}@liverpool.ac.uk

R. Beynon
Institute for Biocomplexity, University of Liverpool, Liverpool L69 3BX, UK. e-mail: R.Beynon@liverpool.ac.uk

J. Hurst
Mammalian Behaviour and Evolution Group, University of Liverpool, Liverpool L69 3BX, UK. e-mail: G.E.Hurst@liverpool.ac.uk

M. Bramer et al. (eds.), *Research and Development in Intelligent Systems XXVIII*,
DOI 10.1007/978-1-4471-2318-7_28, © Springer-Verlag London Limited 2011

buildings [2], transport chains [3], malaria re-emergence in the south of France [6], and urban population growth [7], to give just a few examples. To the best knowledge of the authors there is no work on MABS frameworks to study rodent behaviour. This paper describes some early research regarding issues concerned with the provision of MABS frameworks for rodent control. The focus of this report is a simple "mice in a box" scenario. However, the intention is to develop the framework so that it can be used to support large scale mouse simulations comprising some thousand agents.

2 The Mouse in a Box Scenario

The scenario at which the discussion presented in this paper is directed is that of a number of mice contained in a box. The scenario is founded on the sort of experiments conducted by rodent behaviourists who wish to observe the way that mice interact when placed in a closed environment, namely a $1.22 \times 1.22m$ box[1]. The fundamental idea is that one, two or more mice are placed in a box in which they can "run around". Mice have an affinity to walls [1] (they are *thigmotaxic*) and thus tend to moves along walls (although not exclusively so), thus in the absence of any obstructions a mouse's movements tend to be limited to the edges of the box. The mouse can move round the box in either a clockwise or ant-clockwise direction. It can also stop or turn around, occasionally it may venture into the space in the middle of the box. Mice are also interested in exploring their surroundings, the ultimate goal is the find and maintain an optimum nest location. The stronger Male mice have the best territory (nest locations). Females look for males with the best territory. Males mark their territory with scent, the stronger the male the stronger the scent. In the scenarios considered in this paper only male mice are considered. They are driven by the following desires:

1. A preference for wall locations as opposed to open space locations (in open space they are liable to attack by predators).
2. A desire to explore their environment.
3. A desire to avoid locations which feature the scent of other mice (unless that scent is significantly weaker than the mouse's own scent).
4. A requirement to avoid other mice that come into close proximity.

The above provides for some motivation for a mouse agent to move (to explore its locality), although there is no specific goal (reward). Whether the mouse moves or does not move, how long it moves for (or does not move) and which direction it should take, is a decision influenced partly by the above desires and partly by a random element.

---

[1] The value 1.22 is a result of the fact that the board from which the boxes are typically fashioned comes in $2.44 \times 1.22m$ sheets

3 The MABS Framework

The MABS framework is conceptualised in terms of a "cloud" in which a number of agents exist (Figure 1). From the figure we have three types (classes) of agent: (i) environment agents, (ii) obstruction agents and (iii) mouse (character) agents. The first two are characterised as "dumb" agents in that they do not display any intelligence, while the last has some "thinking" capability. From the figure it can be observed that we have only one environment agent and any number of obstruction and mouse agents (in fact we can have zero obstruction agents, but it would not make any sense to have zero mouse agents). In Figure 1 the arcs indicate communication lines; so the vision is that mouse agents can communicate with one another and the environment agent, while obstruction agents only communicate with the environment. Inspection of Figure 1 indicates that we also have some: (i) house keeping agents to facilitate the operation of the framework, (ii) a simulation interface with which an end user can interact so as to set up individual simulations and (iii) a visualisation unit that allows the end user to observe simulations. Each of the individual classes of agent are described in detail in the following three sections.

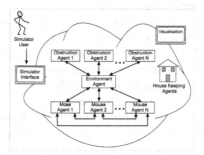

Fig. 1 Proposed MABS Framework

4 The Environment Agent

In the context of the proposed MABS framework an environment agent describes the *playing area*. In the case of the mouse in a box scenario this will be the box. A significant research issue with respect to the desired MABS is how best to represent this playing area. The simplest approach is to represent the playing area as a 2-D grid. However, this may not scale up for large simulations and features the irritation that the centroids of the neighbouring squares of a current square are not equidistant (neighbouring squares on the diagonal are further away than the immediately adjacent squares). Alternative representations include hexagonal grids, vector maps and graphs. However, because of its simplicity, the 2-D grid representation was adopted with respect to the framework described here.

The environment agent thus represents a playing area comprised of a 2-D grid. The dimensions of the environment were defined in terms 1cm units. A mouse was

assumed to measures 7cm in all directions (not true, but the assumption can be upheld for the purpose of the simple mouse in a box scenario). A mouse was deemed to move at the rate of one 1cm per 50 mili-seconds. Each grid square (location) was given a numeric code, a Ground Type Identifier (GTI), indicating the nature of the square. The currently available codes were in the range |0...4| where: 0 indicated a "no-go" square, 1 a "wall" square, 2 a "space" square (non-wall square), 3 a "choice point" and 4 an obstruction (serving to hide the location of other mouse agents). The mouse cannot move into no-go or obstruction locations.

A mouse agent's location is described by its centroid; thus a mouse cannot get closer to a wall or obstruction than 3cm. Therefore all squares within three units of a wall or obstruction were encoded as no-go squares (0), squares exactly four units away from a wall or obstruction were labelled as wall squares (1), and squares more than four units away from walls as space squares (2). Choice points, at their simplest, are then wall squares that coincide with *obtuse* corners; where the mouse might wish to change direction (or stop); or squares where current movement may proceed in more than one wall direction. The corners of the boxes could also have been marked as choice points; however the movement of a mouse agent entering into these locations will be blocked thus, in effect, the location acts as a choice point without actually being marked as such

The current implementation features six types of environment agent: (i) Box, (ii) H-box, (iii) O-box, (iv) Four Box, (v) Four Nest and (vi) Maze. The first represents the simplest scenario. The H-box introduces the concept of obstructions (agents in their own right) into the box scenario, obstructions can be thought of as "bricks" placed into the box environment so as to impede a mouse agent's progress. The four box scenario comprises four occurrences of the box scenario running simultaneously, but described as a single environment with obstructions placed so as to achieve four boxes. The four nest box was used to simulate the interaction of four mouse agents. The maze scenario comprises a box scenario with a set of obstructions arranged to form a "maze", the objective here was to test whether a mouse object could find its way through this environment. Every environment agent has the following fields:

1. *widthX*, the width of the environment, in terms of grid squares, in the X (East-West) direction.
2. *widthY*, the width of the environment, in terms of grid squares, in the Y (North-South) direction.
3. *groundArea*, the two dimensional grid describing the *locations* that make up the ground area (as described above).
4. *gateCoords*, one or more gates where characters can enter the environment (start points).
5. *obstructionList*, a list of zero, one or more obstruction agents that the environment needs to know about.

Each location within the environment has a GTI and a record of any scent at the location, together with the ID for the mouse agent to which the scent sample belongs. Scent is defined in terms of an integer. Scent typically lasts for 8 to 24

hours depending on the dominance of the mouse. We degrade the mouse scent on each iteration of the simulation. To speed up the simulation we can enhance the degradation factor. Currently the maximum scent strength is 255 and it is degraded by 0.25 on each iteration (a more realistic simulation would require a much lower degradation factor).

5 The Obstruction Agent

Obstruction agents are simple agents that, as noted above, can be conceptualised as "bricks" that may be located within an environment. The bricks may be placed in the box as the scenario progresses, hence obstructions are considered to be agents in their own right. The H-box environment contains two obstruction agents so that the environment, when observed in plan view, formed an "H" shape. The O-box contained a single obstruction in the middle of the box so that the environment, when observed in plan view, resembled an "O" shape. The four box and four nest environment also contained two obstruction agents, but arranged to form an intersecting cross so as to divide the environment into four sub-boxes (Our "bricks" can intersect) and to form four "nest area" respectively. The maze environment had eighteen obstruction agents arranged in a "maze" formation. Similar to an environment agent, obstruction agents are dumb agents. The significance of obstruction agents is that mouse agents cannot "see" behind them; they obstruct a mouse agent's "field of view".

6 The Mouse Agent

A mouse agent is the central character in our mouse simulator. Mouse agents have the following fields:

1. *state*, the current state of the mouse agent, either *moving*, *stopped* or *turning*.
2. *stateTime*, the time spent in the current state.
3. *coordX*, the mouse agent's current X location with respect to the environment agent.
4. *coordY*, the mouse agent's current Y location with respect to the environment agent.
5. *direction*, the direction the mouse agent is facing, a number in the range of $|0 \dots 7|$ representing N, NE, E, SE, S, SW, W or NW respectively.
6. *goalDirection*, the direction the agent wishes to face (only applicable when turning).
7. *turnDirection*, the "turning direction", either *clockwise* or *anticlockwise* (also only applicable when turning).
8. *scentStrength*, the strength of its scent.

9. *visionMap*, a disc of locations, with radius *v*, representing the part of the environment which a mouse agent can "see". Thus a mouse agent's field of vision is equivalent to *v*.

Table 1 Action Table

Current State	Event	Action	Comments	New State
stopped	None	Agent decides to move in direction faced	*sateTime* = 0	*moving*
stopped	None	Agent decides to move another direction	*sateTime* = 0	*turning*
moving	At choice point	Agent decides to move in new direction		*turning*
moving	Obstruction	Agent decides to move in new direction		*turning*
moving	Obstruction	Agent decides to stop	*sateTime* = 0	*stopped*
moving	None	Agent decides to stop	*sateTime* = 0	*stopped*
turning	Completed turn	None		*moving*

Mouse agents are dynamic agents in that they can change their location, direction, goal direction, turn direction and state. At the same time they are "intelligent" agents in that they can make decisions about which way to face and where to go.The operation of our mouse agent is founded on the well established concept of a Finite State Machine (FSM) [5, 8]. FSM are used to model processes in terms of a finite set of *states*. A change from one state to another is called a *transition*. Transitions are caused by *events* or *actions* (something happening to the agent or the agent doing something). The possible transitions to a new state, caused by an event or action, are typically described using a *transition table* (*state diagram* or *state table*). FSMs can be conceptualised as graphs (state models) where the vertexes represent states and the edges transitions caused by events or actions. An alternative approach would be to use the Belief-Desire-Intention (BDI) model [4]. This offers the advantage that it is supported by existing logic models. However, planning is typically outside the scope of the model. Given that in our model we think of mouse agents being in a certain state; and that changes from one state to another with an element of randomness as well as intention (expressed in the form of preferences), a finite state machine mechanism of operation was adopted.

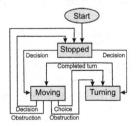

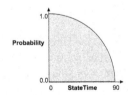

Fig. 2 State Model   **Fig. 3** Cosine Probability

The transition table for the mouse object is given in Table 1, which should be interpreted with respect to the state model presented in Figure 2 . There are seven

different possible transitions. At the start of each simulation the default state for a mouse object is *stopped*. Eventually the mouse will decide to move (how this is determined is discussed below). The mouse object can either move in the direction it is currently facing or turn to face another direction and then move (how this is determined is also discussed below).Thus there are two possible state transitions associated with the *stopped* state.

There are four possible state transitions associated with the *moving* state. The first is when the mouse reaches a choice point. From the above, mice are "wall huggers". A choice point is a location where there are more than one possible next wall locations (as in the case of the maze environment) or the next possible wall location requires a change in direction. In the first case the mouse may decide to continue to move in the current direction, in which case there will be no state change; alternatively the mouse may decide to turn and move in a new direction, thus adopt a *turning* state. The second and third movement state changes are where the mouse's movements are blocked (for example at the corner of a box environment). In this case the mouse can decide to stop (adopt a *stopped* state) or head off in a new direction (change to a *turning* state). Note that in the case of a choice point, in the current implementation, the mouse does not have an option to stop. Finally a mouse in a *moving* state may simply decide to stop (how this is determined is discussed below).

The final state transition in Table 1 occurs when a mouse agent completes a turn, in which case the mouse will move in the direction it is now facing (i.e. adopt a *moving* state). The assumption here is that the only reason for a mouse to turn is to move in a new direction.

At the start of a simulation the state of the mouse agent is always *stopped*. Conceptually the mouse agent can only stay stopped for a finite period of time T. The probability that the mouse will stay stopped decreases as the the current *stateTime* increases (i.e. as the time the mouse agent has spent in its stopped state increases). When $stateTime \equiv T$ the probability that the mouse will stay stopped is 0.0 (definitely decide to move), when $stateTime \equiv 0$ the probability is 1.0 (definitely stay stopped). This probability distribution was modelled using a cosine probability curve (Figure 3); we could have used a linear probability, or some other alternative, however the cosine probability has the feature that the likelihood of the mouse agent staying stopped remains high at low *stateTime* values, and becomes negligible (reducing to 0.0) as *stateTime* approaches T. On each simulation iteration, when the mouse object is stopped, a random number r is generated. A state transition will then occur when:

$$r < cosin\left(\frac{90 \times stateTime}{T}\right) \tag{1}$$

A similar process was applied where a mouse agent's state is *moving*. The assumption is again that the mouse will continue to move for a finite period of time, but in this case the time period was assumed to be $2T$. Thus, on each iteration, when the mouse object is moving a state transition will occur when:

$$r < cosin\left(\frac{90 \times stateTime/2}{T}\right) \qquad (2)$$

7 Selecting a Direction of Travel

When a mouse agent reaches a choice point or discovers an obstruction (i.e. it cannot or may not proceed any further in the current direction) the agent must make a decision. Where an obstruction is reached the mouse has the option to stop or proceed in a new direction (see Figure 2); the decision whether to stop or not is determined using identity 2. Where a change of direction is indicated a mouse agent has between 0 and 8 potential directions it can choose from. A mouse agent cannot enter no-go locations ($GTL = 0$); thus, depending on the mouse agent's current location, some directions will not be permissible. It is possible for a mouse agents movement to be entirely blocked by obstructions and/or the presence of other mouse agents. in which case the mouse will adopt a *stopped* state. Assuming a mouse agent has one or more potential directions it can move in each potential direction has a preference value p of between $|0.0 \dots 1.0|$. The complete set of preference values, P, is then defined as:

$$P = \{p_0, p_1, \dots, p_n\} \qquad (3)$$

such that:

$$\sum_{i=0}^{i=n} p_i = 1.0 \qquad (4)$$

(where n is the number of available directions/locations).

Preference values are made up of a number of components $C = \{c_1, c_2, \dots, c_m\}$, where m is the number of components. Each component describes some factor of the decision making process. A specific component j associated with a specific direction i is indicated as c_{ij}. Each component has a value of $|0.0 \dots 1.0|$. Such that $\sum_{i=0}^{i=n} c_{ij} = 1.0$ (i.e. the set of values describing a particular component across the set of potential directions is equivalent to 1.0). Some components may be considered to have greater significance than others, thus the components are weighted[2]. The weighting associated with a component c_j is indicated by w_j. The preference (p) for a particular location (i) is then calculated as follows:

$$p_i = \frac{\sum_{j=0}^{j=m} w_j p_{ij}}{\sum_{j=0}^{j=m} w_j} \qquad (5)$$

In the current simulation implementation four components are considered ($m = 4$) as follows:

---

[2] Although not a feature of the current implementation, these weighting mat be dynamic (i.e. they may be changed according to circumstances).

c_1 Preference according to GTL (desire for wall locations over space locations).

c_2 Preference for locations not recently or never visited (desire to explore).

c_3 Preference for avoiding locations where the scent of another mouse is significant compared with a mouse agent's own scent strength (desire to avoid the scent trails of other mice).

c_4 Preference for directions that tend to move way from other mouse agents if within sight (desire to avoid other mice).

Algorithm 1 Determination of preference for wall location component (c_1)

$L = Set\ of\ potential\ locations$
$N_n = Number\ of\ nonspace\ locations\ in\ L$
$N_s = Number\ of\ space\ locations\ in\ L$
if $N_s \equiv 0$ **then**
    $p_n = 1.0/N_n$
else
    $p_n = P_n/N_n$
    $p_s = P_s/N_s$
end if
for $i = 0 \rightarrow |L|$ **do**
    if $L_i.groundType \equiv space\ location$ **then**
        $L_i.c_1 = p_s$
    else
        $L_i.c_1 = n_s$
    end if
end for

7.1 Desire for Wall Locations over Space Locations (c_1)

As noted above mice prefer to move along walls, thus a preference should be given to directions (next locations) adjacent to walls. A mouse agent will have potentially N_n wall locations and N_s space locations to choose from, where N_n and N_s are whole numbers in the range of $|0\ldots8|$. Except in the special case where a mouse agent is blocked in, $1 \leq (N_n + N_s) \leq 8$. Of these directions zero, one or more will be space locations, and one or more will be non-space (wall or choice point) locations. The overall probability that a non-space location, L_n, is selected is given by P_n; and the overall probability that a space location, L_s, is selected by P_s, where P_n is assumed to be significantly greater than P_s. If $N_s \equiv 0$ then $P_n = 1.0$. Thus the probability of selecting a specific non space location is given by P_n/N_n, and the probability of selecting a specific space location (if such locations exist) is given by P_s/N_s. The process of determining the values for the preference component that reflects a desire for wall locations is given in algorithm 1.

7.2 Desire to Explore (c_2)

The desire to explore is expressed according to where a mouse agent has been recently, which in turn is expressed according to the scent strength of the mouse agent's own scent strength found at neighbouring locations. A mouse agent prefers locations (directions) where its own scent is not present, or at least weak. Thus the preference for new locations is expressed as a fraction of the inverse of the mouse agent's own scent strength (s_{inv_i}) at a given location i. If no scent is present $s_{inv} = 1.0$. The process for calculating the desire to explore preference component is given in algorithm 2. The c_2 component at a particular candidate location q is given by:

$$c_{q2} = \frac{s_{inv_q}}{\sum_{i=0}^{i=n} s_{inv_i}} \tag{6}$$

In algorithm 2 the factor k is used to reduce the influence of the scent strength at recently visited locations. The current maximum scent strength is 255, and thus the k value has been set to 10; if we simply used the inverse of the scent strength the influence of very recent directions will be negligible, 0.004 ($1/255$) as compared to 0.039 ($10/255$).

Algorithm 2 Determination of desire to explore component (c_2)

$L = Set\ of\ potential\ locations$
$S = Set\ of\ inverses\ scent\ strengths$
$total = 0.0$
for $i = 0 \rightarrow |L|$ **do**
   if $L_i.ownScentStrength \equiv 0$ **then**
     $S_i = 1$
   else
     $S_i = k/L_i.ownScentStrength$
     $total = total + S_i$
   end if
end for
for $i = 0 \rightarrow |L|$ **do**
   $L_i.c_2 = S_i/total$
end for

7.3 Desire to Avoid Scent Trails of other Mice (c_3)

The desire to avoid the scent trails of other mice is encapsulated in a similar manner to the desire to explore new locations. We use the inverse of the strength of the strongest scent belonging to another mouse agent, or 1.0 if there is no such scent. The process is presented in algorithm 3 where *maxScentStrength* is the scent strength associated with the scent strengths at a location belonging to other mice, 0 if there is no such scent strength. The constant K is again used.

7.4 Desire to Avoid other Mice (c_4)

A mouse agent knows nothing about the locations of other mice until they appear on its vision map. In the current simulation the radius of the vision map (v) is set to 20, however if the location of another mouse agent is obscured by an obstruction the current mouse agent will not know anything about this other mouse. To ensure the mouse agents do not actually crash into each other a buffer region of ten units is place round other mouse agents. Our mouse agents are currently programmed to avoid other mouse agents that are on its vision map. The values for this preference component are calculated according to the distance d from each candidate location to the nearest other mouse (if any). The c_4 component at a particular candidate location q is the distance d from the given candidate location q divided by the sum of the distances from all of the locations. Thus:

$$c_{q4} = \frac{d}{\sum_{i=0}^{i=n} d} \tag{7}$$

Algorithm 3 Determination of desire to avoid scent trails of other mice (c_3)

$L = Set\ of\ potential\ locations$
$S = Set\ of\ inverses\ scent\ strengths$
$total = 0.0$
for $i = 0 \rightarrow |L|$ **do**
  if $L_i.maxScentStrength \equiv 0$ **then**
    $S_i = 1$
  else
    $S_i = k/L_i.maxScentStrength$
    $total = total + S_i$
  end if
end for
for $i = 0 \rightarrow |L|$ **do**
  $L_i.c_3 = S_i/total$
end for

Algorithm 4 Next Location Algorithm

$L = Set\ of\ potential\ locations$
$Prob = 0.0$
$R = randomNumberGenerator()$
$L_{final} = -1$
for $i = 0 \rightarrow |L|$ **do**
  $Prob = Prob + L_i.prob$
  if $R < Prob$ **then**
    $L_{final} = L_i$
    break
  end if
end for
$return(L_{final})$

7.5 Decision making process

From the above each location has four components which are used to calculate a preference value for the location. Experiments indicated that the weighting that should be associated with c_1 and c_3 should be higher than those associated with the other components, w_1 and w_3 were therefore set to 2, while the remaining weightings were set to 1. The total preference for a particular location q was this given b:

$$p_q = \frac{2c_1 + c_2 + 2c_3 + c_4}{5} \tag{8}$$

The selection of a new direction was then determined using algorithm 4. The weightings can of course be adjusted as desired by the end user.

7.6 Change of Direction

Having selected a new location it may be necessary to change direction, if so a state transition from moving to turning will occur. Where a turn is initiated the mouse agents *goalDirection* and *turnDirection* fields must be reset. The value for the *turnDirection* field is calculated as follows as shown in algorithm 2 (recall that directions are specified as integers within the range $|0 \ldots 7|$).

Algorithm 5 Direction of Turn Algorithm

$diff = absolute(direction - goalDirection)$
if $if(goalDirection > direction)$ **then**
    if $diff \leq 4$ **then**
        $return("clockwise")$
    else
        $return("anticlockwise")$
    end if
else
    if $diff \leq 4$ **then**
        $return("anticlockwise")$
    else
        $return("clockwise")$
    end if
end if

---

8 Operation

The operation of the simulator was controlled by a Loop which iterated every 50 milliseconds. Thus, given that the mouse agent (when in a moving state) moves at a rate of one grid square per iteration and a grid square measures 1cm, the mouse agent travels at 1200cm per minute (or 72km per hour). Experiments were conducted us-

ing a number of different environments with a turn rate of 45 degrees per iteration, $T = 90$, $P_n = 0.95$, $P_s = 0.05$ and $k = 10$. The Box experiment was intended to establish that the mouse agent behaved in a reasonably realistic manner, as confirmed by domain experts. The H-box was intended to establish that the mouse agent could react to obstructions, the O-box was intended to observe the mouse agent's behaviour should it cross the open space between the outer wall of the box and the obstruction, the Maze experiment was used to evaluate the mouse agent's ability to negotiate choice points and the 4-box to demonstrate that mouse agents did not behave in the same way given four identical spaces. Finally the four nest box simulation was used observe how a group of mouse agents might interact given a hypothetical situation that they each might want to guard their own nest site.

Fig. 4 Box Simulation

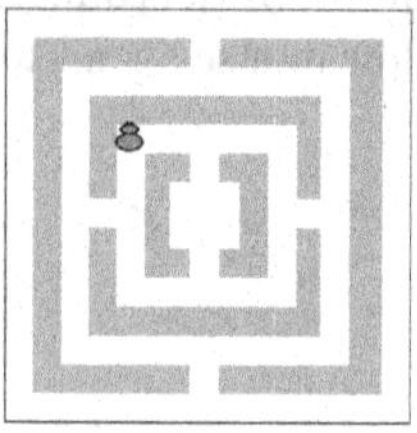

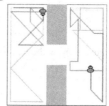

Fig. 5 Maze Simulation

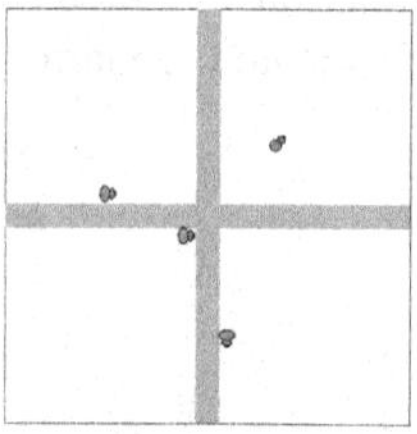

Fig. 6 4 Box Simulation

Fig. 7 O Box Simulation

Fig. 8 H Box Simulation (with scent traces)

Fig. 9 Four Nest Box Simulation (with scent traces)

Figures 4 to 10 illustrating the simulations. Inspection of the figures indicates how mouse agents, when not influenced by the presence of other mouse agents, tend to follow walls. In the case of the O-box environment (Figure 7) the mouse agent has crossed the open space and is now hugging the wall of the obstruction. Figure 8 shows the H-box environment with two mouse agents and Figure 9 the four nest environment with four mouse agents. Both figures include scent trails. The objective in both cases was to observe how mice agents might define there own space. For the benefit of the simulation, and to allow easy observation, the "lifespan" of the scent deposits was kept deliberately shirt. Better results would be achieved by increasing the longevity of the scent trails however in this case the simulation has to be run over a much longer (and more realistic) time period. The experiment demonstrated in Figure 10 was designed to demonstrate that the simulator could function with a reasonable number of mouse agents.

9 Discussion and Conclusions

In this paper we have described a simple Multi-Agent Based Simulation (MABS) framework to describe the mouse in a box scenario. The intention was to provide a simple start point for the development of large scale rodent simulations. Features of the framework are: (i) that it can be used to create sophisticated environments using the concept of obstruction agents, (ii) several mice can operate in these environments and (iii) the mice operate in a sufficiently realistic manner. Experiments indicated that environments were easy to create and that simulations were easy to run and observe. The authors therefore believe that they have established a sound foundation on which to build. Current work is directed at techniques to support more sophisticated scenarios and to allow mouse agents to learn about their environments.

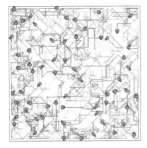

Fig. 10 Large (64 mouse agent) box simulation (with scent trails)

References

1. P. Crowcroft. *Mice All Over*. The Chicago Zoological Society, 1973.
2. P. Davidsson. Multi agent based simulation: Beyond social simulation. In *Proc. Workshop on Multi Agent Based Simulation (MABS) 2000*, pages 141–155. Springer-Verlag, LNCS 1979, 2001.
3. P. Davidsson, J. Holmgren, J.A. Persson, and L. Ramstedt. Multi agent based simulation of transport chains. In *Proc. 7th Int. Joint Conf. on Autonomous Agents and Multi-Agent Systems (AAMAS), Volume 2*, pages 1153–1160. Springer-Verlag, LNAI 3415, 2008.
4. B. Georgeff, M.P. andPell, Pollack M.E., M. Tambe, and M. Wooldridge. The belief-desire-intention model of agency. In *Proc. 5th Int. Workshop on Intelligent Agents: Agent Theories, Architectures and Languages (ATAL'98)*, pages 1–10. Springer-Verlag, London, 1998.
5. A. Gill. *Introduction to the Theory of Finite-state Machines*. McGraw-Hill, 1962.
6. C. Linarda, N. Ponomb, D. Fontenilleb, and E.F. Lambin. A multi-agent simulation to assess the risk of malaria re-emergence in southern france. *Ecology Modelling*, 220(2):160–174, 2009.
7. X. Pan, C.S. Han, K. Dauber, and K.H. Law. A multi-agent based framework for the simulation of human and social behaviors during emergency evacuations. *AI and Society*, 22(2):113–132, 2007.
8. F. Wagner. *Modeling Software with Finite State Machines: A Practical Approach*. Auerbach Publicationsl, 2006.

SHORT PAPERS

Analysis of IDDM Rats

R.Schmidt[1], H.Weiss[2], and G.Fuellen[1]

Abstract The aim of our study is to investigate the mechanism of tolerance induction by the modulatory anti CD4 monoclonal antibody RIB 5/2 in insulin dependent diabetes mellitus rats. By this approach it should be possible to identify the key mechanisms of immune tolerance on the level of T cell, cytokine, and chemokine biomarkers in blood, lymphatic organs, and pancreas; and furthermore to define biomarkers of autoimmunity and tolerance fpr prediction of diabetes onset. So far, decision trees and some other classification algorithms have been applied on data sets of twelve rats.

1 Introduction

Type 1 diabetes is an autoimmune disease in which beta cells are exclusively destroyed by the interaction of antigen presenting cells, T cells, and environmental triggers such as nutrients and viral infection [1]. There are two major challenges for prediction and diagnosis of this disease. First, though the analysis of various beta cell autoantibodies and beta cell specific T cells allows a good risk assessment for the progression of autoimmunity, biomarkers related to mechanisms of T cell mediated beta cell destruction and induction of self-tolerance are missing. Second, intervention strategies to block beta cell autoimmunity are not fully understood.

Induction of immune tolerance is a promising approach to halt autoimmunity in type 1 diabetes. Anti CD3 antibodies and vaccination with modified beta cell antigens such as insulin, GAD65, and hsp60 could block autoimmunity and induce self-tolerance in animal models of autoimmune diabetes [2]. These strategies, however, still show limitations that hamper translation into routine clinical use. First, the mechanisms of T cell modulation are still unclear in particular for transition from temporary immune suppression to induction of

1 University of Rostock, D-18057 Rostock, Germany
rainer.schmidt@uni-rostock.de

2 University of Rostock, D-18057 Rostock, Germany
heike.weiss@uni-rostock.de

M. Bramer et al. (eds.), *Research and Development in Intelligent Systems XXVIII*,
DOI 10.1007/978-1-4471-2318-7_29, © Springer-Verlag London Limited 2011

permanent self-tolerance. Second, despite development of humanized and aglykosylated anti CD3 abs the side effects remain severe and raise ethical concerns for treatment of young type 1 diabetes patients.

The intention of this project is

- To elucidate the mechanisms of the modulating anti CD4 antibody RIB5/2 on prevention of autoimmune destruction of beta cells in the insulin dependent diabetes mellitus (IDDM) rat model.
- To analyse immune cell (bio) markers in peripheral blood during progression of autoimmunity and/or induction of self-tolerance. Decision trees have been applied to calculate relative risk coefficients for development to overt diabetes at different time points of life.

2 Background and Research Status

Beta cell destruction in type 1 diabetes is a complex process comprising a network between beta cells, antigen presenting cells, autoaggressive T cells, and environmental triggers. Beta cells that are under assault are not passive bystanders, but actively participate in their own destruction process [3]. Overall, many of the cytokine- and virus-induced effects involved in inhibition of beta cell function and survival are regulated at the transcriptional and posttranscriptional/translational level [4]. T-cells modulate the autoimmune process and autoreactive T-cells can transfer diseases [5]. Thus, immune intervention during the prodromal phase or at the onset of overt diabetes will affect the balance between autoreactive and regulatory T cells. Currently it is possible to identify ß-cell-specific autoreactive T-cells using standard in vitro proliferation and tetramer assays, but these cell types could also be detected in healthy individuals [6]. Although the analysis of autoantibodies allows an assessment of risk for type 1 diabetes, it is still impossible to draw conclusions about T cell function in the local lymphatic compartment of the pancreas. Notably, there is an extensive knowledge upon activation of T cells and upon induction of self-tolerance on the molecular level of gene expression biomarkers. We hypothesize that biomarkers must be analyzed in a dynamic manner because they shall have specific predictive values for development of autoimmunity at different stages of autoimmunity.

The analysis of gene expression patterns might help to distinguish between T1DM affected subjects and healthy animals at an early stage. In a first experiment, we could demonstrate that analysis of selected genes of T cell differentiation, T cell function, and cytokine expression in whole blood cells at an early prediabetic stage (after 45 days of live), the RT6 T cell proliferation gene was most decisive for diabetes onset in the IDDM rat followed by selectin and

neuropilin at the stage of islet infiltration (after 50 days), and IL-4 during progression of beta cell destruction (after 55 days).

3 Preliminary Data

For recent experiments data from twelve rats were available. They were monitored for gene expression data in blood immune cells for functional gene clusters on the days 30, 35, 40, 45, 50, 55, 60, 65, 70, 80, and 90 of their life. However, just the days between 45 and 60 are assumed to be important of the prediction whether a rat will develop diabetes. Six of the twelve rats developed diabetes, three did not, and another three rats (background strain) were diabetes resistant because of the way they had been bred. Unfortunately, due to problems of the measurement facilities the data quality is rather poor. Many data are missing and some are obviously incorrect, especially for the early and the late measurement time points. However, as mentioned above, the most important measurement time points are in the middle. So, for some measurement time points data from just eleven of the twelve rats were used.

4 First Experimental Results

In the experiments data of the the following measurement time points were used: 45, 50, 55, and 60 days of life. The attributes are eighteen preselected genes and biomarkers. The class labels are "diabetes", "no diabetes", and "background strain".

Since we wanted to get attributes that are most decisive for the classification, we applied decision trees, which do not just provide the most decisive attributes but also their decisive values. The C4.5 decision tree algorithm, which was originally developed by Ross Quinlan [7], was applied in form of its J48 implementation in the WEKA environment [8]. Later on, we also applied other classification algorithms that are provided in WEKA, like "random forest", for example. We decided to use the WEKA environmemt because this has become the standard tool in Bioinformatics.

The result for day 50 is depicted in figure 1. If the gene expression value of selectin is bigger than 2.14 a rat probably belongs to the background strain, otherwise if the gene expression value of neuropilin is bigger than 0.63 a rat probably does not develop diabetes, otherwise it probably develops diabetes.

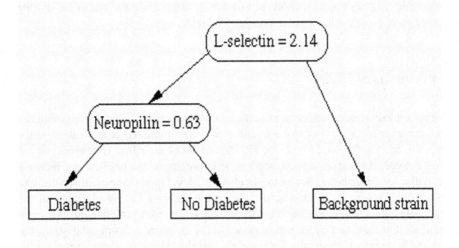

Figure 1 Decision Tree for day 50.

5 Validation

For the IDDM rat model we have started to calculate relative risk coefficients for development for diabetes. Though the data set is very small, the biologists that are involved in the project are very happy with the results and can explain them: At the beginning of infiltration (day 45) the RT6 gene expression, responsible for the correct thymic development of T-cells, may decide whether autoimmunity could develop. At a stage of of islet infiltration (day 50) selectin and neuropilin gene expression decides whether primed T-cells will infiltrate the endocrine pancreas for beta cell destruction. During progression of beta cell destruction (day 55) IL-4 as a T cell stimulating cytokine is crucial for the progression of beta cell infiltration.

However, because of the extremely small data set (twelve rats), the set was not split into a learning and a test set. The trees are just computed on the training set.

So, next Information Gain was considered, on which decision trees are based. WEKA provides them as "attribute selection". Usually, the values are between 0 and 1. In three of four trees the decision was obvious. For day 45, for example, the value of rt6a is 0.811, whereas the values of all other attributes are 0. Just, for day 50 the decison is obvious but the whole situation is not completely clear, because the Information Gain values are 0.959 for l-selection and 0.593 for il-4 and for neuropilin. Furthermore, in the tree neuropilin is used to separate between

"diabetis" and "no diabetis". So, the background strain was excluded and Information Gain was used just to classify "diabetis" and "no diabetis", with the result that neuropilin was the first choice.

Afterwards some standard classification methods provided by WEKA were applied (naïve bayes, nearest neighbor, random forest, J48, and support vector machines). Except for the decision tree algorithm J48 these methods show just the classification results but they do not show which attributes have been used for the classification. In table 1 results are shown just for day 50 as an example. An inner cross validation is provided by WEKA. Because of the small size of the data set 3-fold cross validation was applied instead of the usual 10-fold cross validation. First, the classification algorithms were applied on the whole data sets (table 1) and secondly on the data sets without background strain (table 2). However, the differences are very small.

Table 1. Accuracy and Area Under the Curve for day 50 for the complete data set.

Method	Accuracy (%)	AUC
Naïve Bayes	58.3	0.52
Nearest Neighbor	75.0	0.75
Random Forest	66.7	0.80
J48	66.7	0.76
SVM	58.3	0.65

Table 2. Accuracy and Area Under the Curve for day 50 for the data set without background strain

Method	Accuracy (%)	AUC
Naïve Bayes	55.6	0.42
Nearest Neighbor	77.8	0.67
Random Forest	66.7	0.53
J48	66.7	0.61
SVM	55.6	0.50

6 Discussion

The analysis of gene expression patterns might help to distinguish between T1DM affected subjects and healthy animals at an early stage. In a first experiment, we could demonstrate that analysis of selected genes of T cell differentiation, T cell function, and cytokine expression in whole blood cells at an early prediabetic stage (after 45 days of live), the RT6 T cell proliferation gene was most decisive for diabetes onset in the IDDM rat followed by selectin and neuropilin at the stage

of islet infiltration (after 50 days), and IL-4 during progression of beta cell destruction (after 55 days).

However, so far the data set is very small and, probably because of poor data quality, the cross-validated classification results are not so well (see tables 1 and 2). Nevertheless, the generated decision trees perform well, certainly just on the training set, but nearly all of them can be very well explained by the biochemical experts.

Unfortunately, the breeding and the data collection of these specific rats is expensive and time consuming. At the moment another two dozens of them is going to be bred. So, we shall get a bigger data set and hopefully more convincing results.

References

1. Akerblom, H.K., Vaarala, O., Hyoty, H., Ilonen, J., Knip, M.: Environmental factors in the etiology of type 1 diabetes. Am J Med Genet 115, pp. 18-29 (2002).
2. Ludvigsson, J., Faresjo, M., Hjorth, M., et al.: GAD treatment and insulin secretion in recent-onset type 1 diabetes. N Engl J Med 359, pp. 1909-1920 (2008).
3. D'Hertog, W., Overbergh, L., Lage, K., et al.: Proteomics analysis of cytokine-induced dysfunction and death in insulin-producing INS-1E cells: new insights into the pathways involved. Mol Cell Proteomics 6 (21), pp. 80-99 (2007).
4. Gysemans, C., Callewaert, H., Overbergh, L., Mathieu, C.: Cytokine signalling in the beta-cell: a dual role for IFNgamma. Biochem Soc Trans 36, pp. 328-33 (2008).
5. Lampeter, E.F., McCann, S.R., Kolb, H.: Transfer of diabetes type 1 by bone-marrow transplantation. Lancet 351, pp. 568-9 (1998).
6. Schloot, N.C., Roep, B.O., Wegmann D.R., Yu, L., Wang; T.B., Eisenbarth, G.S.: T-cell reactivity to GAD65 peptide sequences shared with coxsackie virus protein in recent-onset IDDM, post-onset IDDM patients and control subjects. Diabetologia 40, pp. 332-8 (1997).
7. Quinlan, J.R.: C4.5 Programs for Machine Learning. Morgan Kaufmann, San Mateo, (1993).
8. Hall, M. et al.: The WEKA data mining software: An update. SIGKDD Explorations 11(1), pp.10-18 (2009).